Rand McNally

Traveler's
World Atlas
and Guide

Rand McNally & Company
Chicago • New York • San Francisco

QUICK REFERENCE CONTENTS

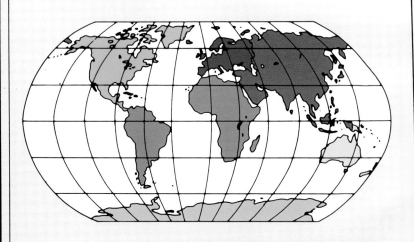

Contents

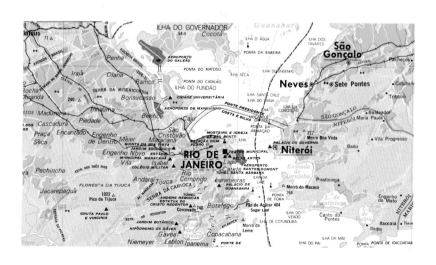

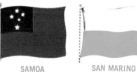

SAINT LUCIA ST. VINCENT/ GRENADINES SAMOA SAN MARINO SAO TOME & PRINCIPE

World Comparison Tables   161 - 168

Index to World Reference Maps   169 - 224

6

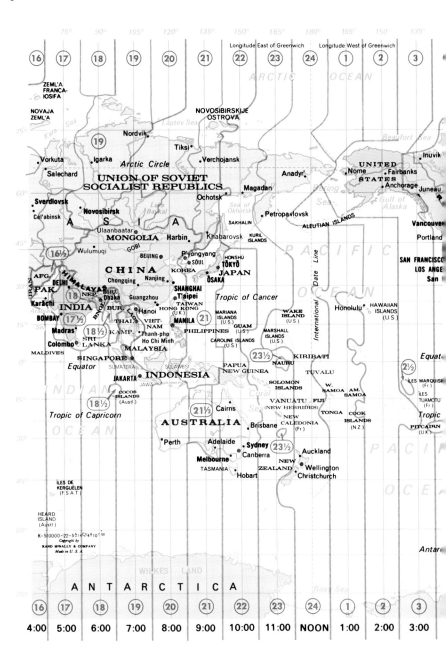

International Dialing Codes
Effective July 1, 1988

To place a call to another country from the U.S., first dial the international access code, "011", and then dial the country code, city code, and the local number.

Country Name	Country Code	City Code
Algeria	213	*
American Samoa	684	*
Andorra	33	All points 628
Anguilla	809	*
Antigua and Barbuda	809	*
Argentina	54	Buenos Aires 1, Córdoba 51, La Plata 21, Rosario 41
Aruba	297	All points 8
Ascension	247	*
Australia	61	Brisbane 7, Canberra 62, Melbourne 3, Sydney 2
Austria	43	Graz 316, Linz 732, Wien (Vienna) 222
Bahamas	809	*
Bahrain	973	*
Bangladesh	880	Chittagong 31, Dhaka 2, Khulna 41, Mymensingh 91
Barbados	809	*
Belgium	32	Antwerpen 3, Bruxelles 2, Gent 91, Liège 41
Belize	501	Belize *, Belmopan 08, Corozal 04, Orange Walk 03
Benin	229	*
Bermuda	809	*
Bolivia	591	Cochabamba 42, La Paz 2, Santa Cruz 33
Botswana	267	Francistown 21, Gaborone 31
Brazil	55	Brasília 61, Rio de Janeiro 21, São Paulo 11
Brunei	673	Bandar Seri Begawan 2, Kuala Belait 3, Tutong 4
Bulgaria	359	Plovdiv 32, Sofija 2, Varna 52
Cameroon	237	*
Canada	†	*
Cape Verde	238	*
Cayman Islands	809	*
Chile	56	Concepción 41, Santiago 2, Valparaíso 32
China	86	Beijing (Peking) 1, Fuzhou 591, Guangzhou (Canton) 20, Jinan 531, Nanjing 25, Shanghai 21
Colombia	57	Barranquilla 5, Bogotá 1, Cali 23, Medellin 4
Costa Rica	506	*
Cyprus	357	Lárnax 41, Lemesós 51, Nicosia (Levkosía) 2
Cyprus, North	90	Ammókhostos (Famagusta) 536, Kirínia 581
Czechoslovakia	42	Bratislava 7, Brno 5, Ostrava 69, Praha (Prague) 2
Denmark	45	Århus 6, København (Copenhagen) 1 or 2, Odense 7
Dominica	809	*
Dominican Republic	809	*
Ecuador	593	Ambato 2, Machala 4, Guayaquil 4, Portoviejo 4, Quito 2
Egypt	20	Al-Iskandarīyah (Alexandria) 3, Al-Qāhirah (Cairo) 2, Aswān 97, Asyūt 88

Country Name	Country Code	City Code
El Salvador	503	*
Ethiopia	251	Adis Abeba 1, Asmera 4, Dese 3, Dire Dawa 5, Harer 5
Faeroe Islands	298	*
Fiji	679	*
Finland	358	Espoo 15, Helsinki 0, Tampere 31, Turku 21
France	33	Bordeaux 56, Lyon 7, Marseille 91, Nice 93, Paris 1, Toulouse 61
French Guiana	594	*
French Polynesia	689	*
Gabon	241	*
Gambia	220	*
German Democratic Republic (East Germany)	37	Berlin 2, Dresden 51, Leipzig 41, Magdeburg 91, Rostock 81
Germany, Federal Republic of (West Germany)	49	Berlin 30, Bonn 228, Essen 201, Frankfurt am Main 69, Hamburg 40, München (Munich) 89
Gibraltar	350	*
Greece	30	Athínai (Athens) 1, Iráklion 81, Lárisa 41, Piraiévs 1, Thessaloníki 31
Greenland	299	Godthåb 2, Thule 50
Grenada	809	*
Guadeloupe	590	*
Guam	671	*
Guatemala	502	Guatemala 2, all other cities 9
Guernsey	44	*
Guyana	592	Bartica 5, Georgetown 2, New Amsterdam 3
Haiti	509	Cap-Haïtien 3, Gonaïves 2, Les Cayes 5, Port-au-Prince 1
Honduras	504	*
Hong Kong	852	Kowloon 3, New Territories 0, Victoria (Hong Kong) 5
Hungary	36	Budapest 1, Debrecen 52, Győr 96, Miskolc 46
Iceland	354	Akureyri 6, Keflavík Naval Base 2, Reykjavík 1
India	91	Bangalore 812, Bombay 22, Calcutta 33, Madras 44, New Delhi 11
Indonesia	62	Bandung 22, Jakarta 21, Medan 61, Surabaya 31
Iran	98	Eşfahān 31, Mashhad 51, Tabrīz 41, Tehrān 21
Ireland	353	Cork 21, Dublin 1, Galway 91, Limerick 61, Waterford 51
Isle of Man	44	*
Israel	972	Hefa (Haifa) 4, Ramat Gan 3, Tel Aviv-Yafo 3, Yerushalayim (Jerusalem) 2
Italy	39	Firenze 55, Genova 10, Milano 2, Napoli 81, Palermo 91, Roma (Rome) 6, Venezia 41
Ivory Coast	255	*
Jamaica	809	*
Japan	81	Kyōto 75, Nagoya 52, Naha 988, Ōsaka 6, Sapporo 11, Tōkyō 3, Yokohama 45
Jersey	44	*
Jordan	962	53 Ammān 6, Az-Zarqā539, Irbid 2, Ma'ān 3

Country Name	Country Code	City Code
Kenya	254	Kisumu 35, Mombasa 11, Nairobi 2, Nakuru 37
Korea, South	82	Inch'ŏn 32, Pusan 51, Sŏul 2, Taegu 53
Kuwait	965	*
Lesotho	266	*
Liberia	231	*
Libya	218	Banghāzī 61, Misrātah 51, Ṭarābulus (Tripoli) 21
Liechtenstein	41	All points 75
Luxembourg	352	*
Macao	853	*
Malawi	265	Blantyre *, Domasi 531, Lilongwe *, Zomba 50
Malaysia	60	Ipoh 5, Johor Baharu 7, Kajang 3, Kuala Lumpur 3
Malta	356	*
Marshall Islands	692	Ebeye 871, Majuro 9
Martinique	596	*
Mexico	52	Acapulco 748, Cancún 988, Chihuahua 14, Ciudad de México 5, Monterrey 83, Puebla 22, Tijuana 66
Micronesia, Federated States of	691	Kosrae 851, Ponape 9, Truk 8319, Yap 841
Monaco	33	All points 93
Montserrat	809	*
Morocco	212	Casablanca *, Fès 6, Marrakech 4, Rabat 7, Tanger 9
Namibia	264	Grootfontein 673, Keetmanshoop 631, Windhoek 61
Nepal	977	*
Netherlands	31	Amsterdam 20, Rotterdam 10, 's-Gravenhage (The Hague) 70, Utrecht 30
Netherlands Antilles	599	Bonaire 7, Curaçao 9, St. Eustatius 3, St. Maarten 5
New Caledonia	687	*
New Zealand	64	Auckland 9, Christchurch 3, Dunedin 24, Hamilton 71, Wellington 4
Nicaragua	505	Chinandega 341, Granada 55, León 311, Managua 2
Niger	227	*
Nigeria	234	Lagos 1
Northern Mariana Is.	670	Capitol Hill 322, Rota 532, Susupe 234, Tinian 433
Norway	47	Bergen 5, Oslo 2, Stavanger 4, Trondheim 7
Oman	968	*
Pakistan	92	Faisalabad 411, Islāmābād 51, Karāchi 21, Lahore 42
Panama	507	*
Papua New Guinea	675	*
Paraguay	595	Asunción 21, Concepción 31, Puerto Presidente Stroessner 61
Peru	51	Arequipa 54, Callao 14, Chiclayo 74, Cuzco 84, Lima 14, Trujillo 44
Philippines	63	Bacolod 34, Cebu 32, Davao 35, Iloilo 33, Manila 2
Poland	48	Gdańsk 58, Katowice 32, Łódź 42, Poznań 61, Kraków 12, Warszawa (Warsaw) 22
Portugal	351	Coimbra 39, Lisboa (Lisbon) 1, Porto 2, Setúbal 65
Qatar	974	*

Country Name	Country Code	City Code
Romania	40	Bucureşti (Bucharest) 0, Constanţa 16, Iaşi 81
St. Christopher-Nevis	809	*
St. Lucia	809	*
St. Pierre and Miquelon	508	*
St. Vincent and the Grenadines	809	*
San Marino	39	All points 541
Saudi Arabia	966	Al-Madīnah 4, Ar-Ridāḍ (Riyadh) 1, Jiddah 2, Makkah (Mecca) 2
Senegal	221	*
Singapore	65	*
South Africa	27	Bloemfontein 51, Cape Town 21, Durban 31, Johannesburg 11, Pretoria 12
Spain	34	Barcelona 3, Madrid 1, Sevilla 54, Valencia 6
Spanish North Africa	34	Ceuta 56, Melilla 52
Sri Lanka	94	Colombo 1, Kandy 8, Kotte 1
Suriname	597	*
Swaziland	268	*
Sweden	46	Göteborg 31, Malmö 40, Stockholm 8, Uppsala 18
Switzerland	41	Basel 61, Bern 31, Genève 22, Lausanne 21, Lucerne 41, Zürich 1
Taiwan	886	Kaohsiung 7, T'ainan 6, T'aipei 2
Tanzania	255	Dar es Salaam 51, Dodoma 61, Mwanza 68, Tanga 53
Thailand	66	Chiang Mai 53, Krung Thep (Bangkok) 2, Nakhon Sawan 56, Ubon Ratchathani 45
Togo	228	*
Trinidad and Tobago	809	*
Tunisia	216	Béja 8, Bizerte 2, El Kairouan 7, Sousse 3, Tunis 1
Turkey	90	Adana 711, Ankara 41, İstanbul 1, İzmir 51
Turks and Caicos Is.	809	*
Uganda	256	Entebbe 42, Jinja 43, Kampala 41
United Arab Emirates	971	Abū Ẓaby (Abu Dhabi) 2, Al-'Ayn 3, Ash-Shāriqah 6, Dubayy 4, 'Ujmān 6
United Kingdom	44	Belfast 232, Birmingham 21, Cardiff 222, Glasgow 41, Liverpool 51, London 1, Manchester 61
United States	1	*
Uruguay	598	Mercedes 532, Montevideo 2, Paysandú 722
Vatican City	39	All points 6
Venezuela	58	Barquisimeto 51, Caracas 2, Maracaibo 61, Valencia 41
Virgin Islands, British	809	*
Yemen	967	Al-Ḥudaydah 3, Ṣan'ā' 2, Ta'izz 4, Yarīm 4, Zabīd 3
Yugoslavia	38	Beograd (Belgrade) 11, Sarajevo 71, Zagreb 41
Zaire	243	Kinshasa 12, Lubumbashi 222
Zambia	260	Chingola 2, Kitwe 2, Luanshya 2, Lusaka 1, Ndola 26
Zimbabwe	263	Bulawayo 9, Harare 4, Mutare 20

* No city code(s).   † No country code. Dial 1 + area code.

Great Circle distances between principal cities in statute miles (black type) and kilometres (blue type)	Beijing, China	Berlin, Germany	Bombay, India	Buenos Aires, Argentina	Cairo (Al-Qāhirah), Egypt	Caracas, Venezuela	Chicago, U.S.	Honolulu, U.S.	Johannesburg, S. Africa
Beijing, China		4,568 7,351	2,960 4,763	11,978 19,277	4,679 7,530	8,922 14,359	6,558 10,554	5,049 8,126	7,269 11,699
Berlin, Germany	4,568 7,351		3,902 6,280	7,410 11,926	1,795 2,888	5,231 8,419	4,404 7,087	7,305 11,756	5,502 8,854
Bombay, India	2,960 4,763	3,902 6,280		9,280 14,935	2,696 4,339	9,014 14,506	8,037 12,934	8,006 12,885	4,324 6,959
Buenos Aires, Argentina	11,978 19,277	7,410 11,926	9,280 14,935		7,360 11,844	3,185 5,125	5,619 9,043	7,556 12,160	5,039 8,109
Cairo (Al-Qāhirah), Egypt	4,679 7,530	1,795 2,888	2,696 4,339	7,360 11,844		6,340 10,203	6,130 9,866	8,823 14,200	3,889 6,258
Caracas, Venezuela	8,922 14,359	5,231 8,419	9,014 14,506	3,185 5,125	6,340 10,203		2,492 4,010	6,009 9,671	6,856 11,034
Chicago, U.S.	6,558 10,554	4,404 7,087	8,037 12,934	5,619 9,043	6,130 9,866	2,492 4,010		4,234 6,814	8,705 14,009
Honolulu, U.S.	5,049 8,126	7,305 11,756	8,006 12,885	7,556 12,160	8,823 14,200	6,009 9,671	4,234 6,814		11,916 19,177
Johannesburg, S. Africa	7,269 11,699	5,502 8,854	4,324 6,959	5,039 8,109	3,889 6,258	6,856 11,034	8,705 14,009	11,916 19,177	
Lagos, Nigeria	7,118 11,455	3,221 5,183	4,733 7,617	4,929 7,932	2,440 3,927	4,799 7,723	5,973 9,613	10,120 16,286	2,810 4,522
London, United Kingdom	5,063 8,148	592 953	4,478 7,207	6,915 11,129	2,194 3,531	4,639 7,466	3,941 6,343	7,220 11,619	5,635 9,068
Los Angeles, U.S.	6,232 10,030	5,793 9,323	8,693 13,990	6,122 9,853	7,588 12,212	3,612 5,813	1,740 2,800	2,551 4,106	10,374 16,695
Mexico City (Ciudad de México), Mexico	7,722 12,427	6,038 9,718	9,714 15,633	4,593 7,391	7,682 12,363	2,220 3,573	1,689 2,718	3,790 6,099	9,065 14,588
Montreal, Canada	6,487 10,440	3,734 6,010	7,499 12,069	5,624 9,051	5,420 8,722	2,439 3,925	744 1,198	4,902 7,889	8,054 12,962
Moscow (Moskva), U.S.S.R.	3,599 5,792	994 1,599	3,136 5,047	8,381 13,488	1,810 2,913	6,152 9,901	4,951 7,968	7,016 11,291	5,694 9,164
New York, U.S.	6,807 10,955	3,961 6,374	7,781 12,523	5,299 8,528	5,598 9,009	2,115 3,403	738 1,187	4,973 8,003	7,967 12,822
Paris, France	5,104 8,214	546 879	4,349 6,999	6,874 11,062	1,995 3,210	4,739 7,627	4,138 6,659	7,424 11,948	5,410 8,707
Rio de Janeiro, Brazil	10,753 17,305	6,209 9,992	8,332 13,409	1,238 1,993	6,147 9,893	2,810 4,523	5,304 8,536	8,285 13,333	4,440 7,146
Rome (Roma), Italy	5,059 8,141	739 1,189	3,828 6,160	6,927 11,148	1,337 2,151	5,175 8,329	4,806 7,734	8,023 12,912	4,802 7,728
Singapore	2,787 4,486	6,164 9,920	2,434 3,917	9,859 15,867	5,129 8,255	11,395 18,339	9,345 15,039	6,699 10,781	5,374 8,649
Sydney, Australia	5,564 8,955	9,997 16,088	6,308 10,152	7,307 11,760	8,945 14,395	9,534 15,344	9,232 14,857	5,073 8,165	6,847 11,019
Tōkyō, Japan	1,325 2,133	5,553 8,937	4,214 6,782	11,362 18,285	5,958 9,588	8,764 14,104	6,255 10,067	3,809 6,130	8,433 13,571

Lagos, Nigeria	London, United Kingdom	Los Angeles, U.S.	Mexico City (Ciudad de México), Mexico	Montreal, Canada	Moscow (Moskva), U.S.S.R.	New York, U.S.	Paris, France	Rio de Janeiro, Brazil	Rome (Roma), Italy	Singapore	Sydney, Australia	Tōkyō, Japan
7,118 / 11,455	5,063 / 8,148	6,232 / 10,030	7,722 / 12,427	6,487 / 10,440	3,599 / 5,792	6,807 / 10,955	5,104 / 8,214	10,753 / 17,305	5,059 / 8,141	2,787 / 4,486	5,564 / 8,955	1,325 / 2,133
3,221 / 5,183	592 / 953	5,793 / 9,323	6,038 / 9,718	3,734 / 6,010	994 / 1,599	3,961 / 6,374	546 / 879	6,209 / 9,992	739 / 1,189	6,164 / 9,920	9,997 / 16,088	5,553 / 8,937
4,733 / 7,617	4,478 / 7,207	8,693 / 13,990	9,714 / 15,633	7,499 / 12,069	3,136 / 5,047	7,781 / 12,523	4,349 / 6,999	8,332 / 13,409	3,828 / 6,160	2,434 / 3,917	6,308 / 10,152	4,214 / 6,782
4,929 / 7,932	6,915 / 11,129	6,122 / 9,853	4,593 / 7,391	5,624 / 9,051	8,381 / 13,488	5,299 / 8,528	6,874 / 11,062	1,238 / 1,993	6,927 / 11,148	9,859 / 15,867	7,307 / 11,760	11,362 / 18,285
2,440 / 3,927	2,194 / 3,531	7,588 / 12,212	7,682 / 12,363	5,420 / 8,722	1,810 / 2,913	5,598 / 9,009	1,995 / 3,210	6,147 / 9,893	1,337 / 2,151	5,129 / 8,255	8,945 / 14,395	5,958 / 9,588
4,799 / 7,723	4,639 / 7,466	3,612 / 5,813	2,220 / 3,573	2,439 / 3,925	6,152 / 9,901	2,115 / 3,403	4,739 / 7,627	2,810 / 4,523	5,175 / 8,329	11,395 / 18,339	9,534 / 15,344	8,764 / 14,104
5,973 / 9,613	3,941 / 6,343	1,740 / 2,800	1,689 / 2,718	744 / 1,198	4,951 / 7,968	738 / 1,187	4,138 / 6,659	5,304 / 8,536	4,806 / 7,734	9,345 / 15,039	9,232 / 14,857	6,255 / 10,067
10,120 / 16,286	7,220 / 11,619	2,551 / 4,106	3,790 / 6,099	4,902 / 7,889	7,016 / 11,291	4,973 / 8,003	7,424 / 11,948	8,285 / 13,333	8,023 / 12,912	6,699 / 10,781	5,073 / 8,165	3,809 / 6,130
2,810 / 4,522	5,635 / 9,068	10,374 / 16,695	9,065 / 14,588	8,054 / 12,962	5,694 / 9,164	7,967 / 12,822	5,410 / 8,707	4,440 / 7,146	4,802 / 7,728	5,374 / 8,649	6,847 / 11,019	8,433 / 13,571
	3,107 / 5,000	7,711 / 12,409	6,861 / 11,042	5,280 / 8,498	3,884 / 6,251	5,244 / 8,440	2,930 / 4,716	3,740 / 6,019	2,490 / 4,007	6,935 / 11,160	9,641 / 15,516	8,392 / 13,506
3,107 / 5,000		5,439 / 8,753	5,530 / 8,899	3,239 / 5,213	1,557 / 2,506	3,440 / 5,536	227 / 365	5,745 / 9,245	895 / 1,441	6,756 / 10,873	10,568 / 17,008	5,956 / 9,585
7,711 / 12,409	5,439 / 8,753		1,551 / 2,496	2,466 / 3,968	6,060 / 9,752	2,467 / 3,970	5,659 / 9,108	6,296 / 10,132	6,335 / 10,195	8,761 / 14,100	7,489 / 12,053	5,436 / 8,749
6,861 / 11,042	5,530 / 8,899	1,551 / 2,496		2,307 / 3,712	6,638 / 10,683	2,092 / 3,366	5,714 / 9,195	4,760 / 7,661	6,348 / 10,216	10,307 / 16,587	8,064 / 12,978	6,989 / 11,247
5,280 / 8,498	3,239 / 5,213	2,466 / 3,968	2,307 / 3,712		4,372 / 7,036	333 / 536	3,429 / 5,519	5,088 / 8,189	4,090 / 6,582	9,192 / 14,793	9,949 / 16,011	6,452 / 10,384
3,884 / 6,251	1,557 / 2,506	6,060 / 9,752	6,638 / 10,683	4,372 / 7,036		4,646 / 7,477	1,540 / 2,479	7,162 / 11,526	1,488 / 2,395	5,246 / 8,443	9,012 / 14,503	4,662 / 7,502
5,244 / 8,440	3,440 / 5,536	2,467 / 3,970	2,092 / 3,366	333 / 536	4,646 / 7,477		3,621 / 5,827	4,799 / 7,723	4,263 / 6,861	9,525 / 15,329	9,943 / 16,002	6,726 / 10,824
2,930 / 4,716	227 / 365	5,659 / 9,108	5,714 / 9,195	3,429 / 5,519	1,540 / 2,479	3,621 / 5,827		5,682 / 9,144	676 / 1,088	6,666 / 10,728	10,520 / 16,931	6,050 / 9,736
3,740 / 6,019	5,745 / 9,245	6,296 / 10,132	4,760 / 7,661	5,088 / 8,189	7,162 / 11,526	4,799 / 7,723	5,682 / 9,144		5,695 / 9,165	9,779 / 15,738	8,398 / 13,516	11,507 / 18,519
2,490 / 4,007	895 / 1,441	6,335 / 10,195	6,348 / 10,216	4,090 / 6,582	1,488 / 2,395	4,263 / 6,861	676 / 1,088	5,695 / 9,165		6,240 / 10,043	10,148 / 16,331	6,150 / 9,897
6,935 / 11,160	6,756 / 10,873	8,761 / 14,100	10,307 / 16,587	9,192 / 14,793	5,246 / 8,443	9,525 / 15,329	6,666 / 10,728	9,779 / 15,738	6,240 / 10,043		3,908 / 6,290	3,326 / 5,353
9,641 / 15,516	10,568 / 17,008	7,489 / 12,053	8,064 / 12,978	9,949 / 16,011	9,012 / 14,503	9,943 / 16,002	10,520 / 16,931	8,398 / 13,516	10,148 / 16,331	3,908 / 6,290		4,863 / 7,826
8,392 / 13,506	5,956 / 9,585	5,436 / 8,749	6,989 / 11,247	6,452 / 10,384	4,662 / 7,502	6,726 / 10,824	6,050 / 9,736	11,507 / 18,519	6,150 / 9,897	3,326 / 5,353	4,863 / 7,826	

Toll Free Numbers

Airlines

AEROLINEAS ARGENTINAS
800/327-0276 (Cont'l US except FL)
800/333-0276 (FL)
800/361-8159 (Canada)

AEROMEXICO
800/237-6639 (Cont'l US)

AEROPERU AIRLINES
800/255-7378 (Cont'l US except FL)
800/494-0022 (FL)

AIR AFRIQUE
800/232-2557 (Cont'l US except CA)
800/221-8156 (CA)

AIR CANADA
800/422-6232 (Cont'l US except NY)

AIR FRANCE
800/237-2747 (Cont'l US)

AIR INDIA
800/223-7776 (Cont'l US except NY)
800/223-9850 (Cont'l US except NY)

AIR JAMAICA
800/523-5585 (US & Ontario)

AIR NEW ZEALAND
800/262-1234 (Cont'l US)
800/521-4059 (AK & HI)
800/663-5494 (Canada)

AIR OVERSEAS INC.
800/327-1031 (Cont'l US except FL)
800/432-7724 (FL)

AIR SEDONA
800/535-4448 (US except AZ)
800/228-7654 (AZ)

ALASKA AIRLINES
800/426-0333 (Cont'l US)

ALITALIA AIRLINES
800/223-5730 (Cont'l US except NY)

ALM ANTILLEAN AIRLINES
800/327-7230 (Cont'l US except FL)
800/432-2849 (FL)

AMERICAN AIRLINES
800/443-7300 (Cont'l US)

AUSTRALIAN AIRLINES
800/922-5122 (US)
800/551-2012 (South Pacific)

AUSTRIAN AIRLINES
800/872-4282 (US except NY)
800/387-1477 (Canada)

CANADIAN AIRLINES INT'L
800/426-7007 (Cont'l US except WA)
800/552-7424 (WA)

CSA CZECHOSLOVAK AIRLINES
800/223-2365 (Cont'l US except NY)

DELTA AIRLINES INC.
800/221-1212 (US except AK)

EASTERN AIRLINES INC.
800/EASTERN (Cont'l US)

EGYPT AIR
800/334-6787 (Cont'l US, Puerto Rico, & Virgin Islands)

EL AL ISRAEL AIRLINES
800/223-6700 (Cont'l US except NY)

IBERIA AIRLINES OF SPAIN
800/772-4642 (Cont'l US)

ICELANDAIR
800/223-5500 (Cont'l US)

JAPAN AIR LINES
800/525-3663 (Cont'l US)

KLM ROYAL DUTCH AIRLINES
800/777-5553 (US)

KOREAN AIR
800/421-8200 (Cont'l US)
800/531-2626 (CA)

LOT POLISH AIRLINES
800/223-0593 (Cont'l US except IL)

LUFTHANSA
800/645-3880 (Cont'l US)

MEXICANA AIRLINES
800/531-7923 (Cont'l US & Canada)

NORTHWEST AIRLINES
800/225-2525 (US)

PAN AM WORLD AIRWAYS
800/221-1111 (Cont'l US)

PHILIPPINE AIRLINES
800/435-9725 (US, Canada, Puerto Rico & Virgin Islands)

PIEDMONT AIRLINES
800/251-5720 (US & Canada A/C 416 & 519)
800/334-5874 (Telecommunications for the Deaf)

QANTAS AIRWAYS
800/227-4500 (US)

SAS SCANDINAVIAN AIR SYSTEM
800/221-2350 (Canada & US except Los Angeles & New York City)

SWISSAIR
800/221-4750 (US)

TRANSWORLD AIRLINES INC.
800/325-4933 (US)
800/392-1673 (MO)

UNITED AIRLINES
800/241-6522 (Cont'l US)

Air Freight & Package Express Service

AER LINGUS
800/223-7660 (US except NY)

AMERICAN AIRLINES INC.
800/334-7400 (US)

CENTRAL AIR FREIGHT, INC.
800/982-3924 (US except MI)
800/621-4377 (MI)

DELTA AIRLINES SMALL PACKAGE PICKUP & DELIVERY SERVICE
800/638-7333 (US except MD)

DYNAMIC AIR FREIGHT INC.
800/631-3484 (US except NJ)

EASTERN AIRLINE SPRINT DELIVERY
800/336-0336 (US)

EMERY WORLDWIDE
800/443-6379 (US)

FEDERAL EXPRESS
800/238-5355 (US)

FIRST CLASS AIR SERVICES
800/422-7461 (US except CA)

FRESH AIR COURIER
800/247-2329 (US except NY)

INTERNATIONAL BONDED COURIERS
800/221-0417 (US except NY)
800/322-3067 (Miami)

MESSENGER AIR FREIGHT
800/421-0063 (US except IL)

QUICKPAK WORLDWIDE SMALL PACKAGE PICK UP & DELIVERY SERVICE
800/638-7237 (US)

SEKO AIR FREIGHT
800/445-8298 (US except MN)

SKYCAB
800/669-9998 (Cont'l US)

TWA NEXT FLIGHT OUT SMALL PACKAGE SERVICE
800/638-7380 (US except MD)
800/492-7363 (MD)

UNITED AIRLINES SMALL PACKAGE DISPATCH
800/241-6522 (US except IL)

Hotel & International Reservation Information

BEST WESTERN INTERNATIONAL RESERVATION CENTER
800/528-1234 (US & Canada)

CANADA PACIFIC HOTELS
800/828-7447 (US)
800/268-9411 (Canada)

CIGA HOTELS/LANDIA INTERNATIONAL SERVICES INC.
800/221-2340 (US)

CLARION HOTELS & RESORTS
800/252-7466 (US)

CLIMAT DE FRANCE
800/237-2623 (US)
800/824-4847 (Canada)

COMFORT INNS
800/228-5150 (US)

CONDO NETWORK INC. (US, Mexico & Caribbean)
800/321-2525 (US except KS)
800/654-6533 (Canada)

DIAL AUSTRIA INSTANT RESERVATIONS
800/221-4980 (Cont'l US except NY)

DIAL BERLIN
800/237-5469 (Cont'l US except TX)

FIESTA AMERICANA HOTELS
(Deluxe Hotels of Mexico)
800/223-2332 (Cont'l US except New York City)

FRIENDSHIP INNS INTERNATIONAL INC.
800/453-4511 (Cont'l US & Canada)

GOLDEN TULIP HOTELS AMERICA
800/344-1212 (US, Canada, & Puerto Rico)

GRAND HOTELS INTERNATIONAL
800/323-7249 (Cont'l US)

HELMSLEY HOTELS
800/221-4982 (US & Canada)

HILTON RESERVATION SERVICE
800/445-8667 (US)

HOLIDAY INN - WORLDWIDE
800/465-4329 (US)

HUNGARY/HUNGARIAN HOTELS
800/448-4321 (US except CA)
800/231-8704 (CA)

HYATT HOTELS
800/228-9000 (US & Canada)

INTERNATIONAL RESERVATION SYSTEM
800/231-0404 (US except NY)

LATIN AMERICA RESERVATION CENTER
800/327-3573 (Cont'l US except FL)

LEADING HOTELS OF THE WORLD
800/223-6800 (US except NY)

LOEWS REPRESENTATION INTERNATIONAL
800/223-0888 (Canada & US except NY)
800/522-5455 (NY)

MEXICO HOTEL & TRAVEL RESERVATION
800/252-0100 (Cont'l US)

PREFERRED HOTELS WORLDWIDE
800/323-7500 (US except IL & Canada)

PRINCE HOTELS INTERNATIONAL
800/223-1818 (Cont'l US)
800/442-8418 (NY)

QUALITY INNS
800/228-5150 (US)

RAMADA INNS INC.
800/272-6232 (Cont'l US)
800/268-8998 (Canada)

REGENT INTERNATIONAL HOTELS LTD.
800/545-4000 (US & Canada)

SCANDINAVIAN RESERVATIONS & INFORMATION SERVICES
800/272-2626 (Cont'l US except CA)
800/972-2626 (CA)

SCOTTISH INNS
800/251-1962 (Cont'l US & Canada)

SONESTA INTERNATIONAL HOTELS
800/343-7170 (US)

ST. CROIX HOTEL ASSOC. INC.
800/524-2026 (Cont'l US)

TRAVELODGE INTERNATIONAL INC.
800/255-3050 (US & Canada)

TRUSTHOUSE FORTE HOTELS
800/223-5672 (Cont'l US & Canada)
800/225-5843 (US)

WESTIN HOTELS
800/228-3000 (US, Canada, & Puerto Rico)

WESTERN TRAVEL
800/423-2917 (Cont'l US except CA)
800/272-3253 (CA except A/C 213)
800/222-2559 (AK & HI)
800/225-5834 (Canada)

Railroads

GERMANRAIL
800/782-2424 (US)

RAILWAYS OF AUSTRAILIA
800/423-2880 (US except CA)
800/232-2121 (CA)

SWISS FEDERAL RAILWAYS
800/223-0448 (Cont'l US except NY)

VIA RAIL CANADA
800/665-0200 (Cont'l US)
800/665-6830 (Canada)

Auto Rentals

AUTO BRITAIN
800/343-0395 (Cont'l US except MA)
800/852-1000 (MA)

AUTO EUROPE
800/223-5555 (Cont'l US except NY)
800/942-1309 (NY)
800/268-8810 (Canada except Ontario)

AUTO GLOBE
800/858-1515 (US except CA)
800/358-9797 (CA)

AUTO IRELAND
800/343-0395 (Cont'l US except MA)
800/852-1000 (MA)

BRENDAN'S SELF DRIVE/NEW ZEALAND
800/421-8446 (Cont'l US)

BUDGET RENT A CAR
800/527-0700 (US & Canada)

EUROPCAR
800/227-7368 (US)

VAN WIJK CAR RENTAL/HOLLAND
800/255-2847 (Cont'l US except NY)

For easy comparison of the major cities of the world, all the metropolitan maps are drawn at a consistent scale of 1:350,000. One inch on the map represents 5.5 miles on the earth's surface.

LEGEND

Major Cities

Inhabited Localities

The symbol represents the number of inhabitants within the locality

- ·   0—10,000
- ○   10,000—25,000
- ◉   25,000—100,000
- ▣   100,000—250,000
- ▣   250,000—1,000,000
- ■   >1,000,000

The size of type indicates the relative economic and political importance of the locality

Écommoy	**St.-Denis**
Trouville	
Lisieux	**PARIS**

■
Hollywood   **Section of a City,**
Westminster   **Neighborhood**
Northland ■
Center   **Major Shopping Center**

Urban Area (area of continuous industrial, commercial, and residential development)

Major Industrial Area

Wooded Area

Political Boundaries

International (First-order political unit)

▬ ▬ ▬ **Demarcated, Undemarcated, and Administrative**

▬ ▬ ▬ **Demarcation Line**

Internal

▬▬▬ **State, Province, etc.**
(Second-order political unit)

▬▬▬ **County, Oblast, etc.**
(Third-order political unit)

‒ ‒ ‒ **Okrug, Kreis, etc.**
(Fourth-order political unit)

‒ ‒ ‒ ‒ **City or Municipality**
(may appear in combination with another boundary symbol)

Capitals of Political Units

BUDAPEST   Independent Nation

Recife   State, Province, etc.

White Plains   County, Oblast, etc.

Iserlohn   Okrug, Kreis, etc.

Transportation

Road

   Primary

BERLINER RING   Secondary

Tertiary

Railway

CANADIAN NATIONAL   Primary

Secondary

Rapid Transit

Airport

LONDON (HEATHROW) AIRPORT

Rail or Air Terminal

■ SÜD BAHNHOF

REICHS-BRÜCKE   **Bridge**

) (**Tunnel**
GREAT ST. BERNARD TUNNEL

Other Features

▲   **Point of Interest**
SORBONNE   (Battlefield, museum, temple, university, etc.)

⌁   **Church, Monastery**
STEPHANSDOM

∴   **Ruins**
UXMAL

Υ
WINDSOR CASTLE   **Castle**

ℑ   **Lighthouse**

ASWĀN DAM \   **Dam**

<>   **Lock**

Mt. Kenya
5199 △   **Elevation Above Sea Level**

Elevations are given in meters

★   Rock

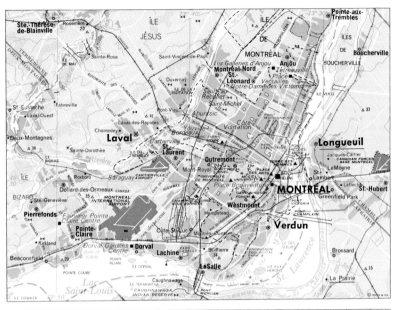

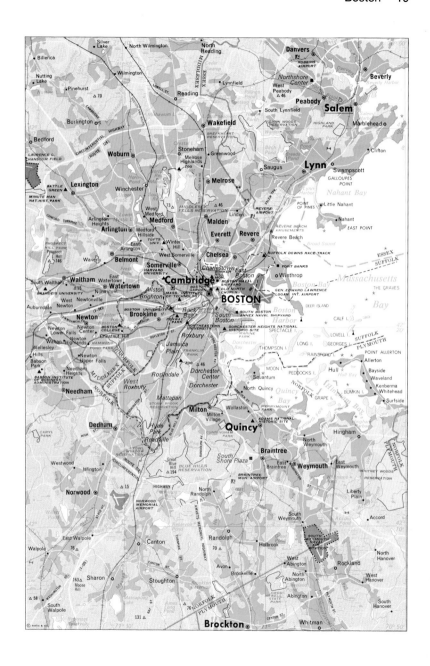

ATLANTIC   OCEAN

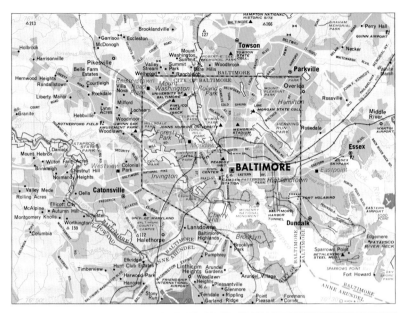

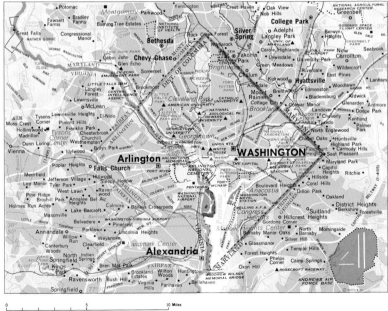

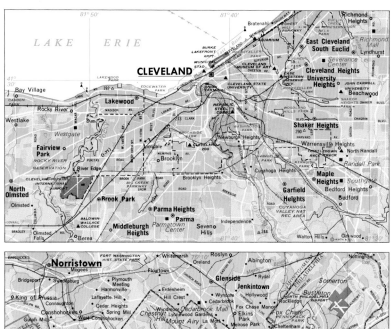

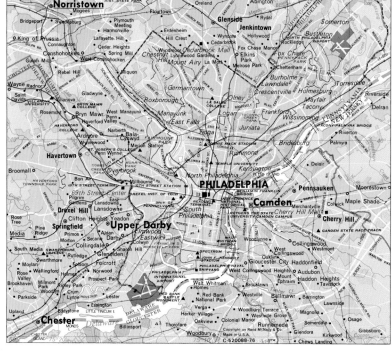

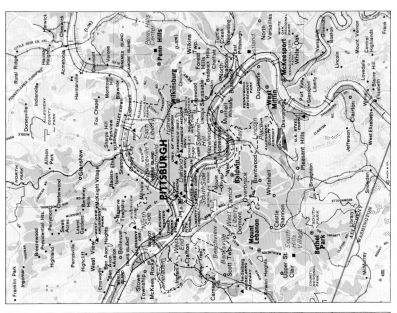

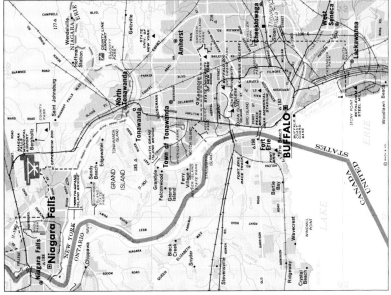

0   5   10 Miles

0   5   10 Kilometers

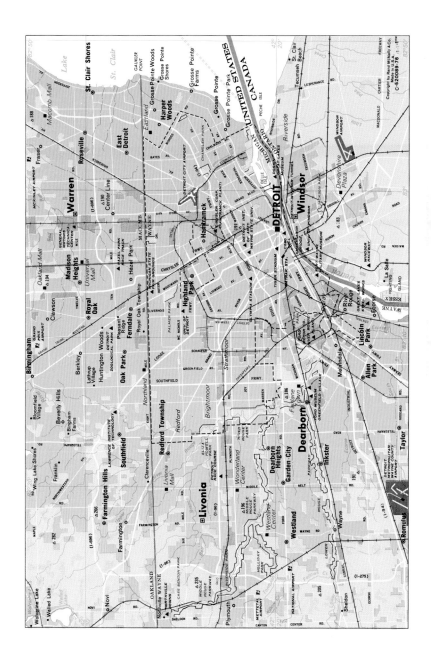

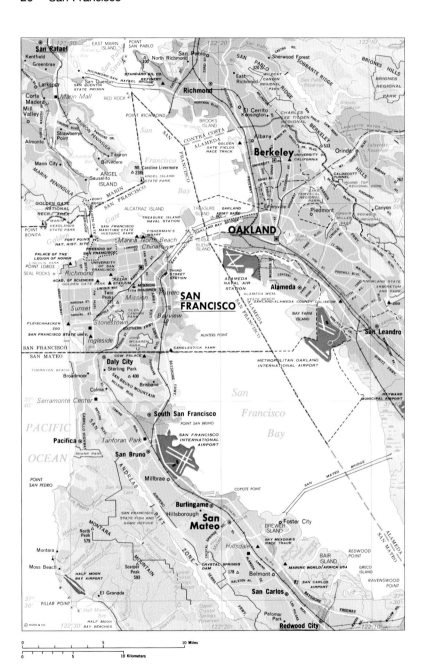

0   5   10 Miles
0   5   10 Kilometers

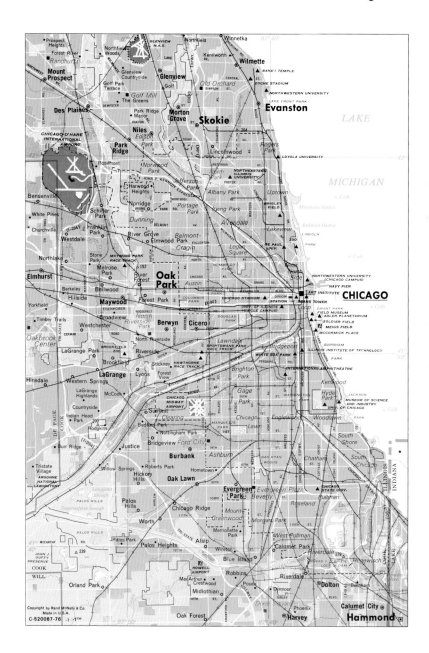

0   5   10 Miles

0   5   10 Kilometers

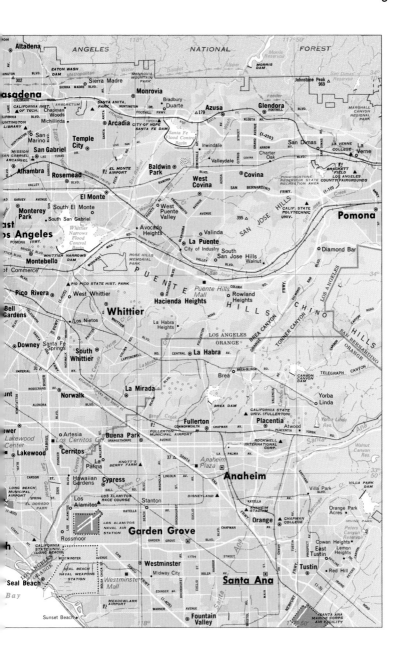

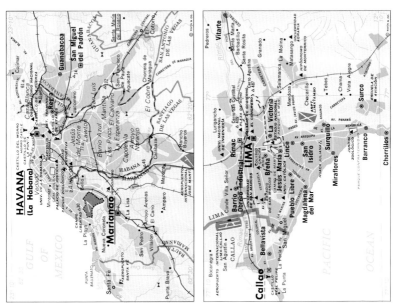

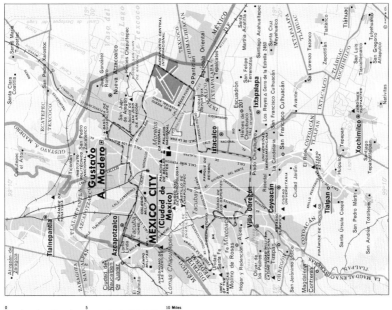

0   5   10 Miles
0   5   10 Kilometers

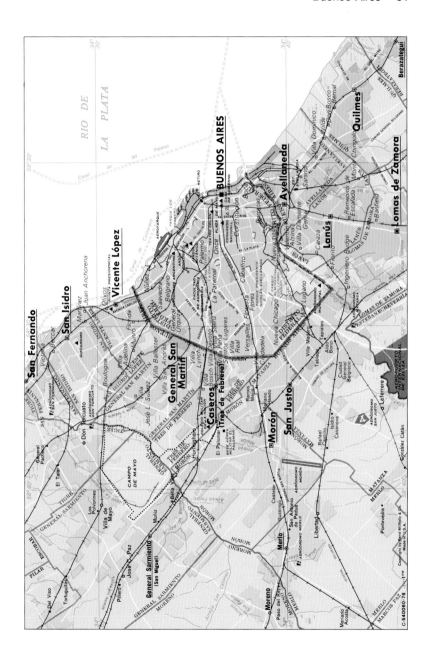

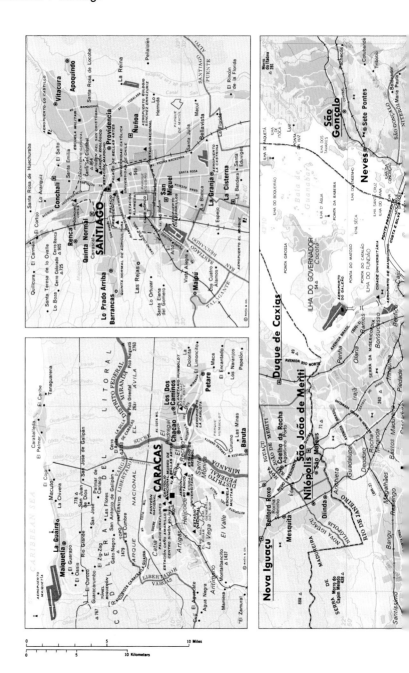

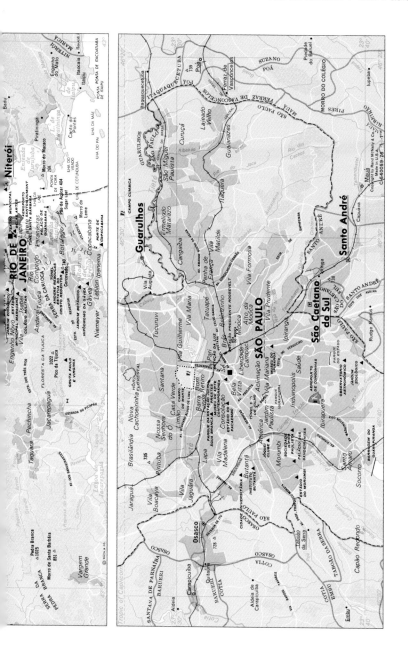

0   5   10 Miles

0   5   10 Kilometers

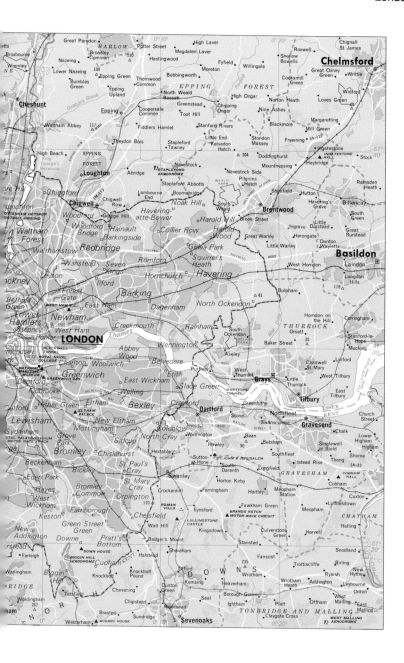

36

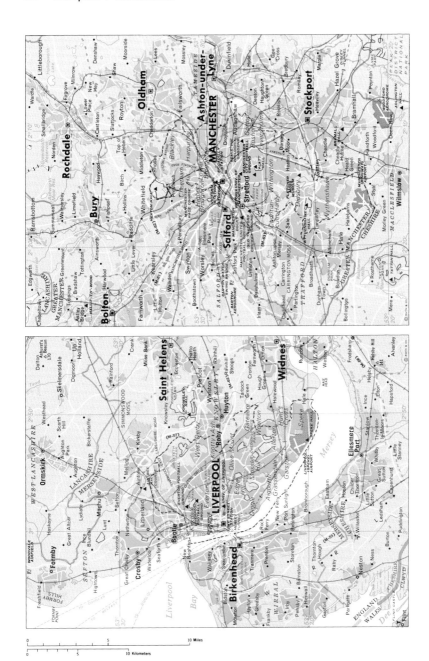

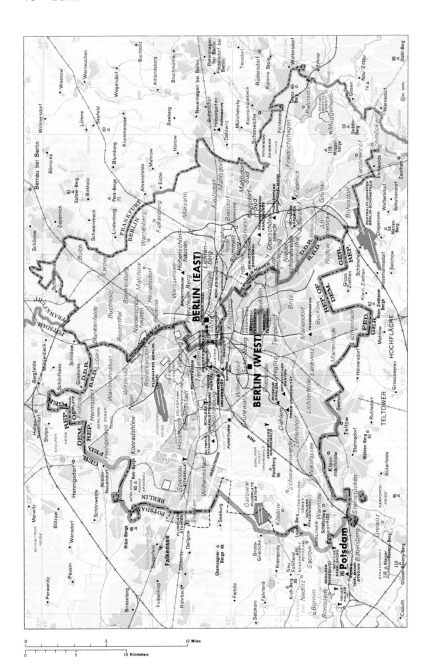

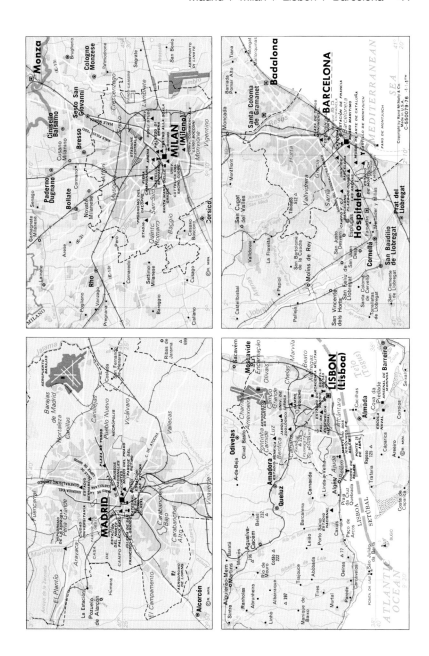

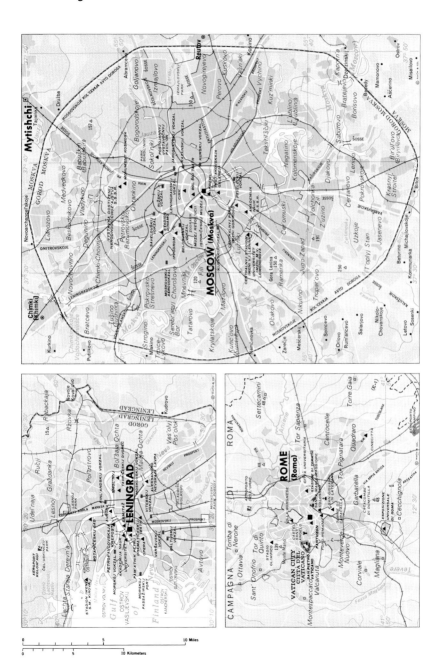

0   5   10 Miles

0   5   10 Kilometers

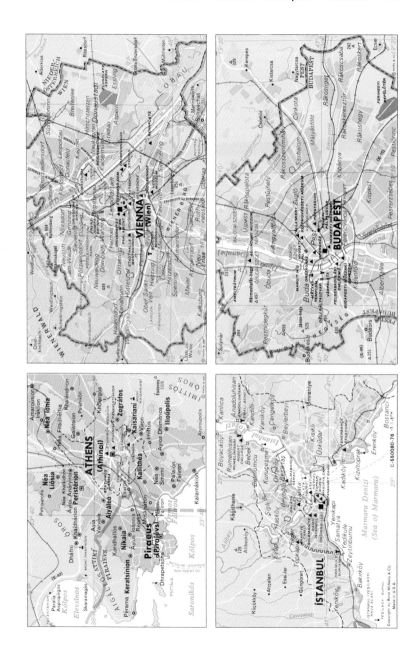

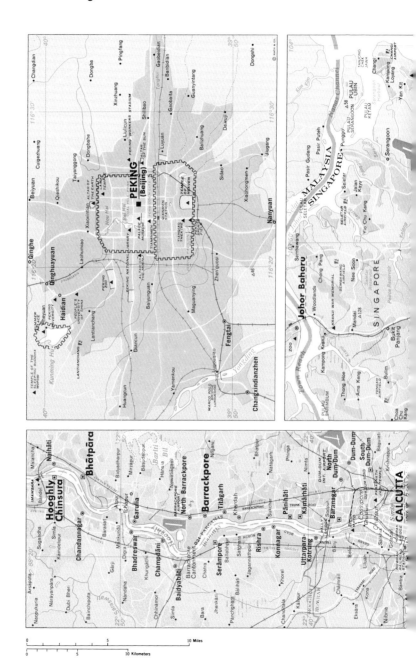

0   5   10 Miles
0   5   10 Kilometers

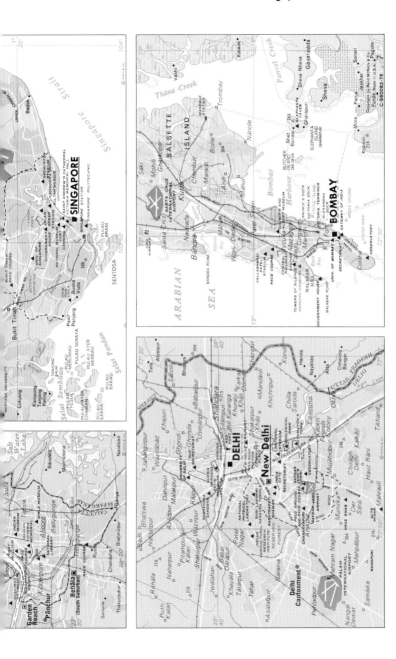

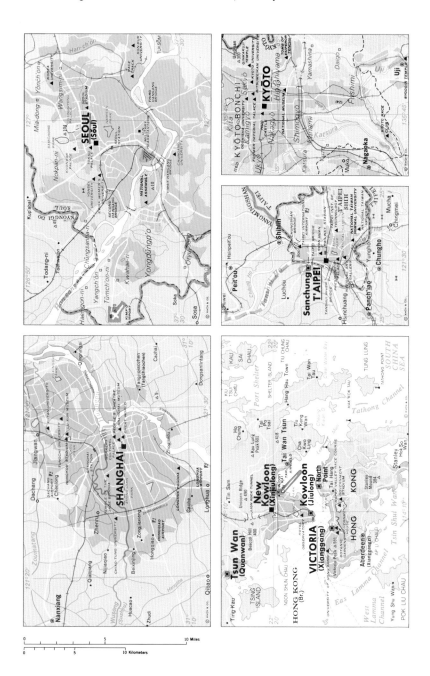

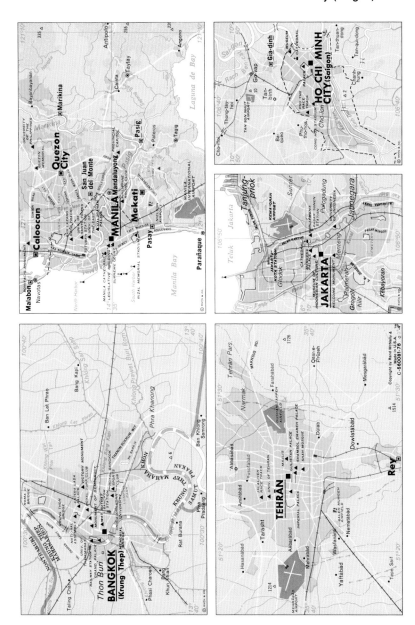

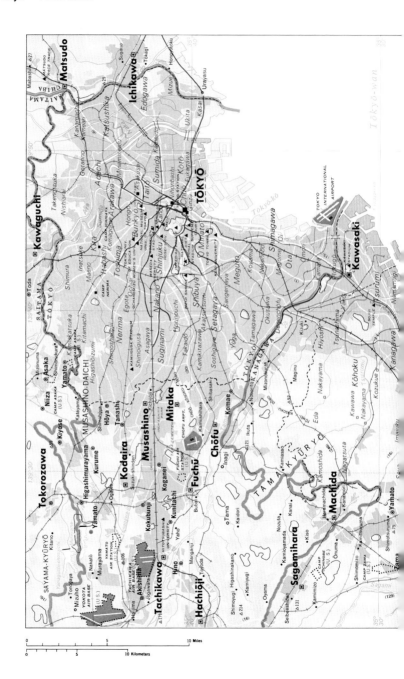

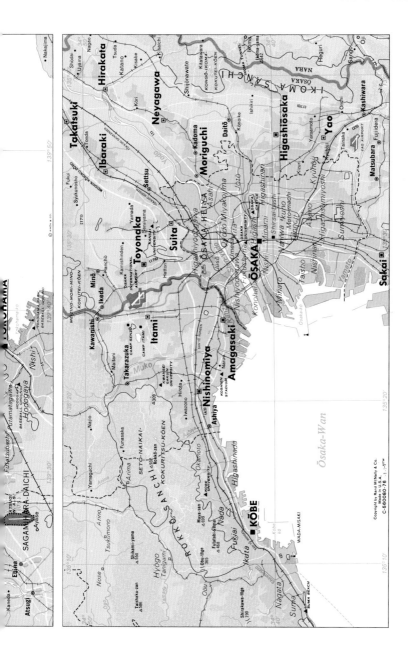

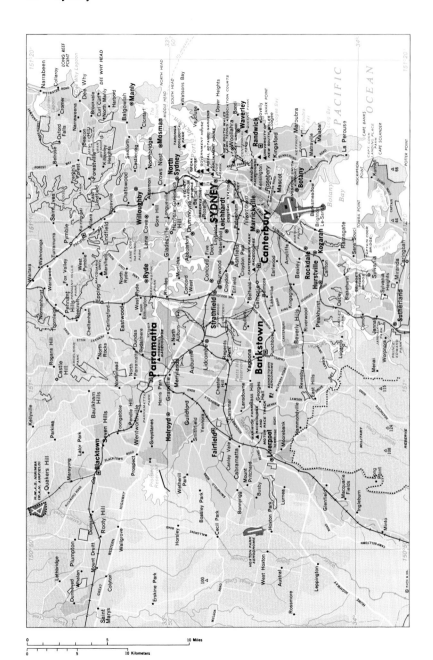

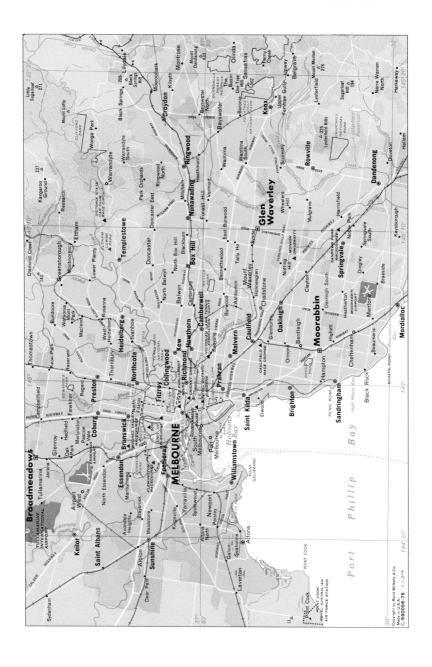

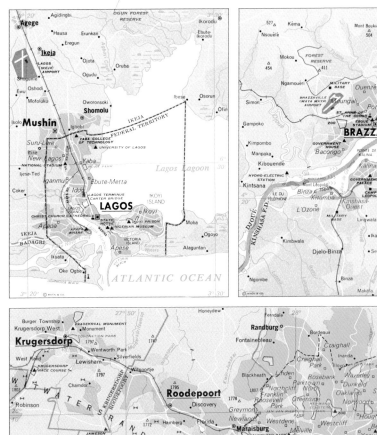

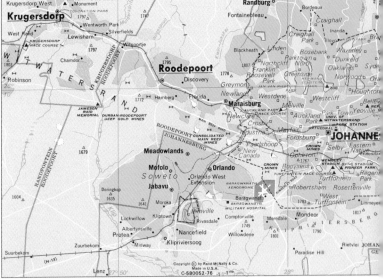

0   5   10 Miles

0   5   10 Kilometers

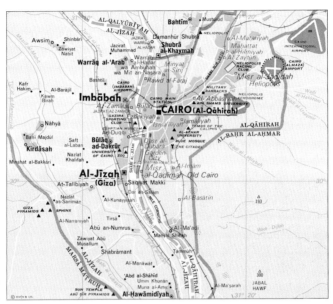
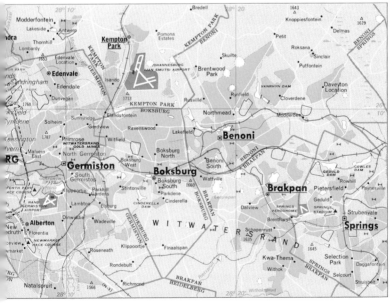

Guide to Selected Cities

This alphabetical guide shows geographical and travel information for major international cities. The list includes metro area population figures, hotels, restaurants, additional information sources, and other details.

Amsterdam, Netherlands

Population: 1,860,000
Altitude: 5 ft. (1.5m.) below sea level
Average Temp.: Jan., 35°F. (2°C.); July, 64°F. (18°C.)
Selected Hotels:
Amstel Intercontinental, Prof. Tulpplein 1
Amsterdam Hilton, 138-140 Apollolaan
L'e Europe, 2-8 Nieuwe Doelenstraat
Krasnapolsku, Dam 9
Marriott, Stadshouderskade
Okura Amsterdam, 175 Ferd. Bolstraat 333
Sonesta, Kattengat 1
Selected Restaurants:
Het Begijntje, Bali, De Boerderij, Molen de Dikkert Amstelveen, De Prinsenkelder, Dikker en Thijs, De Vijff Vlieghen,Excelsior, Sama Sebo, 't Swarte Schaep, De Gravenmolen
Banking: hours are 9 A.M. to 4 P.M. Monday through Friday.
Information Sources:
Amsterdam Tourist Office, 5 Rokin, Amsterdam

Athens (Athínai),Greece

Population: 3,027,331
Altitude: 230 ft. (70m.)
Average Temp.: Jan., 52°F. (11°C.); July, 80°F. (27°C.)
Selected Hotels:
Acropole Palace, 51 Patission St.
Amalia, 10 Amalias Ave.
Athenaeum Intercontinental, 89-93 Syngrou Ave.
Athens Hilton, Queen Sophias Ave.
Electra, 5 Hermou St.
Grande Bretagne, Constitution Sq.
King George, Constitution Sq.
Ledra Marriott, Syngrou Ave.
Meridien, Constitution Sq.
Park, 10 Alexandras Ave.
Selected Restaurants:
Athens Cellar, Corfu, Dionyssos, Gerofinikas, Floca, L'Abreuvoir, Papakia, Prunier, Skorpios, Stagecoach, Ta Nissia, Zonars, Zafiris
Banking: hours are 8 A.M. to 2 P.M. Monday through Saturday.
Information Sources:
Greek National Tourist Office, 1 Constitution Sq., Athens

Atlanta, Georgia

Population: 1,950,000
Altitude: 1,050 feet
Average Temp.: Jan., 52°F. (11°C.); July, 85°F. (29°C.)

Telephone Area Code: 404
Time Zone: Eastern
Selected Hotels:
American Hotel, 160 Spring St., 688-8600
Atlanta Hilton & Towers, 255 Courtland St. NE, 659-2000
Atlanta Marriott Perimeter Center, 246 Perimeter Center Pkwy. NE, 394-6500
Colony Square Hotel, 188 14th St. NE, 892-6000
Holiday Inn-Airport North, 1380 Virginia Ave., 762-8411
Hyatt Regency–Atlanta, 265 Peachtree St. NE, 577-1234
Omni Hotel at CNN Center, 100 CNN Center, 659-0000
Radisson Atlanta, Courtland St. at International Blvd., 659-6500
Westin Peachtree Plaza, 210 Peachtree St., 659-1400
Selected Restaurants:
The Abbey, 163 Ponce de Leon Ave., 876-8831
Bugatti's, in the Omni Hotel at CNN Center, 659-0000
Cafe de la Paix, in the Atlanta Hilton & Towers, 659-2000
Coach And Six, 1776 Peachtree St. NW, 872-6666
La Grotta, 2637 Peachtree Rd. NE, 231-1368
Nikolai's Roof Restaurant, in the Atlanta Hilton & Towers, 659-2000
Pano's and Paul's, 1232 W. Paces Ferry Rd. NW, 261-3662
Terrace Garden, 3405 Lenox Rd. NE, 261-9250
Information Sources:
Atlanta Convention & Visitors Bureau Suite 2000, 233 Peachtree St. NE Atlanta, Georgia 30303 521-6600

Boston, Massachusetts

Population: 3,738,800
Altitude: Sea level to 330 feet
Average Temp.: Jan., 29°F. (-2°C.); July, 72°F. (22°C.)
Telephone Area Code: 617
Time Zone: Eastern
Selected Hotels:
The Colonnade, 120 Huntington Ave., 424-7000
Copley Plaza Hotel, 138 St. James Ave., 267-5300
Hotel Meridien, 250 Franklin St., 451-1900
Logan Airport Hilton, 25 Service Rd., Logan International Airport, 569-9300
Omni Parker House, 60 School St., 227-8600
Selected Restaurants:
Anthony's Pier 4, 140 Northern Ave., 423-6363
The Cafe Budapest, 90 Exeter St., 266-1979
Copley's Restaurant, in the Copley Plaza Hotel, 267-5300
The Dining Room, in The Ritz-Carlton, Boston, 536-5700
Felicia's, 145A Richmond St., up one flight, 523-9885
Genji, 327 Newbury St., 267-5656
Julien, in the Hotel Meridien, 451-1900
Locke-Ober Cafe, 3-4 Winter Pl., 542-1340
Parker's, in the Parker House Hotel, 227-8600
Information Sources:

Greater Boston Convention & Visitors Bureau Inc.
Prudential Plaza West, Box 490 Boston,
Massachusetts 02199   (617) 536-4100

Brussels (Bruxelles), Belgium

Population: 2,395,000
Altitude: 53 ft. (16m.)
Average Temp.: Jan., 38°F. (3°C.); July, 66°F.
(19°C.)
Selected Hotels:
Amigo, 1-3 Rue de l'Amigo
Atlanta, 7 Blvd. Adolphe Max
Brussels Europa, 107 Rue de Loi
Brussels Hilton, 38 Blvd. de Waterloo
Hyatt Regency Brussels, 250 Rue Royale
Metropole, 31 Place de Brouckère
Palace, 22 Place Rogier
Royal Windsor, 5-7 Rue Duquesnoy
Sheraton Brussels, Manhattan Ctr., 3 Place Rogier
Selected Restaurants:
Bruneau, Chez Christopher, Comme Chez Soi,
Dupont, En Plein Ciel, La Pomme Cannelle,
L'Ecailler Du Palais Royal, L'Epaule de Mouton, Le
Cygne, Le Filet De Boeuf, Les Provencaux, Savoy,
Villa Lorraine
Banking: hours are normally 9 A.M. to 1 P.M. and
2:30 P.M. to 3:30 P.M. Tuesday through Thursday; 9
A.M. to 1 P.M. and 2:30 to 4:30 P.M. Monday and
Friday.
Information Sources:
Tourist Information Brussels Rue du Marché-aux-
Herbes 61 Brussels

Buenos Aires, Argentina

Population: 10,750,000
Altitude: 65 ft. (20m.)
Average Temp.: Jan., 75°F. (24°C.); July, 51°F.
(11°C.)
Selected Hotels:
Bauen Hotel, Callao 360
Libertador Hotel, Cordoba 680
Plaza, Plaza San Martín 311
Presidente, Cerrito 846, Avda. 9 de Julio
Selected Restaurants:
Au Bec Fin, Claridge Hotel Grill, Clark's, El Repecho
de San Telmo, La Cabaña, La Chacra, Los Años
Locos, Plaza Hotel Grill
Banking: hours are 10 A.M. to 4 P.M. Monday
through Friday.
Information Sources:
Embassy of the Argentine Republic 1600 New
Hampshire Avenue NW Washington, DC 20009

Cairo (Al-Qāhirah), Egypt

Population: 9,300,000
Altitude: 65 ft. (20m.)
Average Temp.: Jan., 57°F. (14°C.); July, 82°F.
(28°C.)
Selected Hotels:

El Salam Hyatt, 61 Abdel-Hamid Badawy St,
Heliopolis
Holiday Inn Pyramids, Alexandria Desert Rd.
Mena House, in front of Pyramids of Giza
Nile Hilton, Tahrir Square
Cairo Marriott, Saray El Guezira, Zamalek
Cairo Meridien, Roda Island
Cairo-Sheraton, Galae Square, Giza
Sheraton Heliopolis, Orouba St.
Shephaerds, Corniche
El Nil, Garden City
Selected Restaurants:
Aladdin's, A l'Americaine, Cairo Tower, El Haty,
Estoril, Groppi's, Kursaal, Le Grillon, Omar
Khayyam, Sofar, Tamerina, Swiss Restaurant
Banking: hours are 8:30 A.M. to 1 P.M. Saturday
through Thursday; 10 A.M. to noon on Sunday.
Closed Friday.
Information Sources:
Egyptian Tourist Promotion Authority, Misr Travel
Tower, Abbasiyya, Cairo

Calcutta, India

Population: 11,100,000
Altitude: 20 ft. (6m.)
Average Temp.: Jan., 68°F. (20°C.); July, 84°F.
(29°C.)
Selected Hotels:
Airport Ashok, Calcutta Airport
Great Eastern, Old Court House St.
Oberoi Grand, 117 J. Nehru Rd.
Park Hotel, 17 Park St.
Selected Restaurants:
Amber, Blue Fox, Kwality, Mocambo, Moulin Rouge,
Sky Room, Trinca's, Waldorf
Banking: hours are 10 A.M. to 2 P.M. Monday
through Friday;10 A.M. to noon on Saturday.
Information Sources:
Government of India Tourist Office, 4 Shakespeare
Sarani Calcutta

Chicago, Illinois

Population: 7,803,800
Altitude: 579 to 672 feet
Average Temp.: Jan., 27°F. (-3°C.); July, 75°F.
(24°C.)
Telephone Area Code: 312
Time Zone: Central
Selected Hotels:
Ambassador West Hotel, 1300 N. State Pkwy.,
787-7900
Barclay Chicago, 166 E. Superior, 787-6000
Chicago Marriott Hotel, 540 N. Michigan Ave.,
836-0100
Days Inn, 644 N. Lake Shore Dr., 943-9200
Fairmont Hotel, 200 N. Columbus Dr. at Illinois
Center, 565-8000
Holiday Inn, 350 N. Orleans St., 836-5000
Hotel Nikko, 320 N. Dearborn, 744-1900
Hyatt Regency O'Hare, 9300 W. Bryn Mawr Ave.,
Rosemont, 696-1234

Palmer House Towers, 17 E. Monroe St., 726-7500
Park Hyatt, 800 N. Michigan Ave., 280-2222
Tremont Hotel, 100 E. Chestnut St., 751-1900
The Whitehall, 105 E. Delaware Pl., 944-6300
Selected Restaurants:
The Bakery, 2218 N. Lincoln Ave., 472-6942
Biggs Restaurant, 1150 N. Dearborn Pkwy.,
787-0900
Cape Cod Room, in the Drake Hotel, 787-2200
Gordon Restaurant, 500 N. Clark, 467-9780
House of Hunan, 535 N. Michigan Ave., 329-9494
Lawry's The Prime Rib, 100 E. Ontario St.,
787-5000
Le Perroquet Restaurant, 70 E. Walton Pl., 944-7990
Nick's Fishmarket, 1 First National Plaza, Monroe at
Dearborn, 621-0200
Ninety-Fifth, 172 E. Chestnut, in the John Hancock
Center, 787-9596
Pizzeria Uno, 29 E. Ohio St., 321-1000
The Pump Room, Ambassador East Hotel,
1301 State Pkwy., 266-0360
Su Casa, 49 E. Ontario St., 943-4041
Information Sources:
Chicago Convention & Visitors Bureau
McCormick Place-on-the-Lake
Chicago, Illinois 60616 (312) 567 8600

Copenhagen (København), Denmark

Population: 1,685,000
Altitude: 20 ft. (6m.)
Average Temp.: Jan., 33°F. (1°C.); July, 63°F.
(17°C.)
Selected Hotels:
d'Angleterre, 34 Kongens Nytorv
3 Falke, 9 Falkoner Allé
Copenhagen Admiral Hotel, Tolbodgade 24
Palace, 57 Radhuspladsen
The Plaza, 4 Bernstorffsgade
Royal, 1 Hammerichsgade
Hotel Scandinavia, Amager Blvd.
Sheraton-Copenhagen, 6 Vester Søgade
Selected Restaurants:
d'Angleterre Hotel Restaurant, Boef & Ost,
Fiskehuset, Den Gyldne Fortun, Langelinie
Pavillonen Terraces at Royal Yacht Club, Plaza
Hotel Restaurant, Royal Hotel Restaurant
Banking: hours 9:30 A.M. to 4 P.M., Monday
through Friday; close at 6 P.M. Thursday.
Information Sources:
Danish Tourist Board 655 Third Ave., New York,
New York 10017

Dallas-Fort Worth, Texas

Population: 2,974,819
Altitude: 450 to 750 feet
Average Temp.: Jan., 44°F. (7°C.); July, 86°F.
(30°C.)
Telephone Area Code: (Dallas) 214 (Fort Worth) 817
Time Zone: Central
Selected Hotels: DALLAS
Adolphus Hotel, 1321 Commerce St., 742-8200

Dallas Hilton, 1914 Commerce St., 747-7000
Fairmont Hotel, 1717 N. Akard St., 720-2020
Howard Johnson's-Stemmons, 3111 Stemmons
Frwy., 637-0060
Hyatt Regency-Dallas-Fort Worth Airport,
International Pkwy.,453-8400
Le Baron Hotel, 1055 Regal Row, 634-8550
Loews Anatole Hotel, 2201 Stemmons Frwy.,
748-1200
Marriott Hotel Market Center, 2101 Stemmons Frwy.,
748-8551
Plaza of the Americas Hotel, 650 N. Pearl St.,
979-9000
Stouffer Dallas Hotel, 2222 N. Stemmons Frwy.,
631-2222
The Westin Hotel, 13340 Dallas Pkwy., 934-9494
Selected Restaurants: DALLAS
Cafe Royale, Plaza of the Americas Hotel, 979-9000
Il Sorrento, 8616 Turtle Creek Blvd., 352-8759
Mr. Peppe French Cuisine, 5617 W. Lovers Lane,
352-5976
Old Warsaw, 2610 Maple Ave., 528-0032
Plum Blossom, in the Loew's Anatole Hotel,
748-1200
The Pyramid Room, Fairmont Hotel, 748-5454
Information Sources: DALLAS
Dallas Convention & Visitors Bureau 1201 Elm St.,
Suite 2000 Dallas, Texas 75270 (214) 746-6677
Selected Hotels: FORT WORTH
Green Oaks Inn, 6901 W. Frwy., 738-7311
Hyatt Regency Fort Worth, 815 Main St., 870-1234
La Quinta-Fort Worth West, 7888 I-30 W. at Cherry
Ln., 246-5511
Metro Center Hotel, 600 Commerce St., 332-6900
Park Central Inn, 1010 Houston St., 336-2011
Quality Inn South, I-35 W. South at Seminary Exit,
923-8281
Ramada Inn Central, 2000 Beach St., 534-4801
The Worthington, 200 Main St., 870-1000
Selected Restaurants: FORT WORTH
The Balcony, 6100 Camp Bowie Blvd., 731-3719
Bill Martin's Seafood, 251 University Dr., 332-9244
The Castaway, 1900 Ben Ave., 534-4908
Crystal Cactus, in the Hyatt Regency Fort Worth,
870-1234
Mac's House, 2400 Park Hill Dr., 921-4682
Information Sources: FORT WORTH
Fort Worth Convention & Visitors Bureau
100 E. 15th St., Suite 400
Fort Worth, Texas 76102 (817) 336-8791

Denver, Colorado

Population: 1,414,200
Altitude: 5,130 to 5,470 feet
Average Temp.: Jan., 31°F. (-1°C.); July, 74°F.
(23°C.)
Telephone Area Code: 303
Time Zone: Mountain
Selected Hotels:
Brown Palace Hotel, 321 17th St., 297-3111
Burnsley Hotel, 1000 Grant St., 830-1000
Clarion Hotel, 3203 Quebec St., 321-3333
Holiday Inn Downtown, 1450 Glenarm Pl., 573-1450

Hyatt Regency Denver, 1750 Welton St., 295-1200
Radisson Hotel Denver, 1550 Court Pl., 893-3333
Raffles Hotel, I-225 & South Parker Rd., 695-1700
Stapleton Plaza Hotel and Fitness Center, 3333
  Quebec St., 321-3500
Selected Restaurants:
Churchill's, The Writers' Manor Hotel, 1730 S.
  Colorado Blvd., 756-8877
Ellyngton's, at the Brown Palace Hotel, 297-3111
Normandy French Restaurant, 1515 Madison St.,
  321-3311
Palace Arms, at the Brown Palace Hotel, 297-3111
Tante Louise, 4900 E. Colfax Ave., 355-4488
Information Sources:
Denver Metro Convention and Visitors Bureau
  225 W. Colfax Ave., Denver, Colorado 80202
  (303) 892-1112

Detroit, Michigan

Population: 4,399,000
Altitude: 573 to 672 feet
Average Temp.: Jan., 26°F. (-3°C.); July, 73°F.
(28°C.)
Telephone Area Code: 313
Time Zone: Eastern
Selected Hotels:
Holiday Inn Metro Airport, 31200 Industrial Expwy.,
  728-2800
Hotel Pontchartrain, 2 Washington Blvd., 965-0200
Hotel St. Regis, 3071 W. Grand Blvd., 873-3000
Hyatt Regency Dearborn, Fairlane Town Center Dr.,
  Dearborn, 593-1234
Michigan Inn, 16400 J.L. Hudson Dr., Southfield,
  559-6500
Northfield Hilton, 5500 Crooks Rd., Troy, 879-2100
The Westin Hotel, Renaissance Center, 568-8000
Selected Restaurants:
Captains, 260 Schweizer Place, 568-1862
Carl's Chop House, 3020 Grand River Ave.,
  833-0700
Caucus Club, 150 W. Congress St., 965-4970
Charley's Crab, 5498 Crooks Rd., Troy, 879-2060
  559-4230
Joe Muer's, 2000 Gratiot Ave., 567-1088
London Chop House, 155 W. Congress St.,
  962-6735
Mario's Restaurant, 4222 2nd Ave., 833-9425
Pontchartrain Wine Cellars, 234 W. Larned St.,
  963-1785
Van Dyke Place, 649 Van Dyke Ave., 821-2620
Information Sources:
Metropolitan Detroit Convention & Visitors Bureau
  Suite 1950, 100 Renaissance Center
  Detroit, Michigan 48243 (313) 259-4333

Frankfurt am Main, Federal Republic of Germany

Population: 1,855,000
Altitude: 325 ft. (99m.)
Average Temp.: Jan., 34°F. (1°C.); July, 67°F.
(19°C.)
Selected Hotels:

Frankfurter Hof, Kaiserplatz 17
Frankfurt Intercontinental, Wilhelm-Leuschner Str. 43
Hessische Hof, Friedrich-Ebert Anlage 40
Parkhotel, Wiesenhüttenplatz 36
Schlosshotel Kronberg, in Kronberg at Hain Str. 25
Sheraton Rhein-Main, Airport
Steigenberger Airport Hotel
Selected Restaurants:
Chez Henri, Da Franco, Taverne Royale, Weinhaus
  Brückenkeller, Hessische Hof Restaurants,
  Parkhotel Restaurants, Frankfurter Hof Grillroom,
  Kupferpfanne, Silhouette Supper Club in the
  Frankfurt Intercontinental Hotel
Banking: hours 8:30 A.M. to 1 P.M. and 2:30 P.M.
to 4 P.M., Monday through Friday; close at 5:30 P.M.
Thursday.
Information Sources:
German National Tourist Board, Beethovenstrasse
  69, 6000 Frankfurt am Main

Hong Kong (Victoria)

Population: 4,515,000
Altitude: 50 ft., (15m.)
Average Temp.: Jan., 59°F. (15°C.); July, 84°F.
(29°C.)
Selected Hotels:
Excelsior, Gloucester Rd., Causeway Bay
Furama Intercontinental, 1 Connaught Rd.
Holiday Inn Harbour View, 70 Mody Rd., Kowloon
Hong Kong Hilton Hotel, 2 Queen's Rd. Central
Hong Kong Hotel, Harbour City, Kowloon
Hyatt Regency Hong Kong, 67 Nathan Rd., Kowloon
Lee Gardens, Hysan Ave., Causeway Bay
Mandarin, 5 Connaught Rd.
Marco Polo, Harbour City, Kowloon
Miramar, 130 Nathan Rd., Kowloon
Peninsula, Salisbury Rd., Kowloon
Regal Meridien, 71 Mody Rd., Kowloon
Regent, Salisbury Rd., Kowloon
Royal Garden, 69 Mody Rd., East Tsimshatsui,
  Kowloon
Shangri-La, 64 Mody Rd., Kowloon
Sheraton Hong Kong, 20 Nathan Rd., Kowloon
Selected Restaurants:
Chesa, Gaddi's (Peninsula), Harbour Room, Hilton's
  Eagle Nest, Hugo's (Hyatt), Jade Garden, Jimmy's
  Kitchen, Jumbo Floating Restaurant (Aberdeen),
  Juno's Revolving Restaurant, Mandarin Grill,
  Peking Garden, Yung Kee
Banking: hours are 9 A.M. to 3 P.M. Monday
through Friday; 9:00 A.M. to noon on Saturday.
Information Sources:
Hong Kong Tourist Association, 333 N. Michigan
  Ave., Suite 2323 Chicago, Illinois 60601

Honolulu, Hawaii

Population: 762,900
Altitude: Sea level to 4,020 feet
Average Temp.: Jan., 72°F. (22°C.); July, 80°F.
(27°C.)
Telephone Area Code: 808

Time Zone: Hawaiian (Two hours earlier than Pacific standard time)
Selected Hotels:
Halekulani, 2199 Kalia Rd., 923-2311
Hawaiian Regent, 2552 Kalakaua Ave., 922-6611
Hilton Hawaiian Village, 2005 Kalia Rd., 949-4321
Hyatt Regency Waikiki, 2424 Kalakaua Ave., 922-9292
The Ilikai, 1777 Ala Moana Blvd., 949-3811
Moana Surfrider, 2365 Kalakaua Ave., 922-3111
Outrigger Waikiki Hotel, 2335 Kalakaua Ave., 923-0711
Queen Kapiolani, 150 Kapahulu Ave., 922-1941
Royal Hawaiian, 2259 Kalakaua Ave., 923-7311
Sheraton Princess Kaiulani, 120 Kaiulani Ave., 922-5811
Selected Restaurants:
Canlis, 2100 Kalakaua Ave., 923-2324
Foster Towers Furusato, 2500 Kalakaua Ave., 922-5502
Golden Dragon Room (Chinese), in the Hilton Hawaiian Village, 949-4321
Maile Room, in the Kahala Hilton, 734-2211
Michel's, in the Colony Surf Hotel, 2895 Kalakaua Ave., 923-6552
The Third Floor, in the Hawaiian Regent Hotel, 922-6611
The Willows, 901 Hausten St., 946-4808
Information Sources:
Hawaii Visitors Bureau Convention Office 2270 Kalakaua Ave., Suite 801 Honolulu, Hawaii 96815 (808) 923-1811

Istanbul, Turkey

Population: 5,750,000
Altitude: 30 ft. (9m.)
Average Temp.: Jan., 42°F. (6°C.); July, 74°F. (23°C.)
Selected Hotels:
Büyük Tarabya, Tarabya
Carlton Hotel, Yenikoy
Cinar Hotel, Yesilköy
Divan Hotel, Harbiye
ETAP Hotel, Taksim
Istanbul Hilton, Harbiye
Etap Marmara Hotel
Macka Hotel, Emlak Caddesi
Park Hotel, Gümüssuyu Caddesi 6
Sheraton Hotel
Selected Restaurants:
Abdullah Restaurant, Divan Hotel Restaurant, Galata Tower, Etap Marmara Restaurant, Hotel Kalyon Restaurant, Konyali, Le Mangal (Sheraton Hotel), Liman (lunch), Park Hotel Restaurant, Roof Rotisserie, Sadirvan Supper Club at the Hilton Hotel
Banking: hours 9 A.M. to noon and 1:30 P.M. to 5:30 P.M. Monday through Friday.
Information Sources:
Turkish Government Tourism and Information Office, 821 United National Plaza New York, New York 10017

Lisbon (Lisboa), Portugal

Population: 2,250,000
Altitude: 150 ft. (46m.)
Average Temp.: Jan., 51°F. (11°C.); July, 72°F. (22°C.)
Selected Hotels:
Alfa, Av. Columbano Bordalo Pinheiro
Altis, Rua Castilho II
Avenida Palace, Rua 1.° de Dezembro 123
Diplomatico, Rua Castilho 74
Fénix, Praca Marquês de Pombal 8
Flórida, Rua Duque de Palmela 32
Lisbon-Sheraton, Rua Latino Coelho 2
Lisbon Penta, Av. Dos Combatentes
Mundial, Rua D. Duarte 4
Principe Real, Rua da Alegria 53
Ritz, Rua Rodrigo da Fonseca 88-A
Tivoli, Av. da Liberdade 185
Selected Restaurants:
A Gôndola, Altis Hotel Grill Aviz, Bodegon (Fénix Hotel) Cozinha d'el Rey, Escorial, Gambrinus, Hong Kong, Macau, Pabe, Ritz Hotel Grill, Solmar, Tavares
Banking: hours 8:30 A.M. to 11:45 A.M. and 1 to 2:45 P.M. Monday through Friday; closed Saturday.
Information Sources:
Portuguese National Tourist Office, 548 Fifth Avenue, New York, New York 10036

London, England

Population: 11,100,000
Altitude: 20 ft. (6m.)
Average Temp.: Jan., 40°F. (4°C.); July, 64°F. (18°C.)
Selected Hotels:
Berkeley, Wilton Pl., SW 1
Britannia International, Grosvenor Sq., W1
Capital, Basil St., SW 3
Churchill, 30 Portman Sq., W 1
Connaught, Carlos Pl., W 1
Dorchester, Park Lane, W 1
Grosvenor House, Park Lane, W 1
Hilton, Park Lane, W 1
Ritz, Piccadilly, W 1
Savoy, Victoria Embankment, WC 2
Tower, St. Katherine's Way, E1
Waldorf, Aldwych, WC 2
Selected Restaurants:
Café Royal, Mirabelle, Quaglino's, Rules, Simpson's-in-the-Strand, Walton's
Banking: hours in England are 9:30 A.M. to 3:30 P.M. Monday through Friday. Some banks are open Saturday.
Information Sources:
National Tourist Information Centre, Victoria Station Forecourt London SW1
London Tourist Board, 26 Grosvenor Gardens, London SW1W 0DU

Los Angeles, California

Population: 9,840,200
Altitude: Sea level to 5,074 feet
Average Temp.: Jan., 55°F. (13°C.); July, 73°F. (23°C.)
Telephone Area Code: 213
Time Zone: Pacific
Selected Hotels:
Ambassador Garden Hotel, Tennis & Health Club, 3400 Wilshire Blvd., 387-7011
Beverly Hills Hotel, 9641 Sunset Blvd., 276-2251
Biltmore Hotel, 506 S. Grand Ave., 624-1011
Century Plaza, 2025 Avenue of the Stars, 277-2000
Holiday Inn–Hollywood, 1755 N. Highland Ave., 462-7181
Hyatt Los Angeles Airport, 6225 W. Century Blvd., 670-9000
L'Ermitage, 9291 Burton Way, 278-3344
Le Parc Hotel De Luxe, 733 N. West Knoll Dr., 855-8888
Los Angeles Airport Marriott, 5855 W. Century Blvd., 641-5700
Los Angeles Hilton and Towers, 930 Wilshire Blvd., 629-4321
Sheraton Town House, 2961 Wilshire Blvd., 382-7171
Sheraton–Universal, 333 Universal Terrace Pkwy., Universal City, (818) 980-1212
University Hilton, 3540 S. Figueroa St., 748-4141
The Westin Bonaventure Hotel, 404 S. Figueroa St., 624-1000
Selected Restaurants:
Bernard's, in the Biltmore Hotel, 612-1580
Lawry's Prime Rib, 55 N. La Cienega Blvd., 652-2827
Madame Wu's Garden, 2201 Wilshire Blvd., 828-5656
Perino's, 4101 Wilshire Blvd., 487-0000
Scandia, 9040 Sunset Blvd., West Hollywood, 278-3555
The Tower, 1150 S. Olive St., 746-1554
Yamato, in the Century Plaza Hotel, 277-1840
Information Sources:
Greater Los Angeles Visitors & Convention Bureau
515 S. Figueroa, 11th Floor
Los Angeles, California 90071   (213) 624-7300

Madrid, Spain

Population: 4,650,000
Altitude: 2,100 ft. (640m.)
Average Temp.: Jan., 41°F. (5°C.); July, 76°F. (24°C.)
Selected Hotels:
Alameda, Av. Logrono 100
Castellana, Paseo de la Castellana 57
Eurobuilding, Padre Damian 23
Luz Palacio, Castellana 67
Melia Madrid, Princesa 27
Miguel Angel, Miguel Angel 29
Mindanao, S. Francisco De Sales 15
Monte Real, Arroyo Fresno 17
Plaza, Plaza de España 8
Palace, Plaza de las Cortes 7
Princesa Palace, Princesa 40
Villamagna, Castellana 22
Wellington, Velazquez 8
Selected Restaurants:
Club 31, Commodore, Cafe Chinitas, Jockey Club, Las Lanzas, Zalacain Sixt
Banking: hours are 9 A.M. to 2 P.M. Monday through Saturday.
Information Sources:
Spanish National Tourist Office, 665 Fifth Ave., New York, New York 10022

Manila, Philippines

Population: 6,800,000
Altitude: 10 ft. (3m.)
Average Temp.: Jan., 78°F. (26°C.); July, 82°F. (28°C.)
Selected Hotels:
Holiday Inn, 3001 Roxas Blvd.
Hotel Intercontinental, Ayala Av.
Hyatt Regency Manila, 2702 Roxas Blvd.
Manila Hilton, UN Av., Ermita
Manila Hotel, Rizal Park
Manila Mandarin Hotel, Makati Av., Makati
Manila Peninsula, Ayala and Makati Av.
Philippine Plaza, Cultural Center Complex
Silahis International, 1990 Roxas Blvd., Malate
Selected Restaurants:
Aristocrat, Au Bon Vivant, Barrio Fiesta, Champagne Room in Manila Hotel, Hilton Hotel Restaurant, Intercontinental Hotel Restaurant, Kamayan, Maynila
Banking: hours usually are 9 A.M. to 3 P.M. Monday through Friday.
Information Sources:
Convention & Visitors Corp., Embassy of the Philippines, 1617 Massachusetts Ave. NW, Washington, D.C. 20036

Mexico City (Ciudad de México), Mexico

Population: 14,100,000
Altitude: 7,300 ft. (2,225m.)
Average Temp.: Jan., 54°F. (12°C.); July, 64°F. (18°C.)
Selected Hotels:
Alameda, Avenida Juárez 50
Aristos, Paseo de la Reforma 276
Camino Real, Mariano Escobedo 700
El Presidenté, Hamburgo 135
El Presidenté Chapultepec, Paseo de la Reforma and Chapultepec Park
Fiesta Palace, Paseo de la Reforma 80
Gran Hotel, 16 de Septiembre No. 82, Zocalo
Holiday Inn Downtown
Hyatt, Paseo de la Reforma 166
Maria Isabel-Sheraton, Paseo de la Reforma 325
Selected Restaurants:
Ambassadeurs, Anderson's, El Parador, Focolare, Fonda Santa Anita, Hacienda de los Morales, La Cava, Restaurant del Lago, Rivoli, San Angel Inn

Banking: banks are open 9 A.M. to 1 P.M. Monday through Friday; 9 A.M. to 12:30 P.M. on Saturday.
Information Sources:
Ministry of Tourism, Ave. Presidenté Masaryk, 172 Colonia Chapultepec Polanco, Mexico City

Miami, Florida

Population: 2,689,200
Altitude: Sea level to 30 feet
Average Temp.: Jan., 69°F. (21°C.); July, 82°F. (28°C.)
Telephone Area Code: 305
Time Zone: Eastern
Selected Hotels:
Coconut Grove Hotel, 2649 S. Bayshore Dr., 858-2500
Holiday Inn–Civic Center, 1170 NW. 11th St., 324-0800
Marina Park Hotel, 340 Biscayne Blvd., 371-4400
Marriott Hotel, 1201 NW. LeJeune Rd., 649-5000
Miami Lakes Inn, Athletic Club, Golf Resort, Main St. & Bull Run Rd., Miami Lakes, 821-1150
Omni International Hotel, 1601 Biscayne Blvd., 374-0000
Ramada Hotel–Miami International Airport, 3941 NW. 22nd St., 871-1700
Sheraton River House, 3900 NW. 21st St., 871-3800
Selected Restaurants:
Cafe Chauveron, 9561 E. Bay Harbor Dr., 866-8779
Centro Vasco, 2235 SW. 8th St., 643-9606
Cye's Rivergate, 444 Brickell Ave., 358-9100
La Paloma, 10999 Biscayne Blvd., 891-0505
Raimondo, 4612 SW. Le Jeune, 666-9355
Information Sources:
Greater Miami Convention and Visitors Bureau 4770 Biscayne Blvd., Penthouse A
Miami, Florida 33137   (305) 573-4300

Milan (Milano), Italy

Population: 3,775,000
Altitude: 400 ft. (122m.)
Average Temp.: Jan., 34°F. (1°C.); July, 73°F. (23°C.)
Selected Hotels:
Cavalieri, Piazza Missori 1
Continental, Via Manzoni 7
Duomo, Via S. Raffaele 1
Excelsior Gallia, Piazza Duca d'Aosta 9
Grand Hotel et de Milan, Via Manzoni 29
Palace, Piazzale della Repubblica 20
Principe e Savoia, Piazzale della Repubblica 17
Hilton, Via Galvani 12
Selected Restaurants:
Biffi Scala, Giannino, Gourmet, Savini, St. Andrew's
Banking: hours are 8:30 A.M. to 1 P.M. Monday through Friday.
Information Sources:
EPT—Ente Provinciale Turismo
AAST—Azienda Autonoma Soggiorno Turismo

Montréal, Canada

Population: 2,921,357
Altitude: 50 ft. (15m.)
Average Temp.: Jan., 16°F. (-9°C.); July, 71°F. (22°C.)
Telephone Area Number: 514
Selected Hotels:
Le Chateau Champlain, 1 Place du Canada, Lagauchetiere W
Hotel Meridien-Montréal, 4 Complexe Desjardins
Montréal Aeroport Hilton International, 12505 Côte de Liesse Rd. in Dorval
Mt. Royal, 1455 Peel St.
Queen Elizabeth, 900 Blvd. Réné Levesqne
Ritz-Carlton, 1228 Sherbrooke, St. W
Ruby Foo's Motor Hotel, 7815 Decaria Blvd.
Selected Restaurants:
Café de Paris, Café Martin, Chez Bourgetel, Chez Fanny, Des Jardins, Le Castillon in the Bonaventure Hilton International, Le Neufchatel, Le Vieux St. Gabriel, Les Filles du Roy, Les Halles, Ruby Foo's
Banking: hours are generally from 10 A.M. to 3 P.M. Monday through Thursday; 10 A.M. to 6 P.M. on Friday. If Friday is a holiday, Friday hours are observed on Thursday.
Information Sources:
Montréal Convention & Visitors Bureau, 174 Notre Dame St. E at Place Jacques Cartier
Montréal H2Y 1C2

Moscow (Moskva), U.S.S.R.

Population: 12,900,000
Altitude: 395 ft. (120m.)
Average Temp.: Jan., 14°F. (-10°C.); July, 66°F. (19°C.)
Selected Hotels:
Berlin, 3 Zhdanov St.
Intourist, 3/5 Gorky St.
Metropole, 1 Marx Ave.
National, 14-1 Marx Ave.
Rossiya Hotel, 6 Razin St.
Ukraina, 2/1 Kutuzovsky Ave.
Selected Restaurants:
Aragvi, Arbat, Baku, Berlin, Budapest, Peking, Praga, Seventh Heaven, Sofia, Slavyansky Bazaar, Uzbekistan
Banking: banks are open from 9 A.M. to 1 P.M. Monday through Friday, except on days before holidays they close at noon.
Information Sources:
Intourist, 630 Fifth Ave., Suite 868
New York, New York 10111

New Orleans, Louisiana

Population: 1,175,800
Altitude: 5 to 25 feet
Average Temp.: Jan., 55°F. (13°C.); July, 82°F. (28°C.)
Telephone Area Code: 504

Time Zone: Central
Selected Hotels:
Fairmont Hotel, 123 Baronne St., 529-7111
Hyatt Regency New Orleans, 500 Poydras Plaza, 561-1234
The Monteleone, 214 Royal St., 523-3341
New Orleans Hilton Riverside and Towers, Poydras St. at the Mississippi River, 561-0500
New Orleans Marriott, 555 Canal St., 581-1000
The Omni Royal Orleans Hotel, 621 St. Louis St., 529-5333
The Pontchartrain Hotel, 2031 St. Charles Ave., 524-0581
Royal Sonesta Hotel, 300 Bourbon St., 586-0300
Selected Restaurants:
Broussard's, 819 Conti St., 581-3866
Caribbean Room, in The Pontchartrain Hotel, 524-0581
Commander's Palace Restaurant, 1403 Washington Ave., 899-8221
Galatoire's Restaurant, 209 Bourbon St., 525-2021
Louis XVI French Restaurant, 730 Bienville, 581-7000
Masson's Restaurant Français, 7200 Pontchartrain Blvd., 283-2525
Sazerac Restaurant, in the Fairmont Hotel, 529-7111
Information Sources:
Greater New Orleans Tourist & Convention Commission 1520 Sugar Bowl Dr. New Orleans, Louisiana 70112 (504) 566-5011

New York, New York

Population: 16,573,600
Altitude: Sea level to 410 feet
Average Temp.: Jan., 33°F. (-1°C.); July, 75°F. (24°C.)
Telephone Area Code: 212
Time Zone: Eastern
Selected Hotels:
Carlyle, Madison Ave. at E. 76th St., 744-1600
The Helmsley Palace, 455 Madison Ave., 888-7000
The Hotel Pierre, 2 E. 61st St. at 5th Ave., 838-8000
Nikko Essex House, 160 Central Park S, 247-0300
The Plaza, 768 5th Ave., 759-3000
Regency, 540 Park Ave., 759-4100
St. Regis–Sheraton, 5th Ave. at 55th St., 753-4500
Sherry–Netherland, 781 5th Ave., 355-2800
United Nations Plaza Hotel, 1 U.N. Plaza, 355-3400
Selected Restaurants:
The Four Seasons, 99 E. 52nd St., 754-9494
La Cote Basque, 5 E. 55th St., 688-6525
Le Chantilly, 106 E. 57th St., 751-2931
Lutèce, 249 E. 50th St., 752-2225
Mitsukoshi, 461 Park Ave., 935-6444
"21" Club, 21 W. 52nd St., 582-7200
Information Source:
New York Convention and Visitors Bureau, Inc.
Two Columbus Circle
New York City, New York 10019 (212) 397-8200

Paris, France

Population: 9,775,000
Altitude: 140 ft. (43m.)
Average Temp.: Jan., 44°F. (7°C.); July, 76°F. (24°C.)
Selected Hotels:
Le Bristol, 112 Rue du Faubourg St., Honoré 8e
Crillon, 10 Place de la Concorde 8e
George V, 31 Ave. George V 8e
Intercontinental Paris, 3 Rue de Castiglione 1e
Meridien Hotel, 81 Blvd. Gouvion-St. Cyr, Pte. Maillot 17e
Napoleon, 40 Ave. de Friedland 8e
Paris Hilton, 18 Ave. de Suffren, 15e
Plaza Athenée, 25 Ave. Montaigne 8e
Prince de Galles, 33 Ave. George V 8e
Ritz, 15 Place Vendome, overlooking Place Vendome
Selected Restaurants:
Archestrate, Drouant, Grand Vefour, Lasserre, Ledoyen, Le Vivarois, Lucas-Carton, Maxim's, Taillevent, Tour d'Argent, La Marée, Pré Catelan
Banking: from 9 A.M. to 4:30 P.M. Monday through Friday; 9 A.M. to noon day before holidays.
Information Sources:
L'Office de Tourisme de Paris, 127 Champs-Elysées, Paris 8e 75008

Peking (Beijing), China

Population: 6,450,000
Altitude: 165 ft. (50m.)
Average Temp.: Jan., 23°F. (-5°C.); July, 79°F. (26°C.)
Selected Hotels:
Although all travel arrangements are made by the China International Travel Service, here are the leading hotels and their telephone numbers:
Beijing-Toronto Hotel, Yong'anli
Chienmen Hotel, 33-8731
Hsinchiao Hotel, 55-7731
Lidu Hotel, 50-6688
Nationalities Hotel, 66-8541
Great Wall Sheraton Hotel, 50-5566
Peking Hotel, 55-2231
Selected Restaurants:
Peking Duck, Moslem Restaurant, Pei Hai Restaurant, Restaurants of the Summer Palace
Banking: hours vary from one branch to another of Bank of China—9 A.M. to 5 P.M.
Information Sources:
U.S.-China People's Friendship Association Tours (USCPFA) 110 Maryland Avenue NE Washington, D.C. 20002

Philadelphia, Pennsylvania

Population: 5,153,900
Altitude: Sea level to 441 feet
Average Temp.: Jan., 35°F. (17°C.); July, 78°F. (26°C.)
Telephone Area Code: 215
Time Zone: Eastern
Selected Hotels:

Adam's Mark, City Ave. & Monument Rd., 581-5000
The Barclay Hotel, Rittenhouse Sq., 545-0300
The Latham Hotel, 17th & Walnut Sts., 563-7474
The Palace Hotel of Philadelphia, Benjamin Franklin
  Pkwy. at 18th St., 963-2222
Penn Tower Hotel, 34th & Civic Center Blvd.,
  387-8333
Philadelphia Airport Marriott Hotel, 4509 Island Ave.,
  365-4150
Trevose Hilton Inn, 2400 Old Lincoln Hwy., Trevose,
  638-8300
The Warwick Hotel, 17th at Locust St., 735-6000
Wyndham Franklin Plaza Hotel, 2 Franklin Plaza,
  448-2000
Selected Restaurants:
Deja Vu, 1609 Pine St., 546-1190
Deux Cheminees, 1221 Locust St., 790-0200
Di Lullo, 7955 Oxford Ave., 725-6000
La Famiglia, 8 S. Front St., 922-2803
Lautrec, 408 S. Second St., 923-6660
Le Bec Fin, 1523 Walnut St., 567-1000
The Monte Carlo Living Room, 2nd & South Sts.,
  925-2220
Old Original Bookbinders, 125 Walnut St., 925-7027
Information Sources:
Philadelphia Convention & Visitors Bureau
  1515 Market St., Suite 2020
  Philadelphia, Pennsylvania 19102   (215) 636-3300

Rio de Janeiro, Brazil

Population: 1,015,000
Altitude: 30 ft. (9m.)
Average Temp.: Jan., 79°F. (26°C.); July, 69°F.
(21°C.)
Selected Hotels:
Ambassador, Rua Senador Dantas 25
Caesar Park, Ave. Vieria Souto 460
Copacabana Palace, Ave. Atlantica 1702
Everest Rio, Rua Prudente de Morais 1117
Leme Palace, Ave. Atlantica 656
Marina Palace, R. Delfim Moreira 630
Meridien Rio, Ave. Atlantica 1020
Miramar Palace, Ave. Atlantica 3668
Nacional Rio, Ave. Niemeyer 769
Rio Palace, Ave. Atlantica 4240
Sol Ipanema, Ave. Vieira Souto 320
Rio Sheraton, Ave. Niemeyer 128
Selected Restaurants:
Maxim's de Paris, La Streghe, Candido's,
  Antiquarius, Céu, Chalé, La Tour, Mario's, Le Saint
  Honoré, Petronio's, Club Gourmet, Nino, Rio's,
  Sambao e Sinhá
Banking: hours are 10 A.M. to 4:30 P.M. Monday
through Friday.
Information Sources:
Brazilian Tourism Foundation - Funtur, 551 Fifth
  Ave., Suite 421, New York, New York 10176

Rome (Roma), Italy

Population: 3,115,000
Altitude: 80 ft. (24m.)
Average Temp.: Jan., 46°F. (8°C.); July, 75°F.
(24°C.)
Selected Hotels:
Ambasciatori Palace, Via Veneto 70
Bernini Bristol, Piazza Barberini 23
Cavalieri Hilton, Via Cadlolo 101
Eden, Via Ludovisi 49
Excelsior, Via Vittorio Veneto 125
Flora, Via Vittorio Veneto 191
Grand, Via V.E. Orlando 3
Hassler Villa Medici, Trinità dei Monti 6
Mediterraneo, Via Cavour 15
Parco dei Principi, Via G. Frescobaldi 5
Quirinale, Via Nazionale 7
Sheraton Roma, Viale del Pattinaggio
Selected Restaurants:
Capriccio, Da Meo Patacca, George's, Hostaria
  dell'Orso, Passetto, Ranieri, San Souci, 31 al
  Vicaria, Taverna Flavia, Trilussa
Banking: from 8:30 A.M. to 1:30 P.M. Monday
through Friday.
Information Sources:
EPT—Ente Provinciale Turismo, Rome

San Francisco, California

Population: 4,665,500
Altitude: Sea level to 934 feet
Average Temp.: Jan., 50°F. (10°C.); July, 59°F.
(15°C.)
Telephone Area Code: 415
Time Zone: Pacific
Selected Hotels:
The Fairmont Hotel, 950 Mason St., 772-5000
Four Seasons-Clift, 495 Geary St., 775-4700
Hilton Square, 333 O'Farrell St., 771-1400
The Holiday Inn Union Square, 480 Sutter St., 398-
  8900
Huntington Hotel, 1075 California St., 474-5400
Hyatt on Union Square, 345 Stockton St., 398-1234
Hyatt Regency San Francisco, 5 Embarcadero
  Center, 788-1234
Mark Hopkins Intercontinental, 1 Nob Hill, 392-3434
Miyako Hotel, 1625 Post St., 922-3200
Petite Auberge, 863 Bush St., 928-6000
The Phoenix Inn, 601 Eddy St., 776-1380
Queen Anne, 1590 Sutter St., 441-2828
The Westin St. Francis, 335 Powell St., 397-7000
Selected Restaurants:
Amelio's, 1630 Powell St., 397-4339
Blue Fox Restaurant, 659 Merchant St., 981-1177
Doros, 714 Montgomery St., 397-6822
Empress of China, 838 Grant Ave., 434-1345
Ernie's Restaurant, 847 Montgomery St., 397-5969
Fleur de Lys, 777 Sutter St., 673-7779
Fournou's Ovens, in The Stanford Court Hotel,
  989-1910
L'Etoile, 1075 California St., 771-1529
Information Sources:
San Francisco Convention & Visitors Bureau

Convention Plaza 201 Third St., Suite 900 San Francisco, California 94103   (415) 974-6900

Seoul (Sŏul), Korea

Population: 14,100,000
Altitude: 100 ft. (30m.)
Average Temp.: Jan., 24°F. (-4°C.); July, 78°F. (26°C.)
Selected Hotels:
Hotel Lotte, 1 Sokong-dong, Chung-ku
Hotel Shilla, 202, 2-Ga, Jangchung-dong, Chung-ku
Hyatt Regency Hotel, 747-7 Hannam-dong, Yongsam-ku
King Sejong Hotel, 61-3, 2-ka Chung-moo-ro, Chung-ku
Seoul Hilton International, 395, 5-Ka, Namdaemun-ro, Chung-ku
Seoul Plaza Hotel, 23, 2-ga Taipyung-ro, Chung-ku
Sheraton Walker Hill Hotel, 21 Kwangjeng-dong, Sungdong-ku
Westin Chosun Hotel, 87 Sokong-dong, Chung-ku
Selected Restaurants:
Hankuk Hwe Kwan, Hyang Won, Hanil Kwan, Korea House (Korean-style); Asti, Diplomatic Club (Western-style), Four Seasons
Banking: hours are 9:30 A.M. to 4:30 P.M. Monday through Friday; 9:30 A.M. to 1:30 P.M. on Saturday.
Information Sources:
Korea National Tourism Corp., 903, 10 Ta-dong, Chung-gu, Seoul

Singapore, Singapore

Population: 3,000,000
Altitude: 35 ft. (11m.)
Average Temp.: Jan., 79°F. (26°C.); July, 81°F. (27°C.)
Selected Hotels:
Dynasty Singapore, 320 Orchard Rd.
Goodwood Park, 22 Scotts Rd.
Hyatt Singapore, 10-12 Scotts Rd.
The Mandarin Singapore, 333 Orchard Rd.
The Marco Polo, Tanglin Circus
Pavilion Intercontinental Singapore, 1 Cuscaden Rd.
Shangri-La, 22 Orange Grove Rd.
Singapore Hilton, 581 Orchard Rd.
Selected Restaurants:
Cathay, Celestial Room, Islamic, Jubilee, Mandarin Room, Omar Khayyam, Peking Shanghia, Troika
Banking: hours are 10 A.M. to 3 P.M. Monday through Friday; 9:30 A.M. to 11:30 A.M. on Saturday.
Information Sources:
Singapore Tourist Promotion Board, 8484 Wilshire Blvd., Suite 510, Beverly Hills, California 90211

Stockholm, Sweden

Population: 1,449,972
Altitude: 55 ft. (17m.)
Average Temp.: Jan., 27°F. (-3°C.); July, 64°F. (18°C.)
Selected Hotels:
Birger Jarl, Tulegatan 8
Grand Hotel, Södra Blasieholmshamnen 8, opposite the Royal Palace
Strand, Nybrokajen 9
Diplomat, Strandvägen 7 C
Park, Karlavägen 43
Anglais, Humlegärdsgatan 23
Sheraton-Stockholm, Tegelbacken 6
Selected Restaurants:
Den Glydene Freden, Fem Små Hus, Frati's Tre Remmare, Operakällaren, Rådhus Restauranten, Riche, Solliden at Skansen, Stallmästaregarden, Teatergrillen, Veranda of the Grand Hotel
Banking: hours from 9:30 A.M. to 3 P.M. on weekdays.
Information Sources:
Tourist Information Offices, Hamngatan 27, S-103 05, Stockholm

Sydney, Australia

Population: 3,358,550
Altitude: 75 ft. (23m.)
Average Temp.: Jan., 71°F. (22°C.); July, 53°F. (12°C.)
Selected Hotels:
Boulevard Hotel, 90 William St.
Holiday Inn Menzies, 14-28 Carrington St.
Hyatt Kingsgate, Kings Cross Rd.
Regent of Sydney, 199 George St.
Sheraton Wentworth, 61-101 Phillip St.
Hilton International Sydney, 259 Pitt St.
Selected Restaurants:
Argyle Tavern, Beppi's, Chelsea, The Coachmen, Doyle's at Rose & Watson's bays, French Tavern, Hunters Lodge at Double Bay, Le Trianon at King's Cross, Pruniers at Double Bay
Banking: hours are 9:30 A.M. to 4 P.M. Monday through Thursday, 9:30 A.M. to 5 P.M. on Friday. Major branches are open for extended hours.
Information Sources:
Tourism Commission of New South Wales, Shell House, 140 Phillips St., Sydney, N.S.W. 2000

Tel Aviv (Tel Aviv-Yafo), Israel

Population: 1,670,000
Altitude: 35 ft. (11m.)
Average Temp.: Jan., 57°F. (14°C.); July, 77°F. (25°C.)
Selected Hotels:
Carlton, Hayarkon St.
Dan, 99 Hayarkon St.
Diplomat, Hayarkon St.
Hilton, Independence Park
Plaza, Hayarkon St.
Ramada Continental, Hayarkon St.

64

Sheraton, Hayarkon St.
Selected Restaurants:
Apropo, Casba, Zion Exclusive
Banking: hours are 8:30 A.M. to 12:30 P.M. and 4
P.M. to 6 P.M. Sunday, Tuesday and Thursday; 8:30
A.M. to 12:30 P.M. Monday and Wednesday; and
8:30 A.M. to 12 noon Friday. Banks are closed on
eves of holidays and holidays.
Information Sources:
Government Tourist Information Office,
    7 Mendele St., Tel Aviv

Tōkyō, Japan

Population: 27,700,000
Altitude: 20 ft. (6m.)
Average Temp.: Jan., 39°F. (4°C.); July, 77°F.
(25°C.)
Selected Hotels:
Imperial Hotel, 1-chome, Uchisaiwaicho, Chiyoda-ku
Hotel New Otani, 4 Kioicho, Chiyoda-ku
Hotel Okura, 2-10-4 Toranomon, Minato-ku
Keio Plaza Hotel, 2, 2-1, Nishi-Shinjuku, Shinjuku-ku
Palace Hotel, 1-1, 1-chome, Marunouchi, Chiyoda-ku
The Tōkyō Hilton, 10-3, 2-chome, Nagatacho,
    Chiyoda-ku
Selected Restaurants:
Akasaka Misono, Asahi, Chinzan-So, Doh-Hana,
    Hilton Hotel Restaurant, Imperial Hotel Restaurant,
    Inagiku, Mansei, Misono, Okahan, Okura Hotel
    Restaurant, Palace Hotel Restaurant, Steak House
    Ginsen, Suehiro, Ten-ichi, Zakuro
Banking: hours from 9 A.M. to 3 P.M. Monday
through Friday, 9 A.M. to noon on Saturday.
Information Sources:
Japan National Tourist Organization, 2-13,
    Yurakucho, Tōkyō

Toronto, Canada

Population: 3,427,168
Altitude: 275 ft. (84m.)
Average Temp.: Jan., 23°F. (-5°C.); July, 69°F.
(21°C.)
Telephone Area Number: 416
Selected Hotels:
Four Seasons Motor Hotel, 21 Avenue Rd.
Holiday Inn–Downtown, 89 Chestnut St.
Loews Westbury, 475 Yonge St.
Park Plaza, 4 Avenue Rd.
Royal York, 100 Front St. W
Seahorse Hotel, Ltd., 2009 Lakeshore Blvd. W
Sheraton Centre, 123 Queen St.
Sutton Place, 955 Bay St.
Selected Restaurants:
Ed's Warehouse, Fisherman's Wharf, Heritage Room
    in the Toronto Dominion Tower, Imperial Room,
    Old Spaghetti Factory
Banking: hours generally are from 10 A.M. to 3 P.M.
Monday through Friday.
Information Sources:
Metropolitan Toronto Convention & Visitors

Association, 207 Quay West at Harbour Front,
Toronto, Ontario M5J 1A7

Vienna (Wien), Austria

Population: 1,875,000
Altitude: 560 ft. (171m.)
Average Temp.: Jan., 30°F. (-1°C.); July, 68°F.
(20°C.)
Selected Hotels:
Ambassador, Neuer Markt 5, A-1010
Bristol, Kärntner Ring 1, A-1010 opposite Vienna
    Opera
Clima Villenhotel, Nussberggasse 2c, A-1190
Imperial, Kärntner Ring 16, A-1015
Parkhotel Schönbrunn, Hietzinger Haupstr. 12, A-
    1130
Sacher, Philharmonikerstr. 4, A-1015
Vienna Intercontinental, Johannesgasse 28, A-1030
Hilton Wien, Am Stadtpark, A-1030
Selected Restaurants:
Ambassador Hotel Restaurant, Korso in the Bristol
    Hotel, Drei Husaren, Le Palais Schwartzenberg,
    Prinz Eugen Restaurant in the Hilton Hotel, Sacher
    Hotel Restaurant, Wiener Stadtkrug
Banking: hours are 8:00 A.M. to 12:30 P.M. and
1:30 P.M. to 3:30 P.M. Monday, Tuesday,
Wednesday, and Friday. 1:30 P.M. to 5:30 P.M. on
Thursday.
Information Sources:
In Vienna, the Fremdenverkehrsverband (local tourist
    office).
Austrian National Tourist Office, 500 Fifth Ave.,
    New York, New York 10110

West Berlin, Federal Republic of Germany

Population: 3,825,000
Altitude: 115 ft. (35m.)
Average Temp.: Jan., 31°F. (-1°C.); July, 66°F.
(19°C.)
Selected Hotels:
Ambassador, Bayreuther Str. 42-43
Berlin Hotel Intercontinental, Budapester Str. 2
Bristol Hotel Kempinski, Kurfürstendamm 27
Palace Hotel, Europa Center
Schweizerhof, Budapester Str. 21-29
Selected Restaurants:
Aben, Alexander, Bristol Kempinski Grill, Conti-
    Fischstuben, El Panorama, Hotel Berlin Restaurant,
    Kottler's, Maitre, Mampes Gute Stube, Ritz
Banking: hours are from 8:30 A.M. to 1 P.M. and
2:30 P.M.to 4 P.M. weekdays (Thursday to 5:30
P.M.). Closed Saturday and Sunday.
Information Sources:
German National Tourist Office, 747 Third Ave., 33rd
    Floor, New York, New York 10017

Inhabited Localities

The symbol represents the number of inhabitants within the locality

At scales 1:6 000 000 to 1:12 000 000

- · 0—10,000
- ○ 10,000—25,000
- ◎ 25,000—100,000
- ▣ 100,000—250,000
- ▣ 250,000—1,000,000
- ■ >1,000,000

At 1:24 000 000 scale

- · 0—50,000
- ◎ 50,000—100,000
- ▣ 100,000—250,000
- ▣ 250,000—1,000,000
- ■ >1,000,000

Urban Area (area of continuous industrial, commercial, and residential development)

The size of type indicates the relative economic and political importance of the locality

| Écommoy | Lisieux | **Rouen** |
| Trouville | **Orléans** | **PARIS** |

Capitals of Political Units

BUDAPEST   Independent Nation

Cayenne   Dependency (Colony, protectorate, etc.)

Lasa   State, Province, etc.

Alternate Names

MOSKVA 'MOSCOW   English or second official language names are shown in reduced size lettering

Volgograd (Stalingrad)   Historical or other alternates in the local language are shown in parentheses

Political Boundaries

International (First-order political unit)

—··—··—··   Demarcated and Undemarcated

▬▬ ▬▬ ▬▬   Indefinite or Undefined

----------   Demarcation Line (used in Korea)

Internal

State, Province, etc. (Second-order political unit)

MURCIA   Historical Region (No boundaries indicated)

Transportation

————   Primary Road

————   Secondary Road

Canal du Midi   Navigable Canal

—⊐----⊏—   Tunnel

············   Ferry

Hydrographic Features

Intermittent Stream

Rapids, Falls

Irrigation or Drainage Canal

Reef

The Everglades   Swamp

Glacier
VATNAJÖKULL

L. Victoria   Lake, Reservoir

Tuz Gölü   Salt Lake

Intermittent Lake, Reservoir

Dry Lake Bed

Topographic Features

Matterhorn △ 4478   Elevation Above Sea Level

76 ▽   Elevation Below Sea Level

Mount Cook ▲ 3764   Highest Elevation in Country

Khyber Pass ⊐ 1067   Mountain Pass

133 ▼   Lowest Elevation in Country

Elevations are given in metres

The Highest and Lowest Elevation in a continent are underlined

Sand Area

Lava

Salt Flat

66

90° 180° 165° 150° 135° 120° 105° 90° 75° 60° 45° 30° 15° 0°

ARCTIC OCEAN

GREENLAND
(Den.)

ICELAND

75° Beaufort Sea

VICTORIA ISLAND

BAFFIN ISLAND

Godthåb

Arctic Circle

U.S.S.R.

UNITED STATES

Yellowknife

Hudson Bay

NEWFOUNDLAND

UNITED KINGDOM

IRELAND LONDON

FRANCE

60° Bering Sea

Gulf of Alaska

Anchorage

C A N A D A

ALEUTIAN ISLANDS

Vancouver

Winnipeg

Montréal

ROCKY MTS

45° NORTH AMERICA

SAN FRANCISCO

UNITED STATES

CHICAGO

NEW YORK
Washington

ATLANTIC OCEAN

PORTUGAL SPAIN

P A C I F I C

LOS ANGELES

BERMUDA
(U.K.)

AÇORES AZORES
(Port.)

MOROCCO

30° O C E A N

Houston

Mississippi

Gulf of Mexico

Miami

WESTERN SAHARA

ALGERIA

Tropic of Cancer

MEXICO

CUBA

HAITI

DOMINICAN REPUBLIC

MAURI-TANIA

HAWAIIAN ISLANDS
(U.S.)

CIUDAD DE MÉXICO

PUERTO RICO
(U.S.)

SENEGAL

MALI

15° GUATEMALA

HONDURAS

Caribbean Sea

GUINEA

BURKINA FASO

NICARAGUA

TRINIDAD AND TOBAGO

SIERRA LEONE

IVORY COAST

P

PANAMA

VENEZUELA

GUYANA

O

COLOMBIA

FRENCH GUIANA

SURINAME

L

ECUADOR

Equator

Y

ARCHIPIÉLAGO DE COLÓN
GALÁPAGOS ISLANDS
(Ec.)

Amazon

Belém

0° Equator

N

B R A Z I L

ANDES

E

PERU

Recife

S

SOUTH AMERICA

ATLANTIC OCEAN

AM.
SAMOA

I

BOLIVIA

Brasília

15° FIJI

COOK ISLANDS
(N.Z.)

FRENCH POLYNESIA

Tropic of Capricorn

PARAGUAY

RIO DE JANEIRO

TONGA

Asunción

SÃO PAULO

CHILE

30° International Date Line

Santiago

URUGUAY
BUENOS AIRES

P A C I F I C

ARGENTINA

O C E A N

45°

FALKLAND ISLANDS
(U.K.)

CABO DE HORNOS
CAPE HORN

60° Antarctic Circle

Bellingshausen Sea

Weddell Sea

75°

A N T A R C T

90° 180° 165° 150° 135° 120° 105° 90° 75° 60° 45° 30° 15° 0°

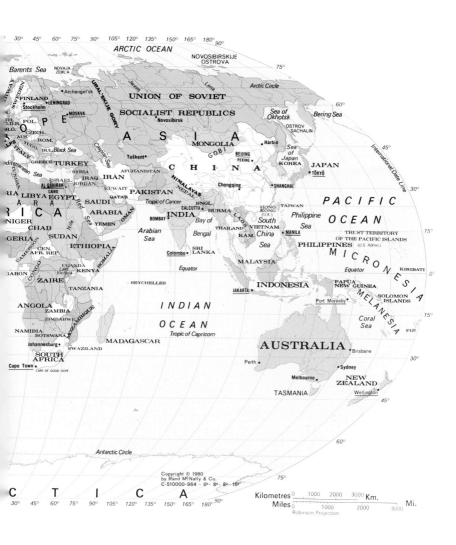

ARCTIC OCEAN
NOVOSIBIRSKIJE
OSTROVA
75°

Barents Sea   NOVAJA
ZEML'A

•Archangel'sk   URAL'SKIJE GORY   Jenisej   Lena   Arctic Circle   60°
FINLAND   •LENINGRAD
Stockholm   •MOSKVA   UNION OF SOVIET   Sea of   Bering Sea
POL.   Novosibirsk   SOCIALIST REPUBLICS   Okhotsk
CZECH.   OSTROV   45°
ROM.   A   S   I   A   SACHALIN
BUL. Black Sea   Caspian Sea   MONGOLIA   Harbin   Sea
GREECE TURKEY   GOBI   of
SYRIA IRAQ IRAN   Taškent•   CHINA   BEIJING   Japan   JAPAN
AL-QĀHIRAH   JORDAN   AFGHANISTAN   PEKING   KOREA   •TŌKYŌ   30°
CAIRO   KUWAIT   PAKISTAN   HIMALAYAS   Chongqing   •SHANGHAI
LIBYA EGYPT   QATAR   NEPAL   PACIFIC
SAUDI   Tropic of Cancer   BNGL.   HONG   TAIWAN
NIGER CHAD   ARABIA OMAN   INDIA   CALCUTTA• BURMA   KONG   Philippine   OCEAN   15°
GERIA   SUDAN   YEMEN   BOMBAY•   LAOS   (U.K.)   Sea
                        Bay of   THAILAND VIETNAM   •MANILA   TRUST TERRITORY
CEN.   ETHIOPIA   Arabian   Bengal   KAM.   South   OF THE PACIFIC ISLANDS
AFR. REP.   Sea   Colombo• SRI   China   PHILIPPINES   (U.S. Admn.)
UGANDA SOMALI   Colombo• LANKA   Sea   M I C R O
ZAIRE KENYA   Equator   MALAYSIA   N   KIRIBATI
Lake   E
Victoria   TANZANIA   SEYCHELLES   Equator   S   I   A
ANGOLA   INDONESIA   PAPUA   A
ZAMBIA   INDIAN   JAKARTA•   NEW GUINEA   SOLOMON   M
NAMIBIA ZIMBABWE   OCEAN   Port Moresby•   ISLANDS   E   L   A
BOTSWANA   Tropic of Capricorn   Coral   N   E   FIJI   15°
Johannesburg•   MADAGASCAR   AUSTRALIA   Sea   S
SWAZILAND   •Brisbane   I   A
SOUTH   Perth •
Cape Town • AFRICA   •Sydney   30°
CAPE OF GOOD HOPE   Melbourne•   NEW
                                TASMANIA   ZEALAND
                                        •Wellington   45°

International Date Line

60°

Antarctic Circle

75°

C   T   I   C   A
30° 45° 60° 75° 90° 105° 120° 135° 150° 165° 180° 90°

Copyright © 1980
by Rand McNally & Co.
C-510000-964 - 6ᵛ- 8ᵛ- 8ᵛ- 15ᵛ

Kilometres   0   1000   2000   3000 Km.
Miles   0   1000   2000   3000 Mi.
Robinson Projection

30° 45° 60° 75° 90° 105° 120° 135° 150° 165° 180°

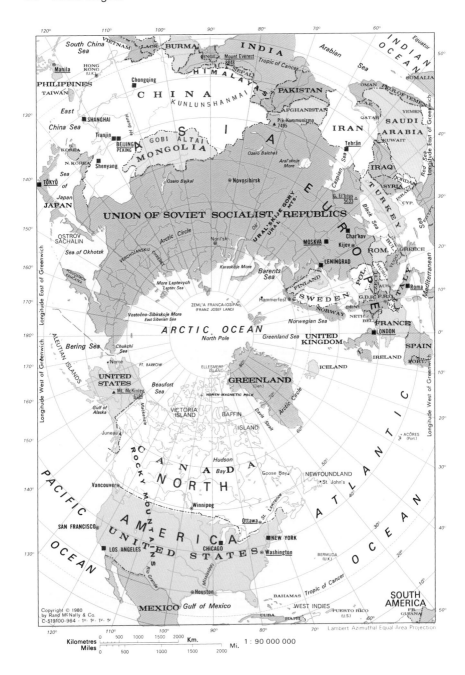

Kilometres
Miles

Km.

Mi.

1 : 90 000 000

Lambert Azimuthal Equal Area Projection

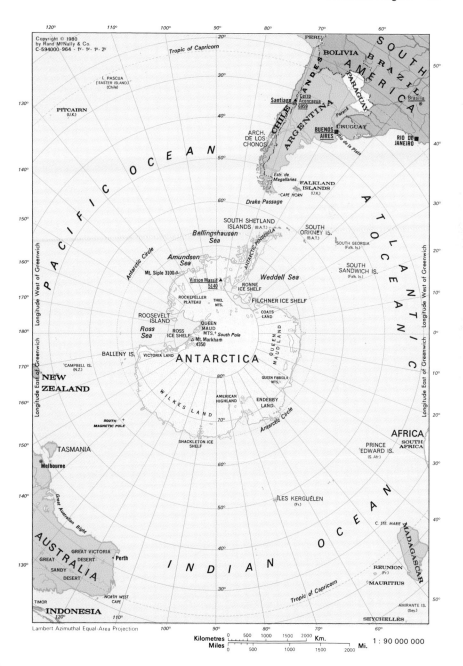

Copyright © 1980
by Rand McNally & Co.
C-594000-964 - 1ᵛ- 1ᵛ- 1ᵛ- 2ᵛ

Tropic of Capricorn

PERU

BOLIVIA

SOUTH

BRAZIL

AMERICA

PARAGUAY

Brasilia

I. PASCUA
(EASTER ISLAND)
(Chile)

PITCAIRN
(U.K.)

Santiago Cerro Aconcagua 6959

ANDES

CHILE

ARGENTINA

Paraná

URUGUAY

BUENOS AIRES

Rio de la Plata

RIO DE JANEIRO

ARCH. DE LOS CHONOS

PACIFIC OCEAN

Estr. de Magallanes

CAPE HORN

FALKLAND ISLANDS
(U.K.)

Drake Passage

SOUTH SHETLAND ISLANDS (B.A.T.)

SOUTH ORKNEY IS.
(B.A.T.)

SOUTH GEORGIA
(Falk. Is.)

Bellingshausen Sea

Antarctic Circle

Amundsen Sea

Mt. Siple 3100

Vinson Massif 5140

ANTARCTIC PENINSULA

Weddell Sea

RONNE ICE SHELF

SOUTH SANDWICH IS.
(Falk. Is.)

ATLANTIC OCEAN

ROCKEFELLER PLATEAU

THIEL MTS.

FILCHNER ICE SHELF

ROOSEVELT ISLAND

Ross Sea

ROSS ICE SHELF

QUEEN MAUD MTS.
South Pole

COATS LAND

QUEEN MAUD LAND

Mt. Markham 4350

BALLENY IS.

CAMPBELL IS.
(N.Z.)

VICTORIA LAND

ANTARCTICA

QUEEN FABIOLA MTS.

NEW ZEALAND

WILKES LAND

AMERICAN HIGHLAND

ENDERBY LAND

Longitude West of Greenwich   Longitude East of Greenwich

SOUTH MAGNETIC POLE

Antarctic Circle

PRINCE EDWARD IS.
(S. Afr.)

AFRICA

SOUTH AFRICA

TASMANIA

SHACKLETON ICE SHELF

Melbourne

ÎLES KERGUÉLEN
(Fr.)

INDIAN OCEAN

Great Australian Bight

C. STE. MARIE

MADAGASCAR

GREAT VICTORIA DESERT

Perth

GREAT SANDY DESERT

AUSTRALIA

REUNION
(Fr.)

MAURITIUS

TIMOR

NORTH WEST CAPE

Tropic of Capricorn

AMIRANTE IS.
(Sey.)

INDONESIA

SEYCHELLES

Lambert Azimuthal Equal-Area Projection

Kilometres 0 500 1000 1500 2000 Km.
Miles 0 500 1000 1500 2000 Mi.

1 : 90 000 000

20° 15° 10° 5° 0° 5° 10° 15° 2

65° FONTUR

ICELAND Akureyri Seydisfjördur

Reykjavík VATNAJÖKULL

Hvannadalshnúkur 2119

Arctic Circle NORWEGIAN SEA

Tromsö 70°

LOFOTEN VESTER

Kebnekais 2111

Jokkmokk

Mo Skelleftea

60° NORWAY

30° Steinkjer Gäddede Tärnaby

Kristiansund Trond heim Örnsköldsvik

FAEROE ISLANDS (Den.) SHETLAND ISLANDS SWEDEN GUL

55° Floro Glittertinden 2472 Sundsvall

25° Bergen Voss Oslo Gävle

ORKNEY ISLANDS Stavanger Skien Uppsala

HEBRIDES Wick Skagerrak Örebro Stockhol

Inverness Kristiansand Göteborg Linköping

Aberdeen DENMARK Borås Balti

SCOTLAND NORTH Álborg Växjö GOTL

50° Glasgow Edinburgh Århus Karlskrona Sea

UNITED Belfast ENGLAND SEA København Kaliningr.

IRELAND ISLE KINGDOM Flensburg Kiel Malmö Gdańsk

20° Galway OF MAN Leeds Hamburg Rostock Olsztyn

Dublin Liverpool Manchester GERMAN Szczecin Bydgoszcz

Cork Birmingham NETHERLANDS Bremen DEM. REP. Poznań POLAN

WALES Amsterdam Münster Hannover BERLIN Leipzig

Cardiff Bristol LONDON FED. REP. Dresden Wrocław

Plymouth Rotterdam Essen OF Częstochowa Kraków

Portsmouth Bruxelles Bonn GER. Frankfurt Ostrava CZECH. Brno

English Channel BELGIUM Mannheim Nürnberg Praha

45° Le Havre LUX. Metz Strasbourg Stuttgart Wien Bratislava

Brest Rouen PARIS München AUSTRIA Vienna Budape

Rennes Le Mans Orléans Basel LIECH. Graz HUNGARY

Lorient Dijon Bern SWITZ. Zürich Szeged

Nantes FRANCE Tours Genève Milano Venezia Zagreb

La Rochelle Limoges Mont Torino Verona Rijeka

40° Bordeaux Clermont- Lyon Blanc Bologna Beograd

La Coruña Oviedo Bay of Ferrand 4807 SAN YUGOSLAV

15° Vigo Orense Biscay Grenoble Genova MARINO Split

León Bilbao Avignon Nice Livorno Firenze Adriatic Sarajev

PORTUGAL Toulouse Montpellier MONACO Sea

Porto PYRENEES Marseille CORSE ITALY Tirane

Coimbra Salamanca Pamplona CORSICA Roma Foggia AL

Valladolid ANDORRA (Fr.) Ajaccio

Lisboa Zaragoza Barcelona SARDEGNA Napoli Bari

Tagus Castellón de la Plana ISLAS BALEARES SARDINIA Salerno Taranto Lecce

Badajoz Madrid BALEARIC ISLANDS (It.) Tyrrhenian Ioan

Valencia Palma Cagliari Sea

SPAIN Córdoba Murcia Alicante Palermo Messina Ionian

35° Sevilla Granada Almería Cartagena Catanzaro Reggio di Sea

CABO DE Cádiz Málaga Catania Calabria

SÃO VICENTE Gibraltar Almería MEDITERRANEAN MALTA SEA

Tanger (U.K.) El Alger Annaba Bizerte Valletta

Ceuta Asnam Algiers (Bône) Tunis

Casablanca (Sp.) Melilla Oran Constantine TUNISIA

Rabat Fès Oujda Sidi MOUNTAINS SAHARIEN Djebel Chambi

Meknès bel Abbès ATLAS 1544

MOROCCO ATLAS ALGERIA ATLAS Biskra

Safi SAHARIEN Sfax

ATLANTIC OCEAN

A T L A N T I C

O C E A N

Copyright © 1980 by Rand McNally & Co. C-550000-964 — 5v- 5v- 5v- 8v

Kilometres 0 200 400 600 Km.

Miles 0 200 400 600 Mi. 1 : 24 000 000

Miller Oblated Stereographic Projection

ATLANTIC

OCEAN

SHETLAND ISLANDS

Melby House

Lerwick

Virkie

ORKNEY ISLANDS
MAINLAND
Stromness   Kirkwall
Burwick

Thurso

Durness   Wick

ISLE OF LEWIS

Ben More Assynt △ 998
Lochinver   Helmsdale

SAINT KILDA

Ullapool   Bonarbridge

Uig   Dingwall   Elgin   Fraserburgh

OUTER HEBRIDES

Kyle of Lochalsh   Inverness   Huntly

NORTH

SEA

ISLAND OF SKYE   Balmoral Castle   Aberdeen

Little Minch

INNER HEBRIDES

Mallaig   △1343 Ben Nevis   Stonehaven

GRAMPIAN MTS.

Tobermory   Arbroath

ISLAND OF MULL   Ben More 1174   Perth   Dundee

Lochgilphead   Kirkcaldy
Firth of Forth

Greenock   Edinburgh

GLASGOW   Motherwell   Berwick-upon-Tweed

Port Ellen   ISLAND OF ARRAN   Kilmarnock   Galashiels

SCOTLAND ENGLAND

Campbeltown   Ayr   Moffat   Hawick

NORTHUMBERLAND NATIONAL

Firth of Clyde

Coleraine   Dumfries   Blyth   Newcastle upon Tyne

Londonderry   Newton Stewart   Carlisle   Durham   Sunderland

North Channel

Lifford   Stranraer   Whitehaven   Penrith   Bishop Auckland   Middlesbrough

Donegal   Omagh   Larne   LAKE DISTRICT NATIONAL PARK   NORTH YORK MOORS NATIONAL PARK

Belmullet   Enniskillen   Bangor   Scarborough

Sligo   Portadown   Belfast   Barrow-in-Furness   YORKSHIRE DALES NATIONAL PARK

ULSTER   Newtownards   ISLE OF MAN (U.K.)   PENNINE

Ballina   N. IRELAND U.K.   Newry   Douglas   York   Kingston upon Hull

Castlebar   Cavan   Dundalk   Castletown   Lancaster

CONNAUGHT   MEATH   Blackpool   Preston   Black-burn   Leeds   Grimsby

Clifden   Roscommon   Drogheda   IRISH   MANCHESTER   Sheffield   Lincoln

CONNEMARA   Athlone   Royal Canal   Southport   Liverpool   Chester   Skegness

ARAN ISLANDS   Dublin   SEA   Bangor   Stoke-on-   Sheringham

Galway   LEINSTER   Dun Laoghaire   Caernarvon   PEAK DIST. NATIONAL PARK   Trent   Nottingham   Cromer

Milltown Malbay   Ennis   Naas   Holy-head   Wrexham   Stafford   Derby   Grantham   Norwich

Shannon   Nenagh   Arklow   IRELAND U.K.   King's Lynn

Limerick   Wicklow   Barmouth   Leicester   Peterborough   Great Yarmouth

Tralee   Tipperary   Kilkenny   WALES   Aberystwyth   BIRMINGHAM   Coventry

Dingle   △1041   Clonmel   Wexford   Stratford-upon-Avon   Cambridge   Ipswich

Carrauntoohil   MUNSTER   Waterford   Rosslare   Worcester   Northampton

Cahirciveen   Cork   Dungarvan   Cardigan   Hereford   Banbury   Luton   Chelmsford

Bantry   Carmarthen   BRECON BEACONS NATIONAL PARK   Gloucester   Oxford   LONDON   Southend-on-Sea

Milford Haven   Merthyr Tydfil   Newport   Thames

PEMBROKESHIRE COAST NATIONAL PARK   Swansea   Cardiff   Bristol   Reading   Windsor

St. George's Channel   Bath   Canterbury   Dover

EXMOOR NATIONAL PARK   Bridgwater   Salisbury   Basingstoke   Guildford   Folkestone

Yeovil   Brighton   Hastings

Exeter   Southampton   Portsmouth   Boulogne-sur-Mer

Weymouth   Bournemouth

DARTMOOR NATIONAL PARK   Newquay   Plymouth   Torquay (Torbay)

ATLANTIC

OCEAN   Saint Austell   English Channel   La Manche   UNITED KINGDOM FRANCE

LAND'S END   Falmouth   Cherbourg   Fécamp   Le Tréport   Dieppe   Tôtes

Le Havre

Conic Projection, Two Standard Parallels

Kilometres 0 50 100 150 Km.
Miles 0   50   100   150 Mi.

1 : 7 500 000

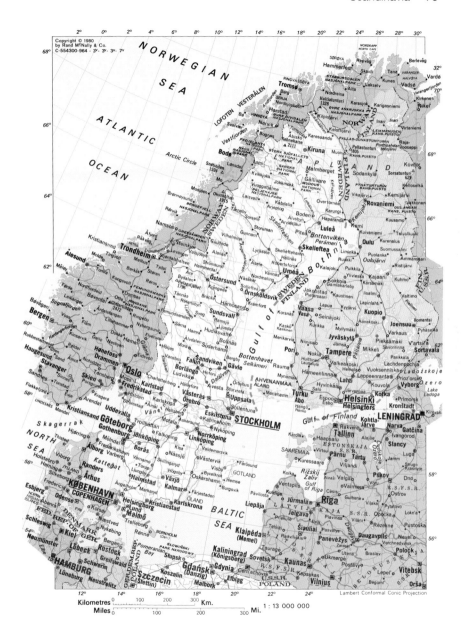

Lambert Conformal Conic Projection

Kilometres 0 100 200 300 Km.
Miles 0 100 200 300 Mi.
1 : 13 000 000

74

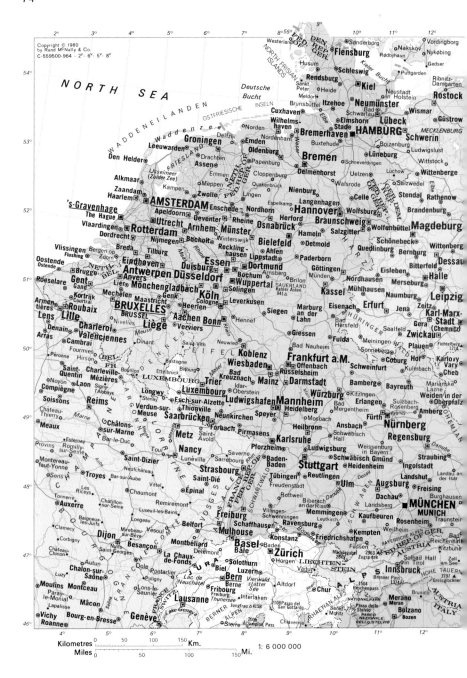

NORTH SEA

WADDENEILANDEN
OSTFRIESISCHE INSELN
NORTH FRISIAN ISLANDS
Deutsche Bucht

Westerland
Husum
Schleswig
Flensburg
Sønderborg
Nakskov
Vordingborg
Nykøbing
Rødbyhavn
Gedser
Puttgarden
Ribnitz-Damgarten
Rendsburg
Sankt Peter
Heide
Meldorf
Itzehoe
Kiel
Neustadt in Holstein
Rostock
Brunsbüttel
Neumünster
Bad Schwartau
Wismar
Güstrow
Cuxhaven
Stade
Elmshorn
Lübeck
MECKLENBURG
Wilhelms- haven
Bremerhaven
Buxtehude
HAMBURG
Schwerin
Nordenham
Boizenburg
Ludwigslust
Norden
Delfzijl
Emden
Oldenburg
Bremen
Lüneburg
Wittstock
Groningen
Leeuwarden
Assen
Papenburg
Delmenhorst
Uelzen
Lüchow
Wittenberge
Den Helder
Drachten
Emmen
Cloppenburg
Walsrode
Salzwedel
IJsselmeer (Zuider Zee)
Kampen
Meppen
Quakenbrück
Nienburg
Celle
Stendal
Rathenow
Alkmaar
Zwolle
Lingen
Langenhagen
Zaandam
Haarlem
's-Gravenhage The Hague
AMSTERDAM
Apeldoorn
Deventer
Enschede
Nordhorn
Rheine
Hannover
Wolfsburg
Brandenburg
Espelkamp
Herford
Utrecht
Arnhem
Münster
Osnabrück
Braunschweig
Magdeburg
Vlaardingen
Rotterdam
Nijmegen
Bocholt
Winterswijk
Bielefeld
Hameln
Salzgitter
Wolfenbüttel
Schöneberg
Dordrecht
Recklinghausen
Ahlen
Lippstadt
Detmold
Paderborn
Quedlinburg
Bernburg
Wittenberg
Dessau
Breda
Tilburg
Vlissingen
Bergen op Zoom
Eindhoven
Essen
Dortmund
Göttingen
Nordhausen
Eisleben
Merseburg
Halle
Flushing
Oostende
Ostende
Brugge
Antwerpen Anvers
Duisburg
Düsseldorf
Wuppertal
Arnsberg
Brilon
Münden
Mühlhausen
Naumburg
Leipzig
Roeselare
Gent
Lier
Mönchengladbach
Köln
Solingen
SAUERLAND
Kahler Asten 841△
Kassel
Erfurt
Jena
Zeitz
Karl-Marx-Stadt (Chemnitz)
Armentières
Roubaix
Kortrijk
Courtrai
Mechelen
Genk
Maastricht
Heerlen
Aachen
Cologne
Leverkusen
Siegen
Marburg an der Lahn
Eisenach
THÜRINGER WALD
Saalfeld
Gera
Zwickau
Lens
Lille
BRUXELLES
BRUSSEL
Liège
Bonn
Hennef
Bad Hersfeld
Meiningen
Plauen
Fichtelberg 1214△
Charleroi
Nivelles
Verviers
Giessen
Fulda
Sonneberg
Hof
Karlovy Vary
Cheb
Denain
Valenciennes
Dinant
EIFEL
Neuwied
Koblenz
Bad Nauheim
Schweinfurt
Coburg
Kulmbach
Cambrai
Fourmies
Hirson
Bastogne
Bitburg
Wiesbaden
Frankfurt a.M.
Offenbach
Bamberg
Bayreuth
Mariánské Lázně
Peronne
Charleville-Mézières
Bouillon
Ettelbruck
Mosel
Bad Kreuznach
Mainz
Rüsselsheim
Darmstadt
Erlangen
Weiden in der Oberpfalz
Saint-Quentin
Laon
Signy l'Abbaye
LUXEMBOURG
Trier
Idar-Oberstein
Würzburg
Kitzingen
Sulzbach-Rosenberg
Amberg
Compiègne
Luxembourg
Esch-sur-Alzette
Fürth
Soissons
Longwy
Thionville
Ludwigshafen
Mannheim
Bad Mergentheim
Nürnberg
Château-Thierry
Reims
Verdun-sur-Meuse
Saarbrücken
Neunkirchen
Speyer
Heidelberg
Mosbach
Ansbach
Regensburg
Meaux
Châlons-sur-Marne
Bar-le-Duc
Metz
Saint-Avold
Forbach
Pirmasens
Heilbronn
Schwäbisch Hall
Weissenburg in Bayern
Straubing
Provins
Romilly-sur-Seine
Esternay
Nancy
Lunéville
Sarrebourg
Karlsruhe
Pforzheim
Ludwigsburg
Ingolstadt
Landau an der Isar
Montereau-faut-Yonne
Saint-Dizier
Saverne
Stuttgart
Schwäbisch Gmünd
Heidenheim
Landshut
Sens
Troyes
Bar-sur-Aube
Saint-Dié
Strasbourg
Baden-Baden
Tübingen
Reutlingen
Ulm
Augsburg
Freising
Dachau
MÜNCHEN MUNICH
Auxerre
Chaumont
Épinal
Vittel
Freudenstadt
Rottweil
Biberach an der Riss
Memmingen
Landsberg
Burghausen
Traunstein
Remiremont
Villingen-Schwenningen
Ravensburg
Kaufbeuren
Rosenheim
Chatillon-sur-Seine
Luxeuil-les-Bains
Freiburg
Leutkirch
Weilheim
Les Riceys
Longeau
Belfort
Schaffhausen
Konstanz
Kempten
Baigneux-les-Juifs
Mulhouse
Friedrichshafen
Füssen
Reichenhall
Bad Tölz
Kitzbühel
Clamecy
Dijon
Besançon
Montbéliard
Basel
Bâle
Baden
Zugspitze 2963
BAYERISCHE ALPEN
Solbad Hall in Tirol
Corbigny
Nuits-Saint-Georges
La Chaux-de-Fonds
Horgen
Zürich
LIECHTENSTEIN
Vaduz
Innsbruck
HOHE TAUERN
Château-Chinon
Autun
Biel
Solothurn
Bern
Berne
Vierwaldstätter See
Altdorf
Chur
ALPS
Brenner Pass
1504
Reschenpass
Grossglockner 3797
1374
AUSTRIA ITALY
Luzy
Lac de Neuchâtel
Pontarlier
Poligny
Fribourg
Thunersee
RHAETIAN ALPS
NATIONAL PARK
Brunico
Bruneck
Moulins
Montceau
Lons-le-Saunier
Lausanne
Interlaken
Jungfrau 4158△
Passo dello Stelvio
St. Moritz
PARCO NAZIONALE DELLO STELVIO
Meran
Merano
Bolzano
Bozen
Paray-le-Monial
Mâcon
Geneve
Lake Geneva
BERNER ALPEN
2108 Passo del San Gottardo
Chiavenna
Lapalisse
Vichy
Bourg-en-Bresse
Sierre
2005 Simplon Pass

Kilometres
Km.
Miles
Mi.
1: 6 000 000

Conic Projection, Two Standard Parallels.

Kilometres 0 50 100 150 Km.
Miles 0 50 100 150 Mi.
1: 6 000 000

Lambert Conformal Conic Projection

Kilometres 0 50 100 150 Km.
Miles 0 50 100 150 Mi.
1: 6 000 000

Conic Projection Two Standard Parallels

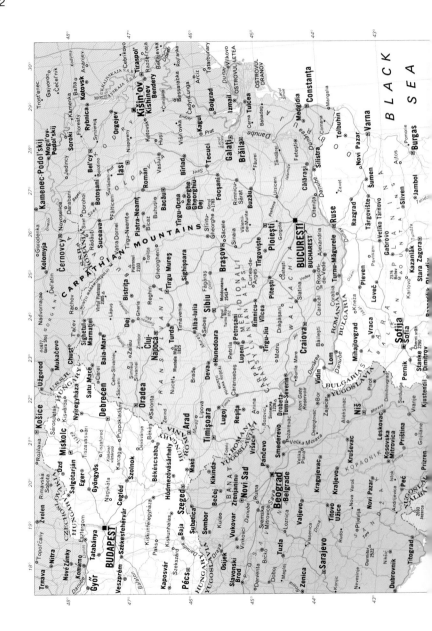

84

Lambert Conformal Conic Projection

Kilometres 0 — 200 — 400 — 600 Km.
Miles 0 — 200 — 400 — 600 Mi.

1 : 24 000 000

Copyright © 1980
by Rand McNally & Co.
C-570000-964 - 2ᵛ- 2ᵛ- 2ᵛ- 3ᵛ

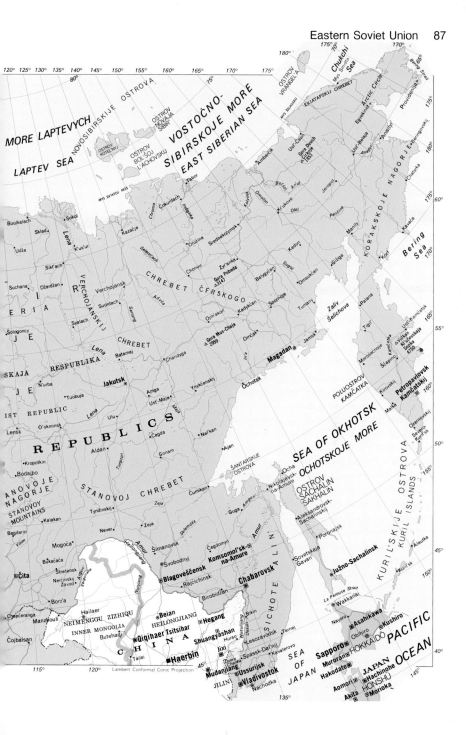

MORE LAPTEVYCH

LAPTEV SEA

NOVOSIBIRSKIJE OSTROVA

VOSTOČNO-SIBIRSKOJE MORE

EAST SIBERIAN SEA

Chukchi Sea

OSTROV VRANGELA

Arctic Circle

Bering Strait

OSTROV NOVAJA SIBIR'

OSTROV BOL'ŠOJ L'ACHOVSKIJ

OSTROV KOTEL'NYJ

EKJATAPSKIJ CHREBET

Providenija

MYS SVJATOJ NOS

Ust-Čaun

Gora Dvuch Cirkov 1853

Ambarčik

Mys Šmidta

Anadyr'

Ust-Belaja

Čalykira

Buolkalach

Sokol

Sklad

Lena

K'us'ur

Kazačje

Čokurdach

Indigirka

Tabor

Bol'šoj Anjuj

Jeropol

Krukovo

Oloj

Penžino

Manily

Kamčatka

Udža

Sikťach

Suchana

Diždžan

VERCHOJANSKIJ

Verchojansk

Suordach

Batagaj

Čoniu

Selennjach

Zyr'anka

Sredněkolymsk

Gora Pobeda 3147

Balygyčan

Sugoj

Omsukčan

Keston

Gižiga

KORAKSKOJE NAGORJ

Korf

Kamča

Bering Sea

Šologoncy

J E

R' S P U B L I K A

SKAJA

Sjalach

Oim'akon

Saring

CHREBET ČERSKOGO

Adyča

Omčak

Gora Mus-Chaia 2959

Zaliv Šelichova

Jama

Tigil'

Ust-Kamčatsk

Vulkan Ključevskaja Sopka 4750

Morošečnoje

Šapino

N'urba

Tuobuja

Jakutsk

Batamaj

Lena

Chandyga

Ina

Ochotsk

Magadan

IST REPUBLIC

Lensk

O'okminsk

Ulu

Amga

Ust-Maja

Cagda

Ynykčanskij

Nel'kan

POLUOSTROV KAMČATKA

Petropavlovsk Kamčatski

Kirovskij

Mal'a

Ozernovskij

Severo-Kuril'sk

R E P U B L I C S

Kropotkin

Bodajbo

Aldan

Gonam

Ajan

ŠANTARSKIJE OSTROVA

SEA OF OKHOTSK

OCHOTSKOJE MORE

KURIL'SKIJE OSTROVA

KURIL ISLANDS

ANOVOJE NAGORJE

STANOVOY MOUNTAINS

STANOVOJ CHREBET

Tynda

Timpton

Ocha

Nikolajevsk-na-Amure

OSTROV SACHALIN

SAKHALIN

Severo-Kuril'sk

Bagdarin

Vitim

Kalakan

Never

Zeja

Šamtoda

Guga

Amgun'

Aleksandrovsk-Sachalinskij

Kuril'sk

Aleutka

Mogoča

Bukačača

Svobodnyj

Šimanovsk

Čegdomyn

Amur

Poronajsk

Čita

Stretensk

Nerčinskij Zavod

Tyndinskij

Zeja

Šimanovsk

Komsomol'sk-na-Amure

Sovetskaja Gavan'

Južno-Sachalinsk

Kuril'sk

Chapceranga

Borz'a

Blagoveščensk

Rajčichinsk

Chabarovsk

SICHOTE ALIN

La Perouse Strait

Wakkanai

Manzhouli

Hailaer

Birobidžan

Terbej

Nayoro

Asahikawa

Kushiro

NEIMENGGU ZIZHIQU

INNER MONGOLIA

Butehadi

Beian

HEILONGJIANG

Hegang

Bikin

Obihiro

Čojbaisan

Qiqihaer Tsitsihar

Shuangyashan

Hurao

Lesozavodsk

Ternej

Muroran

HOKKAIDO

PACIFIC

C H I N A

Huraj

Jixi

Spassk-Dal'nij

Sapporo

Hakodate

OCEAN

Harbin

Mudanjiang

Ussurijsk

Kavalerovo

SEA

Aomori

JAPAN

JILIN

Vladivostok

Nachodka

OF

JAPAN

Hachinohe

HONSHU

Akita

Morioka

115°   120°   Lambert Conformal Conic Projection   135°

88

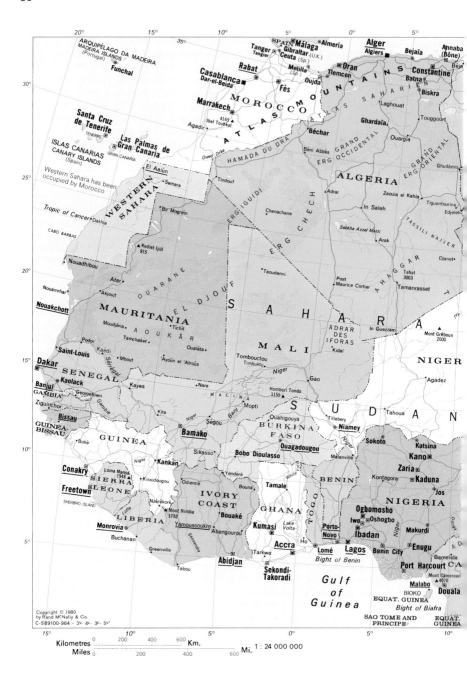

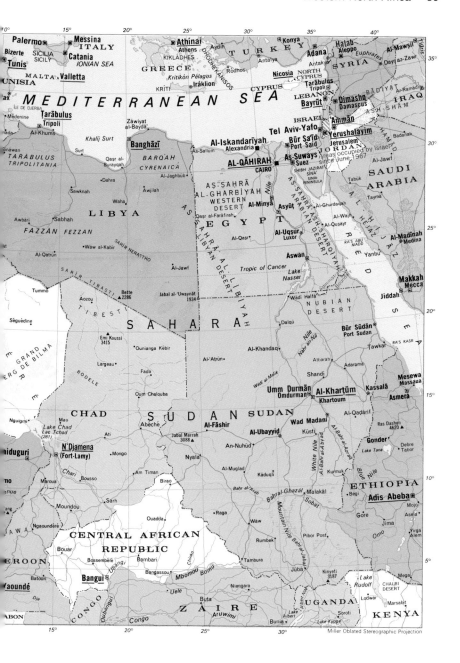

0°   15°   20°   25°   30°   35°   40°

Palermo   Messina   ITALY   Athinai   Konya   Halab   Al-Mawṣil
Bizerte SICILIA Catania IONIAN SEA   Athens   Aydin   Adana Aleppo   Euphrates 35°
Tunis   SICILY   ITALY   KIKLÁDHES   Antakya SYRIA   Dayr az-Zawr
        MALTA•Valletta   GREECE   Rodhos   Antalya   BĀDIYAT
UNISIA   Kritikón Pélagos   Nicosia NORTH   IRAQ
                                     KRITI   Iráklion   CYPRUS CYPRUS Ṭarābulus
ax   M E D I T E R R A N E A N   S E A   CYPRUS LEBANON Tripoli
ÎLE DE DJERBA Ṭarābulus   ISRAEL Bayrūt Dimashq
•Médenine Tripoli   Zāwiyat   Tel Aviv-Yafo Damascus ASH-SHĀM
nada   Al-Khums   Khalīj Surt al-Bayḍā   'Ammān
                        Surt   Banghāzī   Al-Iskandarīyah Būr Sa'īd Yerushalayim
inawan TARĀBULUS   Qaṣr al-   BARQAH   As-Sallūm Alexandria Port Said JORDAN Areas occupied by Israel 30°
        TRIPOLITANIA •Dahra Burayqah CYRENAICA   AL-QĀHIRAH As-Suways since June 1967
                                Al-Jaghbūb   CAIRO   Suez SINAI Al-Jawf SAUDI
        •Sawknah   Wāha• •Awjilah   AṢ-ṢAḤRĀ   SHIBH JAZĪRAT Ṭabūk ARABIA
                                    AL-GHARBĪYAH   Al-Minyā SINAI
Awbārī •Sabhah   L I B Y A   WESTERN Asyūṭ   ARABIAN •Al-Ghurdaqah
FAZZĀN FEZZAN   DESERT   E G Y P T   Tayma• 25°
                        Qaṣr al-Farāfirah Al-Qaṣr Al-Uqṣur DESERT Al-Qusayr
Al-Qaṭrūn •Wāw al-Kabīr   Aswān Luxor   RAS ABU •Al-Wajh AL HIJĀZ Al-Madīnah
                                                    MADD   Medina
Tummo   Bette 2286 Jabal al-'Uwaynāt Tropic of Cancer Lake Yanbu'
        •Aozou   1934   Nasser   MAKKAH Mecca 20°
Séguédine Emi Koussi •Ounianga Kébir   •Al-Jawf   Wādī Ḥalfā Jiddah
        3415   NUBIAN Bur Sūdān
        •Largeau Fada   Al-Khandaq•   DESERT   Port Sudan
BODELE   •Al-'Atrūn Nabr an-Nīl Ţawkar RAS KASR
        •Oum Chalouba   S A H A R A   Atbarah• •Adarama   Mesewa 15°
CHAD   Shandi   Kassalā   Massawa
Nguigmi Mao   Umm Durmān Al-Khartūm   Asmera
Lake Chad Ati Jabal Marrah Al-Fāshir Omdurman Khartoum
Lac Tchad •Abéché 3088▲   Al-Ubayyiḍ Wad Madanī Al-Qaḍārif
N'Djamena   Nyala• An-Nuhūd   Küstī   Ras Dashen Gonder 10°
(Fort-Lamy) •Mongo   Al-Muglad Kādugli   4620▲ Lake Tana Debre
Chari •Bousso   Birao   White Nile   Kurmuk Tabor
•Maroua   Bahr al-'Arab Malakāl Begi ETHIOPIA
Moundou •Sarh   Bahr-Ghazāl Sobat   Gore Adis Abeba
        Ouadda•   •Raga   •Wāw   Jima Mojo•
Ngaoundéré   C E N T R A L   A F R I C A N   Pibor Post• Omo Asela• 5°
                REPUBLIC   Rumbek•   Yirga
EROON Bouar Bossembélé Bambari Tambura Jūbā Kinyeti Lake Alem
Batouri   •Bangassou Mbomou Niangara 3187 Rudolf CHALBI Mega•
aoundé Bangui Bangassou Bonu   Buta Kityeti DESERT
Dja   CONGO   •Uele Z A Ï R E UGANDA Lodwar Marsabit
ABON   Congo   Aruwimi Lake Albert Soroti KENYA
                                Bunia Lake Kyoga

15°   20°   25°   30°   Miller Oblated Stereographic Projection

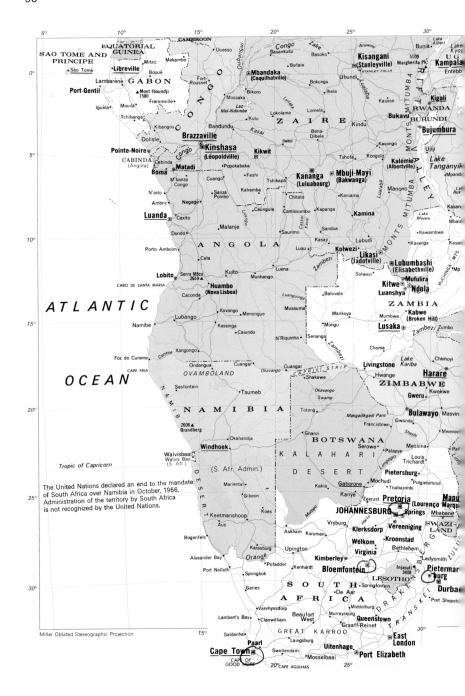

The United Nations declared an end to the mandate
of South Africa over Namibia in October, 1966.
Administration of the territory by South Africa
is not recognized by the United Nations.

ATLANTIC

OCEAN

Tropic of Capricorn

Miller Oblated Stereographic Projection

35°   40°   45°   50°   55°

Soroti
Mbale   SOMALIA   Brava   Equator   0°
DA   Eldoret   Mado
                           Gashi   Afmadu
         Kirinyaga
Lake Nakuru   KENYA   Bura   Kismayu   I N D I A N   O C E A N
ictoria   5199
           Nairobi
                        YATTA PLATEAU   Lamu
SERENGETI   Kilimanjaro
  PLAIN   5895   Voi   SEYCHELLES
Shinyanga   Arusha   Victoria   5°
         MASAI   Mombasa
Singida STEPPE   PEMBA ISLAND
abora   AMIRANTE ISLANDS   PLATTE ISLAND (Sey.)
T A N Z A N I A   Tanga   (Sey.)
   Dodoma Morogoro   Zanzibar   ALPHONSE ISLAND (Sey.)
Kipembawe   ZANZIBAR
                  Dar es Salaam
        Mikumi
Iringa   Utete
      Mahenge   Kilwa Kivinje
Njombe   ALDABRA ISLANDS   PROVIDENCE ISLAND
                 Lindi   (Sey.)   (Sey.)   10°
Manda   Masasi Mtwara   ASTOVE ISLAND   FARQUHAR GROUP   ALDALEGA ISLANDS
Mzuzu Songea   Rovuma   (Sey.)   (Sey.)   (Mauritius)
Lindazi   NJAZIDJA
Lake   Montepuez   Moroni COMOROS   ILES GLORIEUSES   CAP D'AMBRE
Nyasa Lichinga   Pemba   (Fr.)   Antsiranana
ALAWI   MAYOTTE Dzaoudzi
Lilongwe   Maúa   Namapa   (Fr.)   NOSY BE   Iharana
    Mandimba   Andoany   Maromokotro
Vila Malema   Analalava ▲ 2876
outinho   Antalaha
Blantyre Zomba   Nampula   Moçambique   Mahajanga Maroantsetra
te Sapitwa 3000   Port-Bergé
          António Enes   Marovoay   Mananara   TROMELIN
M O Z A M B I Q U E   Pebane   Besalampy   (Fr.)
yangani 2593   Quelimane   Tamborhano Maevatanana
tare Chinde   Toamasina
onte Binga   Ankavandra   Antananarivo
  436 Beira   MADAGASCAR   Belo   Antsirabe
                              Morondava Malaimbandy Mahanoro   MAURITIUS
Nova Mambone   Ambositra   Port Louis   20°
               BASSAS DA INDIA
ssangena   (Fr.)   Morombe Bererоha   Fianarantsoa   Saint-Denis
    PONTA SÃO SEBASTIÃO ÎLE EUROPA   △ Pic Boby   REUNION
                   (Fr.)   Ankazoabo   2658 Manakara   (Fr.)
    PONTA DA BARRA FALSA   MASCARENE
                         Toliara   Betroka Vangaindrano   ISLANDS
Inhambane   Midongy
Inharrime   Bekily Sud   Tropic of Capricorn
Xai-Xai
                   Androka   Faradofay
                     CAP SAINTE-MARIE   25°

                                    I N D I A N   O C E A N

                                         Copyright © 1980
                                         by Rand McNally & Co.
                                         C-589200-964 - 5ᵛ- 8ᵛ- 6ᵛ- 15ᵛ

35°   40°   45°   50°   55°   60°

Kilometres 0   200   400   600 Km.
Miles 0   200   400   600 Mi.   1 : 24 000 000

Copyright © 1980
by Rand McNally & Co.
C-589391-964 - 2v- 2v- 2v- 11v²

Miller Oblated Stereographic Projection

Kilometres 0   200   400   600 Km.
Miles 0   200   400   600 Mi.   1 : 25 300 000

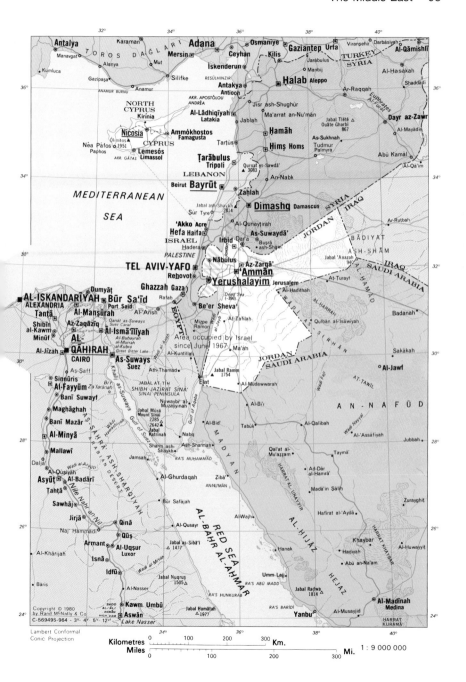

The boundary between India and Pakistan through the disputed state of Jammu and Kashmir follows the "line of control" agreed upon by both countries in 1972.

ARABIAN
SEA

INDIAN

OCEAN

BAY OF

BENGAL

LACCADIVE ISLANDS
(India)

Copyright © 1980
by Rand McNally & Co.
C-569400-964 - 5ᵛ - 5ᵛ - 4ᵛ - 12ᵛ

Kilometres 0 200 400 600 Km.
Miles 0 200 400 600 Mi.

Lambert Conformal
Conic Projection

1 : 24 000 000

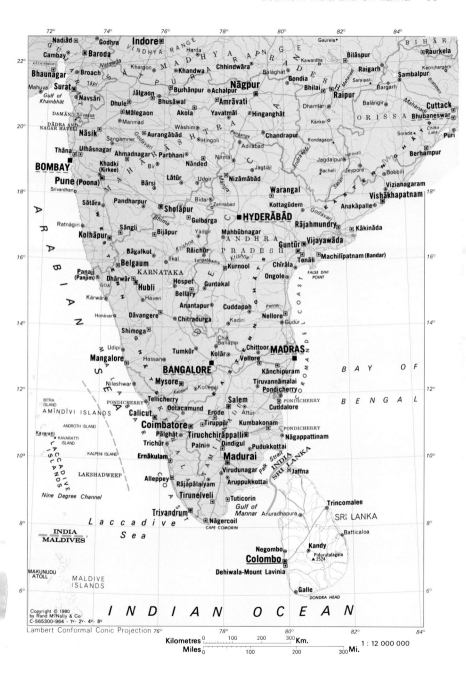

Copyright © 1980
by Rand McNally & Co.
C-565200-964 - 2ᵛ - 2ᵛ - 2ᵛ - 10ᵛˡ

The boundary between India and
Pakistan through the disputed
state of Jammu and Kashmir
follows the "line of control"
agreed to by both countries
in 1972.

ARABIAN SEA

Tropic of Cancer

Kilometres 0   100   200   300 Km.
Miles 0   100   200   300 Mi.

1 : 12 000 000

BAY OF BENGAL

Lambert Conformal Conic Projection

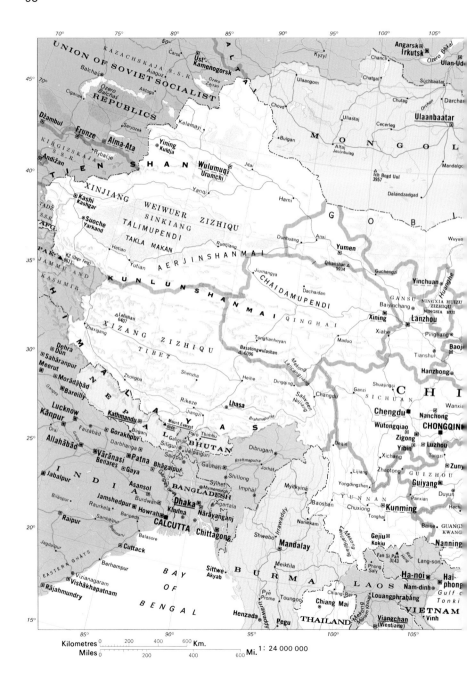

70° 75° 80° 85° 90° 95° 100° 105°

UNION OF SOVIET SOCIALIST REPUBLICS

KAZACHSKAJA S.S.R.

ALTAI

Angarsk
Irkutsk
Ozero Bajkal
Ulan-Ud

Čarsk
Ust'-Kamenogorsk
Kyzyl
Chanch
Chatgal
Süchbaatar
Darchan

Balchaš
Ajaguz
Aktoga
Ozero Zajsan
Ulaangom
Uliastaj
Cecerleg
Orchon
Ulaanbaatar

Ciganak
Ozero Balchaš
Saryozek
Kelamayi
Chovd
M O N G O L

Džambul
Frunze
Alma-Ata
Rybačje
Yining
Kuldja
Bulgan
Altai
Jesönbulag
Mandalgo

KIRGIZSKAJA S.S.R.
TIEN SHAN
Jitai
Ich Bogd Uul
3957
Dalandzadgad

Andižan
Wulumuqi
Ürumchi

TADŽ. S.S.R.
XINJIANG
Yanqi
Hami
G O B I

AFG.
Kashi
Kashgar
WEIWUER
SINKIANG
ZIZHIQU
Dunhuang
Anxi
Yumen
Wuya

PAK
Suoche
Yarkand
TALIMUPENDI
TAKLA MAKAN
Ruoqiang
Qilianshan
5934
Guchengzi
Yinchuan

K2 (Qogir Feng)
8611
JAMMU AND
Hetian
AERJINSHANMAI
Jiumangya
Dachaidan
GANSU
NINGXIA HUIZU ZIZHIQU
NINGSIA HUI
Huanghe

KASHMIR
Yutian
KUNLUN
CHAIDAMUPENDI
Baiyinchang
Xining
Lanzhou

Lelishan
6407
SHANMAI
QINGHAI
Maduo
Xiahe
Pingliang

Dehra Dun
Sahāranpur
Zhaxigang
XIZANG ZIZHIQU
TIBET
Tongtianheyan
Basatongwulashan
6096
Baoji
Tianshui

Meerut
Morādābād
Zhongba
Shenzha
Heihe
Dingqing
Mekong
Lancangjiang
Hanzhong

Bareilly
HIMALAYAS
Rikeze
Jiangzi
Lhasa
Changdu
Salween
Nujiang
Ganzi
SICHUAN
C H I

Lucknow
Kānpur
Kathmandu
Mount Everest
8848
Paro Thimbu
Brahmaputra
Deqin
Shuajingsi
Chengdu
Nanchong
Wanxia

Allahābād
Faizābād
Gorakhpur
NEPAL
Galhtok
BHUTAN
Dibrugarh
Wutongqiao
Zigong
CHONGQIN

Jabalpur
Darbhanga
Siliguri
Jalpaiguri
Brahmaputra
Jorhat
Lijiang
Zhaotong
Yibin
Luzhou

INDIA
Vārānasi
Benares
Patna
Bhāgalpur
Saidpur
Gauhati
Shillong
Yongdingzhen
Chuxiong
GUIZHOU
Tongzi
Zuny

Bilaspur
Jamshedpur
Asansol
Burdwan
Sylhet
Mymensingh
Imphāl
Myitkyina
Baoshan
YUNNAN
Panxian
Guiyang
Duyun

Raurkela
Bāripada
BANGLADESH
Agartala
Tongha
Kunming
Hechi

Raipur
Sambalpur
Howrah
Dhaka
Nārāyanganj
Baose
GUANG
KWANG

Jagdalpur
Balasore
Khulna
CALCUTTA
Chittagong
Namkam
Gejiu
Kokiu
Fan Si Pan
3143
Nanning

Berhampur
Shwebo
Irrawaddy
Lang-son

EASTERN GHATS
Vizianagaram
Vishākhapatnam
BAY
OF
BENGAL
Sittwe
Akyab
B U R M A
Meiktila
Phong Saly
Mekong
Lancangjiang
Ha-noi
Hai-phong

Rājahmundry
Henzada
Pye
Prome
Toungoo
Chiang Rai
Chiang Mai
LAOS
Nam-dinh
VIETNAM
Vinh

Pegu
THAILAND
Louangphrabàng
Viangchan
(Vientiane)
Gulf of
Tonki

Kilometres 0 200 400 600 Km.
Miles 0 200 400 600 Mi.
1 : 24 000 000

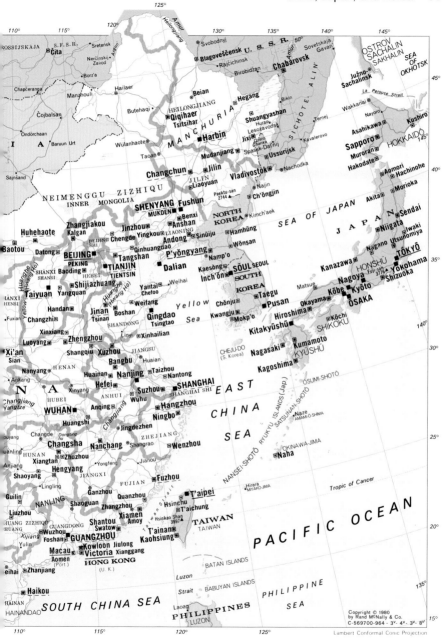

China, Japan, and Korea

Copyright © 1980
by Rand McNally & Co.
C-569700-964 - 3ᵛ- 4ᵛ- 3ᵛ- 8ᵛ

Lambert Conformal Conic Projection

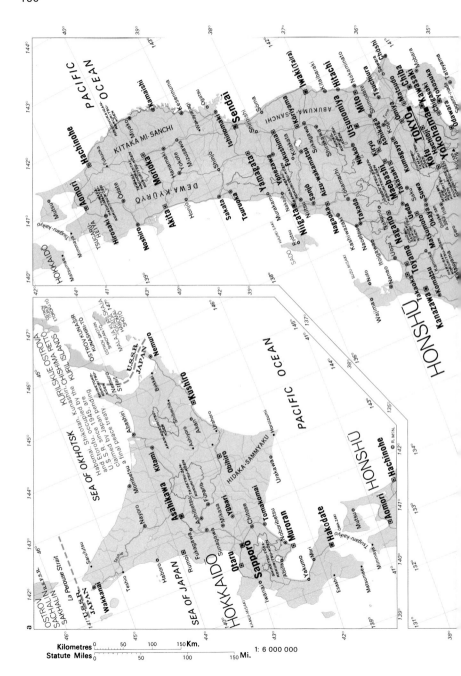

a

Kilometres 0 50 100 150 Km.
Statute Miles 0 50 100 150 Mi.
1 : 6 000 000

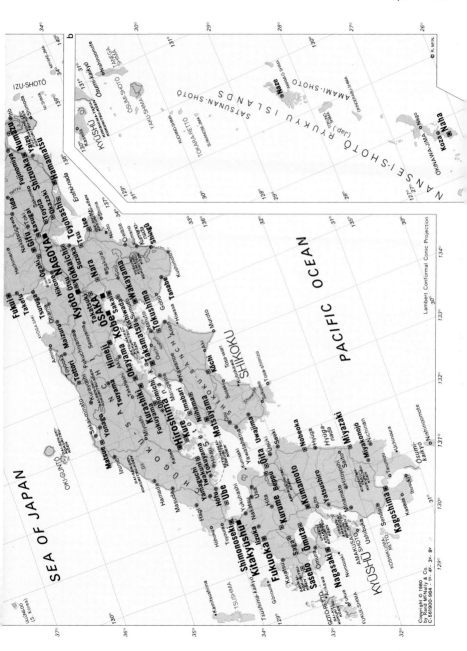

SEA OF JAPAN

PACIFIC OCEAN

IZU-SHOTŌ

SHIKOKU

KYŪSHŪ

NANSEI-SHOTŌ   RYUKYU   ISLANDS

SATSUNAN-SHOTŌ

AMAMI-SHOTŌ

OSUMI-SHOTŌ

TOKARA-RETTŌ

YAKU-SHIMA

OKINAWA-JIMA

Naha
Koza

Naze

Lambert Conformal Conic Projection

Copyright © 1980
by Rand McNally & Co.
C-561900-964 - IV - 4V - 3V - 8V

INDIA Shwebo
Chittagong Mandalay
BANGLA-DESH
Sittwe (Akyab)
BAY OF BENGAL
BURMA
Myingyan
Keng Tung
Prome (Pye)
Henzada
RANGOON
Pegu
Moulmein
Tavoy
Mergui
MERGUI ARCHIPELAGO
Chumphon
ISTHMUS OF KRA
Phuket
Nakhon Si Thammarat
Songkhla

ANDAMAN ISLANDS (India)
ANDAMAN SEA
Port Blair
NICOBAR ISLANDS (India)
Great Channel
Banda Aceh

CHINA
YUNNAN
Gejiu Koktu
GUANGXI ZHUANGZU ZIZHIQU
Nanning
Yulin
Beihai
Fan-si-pan 3143
Phôngsali
Chiang Rai
Louangphabang
Chiang Mai
Viangchan (Vientiane)
Udon Thani
Khon Kaen
Nakhon Sawan
Nakhon Ratchasima
Ha-noi
Nam-dinh
Hai-phong
Gulf of Tonkin
Vinh
Dong-hoi
Hue
Da-nang
Pakxé
Stoeng Trêng

GUANGDONG
GUANGZHOU CANTON
Foshan
Macau Aomen (Port.)
New Kowloon
VICTORIA HONG KONG (U.K.)
Shantou Swatow
Taiwan Strait

LAOS
THAILAND
KRUNG THEP BANGKOK
KAMPUCHEA
Gulf of Thailand
Kâmpóng Saóm
Rach-gia
PHNUM PÉNH
Gia-dinh
Can-tho
THANH-PHO HO CHI MINH (SAI-GON)
VIETNAM
Qui-nhon
Nha-trang
Phan-thiet

Haikou
HAINAN HAINANDAO

SOUTH CHINA SEA

Puerto Princesa
PALAWAN

MALAY PENINSULA
Alor Setar
Kota Baharu
George Town (Pinang)
Medan
Pematangsiantar
MALAYSIA MALAYA
Kuala Lumpur
Melaka
Sibolga
PULAU NIAS
SINGAPORE
SUMATERA
Pakanbaru
SUMATRA
Padang
Gunung Kerinci 3800
Jambi
KEPULAUAN MENTAWAI
Bengkulu
Lahat
Palembang
Pangkalpinang
BELITUNG
KEPULAUAN LINGGA
Pontianak
Kuching
KEPULAUAN BUNGURAN UTARA
TANDJUNG DATU
Sibu
Rajang
Kapuas
Kudat
Kota Kinabalu
Gunung Kinabalu 4094
Sandakan
Bandar Seri Begawan
BRUNEI
Bukit Pagon 1850
Tarakan
MALAYSIA
2053 Kong Kemul
BORNEO
KALIMANTAN
Kayan
Mahakam
Samarinda
Balikpapan
Sampit
Banjarmasin
Selat Makasar
Talok

Equator

GREATER SU
INDONESIA
ISLAND

Telukbetung
LAUT JAWA JAVA SEA
JAKARTA
Bogor
BANDUNG
Cirebon
Semarang
MADURA
SURABAYA
Tasikmalaya
Surakarta
Madiun
Malang
Yogyakarta
JAWA JAVA
BALI
Denpasar
LOMBOK
Laut
SUMBAWA LESSER

INDIAN OCEAN

CHRISTMAS ISLAND (Austr.)

Copyright © 1980 by Rand McNally & Co.
C-569800-964 - 4ᵛ- 7ᵛ- 6ᵛ- 9ᵛ

Kilometres 0 200 400 600 Km.
Miles 0 200 400 600 Mi.
1 : 24 000 000

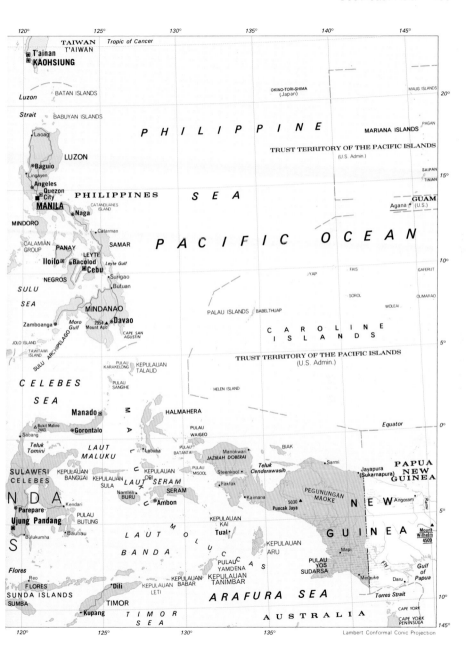

120°   125°   130°   135°   140°   145°

TAIWAN T'AIWAN   Tropic of Cancer
T'ainan
KAOHSIUNG

Luzon   BATAN ISLANDS   OKINO-TORI-SHIMA   MAUG ISLANDS   20°
                                                         (Japan)
Strait   BABUYAN ISLANDS   PAGAN

                    P H I L I P P I N E   MARIANA ISLANDS
Laoag
                                                    TRUST TERRITORY OF THE PACIFIC ISLANDS
LUZON   (U.S. Admin.)
                                                                              SAIPAN   15°
Baguio   TINIAN
Lingayen
Angeles
Quezon   PHILIPPINES   S E A   GUAM
City   Agana (U.S.)
MANILA Naga   CATANDUANES
                    ISLAND

MINDORO   P A C I F I C   O C E A N
              Catarman

CALAMIAN   SAMAR   10°
GROUP   PANAY
Iloilo Bacolod LEYTE   YAP   FAIS   GAFERUT
NEGROS Cebu   Leyte Gulf
              Surigao
SULU   Butuan   SOROL   OLIMARAO
SEA
          MINDANAO   WOLEAI
Zamboanga Moro 2954▲Davao   PALAU ISLANDS BABELTHUAP   5°
         Gulf Mount Apo   C A R O L I N E
                CAPE SAN   I S L A N D S
JOLO ISLAND   AGUSTIN
TAWITAWI
ISLAND   TRUST TERRITORY OF THE PACIFIC ISLANDS
          PULAU   KEPULAUAN   (U.S. Admin.)
          KARAKELONG TALAUD
C E L E B E S   PULAU
                           SANGIHE   HELEN ISLAND
S E A
Manado   M   HALMAHERA
Bukit Malino   A   Equator   0°
2443   PULAU
Sabang   Gorontalo   D   WAIGEO
Teluk   PULAU
Tomini   LAUT   C Labuha   BATANTA   BIAK
          MALUKU   PULAU   Manokwari Sarmi
                           MISOOL JAZIRAH DOBERAI
SULAWESI KEPULAUAN   KEPULAUAN   Steenkool Teluk   Jayapura   PAPUA
CELEBES   BANGGAI KEPULAUAN LAUT SERAM   Cenderawasih   (Sukarnapura) NEW
                  SULA OBI X SERAM   Fakfak   GUINEA
N D A   Namlea   Ambon   Kaimana   PEGUNUNGAN   N E W   Angoram   5°
         Kendari BURU   MAOKE
Parepare   PULAU   5030▲
Ujung Pandang BUTUNG   KEPULAUAN Puncak Jaya
         Baubau   KAI   Tual   G U I N E A Mount
S Bulukumba   LAUT   M O   Wilhelm
                 BANDA   L U C   KEPULAUAN   Mapi   4509
Flores   A S PULAU ARU
Reo   YAMDENA
FLORES   KEPULAUAN BABAR KEPULAUAN   PULAU   Merauke Daru Gulf
SUNDA ISLANDS   LETI   TANIMBAR YOS   of
SUMBA   TIMOR   Dili   SUDARSA   Torres Strait Papua
          Kupang T I M O R   A R A F U R A   S E A   10°
                  S E A   A U S T R A L I A   CAPE YORK
                                                           CAPE YORK
                                                           PENINSULA
120°   125°   130°   135°   Lambert Conformal Conic Projection 145°

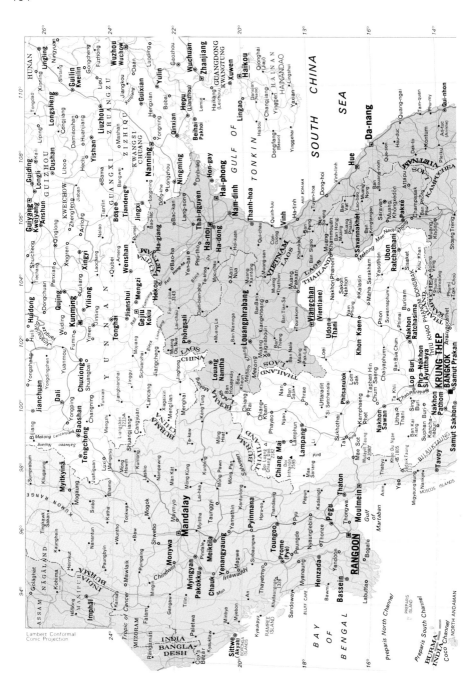

Kilometres 0 — 100 — 200 — 300 Km.
Miles 0 —————— 100 —————— 200 Mi.

1: 12 000 000

SOUTH CHINA SEA

GULF OF THAILAND

THAILAND

MALAYSIA

INDONESIA

SUMATERA

Strait of Malacca

ANDAMAN AND NICOBAR ISLANDS

ANDAMAN SEA

INDIAN OCEAN

BURMA

SINGAPORE

MERGUI ARCHIPELAGO

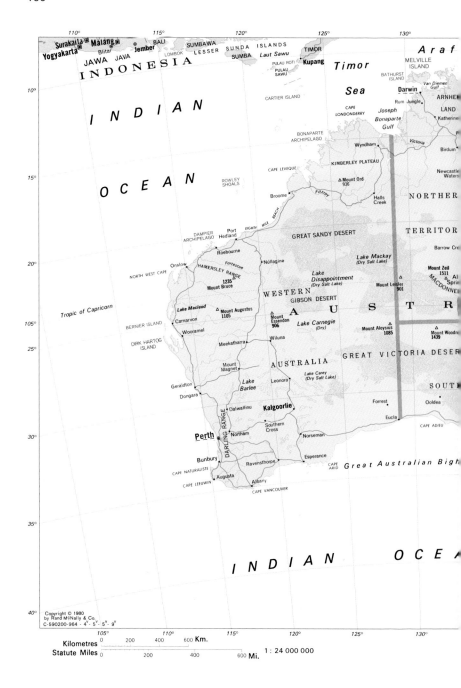

Copyright © 1980
by Rand McNally & Co.
C-590200-964 · 4ᵛ · 5ᵛ · 5ᵛ · 9ᵛ

Kilometres
Statute Miles

1 : 24 000 000

a *Sea*

135°   140°   145°   150°   155°

WESSEL ISLANDS

CAPE ARNHEM

GROOTE
EYLANDT

Limmen Bight

Gulf
of
Carpentaria

BARKLY TABLELAND

nant
eek

Hay

Georgina

Mount
Isa

Flinders

Mitchell

Daru
Gulf of
Papua

Torres   Strait

CAPE
YORK

CAPE

YORK

PENINSULA

MORNINGTON
ISLAND

Normanton

Cloncurry   Hughenden

Winton

QUEENSLAND

GREAT ARTESIAN

BASIN

Quilpie

Charleville

Port
Moresby
PAPUA
NEW GUINEA
NEW GUINEA

OWEN STANLEY RANGE

D'ENTRECASTEAUX ISLANDS

LOUISIADE ARCHIPELAGO

TAGULA
ISLAND

TROBRIAND
ISLANDS

WOODLARK
ISLAND

ROSSEL
ISLAND

VELLA
LAVELLA Gizo
SOLOMON
ISLANDS
Mt. Popomanaseu
2331

NEW
GEORGIA

SANTA
ISABEL

Honiara 160°

Solomon Sea

RENNELL

Coral   *Sea*

WILLIS GROUP
(Austl.)

TREGOSSE ISLETS
(Austl.)

ÎLES
CHESTERFIELD
(N. Cal.)

ÎLE DE SABLE
(N. Cal.)

CAYE DE
L'OBSERVATOIRE
(N. Cal.)

10°

15°

20°

Cooktown

CAPE GRAFTON
Cairns

HINCHINBROOK
ISLAND

Townsville

CUMBERLAND
ISLAND

Mackay

SWAIN
REEFS

SAUMAREZ
REEF

CATO
ISLAND

ILE CHESTERFIELD

Ravenshoe

Emerald

Blackall

Theodore

Rockhampton

CURTIS I.

Bundaberg

Tropic of Capricorn

PACIFIC

OCEAN

GREAT DIVIDING RANGE

GREAT BARRIER REEF

Maryborough

FRASER ISLAND

Mount Kiangarow
1135

Saint George   **Toowoomba**

Brisbane
Ipswich

Tenterfield   Lismore

Round Mountain
1608   Grafton

Walgett

Bourke

Tamworth

Port
Macquarie

MIDDLETON REEF

LORD HOWE ISLAND
(N.S.W.)

25°

30°

35°

40°

SIMPSON

DESERT

GREAT ARTESIAN

Lake Eyre
North
(Dry Salt Lake)
Lake Eyre
South

AUSTRALIA

Lake
Torrens Woomera

Lake
Gairdner
WLER RANGES

Port
Augusta

Port Pirie
Peterborough

FLINDERS RANGE

GREY

RANGE

STURT
DESERT   Milparinka

△Saint Mary
Peak
1165

Broken
Hill

Nyngan

NEW SOUTH WALES

Dubbo

Orange

Newcastle
SYDNEY
Wollongong

Tasman

Sea

RANGE

Paroo

Warrego

Macquarie

Darling

Mildura

Hay

Wagga
Wagga

Albury

Canberra

A.C.T.

Mount
Kosciusko
2228

GREAT DIVIDING RANGE

NINETY MILE BEACH

CAPE HOWE

A L I A

SPENCER GULF

GULF

EYRE PENINSULA

Port
coln

Spencer
Gulf

Gulf
Saint
Vincent

CAPE
ASTROPHE

Adelaide

Murray

Murray

Bordertown

Bendigo

VICTORIA

Encounter
Bay

GEELONG **MELBOURNE**

Warrnambool

Portland

CAPE OTWAY

GAROO
AND

Mount Gambier

SOUTH POINT

KING ISLAND *Bass Strait*

FLINDERS ISLAND

J

5°   140°   145°

Smithton   Burnie   *Banks Strait*

Launceston

Mount Ossa △
1617   TASMANIA

Hobart

SOUTH
WEST
CAPE

SOUTH
EAST
CAPE

150°   155°

165°

160° Lambert Conformal Conic Projection

ANGES

△
DESERT

SIMPSON

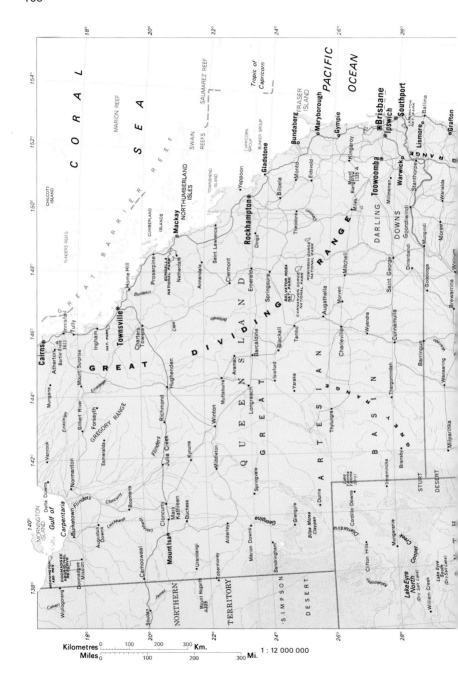

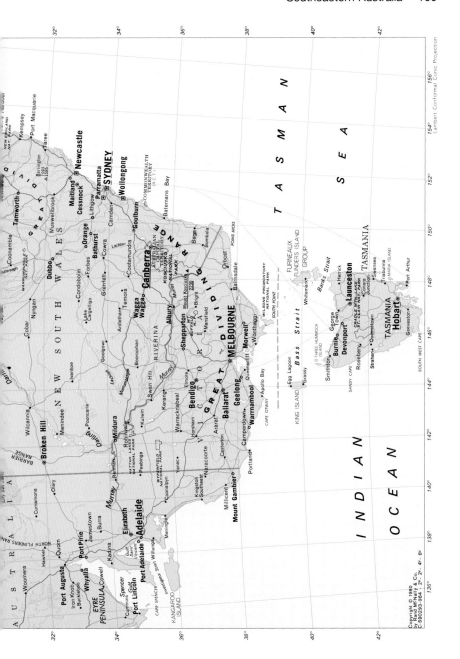

32° 34° 36° 38° 40° 42°

156°
154° Lambert Conformal Conic Projection

T A S M A N

S E A

Kempsey
Port Macquarie
NEW ENGLAND NAT. PARK
Taree
Barrington Tops 5366
Coonamble
Castlereagh
Warrumbungle NAT. PARK
Tamworth
Muswellbrook
Newcastle
Maitland
Cessnock
Lithgow SYDNEY
Parramatta
Wollongong
Goulburn
Camden
COMMONWEALTH TERRITORY (A.C.T.)
Batemans Bay
Bega
POINT HICKS
Orange
Bathurst
Cowra
Dubbo
Forbes
Condobolin
Nyngan
Grenfell
Cootamundra
Canberra
AUSTRALIAN CAPITAL TERRITORY
KOSCIUSKO NATIONAL PARK
Mount Kosciusko 2230
Bright
Orbost
Bombala
Bairnsdale

N E W   S O U T H   W A L E S

D I V I D I N G   R A N G E

G R E A T

Lachlan
Cobar
Ivanhoe
Lake Cargelligo
Ardlethan
Temora
Wagga Wagga
Albury
Shepparton
Mansfield
Elmore
MT. BUFFALO NAT. PARK
Benalla

Wilcannia
Menindee
Pooncarie
Goolgowi
Booroorban
Swan Hill
Kerang
Bendigo
Echuca
G R E A T
Morwell
Wonthaggi
MELBOURNE
Geelong
Queenscliff
WILSONS PROMONTORY NATIONAL PARK
SOUTH POINT

V I C T O R I A

R I V E R I N A

Murrumbidgee
Murray
Kulwin
Robinvale
Mildura
HATTAH LAKES NATIONAL PARK
Ouyen
WYPERFELD NATIONAL PARK
Pinnaroo
Murrayville
Peebinga
Yanac
Kingston Southeast
Millicent
Mount Gambier
Portland
Casterton
Naracoorte
Horsham
Warracknabeal
Ararat
Ballarat
Camperdown
Warrnambool
Apollo Bay
CAPE OTWAY

Egg Lagoon
KING ISLAND
Grassy
Whitemark
FURNEAUX GROUP
FLINDERS ISLAND
Banks Strait
Herrick
Launceston
George Town
CRADLE MTN.-LAKE ST. CLAIR NAT. PARK
Exeter
Burnie
Devonport
Rosebery
Smithton
Strahan
Queenstown
SANDY CAPE
THREE HUMMOCK ISLAND
SOUTH WEST CAPE
TASMANIA
Swansea
Triabunna
MARIA ISLAND
Hobart
Sorell
Geeveston
Port Arthur

B a s s   S t r a i t

I N D I A N

O C E A N

S O U T H   A U S T R A L I A
NORTH FLINDERS RANGES
BARRIER RANGE
Broken Hill
Tibooburra
Olary
Curnamona
Woomera
Iron Knob
Buckleboo
Kimba
EYRE PENINSULA
Port Lincoln
Cummins
CAPE SPENCER
Cowell
Whyalla
Kadina
Quorn
Hawker
Jamestown
Burra
Port Augusta
Port Pirie
Port Adelaide
Elizabeth
Adelaide
Willunga
Meningie
KANGAROO ISLAND
Spencer Gulf
Investigator Strait
Gulf St. Vincent

Darling
Murray
Murray

138° 140° 142° 144° 146° 148° 150° 152°

32° 34° 36° 38° 40° 42°

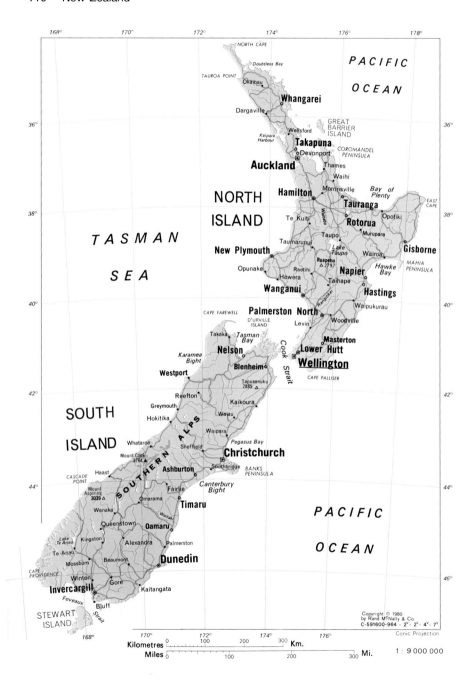

168°   170°   172°   174°   176°   178°

NORTH CAPE

PACIFIC

Doubtless Bay

TAUROA POINT   Okaihau

OCEAN

Whangarei

Dargaville

GREAT
BARRIER
ISLAND

36°   36°

Wellsford

Kaipara
Harbour   **Takapuna**

Devonport   COROMANDEL
PENINSULA

Auckland

Thames

Waihi

Morrinsville   *Bay of
Plenty*

Hamilton   EAST
CAPE

NORTH   Te Kuiti   **Tauranga**

Opotiki

38°   **ISLAND**   **Rotorua**   38°

Taupo   Murupara

TASMAN   Taumarunui   *Lake
Taupo*   Wairoa   **Gisborne**

New Plymouth   *MAHIA
PENINSULA*

SEA   Opunake   Raetihi   Ruapehu
△2797   **Napier**   *Hawke
Bay*

Hawera   Taihape

Wanganui   **Hastings**

40°   CAPE FAREWELL   **Palmerston North**   Waipukurau   40°

D'URVILLE
ISLAND   Levin   Woodville

Takaka   *Tasman
Bay*   **Masterton**

Nelson   *Cook*   **Lower Hutt**

Westport   **Blenheim**   *Strait*   **Wellington**

Tapuaenuku
2885 △   CAPE PALLISER

42°   Reefton   Kaikoura   42°

Greymouth   Waiau

Hokitika   Waipara

SOUTH   Whataroa   Sheffield   *Pegasus Bay*

Mount Cook
3764 △   **Christchurch**

ISLAND   Haast   **Ashburton**   Southbridge   *BANKS
PENINSULA*

CASCADE
POINT   *Canterbury
Bight*

44°   Mount
Aspiring
3039 △   Fairlie   44°

Omarama   **Timaru**

Wanaka

Queenstown   **Oamaru**   *PACIFIC*

*Lake
Te Anau*   Kingston   Alexandra   Palmerston

Te Anau   *OCEAN*

Mossburn   Beaumont   **Dunedin**

CAPE
PROVIDENCE   46°

Winton   Gore   Kaitangata

Invercargill

Foveaux   Bluff

STEWART   *Strait*
ISLAND

168°   Copyright © 1980
by Rand McNally & Co.
C-591600-964 - 2ᵛ - 2ᵛ - 4ᵛ - 7ᵛ

170°   172°   174°   176°   Conic Projection

Kilometres 0   100   200   300 Km.

Miles 0   100   200   300 Mi.   1 : 9 000 000

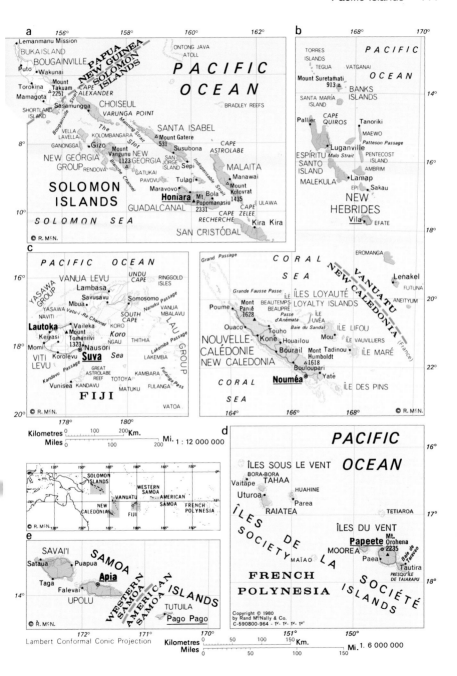

a

156°   158°   160°   162°

Lemanmanu Mission
BUKA ISLAND
BOUGAINVILLE
Puto • Wakunai
Torokina   Mount
Mamagota   Takuam △2251
CAPE
ALEXANDER
SHORTLAND   Sasamungga
ISLAND

PAPUA NEW GUINEA
SOLOMON ISLANDS

ONTONG JAVA
ATOLL

PACIFIC
OCEAN

CHOISEUL
VARUNGA POINT
BRADLEY REEFS

VELLA
LAVELLA   KOLOMBANGARA
GANONGGA   •Gizo   Mount
NEW GEORGIA   Vangunu   NEW
GROUP   RENDOVA   1123   GEORGIA
GATUKAI
PAVOVU•   Tulagi•
SOLOMON   Maravovo•
ISLANDS   Honiara•
GUADALCANAL

The Slot
SANTA ISABEL
△Mount Gatere
531   Susubona
SAN
JORGE   SAN
ISLAND   Sepi
CAPE
ASTROLABE

MALAITA
△Manawai
△Mount
Mt Bola•   Kolovrat
Popomanasiu   1435
2331   CAPE ZELEE
RECHERCHE   Kira Kira
SAN CRISTÓBAL
ULAWA

SOLOMON   SEA

© R. M^cN.

b

168°   170°

TORRES
ISLANDS
TEGUA   VATGANAI
Mount Suretamati
913 △
SANTA MARÍA
ISLAND
Pallier

PACIFIC

OCEAN

BANKS
ISLANDS

CAPE
QUIROS   Tanoriki
MAEWO
Patteson Passage
•Luganville
ESPÍRITU   Malo Strait   PENTECOST
SANTO   ISLAND
ISLAND   AMBRIM
MALEKULA   •Lamap
EPI•   Sakau

NEW
HEBRIDES
Vila•   EFATE

c

16°

PACIFIC   OCEAN
VANUA LEVU
YASAWA
GROUP   Lambasa
Savusavu
YASAWA   Mbua
NAVITI   Vatu-i-Ra Channel
Lautoka   •Vaileka
Keiyasi   △Mount
Momi•   Tomaniivi
1323•
VITI   Korolevu   ⊙Nausori
LEVU   Suva
Kandavu Passage   GREAT
Vunisea   ASTROLABE
KANDAVU   REEF
TOTOYA•

UNDU
CAPE   RINGGOLD
ISLES
Somosomo   Passage
Nanuku
SOUTH   VANUA
CAPE   MBALAVU
KORO
Koro   NGAU   THITHIA
Sea   LAKEMBA
Lakemba Passage   LAU
GROUP
KAMBARA
MATUKU   FULANGA   Fulanga Pass
VATOA

FIJI

© R. M^cN.

EROMANGA

Grand Passage
CORAL
SEA
Grande Fausse Passe
Poume•   Mont
Panié
Ouaco•   1628
NOUVELLE-
CALÉDONIE
NEW CALEDONIA

ÎLE
BEAUTEMPS-
BEAUPRÉ
Passe
d'Anémata
Touho
Koné•   Houailou
•Bourail
CORAL
SEA
Nouméa ⊙

Lenakel
FUTUNA
ÎLES LOYAUTÉ
LOYALTY ISLANDS   ANEITYUM
Passe
du Sandal
UVÉA   ÎLE LIFOU
Mou•   ÎLE VAUVILLIERS
Mont Tadinou•   ÎLE MARÉ
Humboldt
△1618
Bouloupari
•Yaté   ÎLE DES PINS

NEW CALEDONIA
VANUATU (France)

© R. M^cN.

178°   180°

Kilometres 0   100   200 Km.
Miles 0   100   200 Mi. 1 : 12 000 000

164°   166°   168°

20°

d

PACIFIC

16°

ÎLES SOUS LE VENT   OCEAN
BORA-BORA
Vaitape   TAHAA
Uturoa•   HUAHINE
•Parea
RAIATEA   TETIAROA
ÎLES DU VENT
Papeete   Mt.
MOOREA   Orohena
△2235
MAÏAO   Paea•   Baie de Taaroa
Tautira
PRESQU'ÎLE
DE TAIARAPU

17°

ÎLES   DE   LA
SOCIETY
FRENCH
POLYNESIA
SOCIÉTÉ
ISLANDS

18°

e

SAVAI'I
Sataua•   •Puapua
Taga•   Falevai•
UPOLU
14°
© R. M^cN.

SAMOA
Apia
WESTERN SAMOA
AMERICAN
SAMOA
ISLANDS
TUTUILA
•Pago Pago

172°   171°   170°

Lambert Conformal Conic Projection   Kilometres 0   50   100   150 Km.
Miles 0   50   100   150 Mi. 1 : 6 000 000

151°   150°   18°

(inset map)
SOLOMON
ISLANDS
WESTERN
SAMOA
VANUATU   AMERICAN
SAMOA
NEW   FRENCH
CALEDONIA   POLYNESIA
FIJI
© R. M^cN.
135°   150°   165°   180°   165°   150°

SOLOMON SEA / NEW HEBRIDES maps area
SOUTH
SEA
Lambeth Passage
Indispensable Strait
Manning Strait
Bougainville Strait
Blanche Channel
Manioa Strait

116°   114°   112°   110°   108°   106°   104°

San Diego ◙Yuma ARIZONA •Casa Grande   Silver City   WHITE SANDS NATIONAL MONUMENT Alamogordo   Artesia   Hobbs ◙
Tijuana Mexicali San Luis Rio Colorado ORGAN PIPE CACTUS NATIONAL MONUMENT   Lordsburg   NEW MEXICO Las Cruces◙   Carlsbad ◙ Andrews

32° •Ensenada   El Golfo de Santa Clara López Collada Lukeville SAGUARO NATIONAL MONUMENT **Tucson**   CHIRICAHUA NATIONAL MONUMENT Bisbee CARLSBAD CAVERNS NATIONAL PARK   Anthony   Guadalupe Peak 2667   Kermit ◙ Ode

PARQUE NACIONAL SIERRA DE SAN PEDRO MÁRTIR Puerto Peñasco El Cozón Nogales Nogales○ Douglas **Ciudad Juárez**◙ **El Paso**   Guadalupe   Sierra Blanca   Pecos○ Crane

•San Felipe EL Desemboque Caborca• •Altar •Cananea   Ascensión   Nueva Casas Grandes •Villa Ahumada   San Antonio de Bravo   Van Horn Fort Stockton

30° Vicente Guerrero •Rosario   Benjamín Hill •Santa Ana •Arizpe •Nacozari   •Villa Alpine Sanderson•
Puerto Libertad ISLA ÁNGEL DE LA GUARDA •Carbó Mata Ortiz Buenaventura   El Sueco Presidio BIG BEND NATIONAL PARK

Punta Prieta ISLA TIBURÓN •Kino •Moctezuma Las Varas   Cerro Puerto El de Lajas △2978 •Maclovio Herrera PARQU NACIONAL SIERR DEL CARM

28° ISLA CEDROS Bahía Sebastián Vizcaíno El Arco **Hermosillo** Ures• Sahuaripa• •Dolores **Chihuahua** •Aldama
Suaqui Grande• •Yécora Ciudad Guerrero• •Julimes •Tacubaya El Carricito•

•Tastiota •Ocampo• Cuauhtémoc• **Delicias**• Saucillo•

Guaymas •Esperanza •Creel PARQUE NACIONAL BARRANCA DEL COBRE Ciudad Camargo• La Esmeralda•

26° San Ignacio• •Santa Rosalía **Ciudad Obregón**○ Valle de Zaragoza• Ciudad Jiménez•
•Mulegé **Navojoa** •Huatabampo San Francisco del Oro• **Hidalgo del Parral**• Carrillo •Ceballos

PUNTA ABREOJOS •Yávaros Cerro Agua Caliente△ 3315 Las Nieves• Barcelona• **San Ped de las Coloni**

Santo Domingo• ISLA CARMEN •Loreto •San Blas Agua Caliente Grande de Gastelum Cerro Mohinora△ 3992 San Bernardo• La Zarca• **Gómez Palacio** **Torreón**

Los Mochis○ •Guasave Tameapa• Copalquin• Los Herreras• •Pedricena Parras d la Fuent Juan Euger

24° ISLA SANTA MAGDALENA San Luis Gonzaga• ISLA SAN JOSÉ El Médano• **Culiacán** •Tejamen •Abasolo •Acacio

ISLA DE SANTA MARGARITA ISLA CERRALVO •Quilá Altata• Pericos• Francisco I. Madero• Miguel Auza• Camacho•

Tropic of Cancer **La Paz** El Avión• Tayoltita• Coacoyole• **Durango** Villa Vicente Guerrero• Rio Chico Can

Todos Santos• San José del Cabo El Quelite• Ciudad• Nombre de Dios• Cerro 3080

22° CABO SAN LUCAS Agua Caliente• **Mazatlán**○ •Rosario Cerro Candelaria **Fresnillo**•
Zacatecas Jerez de Garcia Salinas•

Teacapán• Rosamorada• Cerro Lechuguilla △2480

P A C I F I C   Tecuala• Santiago Ixcuintla• **Aguascalientes** Cerro El Vigia △2740 •Jalpa

ISLA MARÍA MADRE ISLAS ISLA MARÍA MAGDALENA **MARÍAS** **Tepic**○ Ahuacatlán• Jalostotitlán•

20° ISLA MARÍA CLEOFAS Puerto Vallarta• **Guadalajara** Atotonilco el Alto•
O C E A N CABO CORRIENTES •Mascota Cocula• •Ocotlán Zamora d Hidalgo

de Chapala **Ciudad** Autlán de Navarro• Sayula• PARQUE NACIONAL VOLCÁN DE COLIMA **Guzmán** PARQUE NACIO PICO DE TANCÍT

ISLAS REVILLAGIGEDO (Mex.) ISLA SOCORRO Manzanillo• **Colima** **Apatzingán**•

18° •Pomarc

16° Copyright © 1980 by Rand McNally & Co.
C-531600-964 - 3°- 3°- 4°- 8°

114°   112°   110°   108°   106°   104°

Kilometres 0 ⊢ 100 ⊢ 200 ⊢ 300 Km.
Miles 0 ⊢ 100 ⊢ 200 ⊢ 300 Mi.   1 : 13 300 000

GULF

OF

MEXICO

Tropic of Cancer

Bahía de Campeche

° Lambert Conformal Conic Projection

Golfo
de
Tehuantepec

GUATEMALA

HONDURAS

GULF OF MEXICO

Fort Myers • | UNITED STATES | West Palm Beach | GRAND BAHAMA
FLORIDA | | | GREAT ABACO
Fort Lauderdale | | ELEUTHE
The Everglades | Miami Beach |
MIAMI |
EVERGLADES NATIONAL PARK |
Key West • | | ANDROS ISLAND | Nassau | NEW PROVIDENCE
FLORIDA KEYS | Straits of Florida |

LA HABANA
HAVANA
Marianao • □ •
Artemisa •
Pinar del Río ◉
Golfo de Batabanó
Santa Fe •

Nicholas Channel
Cárdenas
Matanzas
Güines
Sagua la Grande
Santa Clara • Placetas
Cienfuegos Sancti Spíritus
Ciego de Avila
Florida •
Nuevitas

Old Bahama Channel
GREAT BAHAMA BANK
W E S

Río Lagartos •
Progreso •
Mérida ◉ □
Celestún •
Halachó •
Tenabo •
○ Ticul
Campeche ◉
Champotón •
Ciudad del Carmen
Frontera •
Escárcega de Matamoros •
Usumacinta
Palenque •
○ Ocozingo
○ Comitán

YUCATAN
Tizimín •
Chichen Itzá •
○ Peto
Hopelchén •

MEXICO
PENINSULA

CABO CATOCHE
Puerto Juárez •
Cozumel •
ISLA DE COZUMEL
Tulum •
Felipe Carrillo Puerto •
Ciudad Chetuma

CUBA

CAYMAN ISLANDS (U.K.)
Georgetown

Pico Turquino 1994
Santia de Cu

Holguín ◉
Baya
Manzanillo •
Bane

G R E A T E R

BELIZE
Chetumal Bay
Orange Walk
Belize •
Belmopan
○ San Benito
Sayaxché •
1122 Victoria Peak
Gulf of Honduras
ISLAS DE LA BAHÍA

Tiradero •
Piedras Negras •
San Luis •

GUATEMALA
4220 Volcán Tajumulco
Huehuetenango •
El Estor •
SIERRA DE LAS MINAS
Tapachula •
Guatemala □ ◉
Tiquisate •
Santa Ana ◉
Nueva San Salvador ◉
San Salvador •
EL SALVADOR
Chinandega •

Puerto Barrios •
Puerto Cortés ○
El Progreso •
Yoro •
Cerro Las Minas 2865

La Ceiba ○
San Pedro Sula ◉
Juticalpa •
HONDURAS
San Ramón •
Cerro Mogotón 2107
Estelí •
El Sauce •
León ◉
Managua □
Diriamba •

Limón •
Brus Laguna
Patuca
CORDILLERA DE AGALTA
Coco
CABO GRACIAS A DIOS
Waspán •

CORDILLERA ISABELLA
Cerro Piu 1800
Prinzapolca •
Puerto Cabezas •
Río Grande •

San Juan del Norte •
ISLA DE SAN ANDRES (COL.)
San Andrés •

JAMAICA
Montego Bay •
Kingston ◉
Spanish Town

CARI

Tegucigalpa □ ◉
San Miguel ◉
San Vicente •
La Unión •

Matagalpa •
La Cruz •

NICARAGUA
Granada ◉
Rama •
Lago de Nicaragua
Rivas •
ISLA DE OMETEPE
San Carlos
Volcán Miravalles 2028
Liberia •

CORN ISLANDS (NIC.)
Punta Gorda •

PACIFIC OCEAN

PENÍNSULA DE NICOYA
CABO BLANCO
Puntarenas •
San José ◉
Puerto Cortés •
PÉN. DE OSA
Puerto Armuelles •
PUNTA BURICA
ISLA DE COIBA

COSTA RICA
Cartago •
Cerro Chirripó 3819
3475
Volcán Barú
David •
Golfo Chiriquí
PENÍNSULA DE AZUERO

Limón •
Bocas del Toro •
Golfo de los Mosquitos
La Chorrera •
PANAMA
Aguaduíce •
Río Hato •
Gulf of Panama

Colón ◉
Portobelo •
Chepo •
Panamá □ ◉
ISTMO DE PANAMÁ
Mulatupo •
ISLA DEL REY
La Palma •
Yaviza •
Jaqué •

Lori
Monter
Acandi •
Turbo •

CARI

Copyright © 1980 by Rand McNally & Co.
C-530100-964 - 2ᵛ- 6ᵛ- 5ᵛ- 12ᵛⁱ

Kilometres 0 100 200 300 Km.
Miles 0   100   200   300 Mi.   1 : 12 000 000

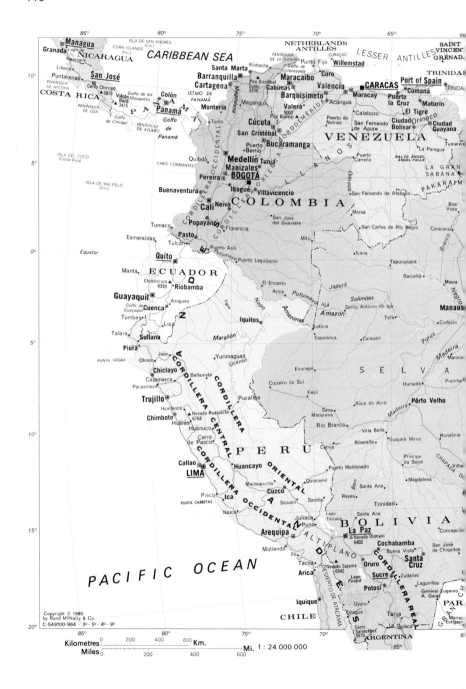

PACIFIC OCEAN

CARIBBEAN SEA

Copyright © 1980
by Rand McNally & Co.
C-549100-964 - 3v- 5v- 4v- 9v

Kilometres 0 200 400 600 Km.
Miles 0 200 400 600 Mi. 1 : 24 000 000

55°   50°   45°   40°   35°

'BARBADOS

AND TOBAGO

10°

ATLANTIC   OCEAN

Morawhanna

Charity
Georgetown
New
Amsterdam   Paramaribo
Wismar
at Roraima   Skeldon
72
ÎLE DU DIABLE
Brokopondo   Cayenne
5°
GUYANA
SURINAME   FRENCH
GUIANA
▲ Juliana Top
1230
Lethem

Cunani

ACARAI MTS   TUMUC-HÚMAC MTS   Caluene
ILHA DE MARACÁ

Macapá   ILHA CAVIANA
Mapuera
ILHA DE MARAJÓ
Pôrto de
Moz   Pará   Belém
Equator   0°
Amazon   Amazonas
Camiranga

Pôrto de   Curralinho
Moz   Pará
Cametá
São Luís
scoatiara   Parintins   Santarém
Rosário   Parnaíba   Acaraú
Altamira
Tucuruí   Monção   Sobral   Fortaleza
Itaituba   Tapajós   Iriri   Maraba   Bacabal   Barras   Batorité   Aracati   ILHA FERNANDO
DE NORONHA
(Brazil)
Tocantins   Barra   Teresina   Crateús   Quixadá   Macau
do Corda   Senador   Mossoró   CABO DE
SÃO ROQUE   5°
Pompeu   Natal
SERRA DO CACHIMBO   Tocantinópolis   Floriano   Iguatu   Currais   Sousa
Novos   Campina   João
Gradaús   Carolina   Loreto   Benedito Leite   Picos   Juàzeiro   Grande   Pessoa
do Norte   Serra   Olinda
Paulistana   Talhada   Pesqueira   Recife
Araguacema   Alto Parnaíba   União dos Palmares   Caruaru
Petrolina   São   Maceió
B   R   A   Z   I   L   Gilbués   Remanso   Paulo   Afonso   Jeremoabo
Xingu   ILHA   Gurupi   Xique-Xique   Tucano   Aracaju
DO
BANANAL   Paraná   Passagem   Alagoinhas
Utiariti   Taguatinga   Feira de Santana
São Domingos   Santo Antônio de Jesus   Salvador
PLANALTO   DO   Posse   Paramirim
MATO   GROSSO   Aruanã   Carinhanha   Guanambi   Jequié   Itabuna   Ilhéus
Pôrto   Rondonópolis   Monte Azul   Vitória
sperdição   Alto Araguaia   Jataí   Brasília   da Conquista   Canavieiras
Roboré   Coxim   Goiânia   Montes   Araçuaí   Pôrto Seguro
Corumbá   Itumbiara   C   E   N   T   R   A   L   Claros   Pirapora   Nanuque   Alcobaça
Pôrto Esperança   Ituiutaba   Corinto   Diamantina   Governador
Valadares   São Mateus
UAY   Aquidauana   Uberlândia   Ibiá   Sete
Lagoas   Colatina
Puerto   Bela   Campo   Uberaba   Belo
Casado   Vista   Grande   São José   Araçatuba   Divinópolis   Horizonte   Vitória
Araçatuba   do Rio Prêto   Barretos   Cachoeiro de
Presidente Prudente   Araraquara   Prêto   Juiz de Fora   Itapemirim
Bauru   Volta   Campos
Campinas   Redonda   Petrópolis
SÃO PAULO   RIO DE   Niterói
JANEIRO
Santos   Tropic of Capricorn

15°

20°
Oblique Conic Conformal Projection

55°   50°   40°

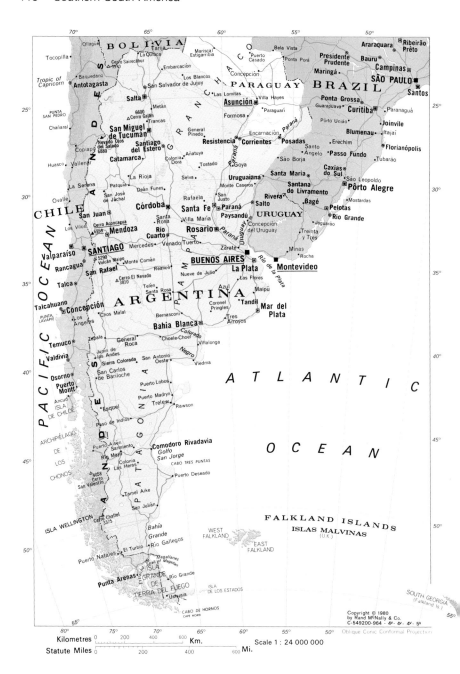

Kilometres 0   200 400 600 Km.
Statute Miles 0   200   400   600 Mi.
Scale 1 : 24 000 000

Copyright © 1980
by Rand McNally & Co.
C-549200-964 - 4V- 4V- 4V- 5V
Oblique Conic Conformal Projection

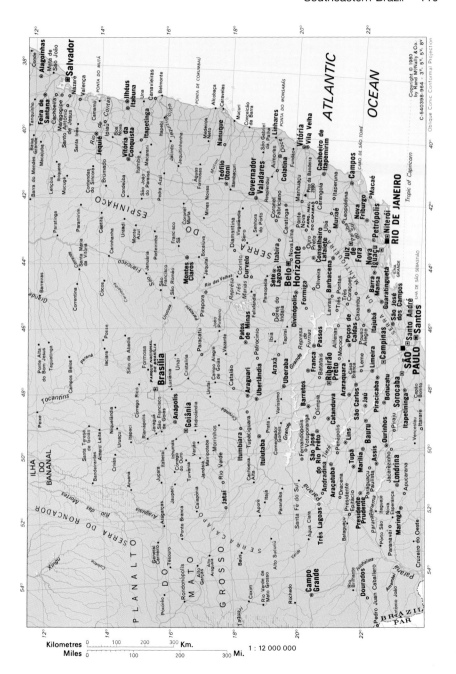

Kilometres 0 100 200 300 Km.

Miles 0 100 200 300 Mi.

1 : 12 000 000

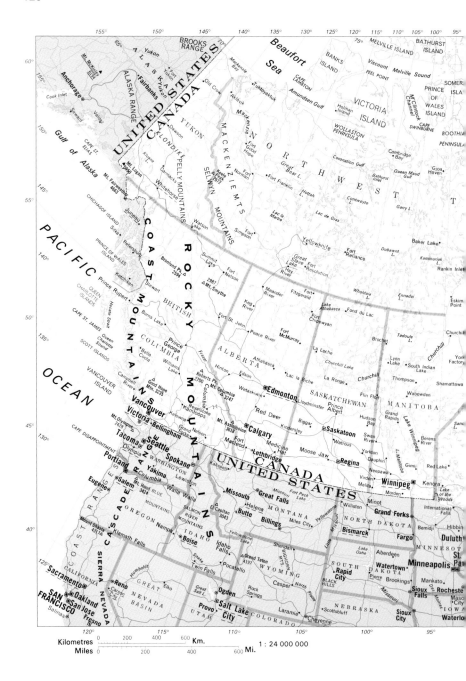

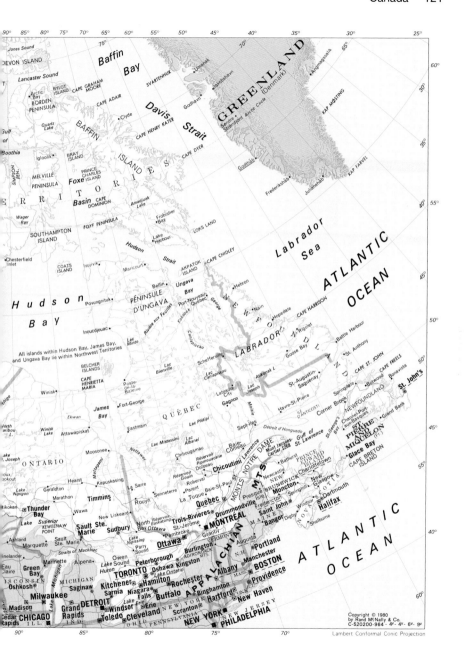

Lambert Conformal Conic Projection

PACIFIC
OCEAN

VANCOUVER ISLAND

BRITISH COLUMBIA
ALBERTA
SASKATCHEWAN
MANITOBA
CANADA
UNITED STATES

WASHINGTON
OREGON
IDAHO
MONTANA
WYOMING
NORTH DAKOTA
SOUTH DAKOTA
NEBRASKA
NEVADA
UTAH
COLORADO
KANSAS
CALIFORNIA
ARIZONA
NEW MEXICO
OKLAHOMA
TEXAS
MEXICO
BAJA CALIFORNIA

Edmonton
Vancouver
Victoria
Tacoma
Seattle
Spokane
Calgary
Winnipeg
Regina
Saskatoon
Great Falls
Billings
Boise
Salt Lake City
Denver
San Francisco
Oakland
Sacramento
San Jose
Fresno
Las Vegas
Bakersfield
LOS ANGELES
San Diego
Tijuana
Phoenix
Tucson
El Paso
Ciudad Juarez
Chihuahua
Hermosillo
Monterrey
Guadalajara

Tropic of Cancer

Kilometres 0 200 400 600 Km.
Miles 0 200 400 600 Mi.
1 : 24 000 000

Kilometres 0 50 100 150 Km.
Miles 0 50 100 150 Mi.
1: 6 000 000

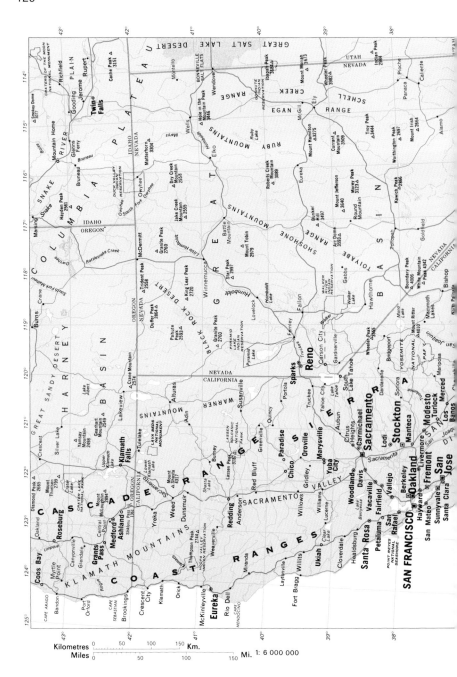

Kilometres 0   50   100   150 Km.
Miles 0   50   100   150 Mi.   1: 6 000 000

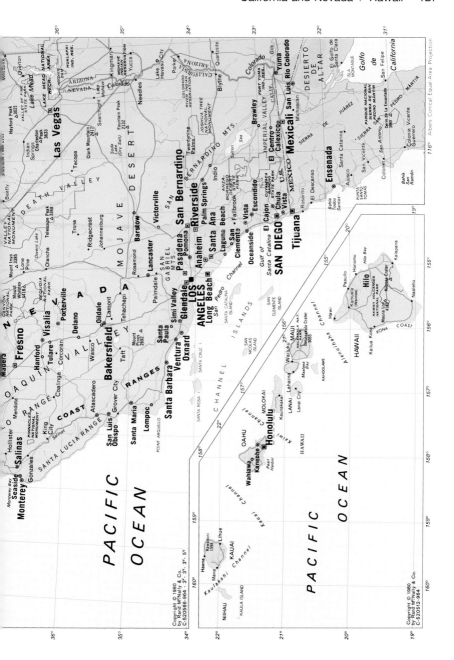

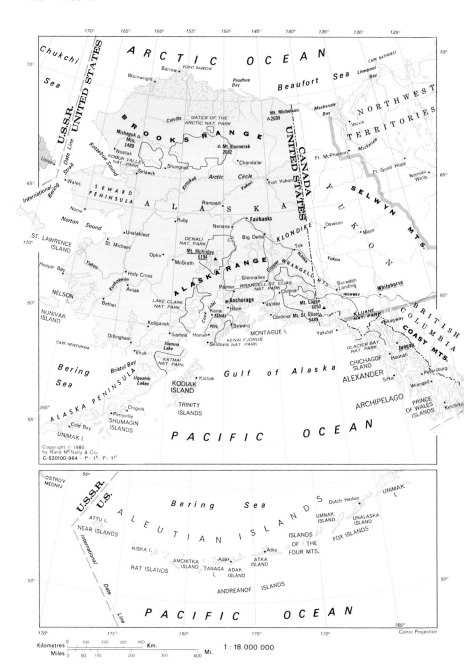

Copyright © 1980
by Rand McNally & Co.
C-520100-964 - 1ᵛ- 1ᵛ- 1ᵛ- 1ᵛⁱ

Kilometres 0 100 200 300 400 Km.
Miles 0 50 100 200 300 400 Mi.

1 : 18 000 000

Conic Projection

Flags of Nations and Country Profiles

This section presents nonmap data for the traveler that supplements the information on the reference maps of the world.

The display of flags enables the traveler to become familiar with a very distinctive and often sacred symbol of the nation for which it stands.

The country profiles furnish important statistical information. The section not only features the 168 independent countries but also gives details on remote, romantic, interesting, and relatively unknown places.

The populations are 1989 estimates. Languages are listed with the official one first, followed by others spoken. Sources for the other information included are from countries official documents.

Documents necessary for international travel may include a passport, proof of citizenship, visa, vaccination certificate, ticket to leave the country, or a letter of recommendation. It is recommended that all travelers check with the embassy of the destination country for the latest requirements. Many countries have other specific, detailed entry requirements.

Passports are available from the national government of the country of origin through regional offices. Visas may be obtained from foreign consulates of the destination countries. An internationally accepted booklet used to document vaccinations is distributed by the World Health Organization.

130

AFGHANISTAN	ALBANIA	ALGERIA	ANGOLA	ARGENTINA
AUSTRALIA	AUSTRIA	BAHAMAS	BAHRAIN	BANGLADESH
BARBADOS	BELGIUM	BELIZE	BENIN	BHUTAN
BOLIVIA	BOTSWANA	BRAZIL	BRUNEI	BULGARIA
BURKINA FASO	BURMA	BURUNDI	CAMBODIA (Kampuchea)	CAMEROON
CANADA	CAPE VERDE	CENTRAL AFRICAN REPUBLIC	CHAD	CHILE
CHINA	COLOMBIA	COMOROS	CONGO	COSTA RICA
CUBA	CYPRUS	CZECHOSLOVAKIA	DENMARK	DJIBOUTI

DOMINICA

 DOMINICAN REPUBLIC

 ECUADOR

 EGYPT

 EL SALVADOR

 EQUATORIAL GUINEA

 ETHIOPIA

 FIJI

 FINLAND

 FRANCE

 GABON

 GAMBIA

 GERMANY (EAST)

 GERMANY (WEST)

 GHANA

 GREECE

 GRENADA

 GUATEMALA

 GUINEA

 GUINEA-BISSAU

 GUYANA

 HAITI

 HONDURAS

 HUNGARY

 ICELAND

 INDIA

 INDONESIA

 IRAN

 IRAQ

 IRELAND

 ISRAEL

 ITALY

 IVORY COAST

 JAMAICA

 JAPAN

 JORDAN

 KENYA

 KOREA (NORTH)

 KOREA (SOUTH)

 KUWAIT

LAOS

LEBANON

LESOTHO

LIBERIA

LIBYA

LIECHTENSTEIN

LUXEMBOURG

MADAGASCAR

MALAWI

MALAYSIA

MALI

MALTA

MAURITANIA

MAURITIUS

MEXICO

MONACO

MONGOLIA

MOROCCO

MOZAMBIQUE

NEPAL

NETHERLANDS

NEW ZEALAND

NICARAGUA

NIGER

NIGERIA

NORWAY

OMAN

PAKISTAN

PANAMA

PAPUA-NEW GUINEA

PARAGUAY

PERU

PHILIPPINES

POLAND

PORTUGAL

QATAR

ROMANIA

RWANDA

SAINT LUCIA

ST. VINCENT AND
THE GRENADINES

SAN MARINO

SAO TOME
AND PRINCIPE

SAUDI ARABIA

SENEGAL

SIERRA LEONE

SINGAPORE

SOLOMON ISLANDS

SOMALIA

SOUTH AFRICA

SPAIN

SRI LANKA

SUDAN

SURINAME

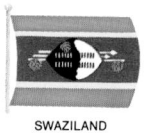

SWAZILAND

SWEDEN

SWITZERLAND

SYRIA

TAIWAN

TANZANIA

THAILAND

TOGO

TRINIDAD AND TOBAGO

TUNISIA

TURKEY

UGANDA

UNION OF SOVIET
SOCIALIST REPUBLICS

UNITED ARAB EMIRATES

UNITED KINGDOM

UNITED STATES

URUGUAY

VATICAN CITY

VENEZUELA

VIETNAM

WESTERN SAMOA

YEMEN

PEOPLE'S DEMOCRATIC
REPUBLIC OF YEMEN

YUGOSLAVIA

ZAIRE

ZAMBIA

ZIMBABWE

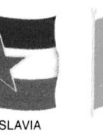

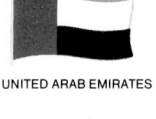

Country Profiles

AFGHANISTAN *(Afghânestân)*
LOCATION: Southern Asia, landlocked
AREA: 251,826 mi² (652,225 km²)
POPULATION: 14,655,000 (URBAN: 19%)
LITERACY: 20%
CAPITAL: Kabul, 972,836
GOVERNMENT: Republic
LANGUAGES: Dari, Pashto
ETHNIC GROUPS: Pathan 50%, Tajik 25%, Uzbek 9%, Hazara 9%
RELIGIONS: Sunni Muslim 74%, Shiite Muslim 15%
CURRENCY: Afghani

ALBANIA *(Shqipëria)*
LOCATION: Southeastern Europe
AREA: 11,100 mi² (28,748 km²)
POPULATION: 3,181,000 (URBAN: 34%)
LITERACY: 75%
CAPITAL: Tiranë, 206,100
GOVERNMENT: Socialist republic
LANGUAGES: Albanian, Greek
ETHNIC GROUPS: Albanian (Illyrian) 96%
RELIGIONS: Officially atheist
CURRENCY: Lek

ALGERIA *(Djazaïr)*
LOCATION: Northern Africa
AREA: 919,595 mi² (2,381,741 km²)
POPULATION: 24,215,000 (URBAN: 43%)
LITERACY: 45%
CAPITAL: Alger (Algiers), 1,721,607
GOVERNMENT: Socialist republic
LANGUAGES: Arabic, Berber dialects, French
ETHNIC GROUPS: Arab-Berber 99%
RELIGIONS: Sunni Muslim 99%, Christian and Jewish
CURRENCY: Dinar
TEL. AREA CODE: 213

AMERICAN SAMOA *(American Samoa (English) / Amerika Samoa (Samoan))*
LOCATION: South Pacific islands
AREA: 77 mi² (199 km²)
POPULATION: 40,000 (URBAN: 48%)
LITERACY: 99%
CAPITAL: Pago Pago, 3,075
GOVERNMENT: Unincorporated territory (U.S.)
LANGUAGES: Samoan, English
ETHNIC GROUPS: Samoan 85%, part Samoan 8%, black 3%, Tongan 2%
RELIGIONS: Congregationalist 50%, other Protestant 30%, Roman Catholic 20%
CURRENCY: U.S. dollar
TEL. AREA CODE: 684

ANDORRA *(Andorra)*
LOCATION: Southwestern Europe, landlocked
AREA: 175 mi² (453 km²)
POPULATION: 51,000
LITERACY: 100%
CAPITAL: Andorra, 14,928
GOVERNMENT: Coprincipality (Spanish and French protection)
LANGUAGES: Spanish, French
ETHNIC GROUPS: Spanish 61%, Andorran 30%, French 6%
RELIGIONS: Roman Catholic
CURRENCY: French franc, Spanish peseta
TEL. AREA CODE: 33

ANGOLA *(Angola)*
LOCATION: Southern Africa
AREA: 481,354 mi² (1,246,700 km²)
POPULATION: 8,385,000 (URBAN: 25%)
LITERACY: 20%
CAPITAL: Luanda, 1,200,000
GOVERNMENT: Socialist republic
LANGUAGES: Portuguese, indigenous
ETHNIC GROUPS: Ovimbundu 37%, Mbundu 25%, Kongo 13%, mulatto 2%, European 1%
RELIGIONS: Roman Catholic 68%, Protestant 20%, indigenous 12%
CURRENCY: Kwanza

ANTIGUA AND BARBUDA *(Antigua and Barbuda)*
LOCATION: Caribbean islands
AREA: 171 mi² (443 km²)
POPULATION: 84,000 (URBAN: 31%)
LITERACY: 90%
CAPITAL: St. Johns, 24,359
GOVERNMENT: Parliamentary state
LANGUAGES: English, local dialects
ETHNIC GROUPS: Black
RELIGIONS: Anglican and other Protestant, Roman Catholic
CURRENCY: East Caribbean dollar
TEL. AREA CODE: 809

ARGENTINA (*Argentina*)

LOCATION: Southern South America
AREA: 1,073,400 mi² (2,780,092 km²)
POPULATION: 32,205,000 (URBAN: 85%)
LITERACY: 93%
CAPITAL: Buenos Aires, 2,922,829
GOVERNMENT: Republic
LANGUAGES: Spanish, English, Italian, German, French
ETHNIC GROUPS: White 85%, mestizo, Amerindian, and others 15%
RELIGIONS: Roman Catholic 90%, Jewish 2%, Protestant 2%
CURRENCY: Austral
TEL. AREA CODE: 54

ARUBA (*Aruba*)

LOCATION: Caribbean island
AREA: 75 mi² (193 km²)
POPULATION: 66,000
LITERACY: 95%
CAPITAL: Oranjestad, 19,800
GOVERNMENT: Self-governing territory (Netherlands protection)
LANGUAGES: Dutch, English, Papiamento, Spanish
ETHNIC GROUPS: Mixed European and West Indian 80%
RELIGIONS: Roman Catholic 82%, Protestant 8%
CURRENCY: Florin
TEL. AREA CODE: 297

AUSTRALIA (*Australia*)

LOCATION: Continent between South Pacific and Indian oceans
AREA: 2,966,155 mi² (7,682,300 km²)
POPULATION: 16,955,000 (URBAN: 86%)
LITERACY: 99%
CAPITAL: Canberra, 243,450
GOVERNMENT: Federal parliamentary state
LANGUAGES: English, indigenous
ETHNIC GROUPS: European 95%, Asian 4%, Aboriginal and other 1%
RELIGIONS: Anglican 26%, Roman Catholic 26%, other Protestant 24%
CURRENCY: Dollar
TEL. AREA CODE: 61

AUSTRIA (*Österreich*)

LOCATION: Central Europe, landlocked
AREA: 32,377 mi² (83,855 km²)
POPULATION: 7,584,000 (URBAN: 56%)
LITERACY: 99%
CAPITAL: Wien (Vienna), 1,489,153
GOVERNMENT: Federal republic
LANGUAGES: German
ETHNIC GROUPS: German 99%
RELIGIONS: Roman Catholic 85%, Protestant 6%
CURRENCY: Schilling
TEL. AREA CODE: 43

BAHAMAS (*Bahamas*)

LOCATION: Caribbean islands
AREA: 5,382 mi² (13,939 km²)
POPULATION: 243,000 (URBAN: 58%)
LITERACY: 89%
CAPITAL: Nassau, 135,000
GOVERNMENT: Parliamentary state
LANGUAGES: English, Creole
ETHNIC GROUPS: Black 85%, white 15%
RELIGIONS: Baptist 29%, Anglican 23%, Roman Catholic 22%
CURRENCY: Dollar
TEL. AREA CODE: 809

BAHRAIN (*Al-Bahrayn*)

LOCATION: Southwestern Asian islands (in Persian Gulf)
AREA: 256 mi² (662 km²)
POPULATION: 458,000 (URBAN: 82%)
LITERACY: 63%
CAPITAL: Al-Manāmah, 108,684
GOVERNMENT: Monarchy
LANGUAGES: Arabic, English, Farsi, Urdu
ETHNIC GROUPS: Bahraini 63%, Asian 13%, other Arab 10%, Iranian 8%
RELIGIONS: Shiite Muslim 70%, Sunni Muslim 30%
CURRENCY: Dinar
TEL. AREA CODE: 973

BANGLADESH (*Bangladesh*)

LOCATION: Southern Asia
AREA: 55,598 mi² (143,998 km²)
POPULATION: 111,390,000 (URBAN: 12%)
LITERACY: 24%
CAPITAL: Dhaka, 1,850,000
GOVERNMENT: Republic
LANGUAGES: Bangla, English
ETHNIC GROUPS: Bengali 98%
RELIGIONS: Muslim 84%, Hindu 15%
CURRENCY: Taka
TEL. AREA CODE: 880

BARBADOS *(Barbados)*
LOCATION: Caribbean island
AREA: 166 mi² (430 km²)
POPULATION: 255,000 (URBAN: 42%)
LITERACY: 99%
CAPITAL: Bridgetown, 7,466
GOVERNMENT: Parliamentary state
LANGUAGES: English
ETHNIC GROUPS: Black 80%, mixed 16%, European 4%
RELIGIONS: Anglican 70%, Methodist 9%, Roman Catholic 4%
CURRENCY: Dollar
TEL. AREA CODE: 809

BELGIUM *(Belgique (French) / België (Flemish))*
LOCATION: Western Europe
AREA: 11,783 mi² (30,518 km²)
POPULATION: 9,862,000 (URBAN: 96%)
LITERACY: 99%
CAPITAL: Bruxelles, 137,738
GOVERNMENT: Constitutional monarchy
LANGUAGES: Dutch (Flemish), French, German
ETHNIC GROUPS: Fleming 55%, Walloon 33%, mixed and others 12%
RELIGIONS: Roman Catholic 75%
CURRENCY: Franc
TEL. AREA CODE: 32

BELIZE *(Belize)*
LOCATION: Central America
AREA: 8,866 mi² (22,963 km²)
POPULATION: 184,000 (URBAN: 50%)
LITERACY: 91%
CAPITAL: Belmopan, 2,935
GOVERNMENT: Parliamentary state
LANGUAGES: English, Spanish, Creole, Mayan, indigenous
ETHNIC GROUPS: Creole 40%, mestizo 33%, Amerindian 16%
RELIGIONS: Roman Catholic 50%, Anglican 12%, Methodist 6%, Mennonite 4%
CURRENCY: Dollar
TEL. AREA CODE: 501

BENIN *(Bénin)*
LOCATION: Western Africa
AREA: 43,484 mi² (112,622 km²)
POPULATION: 4,735,000 (URBAN: 35%)
LITERACY: 17%
CAPITAL: Porto-Novo (designated), 123,000; Cotonou (de facto), 215,000
GOVERNMENT: Socialist republic
LANGUAGES: French, Fon, Adja, indigenous
ETHNIC GROUPS: Fon, Adja, Yoruba, Bariba, others
RELIGIONS: Indigenous 70%, Muslim 15%, Christian 15%
CURRENCY: CFA franc
TEL. AREA CODE: 229

BERMUDA *(Bermuda)*
LOCATION: North Atlantic islands (east of North Carolina)
AREA: 21 mi² (54 km²)
POPULATION: 56,000 (URBAN: 100%)
LITERACY: 98%
CAPITAL: Hamilton, 1,676
GOVERNMENT: Dependent territory (U.K.)
LANGUAGES: English
ETHNIC GROUPS: Black 61%, white 37%
RELIGIONS: Anglican 37%, Roman Catholic 14%, African Methodist Episcopal 10%
CURRENCY: Dollar
TEL. AREA CODE: 809

BHUTAN *(Druk-Yul)*
LOCATION: Southern Asia, landlocked
AREA: 17,954 mi² (46,500 km²)
POPULATION: 1,519,000 (URBAN: 5%)
LITERACY: 5%
CAPITAL: Thimbu, 12,000
GOVERNMENT: Monarchy (Indian protection)
LANGUAGES: Dzongkha, Tibetan and Nepalese dialects
ETHNIC GROUPS: Bhotia 60%, Nepalese 25%, indigenous 15%
RELIGIONS: Buddhist 75%, Hindu 25%
CURRENCY: Ngultrum, Indian rupee

BOLIVIA *(Bolivia)*
LOCATION: Central South America, landlocked
AREA: 424,165 mi² (1,098,581 km²)
POPULATION: 7,184,000 (URBAN: 48%)
LITERACY: 63%
CAPITAL: La Paz (seat of government), 992,592; Sucre (seat of judiciary), 86,609
GOVERNMENT: Republic
LANGUAGES: Spanish, Quechua, Aymara
ETHNIC GROUPS: Quechua 30%, Aymara 25%, mixed 25-30%, European 5-15%
RELIGIONS: Roman Catholic 95%, Methodist and other Protestant
CURRENCY: Boliviano
TEL. AREA CODE: 591

BOTSWANA (Botswana)

LOCATION: Southern Africa, landlocked
AREA: 224,711 mi^2 (582,000 km^2)
POPULATION: 1,230,000 (URBAN: 19%)
LITERACY: 41%
CAPITAL: Gaborone, 95,163
GOVERNMENT: Republic
LANGUAGES: English, Tswana
ETHNIC GROUPS: Tswana 95%, Kalanga, Baswara, and Kgalagadi 4%, white 1%
RELIGIONS: Indigenous 50%, Christian 50%
CURRENCY: Pula
TEL. AREA CODE: 267

BRAZIL (Brasil)

LOCATION: Eastern South America
AREA: 3,286,488 mi^2 (8,511,965 km^2)
POPULATION: 145,930,000 (URBAN: 73%)
LITERACY: 74%
CAPITAL: Brasília, 1,567,709
GOVERNMENT: Federal republic
LANGUAGES: Portuguese, Spanish, English, French
ETHNIC GROUPS: White 55%, mixed 38%, black 6%
RELIGIONS: Roman Catholic 90%
CURRENCY: Cruzado
TEL. AREA CODE: 55

BRUNEI (Brunei)

LOCATION: Southeastern Asia (island of Borneo)
AREA: 2,226 mi^2 (5,765 km^2)
POPULATION: 247,000 (URBAN: 58%)
LITERACY: 78%
CAPITAL: Bandar Seri Begawan, 63,868
GOVERNMENT: Monarchy
LANGUAGES: Malay, English, Chinese
ETHNIC GROUPS: Malay 65%, Chinese 20%, indigenous 8%, Tamil 3%
RELIGIONS: Muslim 63%, Buddhist 14%, Christian 10%
CURRENCY: Dollar
TEL. AREA CODE: 673

BULGARIA (Bâlgarija)

LOCATION: Eastern Europe
AREA: 42,823 mi^2 (110,912 km^2)
POPULATION: 8,997,000 (URBAN: 67%)
LITERACY: 93%
CAPITAL: Sofija (Sofia), 1,114,962
GOVERNMENT: Socialist republic
LANGUAGES: Bulgarian
ETHNIC GROUPS: Bulgarian (Slavic) 85%, Turkish 9%, Gypsy 3%, Macedonian 3%
RELIGIONS: Bulgarian Orthodox, Muslim
CURRENCY: Lev
TEL. AREA CODE: 359

BURKINA FASO (Burkina Faso)

LOCATION: Western Africa, landlocked
AREA: 105,869 mi^2 (274,200 km^2)
POPULATION: 8,596,000 (URBAN: 8%)
LITERACY: 9%
CAPITAL: Ouagadougou, 442,223
GOVERNMENT: Provisional military government
LANGUAGES: French, indigenous
ETHNIC GROUPS: Mossi 30%, Fulani, Lobi, Malinke, Bobo, Senufo, Gurunsi, others
RELIGIONS: Indigenous 65%, Muslim 25%, Roman Catholic and other Christian 10%
CURRENCY: CFA franc

BURMA (Myanmã)

LOCATION: Southeastern Asia
AREA: 261,228 mi^2 (676,577 km^2)
POPULATION: 41,860,000 (URBAN: 24%)
LITERACY: 67%
CAPITAL: Rangoon, 2,458,712
GOVERNMENT: Socialist republic
LANGUAGES: Burmese, indigenous
ETHNIC GROUPS: Burman 68%, Shan 9%, Karen 7%, Raljome 4%, Chinese 3%, Indian 2%
RELIGIONS: Buddhist 85%, indigenous, Christian, and others 15%
CURRENCY: Kyat

BURUNDI (Burundi)

LOCATION: Eastern Africa, landlocked
AREA: 10,745 mi^2 (27,830 km^2)
POPULATION: 5,200,000 (URBAN: 6%)
LITERACY: 25%
CAPITAL: Bujumbura, 229,980
GOVERNMENT: Republic
LANGUAGES: French, Kirundi, Swahili
ETHNIC GROUPS: Hutu 85%, Tutsi 14%, Twa 1%
RELIGIONS: Roman Catholic 62%, indigenous 32%, Protestant 5%, Muslim 1%
CURRENCY: Franc

CAMEROON (Cameroon (English) / Cameroun (French))

LOCATION: Central Africa
AREA: 183,569 mi^2 (475,442 km^2)
POPULATION: 11,495,000   (URBAN: 42%)
LITERACY: 41%
CAPITAL: Yaoundé, 583,000
GOVERNMENT: Republic
LANGUAGES: English, French, indigenous
ETHNIC GROUPS: Cameroon Highlander 31%, Equatorial Bantu 19%, Kirdi 11%, Fulani 10%
RELIGIONS: Indigenous 51%, Christian 33%, Muslim 16%
CURRENCY: CFA franc
TEL. AREA CODE: 237

CANADA (Canada)

LOCATION: Northern North America
AREA: 3,849,674 mi^2 (9,970,610 km^2)
POPULATION: 25,895,000   (URBAN: 76%)
LITERACY: 93%
CAPITAL: Ottawa, 300,763
GOVERNMENT: Federal parliamentary state
LANGUAGES: English, French, indigenous
ETHNIC GROUPS: British origin 40%, French origin 27%, other European 23%, native Canadian 2%
RELIGIONS: Roman Catholic 47%, United Church 16%, Anglican 10%, other Christian
CURRENCY: Dollar

CAPE VERDE (Cabo Verde)

LOCATION: Western African islands
AREA: 1,557 mi^2 (4,033 km^2)
POPULATION: 359,000   (URBAN: 5%)
LITERACY: 37%
CAPITAL: Praia, 37,480
GOVERNMENT: Republic
LANGUAGES: Portuguese, Crioulo
ETHNIC GROUPS: Creole (mulatto) 71%, African 28%, European 1%
RELIGIONS: Roman Catholic 80%, Protestant 10%
CURRENCY: Escudo
TEL. AREA CODE: 238

CAYMAN ISLANDS (Cayman Islands)

LOCATION: Caribbean islands
AREA: 100 mi^2 (259 km^2)
POPULATION: 25,000   (URBAN: 100%)
LITERACY: 98%
CAPITAL: Georgetown, 11,500

GOVERNMENT: Dependent territory (U.K.)
LANGUAGES: English
ETHNIC GROUPS: Mixed 40%, black 20%, white 20%, other 20%
RELIGIONS: United Church, Anglican, Baptist, Roman Catholic, Church of God
CURRENCY: Dollar
TEL. AREA CODE: 809

CENTRAL AFRICAN REPUBLIC (République centrafricaine)

LOCATION: Central Africa, landlocked
AREA: 240,535 mi^2 (622,984 km^2)
POPULATION: 3,089,000   (URBAN: 42%)
LITERACY: 18%
CAPITAL: Bangui, 473,800
GOVERNMENT: Republic
LANGUAGES: French, Sango, Arabic, indigenous
ETHNIC GROUPS: Baya 34%, Banda 27%, Mandja 21%, Sara 10%
RELIGIONS: Protestant 25%, Roman Catholic 25%, indigenous 24%, Muslim 15%
CURRENCY: CFA franc

CHAD (Tchad)

LOCATION: Central Africa, landlocked
AREA: 495,755 mi^2 (1,284,000 km^2)
POPULATION: 4,845,000   (URBAN: 27%)
LITERACY: 17%
CAPITAL: N'Djamena, 303,000
GOVERNMENT: Republic
LANGUAGES: Arabic, French, indigenous
ETHNIC GROUPS: Sara and other African, Arab
RELIGIONS: Muslim 44%, Christian 33%, indigenous 23%
CURRENCY: CFA franc

CHILE (Chile)

LOCATION: Southern South America
AREA: 292,135 mi^2 (756,626 km^2)
POPULATION: 12,925,000   (URBAN: 84%)
LITERACY: 91%
CAPITAL: Santiago, 425,924
GOVERNMENT: Provisional military government
LANGUAGES: Spanish
ETHNIC GROUPS: White and mestizo 95%, Amerindian 3%
RELIGIONS: Roman Catholic 89%, Protestant 11%
CURRENCY: Peso
TEL. AREA CODE: 56

CHINA (Zhongguo)

LOCATION: Eastern Asia
AREA: 3,718,782 mi^2 (9,631,600 km^2)
POPULATION: 1,094,700,000 (URBAN: 21%)
LITERACY: 76%
CAPITAL: Beijing (Peking), 5,860,000
GOVERNMENT: Socialist republic
LANGUAGES: Chinese dialects
ETHNIC GROUPS: Han Chinese 93%, Zhuang, Hui, Uygur, Yi, Miao, Manchu, Tibetan, others
RELIGIONS: Confucian, Taoist, Buddhist, Muslim, Christian
CURRENCY: Yuan
TEL. AREA CODE: 86
NOTES: The above information excludes Taiwan.

COLOMBIA (Colombia)

LOCATION: Northern South America
AREA: 440,831 mi^2 (1,141,748 km^2)
POPULATION: 30,465,000 (URBAN: 67%)
LITERACY: 88%
CAPITAL: Bogotá, 3,967,988
GOVERNMENT: Republic
LANGUAGES: Spanish
ETHNIC GROUPS: Mestizo 58%, white 20%, mulatto 14%, black 4%
RELIGIONS: Roman Catholic 95%
CURRENCY: Peso
TEL. AREA CODE: 57

COMOROS (Al-Qumur (Arabic) / Comores (French))

LOCATION: Southeastern African islands
AREA: 838 mi^2 (2,171 km^2)
POPULATION: 436,000 (URBAN: 25%)
LITERACY: 15%
CAPITAL: Moroni, 20,112
GOVERNMENT: Federal islamic republic
LANGUAGES: Arabic, French, Swahili, Malagasy
ETHNIC GROUPS: African-Arab descent (Antalote, Cafre, Makua, Oimatsaha, Sakalava)
RELIGIONS: Sunni Muslim 86%, Roman Catholic 14%
CURRENCY: Franc
NOTES: The above information excludes Mayotte.

CONGO (Congo)

LOCATION: Central Africa
AREA: 132,047 mi^2 (342,000 km^2)
POPULATION: 2,191,000 (URBAN: 40%)
LITERACY: 80%
CAPITAL: Brazzaville, 595,102
GOVERNMENT: Socialist republic
LANGUAGES: French, indigenous
ETHNIC GROUPS: Kongo 48%, Sangha 20%, Mbochi 12%, Teke 17%
RELIGIONS: Christian 50%, indigenous 42%, Muslim 2%
CURRENCY: CFA franc

COSTA RICA (Costa Rica)

LOCATION: Central America
AREA: 19,730 mi^2 (51,100 km^2)
POPULATION: 2,990,000 (URBAN: 50%)
LITERACY: 88%
CAPITAL: San José, 277,800
GOVERNMENT: Republic
LANGUAGES: Spanish
ETHNIC GROUPS: White and mestizo 96%, black 3%, Amerindian 1%
RELIGIONS: Roman Catholic 95%
CURRENCY: Colon
TEL. AREA CODE: 506

CUBA (Cuba)

LOCATION: Caribbean island
AREA: 42,804 mi^2 (110,861 km^2)
POPULATION: 10,440,000 (URBAN: 72%)
LITERACY: 98%
CAPITAL: La Habana (Havana), 1,914,466
GOVERNMENT: Socialist republic
LANGUAGES: Spanish
ETHNIC GROUPS: Mulatto 51%, white 37%, black 11%, Chinese 1%
RELIGIONS: Roman Catholic, Espiscopalian, Methodist, Baptist
CURRENCY: Peso

CYPRUS (Kípros (Greek) / Kıbrıs (Turkish))

LOCATION: Southern part of the island of Cyprus
AREA: 2,276 mi^2 (5,896 km^2)
POPULATION: 573,000 (URBAN: 50%)
LITERACY: 89%
CAPITAL: Nicosia (Levkosía), 48,221
GOVERNMENT: Republic
LANGUAGES: Greek, Turkish, English
ETHNIC GROUPS: Greek 78%, Turkish 18%
RELIGIONS: Greek Orthodox 78%, Muslim 18%
CURRENCY: Pound
TEL. AREA CODE: 357

CYPRUS, NORTH (Kuzey Kıbrıs)

LOCATION: Northern part of the island of Cyprus
AREA: 1,295 mi^2 (3,355 km^2)
POPULATION: 172,000
CAPITAL: Nicosia (Lefkoşa), 37,400
GOVERNMENT: Republic
LANGUAGES: Turkish
ETHNIC GROUPS: Turkish 99%, Greek, Maronite, and others 1%
RELIGIONS: Sunni Muslim
CURRENCY: Turkish lira
TEL. AREA CODE: 90

CZECHOSLOVAKIA (Československo)

LOCATION: Eastern Europe, landlocked
AREA: 49,384 mi^2 (127,905 km^2)
POPULATION: 15,605,000 (URBAN: 65%)
LITERACY: 99%
CAPITAL: Praha (Prague), 1,193,513
GOVERNMENT: Federal socialist republic
LANGUAGES: Czech, Slovak, Hungarian
ETHNIC GROUPS: Czech 64%, Slovak 31%, Hungarian 4%
RELIGIONS: Roman Catholic 77%, Protestant 20%, Orthodox 2%
CURRENCY: Koruna (Crown)
TEL. AREA CODE: 42

DENMARK (Danmark)

LOCATION: Northern Europe
AREA: 16,638 mi^2 (43,092 km^2)
POPULATION: 5,135,000 (URBAN: 86%)
LITERACY: 99%
CAPITAL: København (Copenhagen), 478,615
GOVERNMENT: Constitutional monarchy
LANGUAGES: Danish
ETHNIC GROUPS: Danish (Scandinavian), German
RELIGIONS: Lutheran 97%
CURRENCY: Krone
TEL. AREA CODE: 45
NOTES: The above information excludes Greenland and the Faeroe Is.

DJIBOUTI (Djibouti)

LOCATION: Eastern Africa
AREA: 8,958 mi^2 (23,200 km^2)
POPULATION: 324,000 (URBAN: 78%)
LITERACY: 20%
CAPITAL: Djibouti, 120,000
GOVERNMENT: Republic
LANGUAGES: French, Afar, Arabic, Somali
ETHNIC GROUPS: Somali (Issa) 60%, Afar 35%
RELIGIONS: Muslim 94%, Christian 6%
CURRENCY: Franc

DOMINICA (Dominica)

LOCATION: Caribbean island
AREA: 290 mi^2 (752 km^2)
POPULATION: 100,000 (URBAN: 27%)
LITERACY: 94%
CAPITAL: Roseau, 9,348
GOVERNMENT: Republic
LANGUAGES: English, French
ETHNIC GROUPS: Black, West Indian
RELIGIONS: Roman Catholic 80%, Anglican, Methodist
CURRENCY: East Caribbean dollar
TEL. AREA CODE: 809

DOMINICAN REPUBLIC (República Dominicana)

LOCATION: Caribbean island (eastern Hispaniola)
AREA: 18,704 mi^2 (48,442 km^2)
POPULATION: 7,069,000 (URBAN: 56%)
LITERACY: 67%
CAPITAL: Santo Domingo, 1,313,172
GOVERNMENT: Republic
LANGUAGES: Spanish
ETHNIC GROUPS: Mulatto 73%, white 16%, black 11%
RELIGIONS: Roman Catholic 95%
CURRENCY: Peso
TEL. AREA CODE: 809

ECUADOR (Ecuador)

LOCATION: Western South America
AREA: 109,484 mi^2 (283,561 km^2)
POPULATION: 10,345,000 (URBAN: 52%)
LITERACY: 84%
CAPITAL: Quito, 890,355
GOVERNMENT: Republic
LANGUAGES: Spanish, Quechua, indigenous
ETHNIC GROUPS: Mestizo 55%, Amerindian 25%, Spanish 10%, black 10%
RELIGIONS: Roman Catholic 95%
CURRENCY: Sucre
TEL. AREA CODE: 593

EGYPT (Miṣr)

LOCATION: Northeastern Africa
AREA: 386,662 mi^2 (1,001,450 km^2)
POPULATION: 52,490,000 (URBAN: 46%)
LITERACY: 38%
CAPITAL: Al-Qāhirah (Cairo), 6,205,000
GOVERNMENT: Socialist republic
LANGUAGES: Arabic
ETHNIC GROUPS: Egyptian (Eastern Hamitic) 90%
RELIGIONS: Muslim 94%, Coptic Christian and others 6%
CURRENCY: Pound
TEL. AREA CODE: 20

EL SALVADOR (El Salvador)

LOCATION: Central America
AREA: 8,124 mi^2 (21,041 km^2)
POPULATION: 5,122,000 (URBAN: 39%)
LITERACY: 62%
CAPITAL: San Salvador, 459,902
GOVERNMENT: Republic
LANGUAGES: Spanish, Nahua
ETHNIC GROUPS: Mestizo 89%, Amerindian 10%, white 1%
RELIGIONS: Roman Catholic 97%
CURRENCY: Colon
TEL. AREA CODE: 503

EQUATORIAL GUINEA (Guinea Ecuatorial)

LOCATION: Central Africa
AREA: 10,831 mi^2 (28,051 km^2)
POPULATION: 438,000 (URBAN: 60%)
LITERACY: 55%
CAPITAL: Malabo, 30,710
GOVERNMENT: Republic
LANGUAGES: Spanish, indigenous, English
ETHNIC GROUPS: Fang 80%, Bubi 15%
RELIGIONS: Roman Catholic 83%, other Christian, indigenous
CURRENCY: CFA franc

ETHIOPIA (Ityopiya)

LOCATION: Eastern Africa
AREA: 483,123 mi^2 (1,251,282 km^2)
POPULATION: 48,470,000 (URBAN: 12%)
LITERACY: 4%
CAPITAL: Adis Abeba, 1,412,575
GOVERNMENT: Socialist republic
LANGUAGES: Amharic, Tigrinya, Orominga, Arabic
ETHNIC GROUPS: Oromo (Galla) 40%, Amhara and Tigrean 32%, Sidamo 9%, Shankella 6%, Somali 6%
RELIGIONS: Muslim 40-45%, Ethiopian Orthodox 35-40%, indigenous 15-20%
CURRENCY: Birr
TEL. AREA CODE: 251

FAEROE ISLANDS (Føroyar)

LOCATION: North Atlantic islands
AREA: 540 mi^2 (1,399 km^2)
POPULATION: 48,000 (URBAN: 29%)
LITERACY: 99%
CAPITAL: Tórshavn, 13,408
GOVERNMENT: Self-governing territory (Danish protection)
LANGUAGES: Danish, Faroese
ETHNIC GROUPS: Faroese (Nordic)
RELIGIONS: Lutheran, Plymouth Bretheren
CURRENCY: Danish krone
TEL. AREA CODE: 298

FIJI (Fiji (French) / Viti (Fijian))

LOCATION: South Pacific islands
AREA: 7,078 mi^2 (18,333 km^2)
POPULATION: 749,000 (URBAN: 41%)
LITERACY: 79%
CAPITAL: Suva, 69,665
GOVERNMENT: Republic
LANGUAGES: English, Fijian, Hindustani
ETHNIC GROUPS: Indian 49%, Fijian 46%, European 5%
RELIGIONS: Christian 51%, Hindu 40%, Muslim 8%
CURRENCY: Dollar
TEL. AREA CODE: 679

FINLAND (Suomi (Finnish) / Finland (Swedish))

LOCATION: Northern Europe
AREA: 130,559 mi^2 (338,145 km^2)
POPULATION: 4,949,000 (URBAN: 64%)
LITERACY: 99%
CAPITAL: Helsinki, 484,263
GOVERNMENT: Republic
LANGUAGES: Finnish, Swedish, Lapp
ETHNIC GROUPS: Finnish (mixed Scandinavian and Baltic), Swedish, Lappic, Gypsy, Tatar
RELIGIONS: Lutheran 89%, Eastern Orthodox 1%
CURRENCY: Markka
TEL. AREA CODE: 358

FRANCE *(France)*

LOCATION: Western Europe
AREA: 211,208 mi^2 (547,026 km^2)
POPULATION: 55,970,000 (URBAN: 73%)
LITERACY: 99%
CAPITAL: Paris, 2,149,900
GOVERNMENT: Republic
LANGUAGES: French
ETHNIC GROUPS: French (mixed Celtic, Latin, and Teutonic)
RELIGIONS: Roman Catholic 90%, Protestant 2%, Jewish 1%, Muslim 1%
CURRENCY: Franc
TEL. AREA CODE: 33
NOTES: The above information excludes French overseas departments

FRENCH GUIANA *(Guyane)*

LOCATION: Northeastern South America
AREA: 35,135 mi^2 (91,000 km^2)
POPULATION: 93,000 (URBAN: 73%)
LITERACY: 88%
CAPITAL: Cayenne, 38,093
GOVERNMENT: Overseas department (France)
LANGUAGES: French
ETHNIC GROUPS: Black or mulatto 66%; white 12%; East Indian, Chinese, and Amerindian 12%
RELIGIONS: Roman Catholic
CURRENCY: French franc
TEL. AREA CODE: 594

FRENCH POLYNESIA *(Polynésie française)*

LOCATION: South Pacific islands
AREA: 1,544 mi^2 (4,000 km^2)
POPULATION: 194,000 (URBAN: 62%)
LITERACY: 98%
CAPITAL: Papeete, 23,496
GOVERNMENT: Overseas territory (France)
LANGUAGES: French, Tahitian
ETHNIC GROUPS: Polynesian 69%, European 12%, Chinese 10%
RELIGIONS: Protestant 55%, Roman Catholic 32%
CURRENCY: CFP franc
TEL. AREA CODE: 689

GABON *(Gabon)*

LOCATION: Central Africa
AREA: 103,347 mi^2 (267,667 km^2)
POPULATION: 1,056,000 (URBAN: 41%)
LITERACY: 65%
CAPITAL: Libreville, 235,700
GOVERNMENT: Republic
LANGUAGES: French, Fang, indigenous
ETHNIC GROUPS: Fang, Eshira, Bapounou, Teke
RELIGIONS: Roman Catholic and other Christian 55-75%, indigenous, Muslim
CURRENCY: CFA franc
TEL. AREA CODE: 241

GAMBIA *(Gambia)*

LOCATION: Western Africa
AREA: 4,361 mi^2 (11,295 km^2)
POPULATION: 789,000 (URBAN: 20%)
LITERACY: 12%
CAPITAL: Banjul, 44,536
GOVERNMENT: Republic
LANGUAGES: English, Malinke, Wolof, Fula, indigenous
ETHNIC GROUPS: Malinke 42%, Fulani 18%, Wolof 16%, Jola 10%, Serahuli 9%
RELIGIONS: Muslim 90%, Christian 9%, indigenous 1%
CURRENCY: Dalasi
TEL. AREA CODE: 220

GERMANY, EAST *(Deutsche Demokratische Republik)*

LOCATION: Eastern Europe
AREA: 41,828 mi^2 (108,333 km^2)
POPULATION: 16,582,000 (URBAN: 77%)
LITERACY: 99%
CAPITAL: Berlin (Ost), 1,236,248
GOVERNMENT: Socialist republic
LANGUAGES: German
ETHNIC GROUPS: German (Teutonic) 99%
RELIGIONS: Lutheran and other Protestant 47%, Roman Catholic 7%
CURRENCY: Mark
TEL. AREA CODE: 37

GERMANY, WEST *(Bundesrepublik Deutschland)*

LOCATION: Western Europe
AREA: 96,027 mi^2 (248,707 km^2)
POPULATION: 61,380,000 (URBAN: 86%)
LITERACY: 99%
CAPITAL: Bonn, 290,769
GOVERNMENT: Federal republic
LANGUAGES: German
ETHNIC GROUPS: German (Teutonic), Danish
RELIGIONS: Roman Catholic 45%, Protestant 44%
CURRENCY: Mark
TEL. AREA CODE: 49

KIRIBATI (Kiribati)

LOCATION: Central Pacific islands
AREA: 280 mi² (726 km²)
POPULATION: 69,000 (URBAN: 34%)
LITERACY: 90%
CAPITAL: Bairiki, 2,086
GOVERNMENT: Republic
LANGUAGES: English, Gilbertese
ETHNIC GROUPS: Micronesian
RELIGIONS: Roman Catholic 53%, Congregationalist 41%, Bahai 2%
CURRENCY: Australian dollar

KOREA, NORTH (Chosŏn-minjujuŭi-inmīn-konghwaguk)

LOCATION: Eastern Asia
AREA: 46,540 mi² (120,538 km²)
POPULATION: 22,250,000 (URBAN: 64%)
LITERACY: 95%
CAPITAL: P'yŏngyang, 1,283,000
GOVERNMENT: Socialist republic
LANGUAGES: Korean
ETHNIC GROUPS: Korean 100%
RELIGIONS: Buddhist, Confucianism, Chondoist, Christian
CURRENCY: Won

KOREA, SOUTH (Taehan-min'guk)

LOCATION: Eastern Asia
AREA: 38,025 mi² (98,484 km²)
POPULATION: 42,840,000 (URBAN: 65%)
LITERACY: 88%
CAPITAL: Sŏul (Seoul), 9,646,000
GOVERNMENT: Republic
LANGUAGES: Korean
ETHNIC GROUPS: Korean
RELIGIONS: Confucian, Christian, Buddhist, Shamanist, Chondoist
CURRENCY: Won
TEL. AREA CODE: 82

KUWAIT (Al-Kuwayt)

LOCATION: Southwestern Asia
AREA: 6,880 mi² (17,818 km²)
POPULATION: 2,002,000 (URBAN: 94%)
LITERACY: 68%
CAPITAL: Al-Kuwayt (Kuwait), 44,335
GOVERNMENT: Constitutional monarchy

LANGUAGES: Arabic, English
ETHNIC GROUPS: Kuwaiti 40%, other Arab 39%, Southern Asian 9%, Iranian 4%
RELIGIONS: Sunni Muslim 45%, Shiite Muslim 30%, Christian 6%
CURRENCY: Dinar
TEL. AREA CODE: 965

LAOS (Lao)

LOCATION: Southeastern Asia, landlocked
AREA: 91,429 mi² (236,800 km²)
POPULATION: 3,892,000 (URBAN: 16%)
LITERACY: 85%
CAPITAL: Viangchan (Vientiane), 377,000
GOVERNMENT: Socialist republic
LANGUAGES: Lao, French, English
ETHNIC GROUPS: Lao 50%; Thai 20%; Phoutheung 15%; Miao, Hmong, Yao, and others 15%
RELIGIONS: Buddhist 85%, indigenous and others 15%
CURRENCY: Kip

LEBANON (Lubnān)

LOCATION: Southwestern Asia
AREA: 4,015 mi² (10,400 km²)
POPULATION: 3,351,000 (URBAN: 80%)
LITERACY: 68%
CAPITAL: Bayrūt (Beirut), 509,000
GOVERNMENT: Republic
LANGUAGES: Arabic, French, Armenian, English
ETHNIC GROUPS: Arab 93%, Armenian 6%
RELIGIONS: Muslim 75%, Christian 25%, Jewish
CURRENCY: Pound

LESOTHO (Lesotho)

LOCATION: Southern Africa, landlocked
AREA: 11,720 mi² (30,355 km²)
POPULATION: 1,689,000 (URBAN: 17%)
LITERACY: 60%
CAPITAL: Maseru, 14,686
GOVERNMENT: Constitutional monarchy
LANGUAGES: English, Sesotho, Zulu, Xhosa
ETHNIC GROUPS: Sotho 100%
RELIGIONS: Roman Catholic and other Christian 80%, indigenous 20%
CURRENCY: Loti
TEL. AREA CODE: 266

LIBERIA (Liberia)

LOCATION: Western Africa
AREA: 38,250 mi² (99,067 km²)
POPULATION: 2,553,000 (URBAN: 40%)
LITERACY: 21%
CAPITAL: Monrovia, 425,000
GOVERNMENT: Republic
LANGUAGES: English, indigenous
ETHNIC GROUPS: Indigenous black 95%, descendants of freed American slaves 5%
RELIGIONS: Indigenous 70%, Muslim 20%, Christian 10%
CURRENCY: U.S. dollar
TEL. AREA CODE: 231

LIBYA (Lībiyā)

LOCATION: Northern Africa
AREA: 679,362 mi² (1,759,540 km²)
POPULATION: 4,019,000 (URBAN: 65%)
LITERACY: 39%
CAPITAL: Tarābulus (Tripoli), 858,500
GOVERNMENT: Socialist republic
LANGUAGES: Arabic
ETHNIC GROUPS: Arab-Berber 97%
RELIGIONS: Sunni Muslim 97%
CURRENCY: Dinar
TEL. AREA CODE: 218

LIECHTENSTEIN (Liechtenstein)

LOCATION: Central Europe, landlocked
AREA: 62 mi² (160 km²)
POPULATION: 29,000 (URBAN: 24%)
LITERACY: 100%
CAPITAL: Vaduz, 4,920
GOVERNMENT: Constitutional monarchy
LANGUAGES: German
ETHNIC GROUPS: Alemannic 95%, Italian and others 5%
RELIGIONS: Roman Catholic 83%, Protestant 7%
CURRENCY: Swiss franc
TEL. AREA CODE: 41

LUXEMBOURG (Luxembourg (French) / Lezebuurg (Luxembourgish))

LOCATION: Western Europe, landlocked
AREA: 998 mi² (2,586 km²)
POPULATION: 368,000 (URBAN: 81%)
LITERACY: 99%
CAPITAL: Luxembourg, 78,924
GOVERNMENT: Constitutional monarchy
LANGUAGES: French, Luxembourgish, German, English

ETHNIC GROUPS: Luxembourger (mixed Celtic, French, and German)
RELIGIONS: Roman Catholic 97%, Jewish and Protestant 3%
CURRENCY: Franc
TEL. AREA CODE: 352

MACAU (Macau)

LOCATION: Eastern Asia (islands and peninsula on China's southeastern coast)
AREA: 6.6 mi² (17 km²)
POPULATION: 432,000 (URBAN: 98%)
LITERACY: 79%
CAPITAL: Macau, 408,500
GOVERNMENT: Chinese territory under Portuguese administration
LANGUAGES: Portuguese, Chinese (Cantonese)
ETHNIC GROUPS: Chinese 95%, Portuguese 3%
RELIGIONS: Buddhist, Roman Catholic
CURRENCY: Pataca
TEL. AREA CODE: 853

MADAGASCAR (Madagasikara (Malagasy))

LOCATION: Southeastern African island
AREA: 226,658 mi² (587,041 km²)
POPULATION: 11,250,000 (URBAN: 22%)
LITERACY: 81%
CAPITAL: Antananarivo, 700,000
GOVERNMENT: Republic
LANGUAGES: Malagasy, French
ETHNIC GROUPS: Merina 15%, Betsimisaraka 9%, Betsileo 7%, Tsimihety 4%, Antaisaka 4%, other tribes
RELIGIONS: Indigenous 52%, Christian 41%, Muslim 7%
CURRENCY: Franc

MALAWI (Malaŵi)

LOCATION: Southern Africa, landlocked
AREA: 45,747 mi² (118,484 km²)
POPULATION: 8,440,000 (URBAN: 12%)
LITERACY: 25%
CAPITAL: Lilongwe, 175,000
GOVERNMENT: Republic
LANGUAGES: Chichewa, English, Tumbuka
ETHNIC GROUPS: Chewa, Nyanja, Tumbuko, Yao, Lomwe, others
RELIGIONS: Protestant 55%, Roman Catholic 20%, Muslim 20%
CURRENCY: Kwacha
TEL. AREA CODE: 265

MALAYSIA (Malaysia)

LOCATION: Southeastern Asia (includes part of the island of Borneo)
AREA: 127,502 mi^2 (330,228 km^2)
POPULATION: 17,255,000 (URBAN: 38%)
LITERACY: 58%
CAPITAL: Kuala Lumpur, 937,817
GOVERNMENT: Federal constitutional monarchy
LANGUAGES: Malay, Chinese dialects, Tamil, English
ETHNIC GROUPS: Malay 65%, Chinese 20%, indigenous 8%, Indian 3%
RELIGIONS: Muslim, Buddhist, Hindu, Christian, Confucian
CURRENCY: Ringgit
TEL. AREA CODE: 60

MALDIVES (Maldives)

LOCATION: Indian Ocean islands
AREA: 115 mi^2 (298 km^2)
POPULATION: 209,000 (URBAN: 20%)
LITERACY: 82%
CAPITAL: Male, 46,334
GOVERNMENT: Republic
LANGUAGES: Divehi
ETHNIC GROUPS: Maldivian (mixed Sinhalese, Dravidian, Arab, and black)
RELIGIONS: Sunni Muslim
CURRENCY: Rufiyaa

MALI (Mali)

LOCATION: Western Africa, landlocked
AREA: 478,767 mi^2 (1,240,000 km^2)
POPULATION: 9,039,000 (URBAN: 18%)
LITERACY: 9%
CAPITAL: Bamako, 502,000
GOVERNMENT: Republic
LANGUAGES: French, Bambara, indigenous
ETHNIC GROUPS: Malinke 50%, Fulani 17%, Voltaic 12%, Songhai 6%
RELIGIONS: Sunni Muslim 90%, indigenous 9%, Christian 1%
CURRENCY: CFA franc

MALTA (Malta)

LOCATION: Mediterranean island
AREA: 122 mi^2 (316 km^2)
POPULATION: 370,000 (URBAN: 85%)
LITERACY: 83%
CAPITAL: Valletta, 9,263
GOVERNMENT: Republic
LANGUAGES: English, Maltese
ETHNIC GROUPS: Maltese (mixed Arab, Sicilian, Norman, Spanish, Italian, and English)
RELIGIONS: Roman Catholic 98%
CURRENCY: Lira
TEL. AREA CODE: 356

MARTINIQUE (Martinique)

LOCATION: Caribbean island
AREA: 425 mi^2 (1,100 km^2)
POPULATION: 338,000 (URBAN: 71%)
LITERACY: 87%
CAPITAL: Fort-de-France, 99,844
GOVERNMENT: Overseas department (France)
LANGUAGES: French, Creole
ETHNIC GROUPS: Black or mulatto 90%, white 5%
RELIGIONS: Roman Catholic 95%, Hindu, African
CURRENCY: French franc
TEL. AREA CODE: 596

MAURITANIA (Mūrītānīyā (Arabic) / Mauritanie (French))

LOCATION: Western Africa
AREA: 397,956 mi^2 (1,030,700 km^2)
POPULATION: 1,948,000 (URBAN: 35%)
LITERACY: 17%
CAPITAL: Nouakchott, 285,000
GOVERNMENT: Provisional military government
LANGUAGES: Arabic, French, indigenous
ETHNIC GROUPS: Mixed Moor and black 40%, Moor 30%, black 30%
RELIGIONS: Sunni Muslim 100%
CURRENCY: Ouguiya

MAURITIUS (Mauritius)

LOCATION: Indian Ocean island
AREA: 788 mi^2 (2,040 km^2)
POPULATION: 1,057,000 (URBAN: 42%)
LITERACY: 67%
CAPITAL: Port Louis, 138,272
GOVERNMENT: Parliamentary state
LANGUAGES: English, Creole, French, Hindi, indigenous
ETHNIC GROUPS: Indo-Mauritian 68%, Creole 27%, Sino-Mauritian 3%, Franco-Mauritian 2%
RELIGIONS: Hindu 51%, Roman Catholic and other Christian 30%, Muslim 17%
CURRENCY: Rupee
NOTES: The above information includes dependencies.

MEXICO (México)

LOCATION: Southern North America
AREA: 761,605 mi² (1,972,547 km²)
POPULATION: 85,300,000 (URBAN: 70%)
LITERACY: 83%
CAPITAL: Ciudad de México (Mexico City), 8,831,079
GOVERNMENT: Federal republic
LANGUAGES: Spanish, indigenous
ETHNIC GROUPS: Mestizo 60%, Amerindian 30%, white 9%
RELIGIONS: Roman Catholic 97%, Protestant 3%
CURRENCY: Peso
TEL. AREA CODE: 52

MONACO (Monaco)

LOCATION: Southern Europe (on the southeastern coast of France)
AREA: 0.7 mi² (1.9 km²)
POPULATION: 29,000 (URBAN: 100%)
LITERACY: 99%
CAPITAL: Monaco, 27,063
GOVERNMENT: Constitutional monarchy
LANGUAGES: French, English, Italian, Monegasque
ETHNIC GROUPS: French 47%, Monegasque 17%, Italian 16%, English 4%, Belgian 2%, Swiss 1%
RELIGIONS: Roman Catholic 95%
CURRENCY: French franc
TEL. AREA CODE: 33

MONGOLIA (Mongol Uls)

LOCATION: Central Asia, landlocked
AREA: 604,250 mi² (1,565,000 km²)
POPULATION: 2,097,000 (URBAN: 51%)
LITERACY: 80%
CAPITAL: Ulaanbaatar, 488,200
GOVERNMENT: Socialist republic
LANGUAGES: Khalkha Mongol, Turkish, Russian, Chinese
ETHNIC GROUPS: Mongol 90%, Kazakh 4%, Chinese 2%, Russian 2%
RELIGIONS: Tibetan Buddhist, Muslim, Shamanic
CURRENCY: Tugrik

MOROCCO (Al-Magrib)

LOCATION: Northwestern Africa
AREA: 172,414 mi² (446,550 km²)
POPULATION: 25,600,000 (URBAN: 45%)
LITERACY: 21%
CAPITAL: Rabat, 518,616
GOVERNMENT: Consitutional monarchy
LANGUAGES: Arabic, Berber dialects, French
ETHNIC GROUPS: Arab-Berber 99%
RELIGIONS: Sunni Muslim 99%
CURRENCY: Dirham
TEL. AREA CODE: 212
NOTES: The above information excludes Western Sahara.

MOZAMBIQUE (Moçambique)

LOCATION: Southern Africa
AREA: 308,642 mi² (799,379 km²)
POPULATION: 17,660,000 (URBAN: 19%)
LITERACY: 27%
CAPITAL: Maputo, 755,300
GOVERNMENT: Socialist republic
LANGUAGES: Portuguese, indigenous
ETHNIC GROUPS: Makua, Lomwe, Thonga, others
RELIGIONS: Indigenous 60%, Christian 30%, Muslim 10%
CURRENCY: Metical

NAMIBIA (Namibia)

LOCATION: Southern Africa
AREA: 317,818 mi² (823,144 km²)
POPULATION: 1,337,000 (URBAN: 51%)
LITERACY: 23%
CAPITAL: Windhoek, 120,000
GOVERNMENT: Under South African administration
LANGUAGES: Afrikaans, English, German, indigenous
ETHNIC GROUPS: Ovambo 49%, Kavango 9%, Damara 8%, Herero 7%, white 7%, mixed 7%
RELIGIONS: Christian, indigenous
CURRENCY: South African rand
TEL. AREA CODE: 264
NOTES: The above information excludes Walvis Bay.

NAURU (Nauru (English) / Naoero (Nauruan))

LOCATION: South Pacific island
AREA: 8.1 mi² (21 km²)
POPULATION: 9,000
LITERACY: 99%
CAPITAL: Yaren District
GOVERNMENT: Republic
LANGUAGES: Nauruan, English
ETHNIC GROUPS: Nauruan 58%, other Pacific Islander 26%, Chinese 8%, European 8%
RELIGIONS: Protestant 67%, Roman Catholic 33%
CURRENCY: Australian dollar

NEPAL (Nepāl)

LOCATION: Southern Asia, landlocked
AREA: 56,827 mi^2 (147,181 km^2)
POPULATION: 18,415,000 (URBAN: 8%)
LITERACY: 21%
CAPITAL: Kathmandu, 235,160
GOVERNMENT: Constitutional monarchy
LANGUAGES: Nepali, Maithili, Bhojpuri, indigenous
ETHNIC GROUPS: Newar, Indian, Tibetan, Gurung, Magar, Tamang, Bhotia, others
RELIGIONS: Hindu 90%, Buddhist 5%, Muslim 3%
CURRENCY: Rupee
TEL. AREA CODE: 977

NETHERLANDS (Nederland)

LOCATION: Western Europe
AREA: 16,133 mi^2 (41,785 km^2)
POPULATION: 14,815,000 (URBAN: 88%)
LITERACY: 99%
CAPITAL: Amsterdam (designated), 679,140; 's-Gravenhage (The Hague) (seat of government), 443,961
GOVERNMENT: Constitutional monarchy
LANGUAGES: Dutch
ETHNIC GROUPS: Dutch (mixed Scandinavian, French, and Celtic) 99%, Indonesian and others 1%
RELIGIONS: Roman Catholic 40%, Dutch Reformed and other Protestant 31%
CURRENCY: Guilder
TEL. AREA CODE: 31

NETHERLANDS ANTILLES (Nederlandse Antillen)

LOCATION: Caribbean islands
AREA: 309 mi^2 (800 km^2)
POPULATION: 194,000 (URBAN: 53%)
LITERACY: 93%
CAPITAL: Willemstad, 31,883
GOVERNMENT: Self-governing territory (Netherlands protection)
LANGUAGES: Dutch, Papiamento, English, Spanish
ETHNIC GROUPS: Mulatto 85%, West Indian, European
RELIGIONS: Roman Catholic, Protestant, Jewish
CURRENCY: Guilder
TEL. AREA CODE: 599

NEW CALEDONIA (Nouvelle-Calédonie)

LOCATION: South Pacific islands
AREA: 7,366 mi^2 (19,079 km^2)
POPULATION: 161,000 (URBAN: 76%)
LITERACY: 91%
CAPITAL: Nouméa, 60,112

GOVERNMENT: Overseas territory (France)
LANGUAGES: French, Malay-Polynesian languages
ETHNIC GROUPS: Melanesian 43%, French 37%, Wallisian 8%, Polynesian 4%, Indonesian 4%, Vietnamese 2%
RELIGIONS: Roman Catholic 60%, Protestant 30%
CURRENCY: CFP franc
TEL. AREA CODE: 687

NEW ZEALAND (New Zealand)

LOCATION: South Pacific islands
AREA: 103,519 mi^2 (268,112 km^2)
POPULATION: 3,391,000 (URBAN: 84%)
LITERACY: 98%
CAPITAL: Wellington, 137,495
GOVERNMENT: Parliamentary state
LANGUAGES: English, Maori
ETHNIC GROUPS: European origin 86%, Maori 9%, Samoan and other Pacific islander 3%
RELIGIONS: Anglican 24%, Presbyterian 18%, Roman Catholic 15%, Methodist 5%
CURRENCY: Dollar
TEL. AREA CODE: 64

NICARAGUA (Nicaragua)

LOCATION: Central America
AREA: 50,193 mi^2 (130,000 km^2)
POPULATION: 3,689,000 (URBAN: 57%)
LITERACY: 58%
CAPITAL: Managua, 644,588
GOVERNMENT: Republic
LANGUAGES: Spanish, English, indigenous
ETHNIC GROUPS: Mestizo 69%, white 17%, black 9%, Amerindian 5%
RELIGIONS: Roman Catholic 95%
CURRENCY: Cordoba
TEL. AREA CODE: 505

NIGER (Niger)

LOCATION: Western Africa, landlocked
AREA: 489,191 mi^2 (1,267,000 km^2)
POPULATION: 7,329,000 (URBAN: 16%)
LITERACY: 10%
CAPITAL: Niamey, 399,100
GOVERNMENT: Provisional military government
LANGUAGES: French, Hausa, Djerma, indigenous
ETHNIC GROUPS: Hausa 56%, Djerma 22%, Fulani 9%, Taureg 8%, Beriberi 4%
RELIGIONS: Muslim 80%, indigenous and Christian 20%
CURRENCY: CFA franc
TEL. AREA CODE: 227

NIGERIA (Nigeria)

LOCATION: Western Africa
AREA: 356,669 mi^2 (923,768 km^2)
POPULATION: 113,580,000 (URBAN: 23%)
LITERACY: 38%
CAPITAL: Lagos (de facto), 1,213,000; Abuja (future)
GOVERNMENT: Provisional military government
LANGUAGES: English, Hausa, Fulani, Yorbua, Ibo, indigenous
ETHNIC GROUPS: Hausa, Fulani, Yoruba, Ibo, others
RELIGIONS: Muslim 50%, Christian 40%, indigenous 10%
CURRENCY: Naira
TEL. AREA CODE: 234

NORWAY (Norge)

LOCATION: Northern Europe
AREA: 149,412 mi^2 (386,975 km^2)
POPULATION: 4,221,000 (URBAN: 73%)
LITERACY: 99%
CAPITAL: Oslo, 448,747
GOVERNMENT: Constitutional monarchy
LANGUAGES: Norwegian, Lapp
ETHNIC GROUPS: Norwegian (Scandinavian), Lappic
RELIGIONS: Lutheran 94%, other Protestant and Roman Catholic 4%
CURRENCY: Krone
TEL. AREA CODE: 47
NOTES: The above information includes Svalbard and Jan Mayen.

OMAN ('Umān)

LOCATION: Southwestern Asia
AREA: 82,030 mi^2 (212,457 km^2)
POPULATION: 1,284,000 (URBAN: 9%)
LITERACY: 20%
CAPITAL: Masqat (Muscat), 50,000
GOVERNMENT: Monarchy
LANGUAGES: Arabic, English, Baluchi, Urdu, Indian dialects
ETHNIC GROUPS: Arab, Baluchi, Zanzibari, Indian
RELIGIONS: Ibadhi Muslim 75%, Sunni Muslim, Shiite Muslim, Hindu
CURRENCY: Rial
TEL. AREA CODE: 968

PAKISTAN (Pākistān)

LOCATION: Southern Asia
AREA: 339,732 mi^2 (879,902 km^2)
POPULATION: 108,990,000 (URBAN: 30%)
LITERACY: 26%
CAPITAL: Islāmābād, 201,000
GOVERNMENT: Federal Islamic Republic

LANGUAGES: English, Urdu, Punjabi, Sindhi, Pashto, Baluchi
ETHNIC GROUPS: Punjabi, Sindhi, Pathan, Baluchi
RELIGIONS: Sunni Muslim 77%, Shiite Muslim 20%, Christian, Hindu, and other 3%
CURRENCY: Rupee
TEL. AREA CODE: 92
NOTES: The above information includes part of Jammu and Kashmir.

PANAMA (Panamá)

LOCATION: Central America
AREA: 29,762 mi^2 (77,082 km^2)
POPULATION: 2,346,000 (URBAN: 52%)
LITERACY: 87%
CAPITAL: Panamá, 389,172
GOVERNMENT: Republic
LANGUAGES: Spanish, English, indigenous
ETHNIC GROUPS: Mestizo 70%, West Indian 14%, white 10%, Amerindian 6%
RELIGIONS: Roman Catholic 93%, Protestant 6%
CURRENCY: Balboa
TEL. AREA CODE: 507

PAPUA NEW GUINEA (Papua New Guinea)

LOCATION: South Pacific islands
AREA: 178,704 mi^2 (462,840 km^2)
POPULATION: 3,639,000 (URBAN: 14%)
LITERACY: 32%
CAPITAL: Port Moresby, 123,624
GOVERNMENT: Parliamentary state
LANGUAGES: English, Motu, Pidgin, indigenous
ETHNIC GROUPS: Melanesian, Papuan, Negrito, Micronesian, Polynesian
RELIGIONS: Indigenous 50%, Lutheran and other Protestant 37%, Roman Catholic 13%
CURRENCY: Kina
TEL. AREA CODE: 675

PARAGUAY (Paraguay)

LOCATION: Central South America, landlocked
AREA: 157,048 mi^2 (406,752 km^2)
POPULATION: 4,210,000 (URBAN: 44%)
LITERACY: 80%
CAPITAL: Asunción, 455,517
GOVERNMENT: Republic
LANGUAGES: Spanish, Guarani
ETHNIC GROUPS: Mestizo 95%, white and Amerindian 5%
RELIGIONS: Roman Catholic 90%, Mennonite and other Protestant
CURRENCY: Guarani
TEL. AREA CODE: 595

PERU (Perú)

LOCATION: Western South America
AREA: 496,225 mi^2 (1,285,216 km^2)
POPULATION: 21,535,000 (URBAN: 67%)
LITERACY: 83%
CAPITAL: Lima, 371,122
GOVERNMENT: Republic
LANGUAGES: Quechua, Spanish, Aymara
ETHNIC GROUPS: Amerindian 45%, mestizo 37%, white 15%
RELIGIONS: Roman Catholic
CURRENCY: Inti
TEL. AREA CODE: 51

PHILIPPINES (Pilipinas (Tagalog) / Philippines (English))

LOCATION: Southeastern Asian islands
AREA: 115,831 mi^2 (300,000 km^2)
POPULATION: 60,110,000 (URBAN: 40%)
LITERACY: 83%
CAPITAL: Manila, 1,630,485
GOVERNMENT: Republic
LANGUAGES: English, Pilipino, Tagalog, Cebuano
ETHNIC GROUPS: Christian Malay 92%, Muslim Malay 4%, Chinese 2%
RELIGIONS: Roman Catholic 83%, Protestant 9%, Muslim 5%, Buddhist and others 3%
CURRENCY: Peso
TEL. AREA CODE: 63

POLAND (Polska)

LOCATION: Eastern Europe
AREA: 120,728 mi^2 (312,683 km^2)
POPULATION: 37,955,000 (URBAN: 61%)
LITERACY: 99%
CAPITAL: Warszawa (Warsaw), 1,664,700
GOVERNMENT: Socialist republic
LANGUAGES: Polish
ETHNIC GROUPS: Polish (mixed Slavic and Teutonic) 99%, Ukrainian, Byelorussian
RELIGIONS: Roman Catholic 95%
CURRENCY: Zloty
TEL. AREA CODE: 48

PORTUGAL (Portugal)

LOCATION: Southwestern Europe
AREA: 35,516 mi^2 (91,985 km^2)
POPULATION: 10,445,000 (URBAN: 32%)
LITERACY: 71%
CAPITAL: Lisboa (Lisbon), 807,167
GOVERNMENT: Republic
LANGUAGES: Portuguese
ETHNIC GROUPS: Portuguese (Mediterranean), black
RELIGIONS: Roman Catholic 97%, Protestant 1%
CURRENCY: Escudo
TEL. AREA CODE: 351

PUERTO RICO (Puerto Rico)

LOCATION: Caribbean island
AREA: 3,515 mi^2 (9,104 km^2)
POPULATION: 3,301,000 (URBAN: 71%)
LITERACY: 88%
CAPITAL: San Juan, 424,600
GOVERNMENT: Commonwealth (U.S. protection)
LANGUAGES: Spanish, English
ETHNIC GROUPS: Puerto Rican (mixed Spanish and black)
RELIGIONS: Roman Catholic 85%
CURRENCY: U.S. dollar

QATAR (Qatar)

LOCATION: Southwestern Asia
AREA: 4,416 mi^2 (11,437 km^2)
POPULATION: 400,000 (URBAN: 88%)
LITERACY: 34%
CAPITAL: Ad-Dawhah (Doha), 217,294
GOVERNMENT: Monarchy
LANGUAGES: Arabic, English
ETHNIC GROUPS: Arab 40%, Pakistani 18%, Indian 18%, Iranian 10%
RELIGIONS: Muslim 95%
CURRENCY: Riyal
TEL. AREA CODE: 974

ROMANIA (România)

LOCATION: Eastern Europe
AREA: 91,699 mi^2 (237,500 km^2)
POPULATION: 23,085,000 (URBAN: 49%)
LITERACY: 96%
CAPITAL: București (Bucharest), 1,989,823
GOVERNMENT: Socialist republic
LANGUAGES: Romanian, Hungarian, German
ETHNIC GROUPS: Romanian (mixed Latin, Thracian, Slavic, and Celtic) 89%, Hungarian 8%, German 2%
RELIGIONS: Romanian Orthodox 80%, Roman Catholic 6%
CURRENCY: Leu
TEL. AREA CODE: 40

RWANDA (Rwanda)

LOCATION: Eastern Africa, landlocked
AREA: 10,169 mi^2 (26,338 km^2)
POPULATION: 7,192,000 (URBAN: 6%)
LITERACY: 35%
CAPITAL: Kigali, 181,600
GOVERNMENT: Republic
LANGUAGES: French, Kinyarwanda
ETHNIC GROUPS: Hutu 89%, Tutsi 10%, Twa
RELIGIONS: Roman Catholic 65%, Protestant 17%, Muslim 1%
CURRENCY: Franc

ST. CHRISTOPHER-NEVIS (St. Christopher-Nevis)

LOCATION: Caribbean islands
AREA: 104 mi^2 (269 km^2)
POPULATION: 47,000 (URBAN: 45%)
LITERACY: 98%
CAPITAL: Basseterre, 14,725
GOVERNMENT: Parliamentary state
LANGUAGES: English
ETHNIC GROUPS: Black 94%, mixed 3%, white 1%
RELIGIONS: Anglican 33%, Methodist 29%, Moravian 9%, Roman Catholic 7%
CURRENCY: East Caribbean dollar
TEL. AREA CODE: 809

ST. LUCIA (St. Lucia)

LOCATION: Caribbean island
AREA: 238 mi^2 (616 km^2)
POPULATION: 148,000 (URBAN: 40%)
LITERACY: 67%
CAPITAL: Castries, 50,798
GOVERNMENT: Parliamentary state
LANGUAGES: English, French
ETHNIC GROUPS: Black 90%, mixed 6%, East Indian 3%, white 1%
RELIGIONS: Roman Catholic 90%, Anglican and other Protestant 10%
CURRENCY: East Caribbean dollar
TEL. AREA CODE: 809

ST. PIERRE AND MIQUELON (St.-Pierre-et-Miquelon)

LOCATION: North Atlantic islands (south of Newfoundland)
AREA: 93 mi^2 (242 km^2)
POPULATION: 6,500 (URBAN: 90%)
LITERACY: 99%
CAPITAL: St. Pierre, 5,371
GOVERNMENT: Overseas department (France)
LANGUAGES: French
ETHNIC GROUPS: French descent
RELIGIONS: Roman Catholic 98%
CURRENCY: French franc
TEL. AREA CODE: 508

ST. VINCENT AND THE GRENADINES (St. Vincent and the Grenadines)

LOCATION: Caribbean islands
AREA: 150 mi^2 (388 km^2)
POPULATION: 125,000 (URBAN: 14%)
LITERACY: 96%
CAPITAL: Kingstown, 18,378
GOVERNMENT: Parliamentary state
LANGUAGES: English, French
ETHNIC GROUPS: Black
RELIGIONS: Anglican, Methodist, Roman Catholic
CURRENCY: East Caribbean dollar
TEL. AREA CODE: 809

SAN MARINO (San Marino)

LOCATION: Southern Europe, landlocked
AREA: 24 mi^2 (61 km^2)
POPULATION: 24,000 (URBAN: 74%)
LITERACY: 96%
CAPITAL: San Marino, 4,137
GOVERNMENT: Republic
LANGUAGES: Italian
ETHNIC GROUPS: Sanmarinese (mixed Latin, Adriatic, and Teutonic), Italian
RELIGIONS: Roman Catholic
CURRENCY: Italian lira
TEL. AREA CODE: 39

SAO TOME AND PRINCIPE (São Tomé e Principe)

LOCATION: Western African islands
AREA: 372 mi^2 (964 km^2)
POPULATION: 119,000 (URBAN: 38%)
LITERACY: 57%
CAPITAL: São Tomé, 17,380
GOVERNMENT: Republic
LANGUAGES: Portuguese, indigenous languages
ETHNIC GROUPS: Black, mixed black and Portuguese, Portuguese
RELIGIONS: Roman Catholic, Protestant, Seventh Day Adventist
CURRENCY: Dobra

SAUDI ARABIA (Al-'Arabīyah as-Su'ūdīyah)

LOCATION: Southwestern Asia
AREA: 864,869 mi^2 (2,240,000 km^2)
POPULATION: 15,775,000 (URBAN: 72%)
LITERACY: 35%
CAPITAL: Ar-Ridād (Riyadh), 1,250,000
GOVERNMENT: Monarchy
LANGUAGES: Arabic
ETHNIC GROUPS: Arab 90%, Afro-Asian 10%
RELIGIONS: Muslim 100%
CURRENCY: Riyal
TEL. AREA CODE: 966

SENEGAL (Sénégal)

LOCATION: Western Africa
AREA: 75,955 mi^2 (196,722 km^2)
POPULATION: 7,394,000 (URBAN: 36%)
LITERACY: 22%
CAPITAL: Dakar, 1,428,084
GOVERNMENT: Republic
LANGUAGES: French, Wolof, indigenous
ETHNIC GROUPS: Wolof 41%, Serer 15%, Fulani 12%, Tukulor 11%, Diola 5%, Malinke 6%
RELIGIONS: Muslim 92%, indigenous 6%, Roman Catholic and other Christian 2%
CURRENCY: CFA franc
TEL. AREA CODE: 221

SEYCHELLES (Seychelles)

LOCATION: Indian Ocean islands
AREA: 175 mi^2 (453 km^2)
POPULATION: 70,000 (URBAN: 50%)
LITERACY: 58%
CAPITAL: Victoria, 23,000
GOVERNMENT: Republic
LANGUAGES: English, French, Creole
ETHNIC GROUPS: Seychellois (mixed Asian, African, and European)
RELIGIONS: Roman Catholic 90%, Anglican 8%
CURRENCY: Rupee

SIERRA LEONE (Sierra Leone)

LOCATION: Western Africa
AREA: 27,925 mi^2 (72,325 km^2)
POPULATION: 4,015,000 (URBAN: 28%)
LITERACY: 15%
CAPITAL: Freetown, 300,000
GOVERNMENT: Republic
LANGUAGES: English, Krio, indigenous
ETHNIC GROUPS: Temne 30%, Mende 30%, Creole 2%, other African
RELIGIONS: Muslim 30%, indigenous 30%, Christian 10%
CURRENCY: Leone

SINGAPORE (Singapore)

LOCATION: Southeastern Asian island
AREA: 239 mi^2 (620 km^2)
POPULATION: 2,663,000 (URBAN. 100%)
LITERACY: 83%
CAPITAL: Singapore, 2,612,800
GOVERNMENT: Republic
LANGUAGES: Chinese (Mandarin), English, Malay, Tamil
ETHNIC GROUPS: Chinese 76%, Malay 15%, Indian 6%
RELIGIONS: Taoist 29%, Buddhist 27%, Muslim 16%, Christian 10%, Hindu 4%
CURRENCY: Dollar
TEL. AREA CODE: 65

SOLOMON ISLANDS (Solomon Islands)

LOCATION: South Pacific islands
AREA: 10,954 mi^2 (28,370 km^2)
POPULATION: 295,000 (URBAN: 10%)
LITERACY: 60%
CAPITAL: Honiara, 30,499
GOVERNMENT: Parliamentary state
LANGUAGES: English, Malay-Polynesian languages
ETHNIC GROUPS: Melanesian 93%, Polynesian 4%, Micronesian 2%
RELIGIONS: Church of Melanesia 34%, Roman Catholic 19%, South Sea Evangelical 17%
CURRENCY: Dollar

SOMALIA (Soomaaliya)

LOCATION: Eastern Africa
AREA: 246,201 mi^2 (637,657 km^2)
POPULATION: 8,118,000 (URBAN: 34%)
LITERACY: 60%
CAPITAL: Mogadishu, 600,000
GOVERNMENT: Socialist republic
LANGUAGES: Arabic, Somali, English, Italian
ETHNIC GROUPS: Somali 85%
RELIGIONS: Sunni Muslim
CURRENCY: Shilling

SOUTH AFRICA (South Africa (English) / Suid-Afrika (Afrikaans))

LOCATION: Southern Africa
AREA: 433,680 mi^2 (1,123,226 km^2)
POPULATION: 35,480,000 (URBAN: 56%)
LITERACY: 70%
CAPITAL: Pretoria (administrative), 435,100; Cape Town (legislative), 859,940; Bloemfontein (judicial), 102,600
GOVERNMENT: Republic
LANGUAGES: Afrikaans, English, indigenous
ETHNIC GROUPS: Black 69%, white 18%, mulatto (coloured) 10%, Indian 3%
RELIGIONS: Christian 55%, indigenous 23%, Hindu 2%, Muslim 1%
CURRENCY: Rand
TEL. AREA CODE: 27
NOTES: The above information includes Walvis Bay.

SPAIN (España)

LOCATION: Southwestern Europe
AREA: 194,885 mi^2 (504,750 km^2)
POPULATION: 39,330,000 (URBAN: 76%)
LITERACY: 93%
CAPITAL: Madrid, 3,200,234
GOVERNMENT: Constitutional monarchy
LANGUAGES: Spanish (Castilian, Catalan, Galician), Basque
ETHNIC GROUPS: Spanish (mixed Mediterranean and Teutonic)
RELIGIONS: Roman Catholic 99%
CURRENCY: Peseta
TEL. AREA CODE: 34

SRI LANKA (Sri Lanka)

LOCATION: Southern Asian island
AREA: 24,962 mi^2 (64,652 km^2)
POPULATION: 16,730,000 (URBAN: 21%)
LITERACY: 86%
CAPITAL: Colombo (de facto), 587,647; Sri Jayawardenapura (future)
GOVERNMENT: Socialist republic
LANGUAGES: English, Sinhala, Tamil
ETHNIC GROUPS: Sinhalese 74%, Ceylon Tamil 12%, Ceylon Moor 7%, Indian Tamil 5%
RELIGIONS: Buddhist 70%, Hindu 15%, Christian 8%, Muslim 7%
CURRENCY: Rupee
TEL. AREA CODE: 94

SUDAN (As-Sūdān)

LOCATION: Eastern Africa
AREA: 967,500 mi^2 (2,505,813 km^2)
POPULATION: 24,255,000 (URBAN: 21%)
LITERACY: 31%
CAPITAL: Al-Khārtūm (Khartoum), 476,218
GOVERNMENT: Republic
LANGUAGES: Arabic, indigenous, English
ETHNIC GROUPS: Black 52%, Arab 39%, Beja 6%
RELIGIONS: Sunni Muslim 70%, indigenous 20%, Christian 5%
CURRENCY: Pound

SURINAME (Suriname)

LOCATION: Northeastern South America
AREA: 63,251 mi^2 (163,820 km^2)
POPULATION: 398,000 (URBAN: 46%)
LITERACY: 65%
CAPITAL: Paramaribo, 67,905
GOVERNMENT: Provisional military government
LANGUAGES: Dutch, Sranan Tongo, English, Hindustani, Javanese
ETHNIC GROUPS: East Indian 37%, Creole 31%, Javanese 15%, black 10%, Amerindian 3%, Chinese 2%
RELIGIONS: Hindu 27%, Protestant 25%, Roman Catholic 23%, Muslim 20%
CURRENCY: Guilder
TEL. AREA CODE: 597

SWAZILAND (Swaziland)

LOCATION: Southern Africa, landlocked
AREA: 6,704 mi^2 (17,364 km^2)
POPULATION: 727,000 (URBAN: 26%)
LITERACY: 55%
CAPITAL: Mbabane (de facto), 53,000; Lobamba (future)
GOVERNMENT: Monarchy
LANGUAGES: English, siSwati
ETHNIC GROUPS: Swazi 95%, European 2%, Zulu 1%
RELIGIONS: Christian 57%, indigenous 43%
CURRENCY: Lilangeni
TEL. AREA CODE: 268

SWEDEN (Sverige)

LOCATION: Northern Europe
AREA: 173,732 mi^2 (449,964 km^2)
POPULATION: 8,444,000 (URBAN: 83%)
LITERACY: 99%
CAPITAL: Stockholm, 663,217
GOVERNMENT: Constitutional monarchy
LANGUAGES: Swedish
ETHNIC GROUPS: Swedish (Scandinavian) 92%, Finnish, Lappic
RELIGIONS: Lutheran (Church of Sweden) 94%, Roman Catholic 2%
CURRENCY: Krona
TEL. AREA CODE: 46

SWITZERLAND (Schweiz (German) / Suisse (French) / Svizzera (Italian))

LOCATION: Central Europe, landlocked
AREA: 15,943 mi^2 (41,293 km^2)
POPULATION: 6,590,000 (URBAN: 58%)
LITERACY: 99%
CAPITAL: Bern, 137,134
GOVERNMENT: Federal republic
LANGUAGES: French, German, Italian, Romansch
ETHNIC GROUPS: German 65%, French 18%, Italian 10%, Romansch 1%
RELIGIONS: Roman Catholic 49%, Protestant 48%
CURRENCY: Franc
TEL. AREA CODE: 41

SYRIA (Sūriyah)

LOCATION: Southwestern Asia
AREA: 71,498 mi^2 (185,180 km^2)
POPULATION: 11,530,000 (URBAN: 50%)
LITERACY: 40%
CAPITAL: Dimashq (Damascus), 1,259,000
GOVERNMENT: Socialist republic
LANGUAGES: Arabic, Kurdish, Armenian, Aramaic, Circassian
ETHNIC GROUPS: Arab 90%, Kurdish, Armenian, and others 10%
RELIGIONS: Sunni Muslim 74%, other Muslim 16%, Christian 10%
CURRENCY: Pound

TAIWAN (T'aiwan)

LOCATION: Eastern Asian island
AREA: 13,900 mi^2 (36,002 km^2)
POPULATION: 20,125,000 (URBAN: 66%)
LITERACY: 90%
CAPITAL: T'aipei, 2,507,620
GOVERNMENT: Republic
LANGUAGES: Chinese dialects
ETHNIC GROUPS: Taiwanese 84%, Chinese 14%, aborigine 2%
RELIGIONS: Buddhist, Confucian, and Taoist 93%, Christian 5%
CURRENCY: Dollar
TEL. AREA CODE: 886

TANZANIA (Tanzania)

LOCATION: Eastern Africa
AREA: 364,900 mi^2 (945,087 km^2)
POPULATION: 24,055,000 (URBAN: 22%)
LITERACY: 46%
CAPITAL: Dar es Salaam (de facto), 757,346; Dodoma (future), 46,000
GOVERNMENT: Republic
LANGUAGES: English, Swahili, indigenous
ETHNIC GROUPS: African 99%
RELIGIONS: Indigenous 35%, Muslim 35%, Christian 30%
CURRENCY: Shilling
TEL. AREA CODE: 255

THAILAND (Prathet Thai)

LOCATION: Southeastern Asia
AREA: 198,115 mi^2 (513,115 km^2)
POPULATION: 55,375,000 (URBAN: 20%)
LITERACY: 88%
CAPITAL: Krung Thep (Bangkok), 5,174,682
GOVERNMENT: Constitutional monarchy
LANGUAGES: Thai, indigenous
ETHNIC GROUPS: Thai 84%, Chinese 12%
RELIGIONS: Buddhist 98%, Muslim 1%
CURRENCY: Baht
TEL. AREA CODE: 66

TOGO (Togo)

LOCATION: Western Africa
AREA: 21,925 mi^2 (56,785 km^2)
POPULATION: 3,393,000 (URBAN: 22%)
LITERACY: 16%
CAPITAL: Lomé, 369,926
GOVERNMENT: Republic
LANGUAGES: French, indigenous
ETHNIC GROUPS: Ewe 25%, Kabye 15%, Mina, others
RELIGIONS: Indigenous 70%, Christian 20%, Muslim 10%
CURRENCY: CFA franc
TEL. AREA CODE: 228

TRINIDAD AND TOBAGO (Trinidad and Tobago)

LOCATION: Caribbean islands
AREA: 1,980 mi^2 (5,128 km^2)
POPULATION: 1,295,000 (URBAN: 64%)
LITERACY: 95%
CAPITAL: Port of Spain, 65,906
GOVERNMENT: Republic
LANGUAGES: English, Hindi, French, Spanish
ETHNIC GROUPS: Black 41%, East Indian 41%, mixed 16%, white 1%
RELIGIONS: Roman Catholic 33%, Anglican and other Protestant 29%, Hindu 25%
CURRENCY: Dollar
TEL. AREA CODE: 809

TUNISIA (Tunisie (French) / Tunis (Arabic))

LOCATION: Northern Africa
AREA: 63,170 mi^2 (163,610 km^2)
POPULATION: 7,876,000 (URBAN: 57%)
LITERACY: 46%
CAPITAL: Tunis, 596,654
GOVERNMENT: Republic
LANGUAGES: Arabic, French
ETHNIC GROUPS: Arab 98%, European 1%
RELIGIONS: Muslim 98%, Christian 1%
CURRENCY: Dinar
TEL. AREA CODE: 216

TURKEY (Türkiye)

LOCATION: Southeastern Europe and southwestern Asia
AREA: 300,948 mi^2 (779,452 km^2)
POPULATION: 51,970,000 (URBAN: 46%)
LITERACY: 69%
CAPITAL: Ankara, 2,235,035
GOVERNMENT: Republic
LANGUAGES: Turkish, Kurdish, Arabic
ETHNIC GROUPS: Turkish 85%, Kurdish 12%
RELIGIONS: Muslim 98%
CURRENCY: Lira
TEL. AREA CODE: 90

TUVALU (Tuvalu)

LOCATION: South Pacific islands
AREA: 10 mi^2 (26 km^2)
POPULATION: 8,700
LITERACY: 50%
CAPITAL: Funafuti, 2,191
GOVERNMENT: Parliamentary state
LANGUAGES: Tuvaluan, English
ETHNIC GROUPS: Polynesian 96%
RELIGIONS: Christian
CURRENCY: Australian dollar

UGANDA (Uganda)

LOCATION: Eastern Africa, landlocked
AREA: 93,104 mi^2 (241,139 km^2)
POPULATION: 16,725,000 (URBAN: 10%)
LITERACY: 52%
CAPITAL: Kampala, 460,000
GOVERNMENT: Republic
LANGUAGES: English, Luganda, Swahili, indigenous
ETHNIC GROUPS: Ganda, Nkole, Gisu, Soga, Turkana, Chiga, Lango, Acholi
RELIGIONS: Roman Catholic 33%, Protestant 33%, Muslim 16%, indigenous

CURRENCY: Shilling
TEL. AREA CODE: 256

UNION OF SOVIET SOCIALIST REPUBLICS (Sovetskiy Soyuz)

LOCATION: Eastern Europe and northern Asia
AREA: 8,600,387 mi^2 (22,274,900 km^2)
POPULATION: 287,550,000 (URBAN: 66%)
LITERACY: 100%
CAPITAL: Moskva (Moscow), 8,614,000
GOVERNMENT: Federal socialist republic
LANGUAGES: Russian and other Slavic languages, various ethnic languages
ETHNIC GROUPS: Russian 52%, Ukrainian 16%, Uzbek 5%, Byelorussian 4%
RELIGIONS: Russian Orthodox 18%, Muslim 9%
CURRENCY: Ruble

UNITED ARAB EMIRATES (Al-Imārāt al-'Arabīyah al-Muttahidah)

LOCATION: Southwestern Asia
AREA: 32,278 mi^2 (83,600 km^2)
POPULATION: 2,047,000 (URBAN: 78%)
LITERACY: 68%
CAPITAL: Abū Ẓaby (Abu Dhabi), 242,975
GOVERNMENT: Federation of monarchs
LANGUAGES: Arabic, English, Farsi, Hindi, Urdu
ETHNIC GROUPS: South Asian 50%, native Emirian 19%, other Arab 23%
RELIGIONS: Muslim 89%, Christian 6%
CURRENCY: Dirham
TEL. AREA CODE: 971

UNITED KINGDOM (United Kingdom)

LOCATION: Northwestern European islands
AREA: 93,629 mi^2 (242,496 km^2)
POPULATION: 57,090,000 (URBAN: 92%)
LITERACY: 99%
CAPITAL: London, 6,851,400
GOVERNMENT: Constitutional monarchy
LANGUAGES: English, Welsh, Gaelic
ETHNIC GROUPS: English 82%, Scottish 10%, Irish 2%, Welsh 2%
RELIGIONS: Anglican 45%, Roman Catholic 9%, Presbyterian 3%, Methodist 1%
CURRENCY: Pound sterling
TEL. AREA CODE: 44

UNITED STATES (United States)

LOCATION: Central North America
AREA: 3,679,245 mi^2 (9,529,202 km^2)
POPULATION: 247,410,000 (URBAN: 74%)
LITERACY: 91%
CAPITAL: Washington, D.C., 638,432
GOVERNMENT: Federal republic
LANGUAGES: English, Spanish
ETHNIC GROUPS: White 85%, black 12%
RELIGIONS: Baptist and other Protestant 32%,
    Roman Catholic 22%, Jewish 2%
CURRENCY: Dollar
TEL. AREA CODE: 1

URUGUAY (Uruguay)

LOCATION: Eastern South America
AREA: 67,574 mi^2 (175,016 km^2)
POPULATION: 3,184,000 (URBAN: 85%)
LITERACY: 94%
CAPITAL: Montevideo, 1,247,920
GOVERNMENT: Republic
LANGUAGES: Spanish
ETHNIC GROUPS: White 88%, mestizo 8%, black
    4%
RELIGIONS: Roman Catholic 66%, Protestant 2%,
    Jewish 2%
CURRENCY: New Peso
TEL. AREA CODE: 598

VANUATU (Vanuatu)

LOCATION: South Pacific islands
AREA: 4,706 mi^2 (12,189 km^2)
POPULATION: 155,000 (URBAN: 25%)
LITERACY: 20%
CAPITAL: Port-Vila, 13,067
GOVERNMENT: Republic
LANGUAGES: Bislama, English, French
ETHNIC GROUPS: Ni-Vanuatu 94%, European 2%,
    other Pacific Islander 1%
RELIGIONS: Christian
CURRENCY: Vatu

VATICAN CITY (Città del Vaticano)

LOCATION: Southern Europe, landlocked (within the
    city of Rome, Italy)
AREA: 0.2 mi^2 (0.4 km^2)
POPULATION: 800 (URBAN: 100%)
LITERACY: 100%
CAPITAL: Vatican City, 700
GOVERNMENT: Ecclesiastical city-state
LANGUAGES: Italian, Latin
ETHNIC GROUPS: Italian, Swiss
RELIGIONS: Roman Catholic
CURRENCY: Italian lira
TEL. AREA CODE: 39

VENEZUELA (Venezuela)

LOCATION: Northern South America
AREA: 352,145 mi^2 (912,050 km^2)
POPULATION: 19,010,000 (URBAN: 87%)
LITERACY: 84%
CAPITAL: Caracas, 3,041,000
GOVERNMENT: Federal republic
LANGUAGES: Spanish, indigenous
ETHNIC GROUPS: Mestizo 67%, white 21%, black
    10%, Indian 2%
RELIGIONS: Roman Catholic 96%, Protestant 2%
CURRENCY: Bolivar
TEL. AREA CODE: 58

VIETNAM (Viet Nam)

LOCATION: Southeastern Asia
AREA: 127,242 mi^2 (329,556 km^2)
POPULATION: 66,030,000 (URBAN. 20%)
LITERACY: 84%
CAPITAL: Ha-noi, 819,913
GOVERNMENT: Socialist republic
LANGUAGES: Vietnamese, French, Chinese, English,
    Khmer, indigenous
ETHNIC GROUPS: Vietnamese 85-90%, Chinese 3%
RELIGIONS: Buddhist, Confucian, Taoist, Roman
    Catholic, indigenous, Muslim
CURRENCY: Dong

VIRGIN ISLANDS (U.S.) (Virgin Islands (U.S.))

LOCATION: Caribbean islands
AREA: 133 mi^2 (344 km^2)
POPULATION: 106,000 (URBAN: 47%)
LITERACY: 90%
CAPITAL: Charlotte Amalie, 11,842
GOVERNMENT: Unincorporated territory (U.S.)
LANGUAGES: English, Spanish, Creole
ETHNIC GROUPS: West Indian 74%, American 13%,
    Puerto Rican 5%
RELIGIONS: Baptist 42%, Roman Catholic 34%,
    Anglican 17%
CURRENCY: U.S. dollar

VIRGIN ISLANDS, BRITISH (British Virgin Islands)

LOCATION: Caribbean islands
AREA: 59 mi^2 (153 km^2)
POPULATION: 13,000 (URBAN: 12%)
LITERACY: 98%
CAPITAL: Road Town, 2,479
GOVERNMENT: Dependent territory (U.K.)
LANGUAGES: English
ETHNIC GROUPS: Black 90%
RELIGIONS: Methodist, Anglican, Church of God
CURRENCY: U.S. dollar
TEL. AREA CODE: 809

*WESTERN SAMOA (Western Samoa (English) /
Samoa i Sisifo (Samoan))*

LOCATION: South Pacific islands
AREA: 1,097 mi^2 (2,842 km^2)
POPULATION: 180,000 (URBAN: 22%)
LITERACY: 98%
CAPITAL: Apia, 33,170
GOVERNMENT: Constitutional monarchy
LANGUAGES: English, Samoan
ETHNIC GROUPS: Samoan, mixed European and Polynesian
RELIGIONS: Christian (Congregational, Roman Catholic, Methodist, others) 97%
CURRENCY: Tala

YEMEN (Al-Yaman)

LOCATION: Southwestern Asia
AREA: 75,290 mi^2 (195,000 km^2)
POPULATION: 10,110,000 (URBAN: 20%)
LITERACY: 13%
CAPITAL: San'ā', 277,818
GOVERNMENT: Islamic republic
LANGUAGES: Arabic
ETHNIC GROUPS: Arab 90%, Afro-Arab 10%
RELIGIONS: Muslim 100%
CURRENCY: Riyal
TEL. AREA CODE: 967

*YEMEN, PEOPLE'S DEMOCRATIC REPUBLIC
OF (Jumhūrīyat al-Yaman ad-Dīmuqrātīyah ash-
Sha'bīyah)*

LOCATION: Southwestern Asia
AREA: 130,066 mi^2 (336,869 km^2)
POPULATION: 2,551,000 (URBAN: 40%)
LITERACY: 27%
CAPITAL: Aden, 176,100
GOVERNMENT: Socialist republic
LANGUAGES: Arabic
ETHNIC GROUPS: Arab
RELIGIONS: Sunni Muslim, Christian, Hindu
CURRENCY: Dinar

YUGOSLAVIA (Jugoslavija)

LOCATION: Eastern Europe
AREA: 98,766 mi^2 (255,804 km^2)
POPULATION: 23,970,000 (URBAN: 46%)
LITERACY: 84%
CAPITAL: Beograd (Belgrade), 936,200
GOVERNMENT: Federal socialist republic
LANGUAGES: Macedonian, Serbo-Croatian, Slovene, Albanian, Hungarian
ETHNIC GROUPS: Serbian 36%, Croatian 20%, Bosnian 9%, Slovene 8%, Albanian 8%, Macedonian 6%
RELIGIONS: Eastern Orthodox 50%, Roman Catholic 30%, Muslim 10%, Protestant 1%
CURRENCY: Dinar
TEL. AREA CODE: 38

ZAIRE (Zaïre)

LOCATION: Central Africa
AREA: 905,568 mi^2 (2,345,409 km^2)
POPULATION: 33,795,000 (URBAN: 37%)
LITERACY: 46%
CAPITAL: Kinshasa, 2,653,558
GOVERNMENT: Republic
LANGUAGES: French, Kikongo, Lingala, Swahili, Tshiluba
ETHNIC GROUPS: Mongo, Luba, Kongo, Mangbetu-Azande, others
RELIGIONS: Roman Catholic 50%, Protestant 20%, Kimbanguist 10%, Muslim 10%
CURRENCY: Zaire
TEL. AREA CODE: 243

ZAMBIA (Zambia)

LOCATION: Southern Africa, landlocked
AREA: 290,586 mi^2 (752,614 km^2)
POPULATION: 7,682,000 (URBAN: 50%)
LITERACY: 52%
CAPITAL: Lusaka, 535,830
GOVERNMENT: Republic
LANGUAGES: English, Bemba, Nyanja, Tonga, indigenous
ETHNIC GROUPS: African 99%, European 1%
RELIGIONS: Christian 50-75%, indigenous 20-45%, Muslim and Hindu 1%
CURRENCY: Kwacha
TEL. AREA CODE: 260

ZIMBABWE (Zimbabwe)

LOCATION: Southern Africa, landlocked
AREA: 150,873 mi^2 (390,759 km^2)
POPULATION: 9,003,000 (URBAN: 25%)
LITERACY: 55%
CAPITAL: Harare, 656,011
GOVERNMENT: Republic
LANGUAGES: English, ChiShona, SiNdebele
ETHNIC GROUPS: Shona 71%, Ndebele 16%, white 1%
RELIGIONS: Indigenous, Christian (Anglican, Roman Catholic, and others)
CURRENCY: Dollar
TEL. AREA CODE: 263

THE CONTINENTS

Continent	Area	Estimated Population	Population Density	Mean Elevation	Highest Elevation	Lowest Elevation
Africa	11,700,000 sq. mi. (30,300,000 sq. km.)	642,100,000	55/sq. mi. (22/sq. km.)	1,900 ft. (600 m.)	Kilimanjaro, Tanzania, 19,341 ft. (5,895 m.)	Lac Assal, Djibouti, -502 ft. (-153 m.)
Antarctica	5,400,000 sq. mi. (14,000,000 sq. km.)	. . .	. . .	6,000 ft. (1,800 m.)	Vinson Massif, 16,864 ft. (5,140 m.)	Sea level
Asia	17,400,000 sq. mi. (45,000,000 sq. km.)	3,130,600,000	180/sq. mi. (70/sq. km.)	3,000 ft. (900 m.)	Mt. Everest, China (Tibet)-Nepal, 29,028 ft. (8,848 m.)	Dead Sea, Israel-Jordan, -1,299 ft. (-396 m.)
Australia	2,966,155 sq. mi. (7,682,300 sq. km.)	16,955,000	5.7/sq. mi. (2.2/sq. km.)	1,000 ft. (300 m.)	Mt. Kosciusko, New South Wales, 7,310 ft. (2,228 m.)	Lake Eyre, South Australia, -52 ft. (-16 m.)
Europe	3,800,000 sq. mi. (9,900,000 sq. km.)	685,400,000	180/sq. mi. (69/sq. km.)	1,000 ft. (300 m.)	Gora El'brus, U.S.S.R., 18,481 ft. (5,633 m.)	Caspian Sea, U.S.S.R., -92 ft. (-28 m.)
North America	9,400,000 sq. mi. (24,400,000 sq. km.)	420,100,000	45/sq. mi. (17/sq. km.)	2,000 ft. (600 m.)	Mt. McKinley, U.S. (Alaska), 20,320 ft. (6,194 m.)	Death Valley, U.S. (Calif.), -282 ft. (-86 m.)
Oceania, incl. Australia	3,300,000 sq. mi. (8,500,000 sq. km.)	26,300,000	8.0/sq. mi. (3.1/sq. km.)	. . .	Mt. Wilhelm, Papua New Guinea, 14,793 ft. (4,509 m.)	Lake Eyre, South Australia, -52 ft. (-16 m.)
South America	6,900,000 sq. mi. (17,800,000 sq. km.)	287,500,000	42/sq. mi. (16/sq. km.)	1,800 ft. (550 m.)	Cerro Aconcagua, Argentina, 22,831 ft. (6,959 m.)	Salinas Chicas, Argentina, -138 ft. (-42 m.)
WORLD	57,900,000 sq. mi. (149,900,000 sq. km.)	5,192,000,000	90/sq. mi. (35/sq. km.)	. . .	Mt. Everest, China (Tibet)-Nepal, 29,028 ft. (8,843 m.)	Dead Sea, Israel-Jordan, -1,299 ft. (-396m.)

Principal Mountains

Mountains	Location	Feet	Meters
Aconcagua, Cerro	Argentina	22,831	6,959
Adams, Mt.	U.S.	12,276	3,742
Annapurna	Nepal	26,503	8,078
Apo, Mt.	Philippines	9,692	2,954
Barú, Volcán	Panama	11,401	3,475
Blanc, Mont	France-Italy	15,771	4,807
Bolívar, Pico	Venezuela	16,411	5,002
Boundary Pk.	U.S.	13,143	4,006
Büyük Aği Daği (Mt. Ararat)	Turkey	17,011	5,185
Cameroun, Mont	Cameroon	13,353	4,070
Chimborazo	Ecuador	20,702	6,310
Chirripó, Cerro	Costa Rica	12,530	3,819
Citlaltépetl, Volcán	Mexico	18,701	5,700
Columbia, Mt.	Canada	12,293	3,747
Cook, Mt.	New Zealand	12,349	3,764
Cristóbal Colón, Pico	Colombia	18,947	5,775
Dhaulāgiri	Nepal	26,811	8,172
Dimlang	Nigeria	6,699	2,042
Duarte, Pico	Dominican Republic	10,417	3,175
Dufour Spitze	Italy-Switzerland	15,203	4,634
Elbert, Mt.	U.S.	14,433	4,399
El'brus, Gora	U.S.S.R.	18,481	5,633
Etna, Monte	Italy	10,902	3,323
Everest, Mt.	China-Nepal	29,028	8,848
Fuji-san	Japan	12,388	3,776
Gannett Pk.	U.S.	13,804	4,207
Glittertinden	Norway	8,110	2,472
Grand Teton	U.S.	13,770	4,197
Grossglockner	Austria	12,457	3,797
Guadalupe Pk.	U.S.	8,749	2,667
Hood, Mt.	U.S.	11,234	3,424
Huascarán, Nevado	Peru	22,205	6,768
Humphreys Pk.	U.S.	12,633	3,851
Hvannadalshnúkur	Iceland	6,952	2,119
Illimani, Nevado	Bolivia	21,004	6,402
Inthanon, Doi	Thailand	8,513	2,595
Inyangani	Zimbabwe	8,507	2,593
Jaya, Puncak	Indonesia	16,503	5,030
Jungfrau	Switzerland	13,642	4,158
K2 (Qogir Feng)	China-Pakistan	28,251	8,611
Kānchenjunga	Nepal-India	28,209	8,598
Kāmet	China-India	25,446	7,756
Katrīnah, Jabal	Egypt	8,668	2,642
Kebnekaise	Sweden	6,926	2,111
Kerinci, Gunung	Indonesia	12,467	3,800
Kilimanjaro	Tanzania	19,341	5,895
Kinabalu, Gunong	Malaysia	13,432	4,094
Kirinyaga (Mt. Kenya)	Kenya	17,057	5,199
Kommunizma, Pik	U.S.S.R.	24,590	7,495
Kosciusko, Mt.	Australia	7,310	2,228
Koussi, Emi	Chad	11,204	3,415
Kula Kangri	Bhutan	24,783	7,554
Las Minas, Cerro	Honduras	9,400	2,865
Lassen Pk.	U.S.	10,457	3,187
Logan, Mt.	Canada	19,521	5,950
Makālu	China-Nepal	27,825	8,481
Marcy, Mt.	U.S.	5,344	1,629
Margherita Pk.	Uganda-Zaire	16,762	5,109
Maromokotro	Madagascar	9,436	2,876
Matterhorn	Italy-Switzerland	14,692	4,478
Mauna Loa	U.S.	13,679	4,169
McKinley, Mt.	U.S. (Alaska)	20,320	6,194
Mitchell, Mt.	U.S.	6,684	2,037
Mogotón, Cerro	Nicaragua	6,913	2,107
Mulhacén	Spain	11,411	3,478
Nanda Devi	India	25,646	7,817
Nānga Parbat	Pakistan	26,660	8,126
Narodnaja, Gora	U.S.S.R.	6,214	1,894
Nevis, Ben	U.K.	4,406	1,343
Ojos del Salado, Nevado	Argentina-Chile	22,572	6,880
Ólimbos (Mt. Olympus)	Greece	9,570	2,917
Olympus, Mt.	U.S.	7,965	2,428
Orohena, Mt.	French Polynesia	7,333	2,235
Ossa, Mt.	Australia	5,305	1,617
Pelée, Montagne	Martinique	4,583	1,397
Pidurutalagala	Sri Lanka	8,281	2,524
Pikes Pk.	U.S.	14,110	4,301
Pobedy, pik	China-U.S.S.R.	24,406	7,439
Popocatépetl, Volcán	Mexico	17,887	5,452
Rainier, Mt.	U.S.	14,410	4,392
Ras Dashen	Ethiopia	15,157	4,620
Sajama, Nevado	Bolivia	21,463	6,540
Selle, Châine de la	Haiti	8,773	2,674
Shasta, Mt.	U.S.	14,162	4,317
Tahat	Algeria	9,852	3,003
Tajumulco, Volcán	Guatemala	13,845	4,220
Toubkal, Jbel	Morocco	13,665	4,165
Triglav	Yugoslavia	9,393	2,863
Uncompahgre Pk.	U.S.	14,309	4,361
Vesuvio	Italy	4,190	1,277
Vinson Massif	Antarctica	16,864	5,140
Washington, Mt.	U.S.	6,288	1,917
Whitney, Mt.	U.S.	14,495	4,418
Wilhelm, Mt.	Papua New Guinea	14,793	4,509
Xixabangma Mtn.	China	26,289	8,013

Oceans, Seas, and Gulfs

Name	Location	Sq. Mi.	Sq. Km.	Name	Location	Sq. Mi.	Sq. Km.
Arabian Sea	Asia-Africa	1,492,000	3,864,000	Indian Ocean	. . .	28,900,000	74,900,000
Arctic Ocean	. . .	5,400,000	14,000,000	Mediterranean Sea	. . .	967,000	2,505,000
Atlantic Ocean	. . .	31,800,000	82,400,000	Mexico, Gulf of	N.A.	596,000	1,544,000
Baltic Sea	Eur.	163,000	422,000	North Sea	Eur.	222,000	575,000
Bengal, Bay of	Asia	839,000	2,173,000	Norwegian Sea	Eur.-N.A.	597,000	1,546,000
Bering Sea	Asia-N.A.	876,000	2,269,000	Pacific Ocean	. . .	63,800,000	165,200,000
Black Sea	Eur.-Asia	178,000	461,000	Red Sea	Africa-Asia	169,000	438,000
Caribbean Sea	N.A.-S.A.	1,063,000	2,753,000	South China Sea	Asia	1,331,000	3,447,000
Greenland Sea	Eur.-N.A.	465,000	1,204,000	Yellow Sea	China-Korea	480,000	1,200,000
Hudson Bay	Canada	475,000	1,230,000				

Principal Islands

Name	Location	Sq. Mi.	Sq. Km.	Name	Location	Sq. Mi.	Sq. Km.
Baffin I.	Canada	195,928	507,451	Newfoundland	Canada	42,031	108,860
Banks I.	Canada	27,038	70,028	New Guinea	Oceania	309,000	800,000
Borneo	Asia	287,300	744,100	North I.	New Zealand	44,274	114,669
Bougainville	Papua New Guinea	3,600	9,300	Novaja Zeml'a	U.S.S.R.	31,900	82,600
Cape Breton I.	Canada	3,981	10,311	Palawan	Philippines	4,550	11,785
Corse (Corsica)	France	3,352	8,681	Panay	Philippines	4,446	11,515
Cuba	N.A.	42,800	110,800	Prince of Wales I.	Canada	12,872	33,339
Devon I.	Canada	21,331	55,247	Puerto Rico	N.A.	3,500	9,100
Ellesmere I.	Canada	75,767	196,236	Sachalin, Ostrov	U.S.S.R.	29,500	76,400
Great Britain	United Kingdom	88,795	229,978	Samar	Philippines	5,100	13,080
Greenland	N.A.	840,000	2,175,600	Sardegna (Sardinia)	Italy	9,301	24,090
Guadalcanal	Solomon Is.	2,060	5,336	Seram (Ceram)	Indonesia	45,801	118,625
Hainan Dao	China	13,100	34,000	Shikoku	Japan	7,258	18,799
Hawaii	U.S.	4,034	10,448	Sicilia (Sicily)	Italy	9,926	25,708
Hispaniola	N.A.	29,300	76,000	Somerset I.	Canada	9,570	24,786
Hokkaidō	Japan	32,245	83,515	Southampton I.	Canada	15,913	41,214
Honshū	Japan	89,176	230,966	South I.	New Zealand	57,870	149,883
Ireland	Europe	32,600	84,400	Spitsbergen	Norway	15,260	39,523
Ísland	Europe	39,800	103,000	Sri Lanka	Asia	24,900	64,600
Jamaica	N.A.	4,200	11,000	Sulawesi (Celebes)	Indonesia	73,057	189,216
Jawa (Java)	Indonesia	51,038	132,187	Sumatera (Sumatra)	Indonesia	182,860	473,606
Kípros / Kıbrıs	Asia	3,572	9,251	T'aiwan	Asia	13,900	36,000
Kodiak I.	U.S.	3,670	9,505	Tasmania	Austl.	26,200	67,800
Kríti (Crete)	Greece	3,189	8,259	Tierra del Fuego, Isla Grande de	S.A.	18,600	48,200
Kyūshū	Japan	17,129	44,363	Timor	Indonesia	5,743	14,874
Long I.	U.S.	1,377	3,566	Vancouver I.	Canada	12,079	31,285
Luzon	Philippines	40,420	104,688	Victoria I.	Canada	83,897	217,291
Madagascar	Africa	227,000	587,000	Vrangel'a, Ostrov (Wrangel I.)	U.S.S.R.	2,800	7,300
Melville I.	Canada	16,274	42,149				
Mindanao	Philippines	36,537	94,630				
Mindoro	Philippines	3,759	9,735				
Negros	Philippines	4,907	12,710				
New Britain	Papua New Guinea	14,093	36,500				
New Caledonia	Oceania	6,252	16,192				

Principal Lakes

Name	Location	Sq. Mi.	Sq. Km.
Albert, L.	Uganda-Zaire	2,160	5,594
Aral'skoje More (Aral Sea)	U.S.S.R.	24,700	64,100
Athabasca, L.	Canada	3,064	7,935
Bajkal, Ozero (L. Baikal)	U.S.S.R.	12,200	31,500
Balchaš, Ozero (L. Balkhash)	U.S.S.R.	7,100	18,300
Caspian Sea	Iran-U.S.S.R.	143,240	370,990
Chad, L.	Cameroon-Chad-Nigeria	6,300	16,300
Erie, L.	Canada-U.S.	9,910	25,667
Eyre, L.	Australia	3,700	9,500
Great Bear L.	Canada	12,095	31,326
Great Salt L.	U.S.	1,680	4,351
Great Slave L.	Canada	11,030	28,568
Huron, L.	Canada-U.S.	23,000	60,000
Mai-Ndombe, Lac	Zaire	3,100	8,000
Michigan, L.	U.S.	22,300	57,800
Nicaragua, Lago de	Nicaragua	3,150	8,158
Nyasa, L.	Malawi-Mozambique-Tanzania	11,150	28,878
Ontario, L.	Canada-U.S.	7,540	19,529
Rudolf, L.	Ethiopia-Kenya	2,473	6,405
Superior, L.	Canada-U.S.	31,700	82,100
Tanganyika. L.	Africa	12,350	31,986
Titicaca, Lago	Bolivia-Peru	3,200	8,300
Tônlé Sab	Kampuchea	2,500	6,500
Vänern	Sweden	2,156	5,584
Victoria, L.	Kenya-Tanzania-Uganda	26,820	69,463
Winnipeg, L.	Canada	9,416	24,387
Woods, Lake of the	Canada-U.S.	1,727	4,472

Principal Rivers

Name	Location	Mi.	Km.
Amazon-Ucayali	S.A.	4,000	6,400
Amur (Heilong)	Asia	2,744	4,416
Angara	Asia	1,105	1,779
Araguaia	S.A.	1,400	2,200
Arkansas	N.A.	1,459	2,348
Brahmaputra	Asia	1,770	2,849
Changjiang (Yangtze)	Asia	3,900	6,300
Churchill	N.A.	1,000	1,600
Colorado	N.A.	1,450	2,334
Columbia	N.A.	1,200	2,000
Congo (Zaïre)	Africa	2,900	4,700
Danube	Europe	1,776	2,858
Darling	Australia	864	1,390
Dnepr	Europe	1,400	2,200
Dnestr	Europe	840	1,352
Don	Europe	1,162	1,870
Euphrates (Al-Furāt)	Asia	1,510	2,430
Ganges	Asia	1,560	2,511
Grande, Rio	N.A.	1,885	3,034
Huanghe (Yellow)	Asia	3,395	5,464
Indus	Asia	1,800	2,900
Irrawaddy	Asia	1,300	2,100
Jenisej (Yenisey)	Asia	2,543	4,092
Kasai	Africa	1,338	2,153
Lena	Asia	2,700	4,400
Limpopo	Africa	1,100	1,800
Mackenzie	N.A.	2,635	4,241
Madeira	S.A.	2,013	3,240
Mekong	Asia	2,600	4,200
Mississippi	N.A.	2,348	3,779
Mississippi-Missouri	N.A.	3,740	6,019
Murray	Australia	1,566	2,520
Negro	S.A.	1,300	2,100
Niger	Africa	2,600	4,200
Nile	Africa	4,145	6,671
Ob'-Irtyš	Asia	3,362	5,410
Ohio	N.A.	981	1,579
Orange	Africa	1,300	2,100
Orinoco	S.A.	1,600	2,600
Paraguay	S.A.	1,610	2,591
Peace	N.A.	1,195	1,923
Pečora	Europe	1,124	1,809
Purus	S.A.	1,860	2,993
Red	N.A.	1,270	2,044
Rhine (Rhein)	Europe	820	1,320
Rio de la Plata-Paraná	S.A.	3,030	4,876
St. Lawrence	N.A.	800	1,300
Salween (Nu)	Asia	1,750	2,816
São Francisco	S.A.	1,988	3,199
Saskatchewan-Bow	N.A.	1,205	1,939
Snake	N.A.	1,038	1,670
Tennessee	N.A.	652	1,049
Tigris	Asia	1,180	1,899
Ural	Asia	1,509	2,428
Uruguay	S.A.	1,025	1,650
Volga	Europe	2,194	3,531
Yukon	N.A.	1,770	2,849
Zambezi	Africa	1,700	2,700

Largest Countries: Area

	Country	Sq. Mi.	Sq. Km.
1	U.S.S.R.	8,600,387	22,274,900
2	Canada	3,849,674	9,970,610
3	China	3,718,782	9,631,600
4	United States	3,679,245	9,529,202
5	Brazil	3,286,488	8,511,965
6	Australia	2,966,155	7,682,300
7	India	1,237,062	3,203,975
8	Argentina	1,073,400	2,780,092
9	Sudan	967,500	2,505,813
10	Algeria	919,595	2,381,741
11	Zaire	905,568	2,345,409
12	Saudi Arabia	864,869	2,240,000
13	Greenland	840,004	2,175,600
14	Mexico	761,605	1,972,547
15	Indonesia	741,101	1,919,443
16	Libya	679,362	1,759,540
17	Iran	636,296	1,648,000
18	Mongolia	604,250	1,565,000
19	Peru	496,225	1,285,216
20	Chad	495,755	1,284,000
21	Niger	489,191	1,267,000
22	Ethiopia	483,123	1,251,282
23	Angola	481,354	1,246,700
24	Mali	478,767	1,240,000
25	Colombia	440,831	1,141,748
26	South Africa	433,680	1,123,226
27	Bolivia	424,165	1,098,581
28	Mauritania	397,956	1,030,700
29	Egypt	386,662	1,001,450
30	Tanzania	364,900	945,087
31	Nigeria	356,669	923,768
32	Venezuela	352,145	912,050
33	Pakistan	339,732	879,902
34	Mozambique	308,642	799,379
35	Turkey	300,948	779,452
36	Chile	292,135	756,626
37	Zambia	290,586	752,614
38	Burma	261,228	676,577
39	Afghanistan	251,826	652,225
40	Somalia	246,201	637,657
41	Central African Republic	240,535	622,984
42	Madagascar	226,658	587,041
43	Kenya	224,961	582,646
44	Botswana	224,711	582,000
45	France	211,208	547,026
46	Thailand	198,115	513,115
47	Spain	194,885	504,750
48	Cameroon	183,569	475,442
49	Papua New Guinea	178,704	462,840
50	Sweden	173,732	449,964
51	Morocco	172,414	446,550
52	Iraq	169,235	438,317
53	Paraguay	157,048	406,752
54	Zimbabwe	150,873	390,759
55	Norway	149,412	386,975

Smallest Countries: Area

	Country	Sq. Km.	Sq. Mi.
1	Vatican City	0.2	0.4
2	Monaco	0.7	1.9
3	Nauru	8.1	21
4	Tuvalu	10	26
5	San Marino	24	61
6	Anguilla	35	91
7	Liechtenstein	62	160
8	Marshall Islands	70	181
9	Aruba	75	193
10	Cook Islands	91	236
11	Niue	102	263
12	St. Christopher-Nevis	104	269
13	Maldives	115	298
14	Malta	122	316
15	Grenada	133	344
16	St. Vincent and the Grenadines	150	388
17	Barbados	166	430
18	Antigua and Barbuda	171	443
19	Andorra	175	453
	Seychelles	175	453
20	Palau	196	508
21	Isle of Man	221	572
22	St. Lucia	238	616
23	Singapore	239	620
24	Bahrain	256	662
25	Tonga	270	699
26	Micronesia, Fed. States of	271	702
27	Kiribati	280	726
28	Dominica	290	752
29	Netherlands Antilles	309	800
30	Sao Tome and Principe	372	964
31	Faeroe Islands	540	1,399
32	Pacific Islands, Trust Terr. of the	721	1,868
33	Mauritius	788	2,040
34	Comoros	838	2,171
35	Luxembourg	998	2,586
36	Western Samoa	1,097	2,842
37	Cyprus, North	1,295	3,355
38	Cape Verde	1,557	4,033
39	Trinidad and Tobago	1,980	5,128
40	Brunei	2,226	5,765
41	Cyprus	2,276	5,896
42	Venda	2,654	6,875
43	Ciskei	3,008	7,790
44	Puerto Rico	3,515	9,104
45	Lebanon	4,015	10,400
46	Jamaica	4,244	10,991
47	Gambia	4,361	11,295
48	Qatar	4,416	11,437
49	Vanuatu	4,706	12,189
50	Bahamas	5,382	13,939
51	Swaziland	6,704	17,364
52	Kuwait	6,880	17,818

Largest Countries: Population

	Country	Population
1	China	1,094,700,000
2	India	825,000,000
3	U.S.S.R.	287,550,000
4	United States	247,410,000
5	Indonesia	185,860,000
6	Brazil	145,930,000
7	Japan	123,010,000
8	Nigeria	113,580,000
9	Bangladesh	111,390,000
10	Pakistan	108,990,000
11	Mexico	85,300,000
12	Vietnam	66,030,000
13	Germany, Fed. Rep. of	61,380,000
14	Philippines	60,110,000
15	Italy	57,500,000
16	United Kingdom	57,090,000
17	France	55,970,000
18	Thailand	55,375,000
19	Iran	52,760,000
20	Egypt	52,490,000
21	Turkey	51,970,000
22	Ethiopia	48,470,000
23	Korea, South	42,840,000
24	Burma	41,860,000
25	Spain	39,330,000
26	Poland	37,955,000
27	South Africa	35,480,000
28	Zaire	33,795,000
29	Argentina	32,205,000
30	Colombia	30,465,000
31	Canada	25,895,000
32	Kenya	25,825,000
33	Morocco	25,600,000
34	Sudan	24,255,000
35	Algeria	24,215,000
36	Tanzania	24,055,000
37	Yugoslavia	23,970,000
38	Romania	23,085,000
39	Korea, North	22,250,000
40	Peru	21,535,000
41	Taiwan	20,125,000
42	Venezuela	19,010,000
43	Nepal	18,415,000
44	Iraq	17,900,000
45	Mozambique	17,660,000
46	Malaysia	17,255,000
47	Australia	16,955,000
48	Sri Lanka	16,730,000
49	Uganda	16,725,000
50	German Dem. Rep.	16,582,000
51	Saudi Arabia	15,775,000
52	Czechoslovakia	15,605,000
53	Netherlands	14,815,000
54	Afghanistan	14,655,000
55	Ghana	14,575,000

Smallest Countries: Population

	Country	Population
1	Vatican City	800
2	Niue	2,400
3	Anguilla	7,000
4	Tuvalu	8,700
5	Nauru	9,000
6	Palau	15,000
7	Cook Islands	17,000
8	San Marino	24,000
9	Liechtenstein	29,000
	Monaco	29,000
10	Marshall Islands	40,000
11	St. Christopher-Nevis	47,000
12	Faeroe Islands	48,000
13	Andorra	51,000
14	Greenland	55,000
15	Isle of Man	62,000
16	Aruba	66,000
17	Kiribati	69,000
18	Seychelles	70,000
19	Antigua and Barbuda	84,000
20	Grenada	95,000
21	Dominica	100,000
	Tonga	100,000
22	Micronesia, Fed. States of	108,000
23	Sao Tome and Principe	119,000
24	St. Vincent and the Grenadines	125,000
25	St. Lucia	148,000
26	Vanuatu	155,000
27	Cyprus, North	172,000
28	Western Samoa	180,000
29	Belize	184,000
30	Pacific Islands, Trust Terr. of the	185,000
31	Netherlands Antilles	194,000
32	Maldives	209,000
33	Bahamas	243,000
34	Brunei	247,000
35	Iceland	248,000
36	Barbados	255,000
37	Solomon Islands	295,000
38	Djibouti	324,000
39	Cape Verde	359,000
40	Luxembourg	368,000
41	Malta	370,000
42	Suriname	398,000
43	Qatar	400,000
44	Comoros	436,000
45	Equatorial Guinea	438,000
46	Bahrain	458,000
47	Venda	556,000
48	Cyprus	573,000
49	Swaziland	727,000
50	Fiji	749,000

Highest Urban Population

Country	Percent Urban
1 Monaco	100%
Singapore	100%
Vatican City	100%
2 Belgium	96%
3 Kuwait	94%
4 United Kingdom	92%
5 Israel	90%
6 Iceland	89%
7 Netherlands	88%
Qatar	88%
8 Venezuela	87%
9 Australia	86%
Denmark	86%
Germany, Fed. Rep. of	86%
10 Argentina	85%
Malta	85%
Uruguay	85%
11 Chile	84%
New Zealand	84%
12 Sweden	83%
13 Bahrain	82%
14 Luxembourg	81%
15 Lebanon	80%

Lowest Urban Population

Country	Percent Urban
1 Bhutan	5%
Cape Verde	5%
2 Burundi	6%
Rwanda	6%
3 Burkina Faso	8%
Nepal	8%
4 Oman	9%
5 Solomon Islands	10%
Uganda	10%
6 Kampuchea (Cambodia)	11%
7 Bangladesh	12%
Ethiopia	12%
Malawi	12%
8 Papua New Guinea	14%
St. Vincent and the Grenadines	14%
9 Grenada	15%
10 Laos	16%
Niger	16%
Northern Mar. Islands	16%
11 Lesotho	17%
12 Mali	18%
13 Afghanistan	19%
14 Botswana	19%

Highest Life Expectancy

Country	Years M	F
1 Iceland	74	80
Japan	74	80
2 Norway	73	80
Netherlands	73	80
Switzerland	73	80
3 Faeroe Islands	73	79
Sweden	73	79
4 Israel	73	76
5 Australia	72	79
Canada	72	79
6 Denmark	72	78
7 Cyprus	72	76
Greece	72	76
8 Cuba	72	75
9 France	71	79
10 Italy	71	78
Puerto Rico	71	78
Spain	71	78
United States	71	78
11 New Zealand	71	77
United Kingdom	71	77

Lowest Life Expectancy

Country	Years M	F
1 Sierra Leone	33	36
2 Gambia	34	37
3 Afghanistan	37	37
4 Guinea	39	42
5 Ethiopia	39	43
Somalia	39	43
6 Angola	40	44
Mali	40	44
7 Niger	41	44
8 Central African Rep.	41	45
Chad	41	45
Guinea-Bissau	41	45
9 Benin	42	46
Equatorial Guinea	42	46
Mauritania	42	46
10 Kampuchea (Cambodia)	42	45
Senegal	42	45
11 Sao Tome and Principe	43	45
12 Malawi	44	46
Mozambique	44	46
13 Burkina Faso	44	47

Highest Literacy

Country	Percent Literate
1 Andorra	100%
Iceland	100%
Liechtenstein	100%
Tonga	100%
U.S.S.R.	100%
Vatican City	100%
2 Australia	99%
Austria	99%
Barbados	99%
Belgium	99%
Czechoslovakia	99%
Denmark	99%
Faeroe Islands	99%
Finland	99%
France	99%
German Democratic Republic	99%
Germany, Federal Republic of	99%
Greenland	99%
Hungary	99%
Japan	99%
Luxembourg	99%
Monaco	99%
Nauru	99%
Netherlands	99%
Norway	99%
Poland	99%
Sweden	99%
Switzerland	99%
United Kingdom	99%

Lowest Literacy

Country	Percent Literate
1 Ethiopia	4%
2 Bhutan	5%
3 Burkina Faso	9%
Mali	9%
5 Niger	10%
6 Gambia	12%
7 Yemen	13%
8 Comoros	15%
Sierra Leone	15%
9 Togo	16%
10 Benin	17%
Chad	17%
Mauritania	17%
11 Central African Republic	18%
12 Afghanistan	20%
Angola	20%
Djibouti	20%
Guinea-Bissau	20%
Oman	20%
Vanuatu	20%
13 Haiti	21%
Liberia	21%
Morocco	21%
Nepal	21%
14 Senegal	22%
15 Bangladesh	24%
16 Burundi	25%
Ivory Coast	25%
Malawi	25%

Highest GDP U.S. $ / Capita

Country	GDP/ Capita
1 Liechtenstein	26,296
2 Qatar	23,956
3 United Arab Emirates	23,242
4 Nauru	*19,512*
5 Brunei	16,293
6 United States	15,452
7 Switzerland	14,080
8 Canada	13,416
9 Norway	13,217
10 Kuwait	12,731
11 Australia	11,724
12 Sweden	11,356
13 Iceland	10,953
14 Bahrain	10,852
15 Denmark	10,691
16 Saudi Arabia	10,595
17 German Dem. Republic	*10,486*
18 Finland	10,424
19 Germany, Fed. Republic of	9,977
20 Japan	9,717

Lowest GDP U.S. $ / Capita

Country	GDP/ Capita
1 Chad	135
2 Mali	140
3 Mozambique	142
4 Nepal	145
5 Zaire	150
6 Burkina Faso	153
Ethiopia	153
7 Bangladesh	165
8 Burma	172
9 Guinea-Bissau	184
10 Malawi	185
11 Laos	*190*
12 Equatorial Guinea	*195*
13 Bhutan	214
14 Afghanistan	*240*
15 Burundi	241
16 Madagascar	247
Tanzania	247

Figures in italics are GNP.

Introduction to the Index

This universal index includes in a single alphabetical list more than 7,000 names of features that appear on the reference maps on pages 66 through 128. Each name is followed by latitude and longitude coordinates and a page reference.

Names Local official names are used on the maps and in the index. The names are shown in full, including diacritical marks. Features that extend beyond the boundaries of one country and have no single official name are usually named in English. Many conventional English names and former names are cross-referenced to the official names. Names that appear in shortened versions on the maps due to space limitiations are spelled out in full in the index. The portions of these names omitted from the maps are enclosed in brackets—for example, Acapulco [de Juárez].

Transliteration For names in languages not written in the Roman alphabet, the locally official transliteration system has been used where one exists. Thus, names in the Soviet Union and Bulgaria have been transliterated according to the systems adopted by the academies of science of these countries. Similarly, the transliteration for mainland Chinese names follows the Pinyin system, which has been officially adopted in mainland China. For languages with no one locally accepted system, notably Arabic, transliteration closely follows a system adopted by the United States Board on Geographic Names.

Abbreviation and Capitalization Abbreviations of names on the maps have been standardized as much as possible. Names that are abbreviated on the maps are generally spelled out in full in the index. Periods are used after all abbreviations regardless of local practice. The abbreviation "St." is used only for "Saint". "Sankt" and other forms of this term are spelled out.

Most initial letters of names are capitalized, except for a few Dutch names, such as "'s-Gravenhage". Capitalization of noninitial words in a name generally follows local practice.

Alphabetization Names are alphabetized in the order of the letters of the English alphabet. Spanish *ll* and *ch*, for example, are not treated as distinct letters. Furthermore, diacritical marks are disregarded in alphabetization—German or Scandinavian *ä* or *ö* are treated as *a* or *o*.

The names of physical features may appear inverted, since they are always alphabetized under the proper, not the generic, part of the name, thus: "Gibraltar, Strait of ⥜". Otherwise every entry, whether consisting of one word or more, is alphabetized as a single continuous entity. "La Habana," for example, appears after "Lagunillas" and before "Lahaina." Names beginning with articles (Le Havre, Den Helder, Al-Qāhirah, As-Suways) are not inverted. Names beginning "Mc" are alphabetized as though spelled "Mac," and names beginning "St.", "Ste." and "Sainte" as though spelled "Saint."

In the case of identical names, towns are listed first, then political divisions, then physical features. Entries that are completely identical (including symbols, discussed below) are distinguished by abbreviations of their official country names. The country abbreviations used for places in the United States, Canada and United Kingdom indicate the state, province or political division in which the feature is located. (See List of Abbreviations below).

Symbols City names are not followed by symbols. The names of all other features are followed by symbols that graphically represent broad categories of features, for example, ⋀ for mountain (Everest, Mount ⋀). Superior numbers indicate finer distinctions, for example, ⋀[1] for volcano (Fuji-san ⋀[1]). A complete list of symbols, including those with superior numbers, follows the List of Abbreviations.

All cross-references are indicated by the symbol →.

Page References and Geographical Coordinates The page references and geographical coordinates are found in the last three columns of each entry.

The page number generally refers to the map that shows the feature at the best scale. Countries, mountain ranges and other extensive features are usually indexed to maps that both show the features completely and also show them in their relationship to broad areas. Page references to two-page maps always refer to the left-hand page. If a page contains several maps or insets, a lowercase letter may identify the specific map or inset.

Latitude and longitude coordinates for point features, such as cities and mountain peaks, indicate the locations of the symbols. For extensive areal features, such as countries or mountain ranges, locations are given for the approximate center of the feature. Those for linear features, such as canals and rivers, are given to the mouth or terminal point.

List of Abbreviations

	LOCAL NAME	ENGLISH		LOCAL NAME	ENGLISH
Ab., Can.	Alberta	Alberta	**Alg.**	Algérie / Djazair	Algeria
Afg.	Afghānestān	Afghanistan	**Am. Sam.**	American Samoa /	American Samoa
Afr.	—	Africa		Amerika Samoa	
Ak., U.S.	Alaska	Alaska	**And.**	Andorra	Andorra
Al., U.S.	Alabama	Alabama	**Ang.**	Angola	Angola

	LOCAL NAME	ENGLISH
Anguilla	Anguilla	Anguilla
Ant.	—	Antarctica
Antig.	Antigua and Barbuda	Antigua and Barbuda
Ar., U.S.	Arkansas	Arkansas
Arc. O.	—	Arctic Ocean
Arg.	Argentina	Argentina
Ar. Su.	Al-'Arabīyah as-Su'ūdīyah	Saudi Arabia
Aruba	Aruba	Aruba
Asia	—	Asia
Atl. O.	—	Atlantic Ocean
Austl.	Australia	Australia
Az., U.S.	Arizona	Arizona
Ba.	Bahamas	Bahamas
Bahr.	Al-Bahrayn	Bahrain
Barb.	Barbados	Barbados
B.A.T.	British Antarctic Territory	British Antarctic Territory
B.C., Can.	British Columbia / Colombie-Britannique	British Columbia
Bdi.	Burundi	Burundi
Bel.	Belgique / België	Belgium
Belize	Belize	Belize
Bénin	Bénin	Benin
Ber.	Bermuda	Bermuda
Ber. S.	—	Bering Sea
B.I.O.T.	British Indian Ocean Territory	British Indian Ocean Territory
Blg.	Bâlgarija	Bulgaria
Bngl.	Bangladesh	Bangladesh
Bol.	Bolivia	Bolivia
Boph.	Bophuthatswana	Bophuthatswana
Bots.	Botswana	Botswana
Bra.	Brasil	Brazil
B.R.D.	Bundesrepublik Deutschland	Federal Republic of Germany
Bru.	Brunei	Brunei
Br. Vir. Is.	British Virgin Islands	British Virgin Islands
Burkina	Burkina Faso	Burkina Faso
Ca., U.S.	California	California
Cam.	Cameroun / Cameroon	Cameroon
Can.	Canada	Canada
Carib. S.	—	Caribbean Sea
Cay. Is.	Cayman Islands	Cayman Islands
Centraf.	République centrafricaine	Central African Republic
Cesko.	Ceskoslovensko	Czechoslovakia
Chile	Chile	Chile
Christ. I.	Christmas Island	Christmas Island
Ciskei	Ciskei	Ciskei
C. Iv.	Côte d'Ivoire	Ivory Coast
C.M.I.K.	Choson-minjujuui-inmīn-konghwaguk	North Korea
Co., U.S.	Colorado	Colorado
Cocos Is.	Cocos (Keeling) Islands	Cocos (Keeling) Islands
Col.	Colombia	Colombia
Comores	Comores / Al-Qumur	Comoros
Congo	Congo	Congo
Cook Is.	Cook Islands	Cook Islands
C.R.	Costa Rica	Costa Rica
Ct., U.S.	Connecticut	Connecticut

	LOCAL NAME	ENGLISH
Cuba	Cuba	Cuba
C.V.	Cabo Verde	Cape Verde
Dan.	Danmark	Denmark
D.C., U.S.	District of Columbia	District of Columbia
D.D.R.	Deutsche Demokratische Republik	German Democratic Republic
De., U.S.	Delaware	Delaware
Dji.	Djibouti	Djibouti
Dom.	Dominica	Dominica
D.Y.	Druk-Yul	Bhutan
Ec.	Ecuador	Ecuador
Ellás	Ellás	Greece
El Sal.	El Salvador	El Salvador
Eng., U.K.	England	England
Esp.	España	Spain
Europe	—	Europe
Falk. Is.	Falkland Islands / Islas Malvinas	Falkland Islands
Fiji	Fiji	Fiji
Fl., U.S.	Florida	Florida
Fr.	Føroyar	Faeroe Islands
Fr.	France	France
Ga., U.S.	Georgia	Georgia
Gabon	Gabon	Gabon
Gam.	Gambia	Gambia
Ghana	Ghana	Ghana
Gib.	Gibraltar	Gibraltar
Gren.	Grenada	Grenada
Guad.	Guadeloupe	Guadeloupe
Guam	Guam	Guam
Guat.	Guatemala	Guatemala
Guernsey	Guernsey	Guernsey
Gui.-B.	Guiné-Bissau	Guinea-Bissau
Gui. Ecu.	Guinea Ecuatorial	Equatorial Guinea
Guinée	Guinée	Guinea
Guy.	Guyana	Guyana
Guy. fr.	Guyane francaise	French Guiana
Hai.	Haiti	Haiti
Hi., U.S.	Hawaii	Hawaii
H.K.	Hong Kong	Hong Kong
Hond.	Honduras	Honduras
Ia., U.S.	Iowa	Iowa
Id., U.S.	Idaho	Idaho
I.I.A.	Ittihād al-Imārāt al-'Arabīyah	United Arab Emirates
Il., U.S.	Illinois	Illinois
In., U.S.	Indiana	Indiana
India	India / Bharat	India
Ind. O.	—	Indian Ocean
Indon.	Indonesia	Indonesia
I. of Man	Isle of Man	Isle of Man
Iran	Īrān	Iran
Iraq	Al-'Irāq	Iraq
Ire.	Ireland / Éire	Ireland
Ísland	Ísland	Iceland
Isr. Occ.	—	Israeli Occupied Areas
It.	Italia	Italy
Ityo.	Ityopiya	Ethiopia
Jam.	Jamaica	Jamaica
Jersey	Jersey	Jersey
Jugo.	Jugoslavija	Yugoslavia
J.Y.D.S.	Jumhūrīyat al-Yaman ad-Dīmuqrāṭīyah ash-Sha'bīyah	People's Democratic Republic of Yemen

	LOCAL NAME	ENGLISH		LOCAL NAME	ENGLISH
Kal. Nun.	Kalaallit Nunaat / Grønland	Greenland	Ned. Ant.	Nederlandse Antillen	Netherlands Antilles
Kam.	Kâmpuchéa Prâchéathıpâtèyy	Kampuchea (Cambodia)	Nepal	Nepāl	Nepal
Kenya	Kenya	Kenya	Nf., Can.	Newfoundland / Terre-Neuve	Newfoundland
Kıbrıs	Kuzey Kıbrıs	North Cyprus (Turkish Republic of Northern Cyprus)	N.H., U.S.	New Hampshire	New Hampshire
			Nic.	Nicaragua	Nicaragua
			Nig.	Nigeria	Nigeria
			Niger	Niger	Niger
			Nihon	Nihon	Japan
Kípros	Kípros / Kıbrıs	Cyprus	N. Ire., U.K.	Northern Ireland	Northern Ireland
Kiribati	Kiribati	Kiribati	Niue	Niue	Niue
Ks., U.S.	Kansas	Kansas	N.J., U.S.	New Jersey	New Jersey
Kuwayt	Al-Kuwayt	Kuwait	N.M., U.S.	New Mexico	New Mexico
Ky., U.S.	Kentucky	Kentucky	Nor.	Norge	Norway
La., U.S.	Louisiana	Louisiana	Norf. I.	Norfolk Island	Norfolk Island
Lao	Lao	Laos	N.S., Can.	Nova Scotia / Nouvelle-Écosse	Nova Scotia
Leso.	Lesotho	Lesotho			
Liber.	Liberia	Liberia	N.T., Can.	Northwest Territories / Territoires du Nord-Ouest	Northwest Territories
Lıbiya	Lĩbiyā	Libya			
Liech.	Liechtenstein	Liechtenstein			
Lubnan	Al-Lubnān	Lebanon			
Lux.	Luxembourg	Luxembourg	Nv., U.S.	Nevada	Nevada
Ma., U.S.	Massachusetts	Massachusetts	N.Y., U.S.	New York	New York
Macau	Macau	Macau	N.Z.	New Zealand	New Zealand
Madag.	Madagasikara / Madagascar	Madagascar	Oc.	—	Oceania
			Oh., U.S.	Ohio	Ohio
Magreb	Al-Magreb	Morocco	Ok., U.S.	Oklahoma	Oklahoma
Magy.	Magyarország	Hungary	On., Can.	Ontario	Ontario
Malaŵi	Malaŵi	Malawi	Or., U.S.	Oregon	Oregon
Malay.	Malaysia	Malaysia	Öst.	Österreich	Austria
Mald.	Maldives	Maldives	Pa., U.S.	Pennsylvania	Pennsylvania
Mali	Mali	Mali	Pac. O.	—	Pacific Ocean
Malta	Malta	Malta	Pak.	Pākistān	Pakistan
Mart.	Martinique	Martinique	Pan.	Panamá	Panama
Maur.	Mauritanie / Mūrĩtāniyā	Mauritania	Pap. N. Gui.	Papua New Guinea	Papua New Guinea
			Para.	Paraguay	Paraguay
Maus.	Mauritius	Mauritius	P.E., Can.	Prince Edward Island / Île-du-Prince-Édouard	Prince Edward Island
Mayotte	Mayotte	Mayotte			
Mb., Can.	Manitoba	Manitoba			
Md., U.S.	Maryland	Maryland			
Me., U.S.	Maine	Maine	Perú	Perú	Peru
Medit. S.	—	Mediterranean Sea	Pil.	Pilipinas	Philippines
Méx.	México	Mexico	Pit.	Pitcairn	Pitcairn
Mi., U.S.	Michigan	Michigan	Pol.	Polska	Poland
Mid. Is.	Midway Islands	Midway Islands	Poly. fr.	Polynésie française	French Polynesia
Misr	Mişr	Egypt	Port.	Portugal	Portugal
Mn., U.S.	Minnesota	Minnesota	P.Q., Can.	Québec	Quebec
Mo., U.S.	Missouri	Missouri	P.R.	Puerto Rico	Puerto Rico
Moc.	Moçambique	Mozambique	P.S.N.Á.	Plazas de Soberanía en el Norte de África	Spanish North Africa
Monaco	Monaco	Monaco			
Mong.	Mongol Ard Uls	Mongolia			
Monts.	Montserrat	Montserrat	Qatar	Qatar	Qatar
Ms., U.S.	Mississippi	Mississippi	Rep. Dom.	República Dominicana	Dominican Republic
Mt., U.S.	Montana	Montana			
Mya.	Myanmā	Burma	Réu.	Réunion	Reunion
N.A.	—	North America	R.I., U.S.	Rhode Island	Rhode Island
Namibia	Namibia	Namibia	Rom.	Românĩa	Romania
Nauru	Nauru / Naoero	Nauru	Rw.	Rwanda	Rwanda
N.B., Can.	New Brunswick / Nouveau-Brunswick	New Brunswick	S.A.	—	South America
			S. Afr.	South Africa / Suid-Afrika	South Africa
N.C., U.S.	North Carolina	North Carolina	S.C., U.S.	South Carolina	South Carolina
N. Cal.	Nouvelle-Calédonie	New Caledonia	S. Ch. S.	—	South China Sea
N.D., U.S.	North Dakota	North Dakota	Schw.	Schweiz / Suisse / Svizzera	Switzerland
Ne., U.S.	Nebraska	Nebraska	Scot., U.K.	Scotland	Scotland
Ned.	Nederland	Netherlands	S.D., U.S.	South Dakota	South Dakota
			Sén.	Sénégal	Senegal

	LOCAL NAME	ENGLISH
Sey.	Seychelles	Seychelles
Shq.	Shqipëri	Albania
Sing.	Singapore	Singapore
Sk., Can.	Saskatchewan	Saskatchewan
S.L.	Sierra Leone	Sierra Leone
S. Lan.	Sri Lanka	Sri Lanka
S. Mar.	San Marino	San Marino
Sol. Is.	Solomon Islands	Solomon Islands
Som.	Somaliya	Somalia
S.S.S.R.	Sojuz Sovetskich Socialističeskich Respublik	Union of Soviet Socialist Republics
St. C.-N.	St. Christopher-Nevis	St. Christopher-Nevis
St. Hel.	St. Helena	St. Helena
St. Luc.	St. Lucia	St. Lucia
S. Tom./P.	São Tomé e Príncipe	Sao Tome and Principe
St. P./M.	St.-Pierre-et-Miquelon	St. Pierre and Miquelon
St. Vin.	St. Vincent and the Grenadines	St. Vincent and the Grenadines
Sud.	As-Sūdān	Sudan
Suomi	Suomi / Finland	Finland
Sur.	Suriname	Suriname
Surıy.	As-Sūrīyah	Syria
Sve.	Sverige	Sweden
Swaz.	Swaziland	Swaziland
T.a.a.f.	Terres australes et antarctiques francaises	French Southern and Antarctic Territories
Taehan	Taehan-min'guk	South Korea
T'aiwan	T'aiwan	Taiwan
Tan.	Tanzania	Tanzania
Tchad	Tchad	Chad
T./C. Is.	Turks and Caicos Islands	Turks and Caicos Islands
Thai	Prathet Thai	Thailand
Tn., U.S.	Tennessee	Tennessee
Togo	Togo	Togo
Tok.	Tokelau	Tokelau
Tonga	Tonga	Tonga
Transkei	Transkei	Transkei

	LOCAL NAME	ENGLISH
Trin.	Trinidad and Tobago	Trinidad and Tobago
T.T.P.I.	Trust Territory of the Pacific Islands	Trust Territory of the Pacific Islands
Tun.	Tunisie / Tunis	Tunisia
Tur.	Türkiye	Turkey
Tuvalu	Tuvalu	Tuvalu
Tx., U.S.	Texas	Texas
Ug.	Uganda	Uganda
U.K.	United Kingdom	United Kingdom
'Uman	'Umān	Oman
Ur.	Uruguay	Uruguay
Urd.	Al-Urdunn	Jordan
U.S.	United States	United States
Ut., U.S.	Utah	Utah
Va., U.S.	Virginia	Virginia
Vanuatu	Vanuatu	Vanuatu
Vat.	Città del Vaticano	Vatican City
Ven.	Venezuela	Venezuela
Venda	Venda	Venda
Viet.	Viet-nam	Vietnam
Vir. Is., U.S.	Virgin Islands (U.S.)	Virgin Islands (U.S.)
Vt., U.S.	Vermont	Vermont
Wa., U.S.	Washington	Washington
Wake I.	Wake Island	Wake Island
Wales, U.K.	Wales	Wales
Wal./F.	Wallis et Futuna	Wallis and Futuna
Wi., U.S.	Wisconsin	Wisconsin
W. Sah.	—	Western Sahara
W. Sam.	Western Samoa / Samoa i Sisifo	Western Samoa
W.V., U.S.	West Virginia	West Virginia
Wy., U.S.	Wyoming	Wyoming
Yaman	Al-Yaman	Yemen
Yis.	Yisra'el / Isrā'īl	Israel
Yk., Can.	Yukon Territory	Yukon
Zaire	Zaire	Zaire
Zam.	Zambia	Zambia
Zhg.	Zhongguo	China
Zimb.	Zimbabwe	Zimbabwe

Key to Symbols

∧	**Mountain**	‖	**Islands**
∧¹	Volcano	±	**Other Topographic Features**
∧²	Hill		
⋇	**Mountains**	±¹	Continent
⋇¹	Plateau	±²	Coast, Beach
⋇²	Hills	±³	Isthmus
)(	**Pass**	±⁴	Cliff
		±⁶	Crater
∨	**Valley, Canyon**	±⁸	Dunes
		±⁹	Lava Flow
⋍	**Plain**		
⋍¹	Basin	∽	**River**
⋍²	Delta	≖	**Canal**
⋎	**Cape**	∟	**Waterfall, Rapids**
⋎¹	Peninsula	⊔	**Strait**
I	**Island**	⊂	**Bay, Gulf**
I¹	Atoll		

⊂¹	Estuary	▯³	State, Canton, Republic
⊂²	Fjord		
⊂³	Bight	▯⁴	Province, Region, Oblast
⊜	**Lake, Lakes**	▯⁵	Department, District, Prefecture
⊜¹	Reservoir		
⊞	**Swamp**	▯⁸	Miscellaneous
⊠	**Ice Features, Glacier**	▯⁹	Historical
⊤	**Other Hydrographic Features**	♦	**Recreational Site**
⊤¹	Ocean	✦	**Miscellaneous**
⊤²	Sea	✦¹	Region
⊤⁴	Oasis, Well, Spring	✦²	Desert
▯	**Political Unit**	✦³	Forest, Moor
▯¹	Independent Nation	✦⁴	Reserve, Reservation
▯²	Dependency	✦⁶	Dam
		✦⁸	Neighborhood

Index

Name	Page No.	Lat.	Long.
Anina	82	45.05N	21.51 E
Ankara	70	39.56N	32.52 E
Annaba (Bône)	88	36.54N	7.46 E
An-Nafūd ◆²	93	28.30N	41.00 E
An-Najaf	92	31.59N	44.20 E
Annapolis	124	38.58N	76.29W
Annapurna ʌ	96	28.34N	83.50 E
Ann Arbor	124	42.16N	83.43W
Annecy	76	45.54N	6.07 E
An-Nuhūd	88	12.42N	28.26 E
Anqing	98	30.31N	117.02 E
Ansbach	74	49.17N	10.34 E
Anshan	98	41.08N	122.59 E
Antalaha	90	14.53S	50.16 E
Antalya	70	36.53N	30 42 E
Antananarivo	90	18.55S	47.31 E
Antarctica ±¹	69	90.00S	0.00
Antarctic Peninsula ≻¹	69	69.30S	65.00W
Antequera	78	37.01N	4.33W
Anticosti, Île d' ı	122	49.30N	63.00W
Antigua and Barbuda □¹	114	17.03N	61.48W
Antofagasta	118	23.39S	70.24W
António Enes	90	16.14S	39.54 E
Antsirabe	90	19.51S	47.02 E
Antsiranana	90	12.16S	49.17 E
Antwerp → Antwerpen	74	51.13N	4.25 E
Antwerpen (Anvers)	74	51.13N	4.25 E
Anvers → Antwerpen	74	51.13N	4.25 E
Aomori	100	40.49N	140.45 E
Aôral, Phnum ʌ	104	12.02N	104.10 E
Aosta	80	45.44N	7.20 E
Aoukâr ◆¹	88	18.00N	9.30W
Apatzingán [de la Constitución]	112	19.05N	102.21W
Apeldoorn	74	52.13N	5.58 E
Apia	111e	13.50S	171.44W
Apo, Mount ʌ	102	6.59N	125.16 E
Apostólou Andréa, Akrotírion ≻	93	35.42N	34.35 E
Appalachian Mountains ◄	122	41.00N	77.00W
Appennino (Apennines) ◄	80	43.00N	13.00 E
Appennino Abruzzese ◄	80	42.00N	14.00 E
Appennino Calabrese ◄	80	39.00N	16.30 E
Appennino Ligure ◄	80	44.30N	9.00 E
Appennino Tosco-Emiliano ◄	80	44.00N	11.30 E
Appennino Umbro-Marchigiano ◄	80	43.00N	13.00 E
Apure ≏	114	7.37N	66.25W
Aqaba, Gulf of c	93	29.00N	34.40 E
'Arab, Bahr al- ≏	88	9.02N	29.28 E
Arabian Sea ⊤²	66	15.00N	65.00 E
Aracaju	116	10.55S	37.04W
Araçatuba	116	21.12S	50.25W
Arad	82	46.11N	21.20 E
Arafura Sea ⊤²	102	11.00S	135.00 E
Arago, Cape ≻	126	43.18N	124.25W
Aragón □⁹	78	41.00N	1.00W
Aragón ≏	78	42.13N	1.44W
Araguaia ≏	116	5.21S	48.41W
Araguari	119	18.38S	48.11W
Árakhthos ≏	82	39.01N	21.03 E
Aral'skoje More ⊤²	70	45.00N	59.00 E
Aran Islands ıı	72	53.07N	9.43W
Aranjuez	78	40.02N	3.36W
Aranyaprathet	104	13.41N	102.30 E
Araraquara	116	21.47S	48.10W
Araxá	119	19.35S	46.55W
Arbroath	72	56.34N	2.35W
Arc Dome ʌ	126	38.51N	117.22W
Archangel'sk (Archangel)	70	64.34N	40.32 E
Arctic Bay	120	73.02N	85.11W
Arctic Ocean ⊤¹	68	85.00N	170.00 E
Ardennes ◆¹	76	50.10N	5.45 E
Arecibo	114	18.28N	66.43W
Arendal	73	58.27N	8.48 E
Arequipa	116	16.24S	71.33W
Arezzo	80	43.25N	11.53 E
Argentina □¹	118	34.00S	64.00W
Argonne ◆¹	76	49.30N	5.00 E
Árgos	82	37.39N	22.44 E
Arguello, Point ≻	126	34.35N	120.39W
Argun' (Ergu'nahe) ≏	98	53.20N	121.28 E
Århus	73	56.09N	10.13 E
Arica, Chile	116	18.29S	70.20W
Arica, Col.	116	2.08S	71.47W
'Arīsh, Wādī al- ᴠ	93	31.09N	33.49 E
Arismendi	114	8.29N	68.22W
Arizona □³	122	34.00N	112.00W
Arjona	114	10.15N	75.21W
Arkansas □³	122	34.50N	93.40W
Arkansas ≏	122	33.48N	91.04W
Arm'anskaja Sovetskaja Socialistíčeskaja Respublika □³	70	40.00N	45.00 E
Armant	93	25.37N	32.32 E
Armavir	70	45.00N	41.08 E
Armentières	76	50.41N	2.53 E
Arnhem	74	51.59N	5.55 E
Arnhem Land ◆¹	106	13.10S	134.30 E
Arran, Island of ı	72	55.35N	5.15W
Arras	76	50.17N	2.47 E
Ar-Riyāḍ (Riyadh)	92	24.38N	46.43 E
Ar-Rub' al-Khālī ◆²	92	20.00N	51.00 E
Artemisa	114	22.49N	82.46W
Artesia	112	32.50N	104.24W
Aru, Kepulauan ıı	102	6.00S	134.30 E
Aruba □²	114	12.30N	69.58W
Arunachal Pradesh □⁸	96	28.30N	95.00 E
Arusha	90	3.22S	36.41 E
Aruwimi ≏	90	1.13N	23.36 E
Asahikawa	100a	43.46N	142.22 E
Asansol	96	23.41N	86.59 E
Asbestos	124	45.46N	71.57W
Ascensión	112	31.06N	107.59W
Aseb	92	13.00N	42.45 E
Asenovgrad	82	42.01N	24.52 E
Ashburton	110	43.55S	171.45 E
Asheville	122	35.36N	82.33W
Ashikaga	100	36.20N	139.27 E
Ashland, Ky., U.S.	124	38.28N	82.38W
Ashland, N.H., U.S.	124	43.41N	71.37W
Ashland, Or., U.S.	126	42.11N	122.42W
Ashland, Wi., U.S.	122	46.35N	90.53W
Ashtabula	124	41.51N	80.47W
Ashville	124	39.42N	82.57W
Asia ±¹	66	50.00N	100.00 E
Asia Minor ◆¹	70	39.00N	32.00 E
Askham	90	26.59S	20.47 E
Asmera	92	15.20N	38.53 E
Aspiring, Mount ʌ	110	44.23S	168.44 E
Assam □³	96	26.00N	92.00 E
Assen	74	52.59N	6:34 E
Assiniboine, Mount ʌ	120	50.52N	115.39W
As-Sulaymānīyah	70	35.33N	45.26 E
As-Suwaydā'	93	32.42N	36.34 E
As-Suways (Suez)	88	29.58N	32.33 E
Asti	80	44.54N	8.12 E
Astrachan'	70	46.21N	48.03 E
Astrolabe, Cape ≻	111a	8.20S	160.34 E
Asunción	118	25.16S	57.40W
Aswān	88	24.05N	32.53 E
Aswān High Dam ◆⁶	92	24.05N	32.53 E
Asyūṭ	88	27.11N	31.11 E

Name	Page No.	Lat.	Long.
Atacama, Desierto de ← ²	116	20.00S	69.15W
Atar	88	20.31N	13.03W
Atbarah	88	17.42N	33.59 E
Atbasar	86	51.48N	68.20 E
Athabasca	120	54.43N	113.17W
Athabasca, Lake ⊜	120	59.07N	110.00W
Athens			
→ Athínai, Ellás	82	37.58N	23.43 E
Athens, Ga., U.S.	122	33.57N	83.22W
Athens, Oh., U.S.	124	39.19N	82.06W
Athens, Pa., U.S.	124	41.57N	76.31W
Athínai (Athens)	82	37.58N	23.43 E
Athlone	72	53.25N	7.56W
Atikokan	120	48.45N	91.37W
Atikonak Lake ⊜	120	52.40N	64.30W
Atka Island I	128	52.15N	174.30W
Atlanta	122	33.44N	84.23W
Atlantic City	124	39.21N	74.25W
Atlantic Ocean ▼ ¹	66	0.00	25.00W
Atlas Mountains ⋌	88	33.00N	2.00W
Atlas Saharien ⋌	88	33.25N	1.20 E
Atotonilco el Alto	112	20.33N	102.31W
Atrato ≏	114	8.17N	76.58W
Attawapiskat	120	52.55N	82.26W
Attu Island I	128	52.55N	173.00 E
Auburn	124	42.55N	76.33W
Auckland	110	36.52S	174.46 E
Augsburg	74	48.23N	10.53 E
Augusta, Austl.	106	34.19S	115.10 E
Augusta, It.	80	37.13N	15.13 E
Augusta, Ga., U.S.	122	33.28N	82.01W
Augusta, Ky., U.S.	124	38.46N	84.00W
Augusta, Me., U.S.	124	44.18N	69.46W
Augustus, Mount ⋀	106	24.20S	116.50 E
Aurillac	76	44.56N	2.26 E
Aurora	124	44.00N	79.28W
Aus	90	26.40S	16.15 E
Austin	122	30.16N	97.44W
Australia □ ¹	106	25.00S	135.00 E
Australian Capital Territory □ ⁸	108	35.30S	149.00 E
Austria □ ¹	70	47.20N	13.20 E
Autlán de Navarro	112	19.46N	104.22W
Auvergne □ ⁹	76	45.25N	2.30 E
Auxerre	76	47.48N	3.34 E
Aveiro	78	40.38N	8.39W
Avellino	80	40.54N	14.47 E
Avesta	73	60.09N	16.12 E
Avezzano	80	42.02N	13.25 E
Avignon	76	43.57N	4.49 E
Ávila	78	40.39N	4.42W
Avilés	78	43.33N	5.55W
Avon	124	42.54N	77.44W
Axiós (Vardar) ≏	82	40.31N	22.43 E
Aydın	82	37.51N	27.51 E
Aylmer West	124	42.46N	80.59W
Ayr	72	55.28N	4.38W
Azerbajdžanskaja Sovetskaja Socialističeskaja Respublika □ ³	70	40.30N	47.30 E
Azogues	116	2.44S	78.50W
Azores			
→ Açores II	66	38.30N	28.00W
Azovskoje More ▼ ²	70	46.00N	36.00 E
Azraq, Al-Bahr al- (Blue Nile) ≏	88	15.38N	32.31 E
Azua	114	18.27N	70.44W
Azuaga	78	38.16N	5.41W
Azuero, Península de ⅃ ¹	114	7.40N	80.35W
Azul	118	36.47S	59.51W
Az-Zaqāzīq	88	30.35N	31.31 E
Az-Zarqā'	93	32.05N	36.06 E

Name	Page No.	Lat.	Long.
B			
Babaeski	82	41.26N	27.06 E
Babelthuap I	102	7.30N	134.36 E
Babuyan Islands II	102	19.10N	121.40 E
Bacău	82	46.34N	26.55 E
Bac-lieu (Vinh-loi)	104	9.17N	105.44 E
Bacolod	102	10.40N	122.57 E
Badajoz	78	38.53N	6.58W
Badalona	78	41.27N	2.15 E
Baden, Öst.	74	48.00N	16.14 E
Baden, Schw.	76	47.29N	8.18 E
Baden-Baden	74	48.46N	8.14 E
Bad Ischl	74	47.43N	13.37 E
Bad Kreuznach	74	49.52N	7.51 E
Baffin Bay ⊂	120	73.00N	66.00W
Baffin Island I	120	68.00N	70.00W
Bāgalkot	95	16.11N	75.42 E
Bagdad			
→ Baghdād	92	33.21N	44.25 E
Bagé	118	31.20S	54.06W
Baghdād	92	33.21N	44.25 E
Bagheria	80	38.05N	13.30 E
Baghlān	96	36.13N	68.46 E
Baguio	102	16.25N	120.36 E
Bahamas □ ¹	114	24.15N	76.00W
Bahāwalnagar	96	29.59N	73.16 E
Bahāwalpur	94	29.24N	71.41 E
Bahía, Islas de la II	114	16.20N	86.30W
Bahía Blanca	118	38.43S	62.17W
Bahrain □ ¹	92	26.00N	50.30 E
Baia-Mare	82	47.40N	23.35 E
Baidoa	92	3.04N	43.48 E
Baie-Comeau	120	49.13N	68.10W
Baie-Saint-Paul	120	47.27N	70.30W
Băilești	82	44.02N	23.21 E
Baja	74	46.11N	18.57 E
Baja California ⅃ ¹	112	28.00N	113.30W
Bajkal, Ozero (Lake Baykal) ⊜	86	53.00N	107.40 E
Baker, Mt., U.S.	122	46.22N	104.17W
Baker, Or., U.S.	122	44.46N	117.49W
Baker Lake	120	64.15N	96.00W
Bakersfield	126	35.22N	119.01W
Bakhtaran	92	34.19N	47.04 E
Baku	70	40.23N	49.51 E
Balakovo	70	52.02N	47.47 E
Balaton ⊜	74	46.50N	17.45 E
Balchaš	86	46.49N	74.59 E
Balchaš, Ozero ⊜	86	46.00N	74.00 E
Bâle			
→ Basel	76	47.33N	7.35 E
Baleares, Islas (Balearic Islands) II	78	39.30N	3.00 E
Bali I	102	8.20S	115.00 E
Balıkesir	82	39.39N	27.53 E
Balikpapan	102	1.17S	116.50 E
Balkan Mountains			
→ Stara Planina ⋌	82	43.15N	25.00 E
Ballina	72	54.07N	9.09W
Ballinger	112	31.44N	99.56W
Balmoral Castle	72	57.02N	3.15W
Balsas ≏	112	17.55N	102.10W
Baltic Sea ▼ ²	73	57.00N	19.00 E
Baltimore	124	39.17N	76.36W
Baluchistan □ ⁹	94	28.00N	63.00 E
Bamako	88	12.39N	8.00W
Bambari	88	5.45N	20.40 E
Bamenda	88	5.56N	10.10 E
Banbury	72	52.04N	1.20W
Banda, Laut (Banda Sea) ▼ ²	102	5.00S	128.00 E
Banda Aceh	102	5.34N	95.20 E

Name	Page No.	Lat.	Long.
Broken Hill, Austl.	106	31.57S	141.27 E
Broken Hill			
→ Kabwe, Zam.	90	14.27S	28.27 E
Brokopondo	116	5.04N	54.58W
Bronlund Peak ʌ	120	57.26N	126.38W
Brookings, Or., U.S.	126	42.03N	124.16W
Brookings, S.D., U.S.	122	44.18N	96.47W
Brooks Range ⚲	128	68.00N	154.00W
Broome	106	17.58S	122.14 E
Brown City	124	43.12N	82.59W
Brownsville	122	25.54N	97.29W
Brownville Junction	124	45.21N	69.03W
Brownwood	112	31.42N	98.59W
Bruce, Mount ʌ	106	22.36S	118.08 E
Bruce Peninsula ⪢[1]	124	44.50N	81.20W
Brugge	74	51.13N	3.14 E
Bruneau	126	42.52N	115.47W
Bruneau ⪦	126	42.57N	115.58W
Brunei □[1]	102	4.30N	114.40 E
Brus Laguna	114	15.47N	84.35W
Brussel			
→ Bruxelles	74	50.50N	4.20 E
Bruxelles (Brussel)	74	50.50N	4.20 E
Bryan	124	41.28N	84.33W
Brzeg	74	50.52N	17.27 E
Bucaramanga	116	7.08N	73.09W
Buchanan	88	5.57N	10.02W
Bucharest			
→ București	82	44.26N	26.06 E
Buckhannon	124	38.59N	80.13W
Buckingham	124	45.35N	75.25W
București (Bucharest)	82	44.26N	26.06 E
Budapest	74	47.30N	19.05 E
Buenaventura	116	3.53N	77.04W
Buena Vista	116	17.27S	63.40W
Buenos Aires	118	34.36S	58.27W
Buffalo	124	42.53N	78.52W
Bug ⪦	70	52.31N	21.05 E
Buhuși	82	46.43N	26.41 E
Bujumbura	90	3.23S	29.22 E
Buka Island I	111a	5.15S	154.35 E
Bukavu	90	2.30S	28.52 E
Bukovina □[9]	82	48.00N	25.30 E
Bulawayo	90	20.09S	28.36 E
Bulgan	98	48.45N	103.34 E
Bulgaria □[1]	70	43.00N	25.00 E
Bunbury	106	33.19S	115.38 E
Bundaberg	106	24.52S	152.21 E
Bunguran Utara,			
Kepulauan II	102	4.40N	108.00 E
Bunia	90	1.34N	30.15 E
Burgas	82	42.30N	27.28 E
Burgos	78	42.21N	3.42W
Buriram	104	15.00N	103.07 E
Burkina Faso □[1]	88	13.00N	2.00W
Burlington, Ia., U.S.	122	40.48N	91.06W
Burlington, Vt., U.S.	124	44.28N	73.12W
Burma □[1]	102	22.00N	98.00 E
Burnie	106	41.04S	145.54 E
Burns	126	43.35N	119.03W
Burns Lake	120	54.14N	125.46W
Bursa	82	40.11N	29.04 E
Būr Saʿīd (Port Said)	88	31.16N	32.18 E
Būr Sūdān (Port Sudan)	88	19.37N	37.14 E
Burton	124	43.02N	83.36W
Buru I	102	3.24S	126.40 E
Burundi □[1]	90	3.15S	30.00 E
Burwick	72	58.44N	2.57W
Buta	88	2.48N	24.44 E
Butler, Oh., U.S.	124	40.35N	82.25W
Butler, Pa., U.S.	124	40.51N	79.53W
Butte	122	46.00N	112.32W
Butterworth	104	5.25N	100.24 E
Butung, Pulau I	102	5.00S	122.55 E
Büyükmenderes ⪦	82	37.27N	27.11 E
Buzău	82	45.09N	26.49 E
Buzuluk	70	52.47N	52.15 E
Bydgoszcz	74	53.08N	18.00 E
Bytom (Beuthen)	74	50.22N	18.54 E

C

Name	Page No.	Lat.	Long.
Cabimas	116	10.23N	71.28W
Cabinda □[5]	90	5.00S	12.30 E
Cáceres, Col.	114	7.35N	75.20W
Cáceres, Esp.	78	39.29N	6.22W
Cache Peak ʌ	126	42.11N	113.40W
Cachoeira	119	12.36S	38.58W
Cachoeiro de Itapemirim	116	20.51S	41.06W
Cadillac	124	44.15N	85.24W
Cádiz	78	36.32N	6.18W
Cádiz, Golfo de c	78	36.50N	7.10W
Caen	76	49.11N	0.21W
Caenarvon	72	53.08N	4.16W
Cagliari	80	39.20N	9.00 E
Caguas	114	18.14N	66.02W
Caiapó, Serra ⚲	119	17.00S	52.00W
Caicos Islands II	114	21.56N	71.58W
Cairns	106	16.55S	145.46 E
Cairo			
→ Al-Qāhirah	88	30.03N	31.15 E
Cairo	122	37.00N	89.10W
Cajamarca	116	7.10S	78.31W
Calabozo	116	8.56N	67.26W
Calais, Fr.	76	50.57N	1.50 E
Calais, Me., U.S.	124	45.11N	67.16W
Calais, Pas de (Strait of			
Dover) ᴜ	76	51.00N	1.30 E
Calamian Group II	102	12.00N	120.00 E
Călărași	82	44.11N	27.20 E
Calcutta	96	22.32N	88.22 E
Caldas da Rainha	78	39.24N	9.08W
Calexico	126	32.40N	115.29W
Calgary	120	51.03N	114.05W
Cali	116	3.27N	76.31W
Calicut	95	11.15N	75.46 E
Caliente	126	37.36N	114.30W
California □[3]	122	37.30N	119.30W
California, Golfo de c	112	28.00N	112.00W
Callao	116	12.04S	77.09W
Caltagirone	80	37.14N	14.31 E
Caltanissetta	80	37.29N	14.04 E
Camacho	112	24.25N	102.18W
Camagüey	114	21.23N	77.55W
Ca-mau, Mui ⪢	104	8.38N	104.44 E
Cambodia			
→ Kampuchea □[1]	102	13.00N	105.00 E
Cambrian Mountains ⚲	72	52.35N	3.35W
Cambridge, On., Can.	124	43.22N	80.19W
Cambridge, Eng., U.K.	72	52.13N	0.08 E
Cambridge, Md., U.S.	124	38.33N	76.04W
Cambridge, Oh., U.S.	124	40.02N	81.35W
Cambridge Bay	120	69.03N	105.05W
Camden, Me., U.S.	124	44.12N	69.03W
Camden, N.J., U.S.	124	39.55N	75.07W
Cameroon □[1]	88	6.00N	12.00 E
Cameroun, Mont ʌ	88	4.12N	9.11 E
Campbell Island I	69	52.30S	169.05 E
Campbell River	120	50.01N	125.15W
Campbells Bay	124	45.44N	76.36W
Campbeltown	72	55.26N	5.36W
Campeche	112	19.51N	90.32W
Campeche, Bahía de c	112	20.00N	94.00W
Campina Grande	116	7.13S	35.53W
Campinas	116	22.54S	47.05W
Campobasso	80	41.34N	14.39 E

Name	Page No.	Lat.	Long.
Campo Grande	**116**	20.27S	54.37W
Campos	**116**	21.45S	41.18W
Cam-ranh	**104**	11.54N	109.09E
Canada □[1]	**120**	60.00N	95.00W
Çanakkale	**82**	40.09N	26.24E
Çanakkale Boğazı (Dardanelles) ⊔	**82**	40.15N	26.25E
Cananea	**112**	30.57N	110.18W
Canarias, Islas (Canary Islands) II	**88**	28.00N	15.30W
Canaveral, Cape ›	**122**	28.27N	80.32W
Canavieiras	**119**	15.39S	38.57W
Canberra	**106**	35.17S	149.08E
Caniapiscau ≃	**120**	57.40N	69.30W
Caniapiscau, Lac ⊜	**120**	54.10N	69.55W
Cannes	**76**	43.33N	7.01E
Cantábrica, Cordillera ⋏	**78**	43.00N	5.00W
Cantaura	**114**	9.19N	64.21W
Canterbury	**72**	51.17N	1.05E
Canterbury Bight ⊂[3]	**110**	44.15S	171.38E
Canton, Oh., U.S.	**124**	40.47N	81.22W
Canton → Guangzhou, Zhg.	**98**	23.06N	113.16E
Canyonville	**126**	42.55N	123.16W
Cape Breton Island I	**120**	46.00N	60.30W
Cape Cod National Seashore ♦	**124**	41.56N	70.06W
Cape Girardeau	**122**	37.18N	89.31W
Cape May	**124**	38.56N	74.54W
Cape Town (Kaapstad)	**90**	33.55S	18.22E
Cape York Peninsula ›[1]	**106**	14.00S	142.30E
Cap-Haïtien	**114**	19.45N	72.12W
Caprivi Strip □[9]	**90**	17.59S	23.00E
Caracal	**82**	44.07N	24.21E
Caracas	**116**	10.30N	66.56W
Carangola	**119**	20.44S	42.02W
Caratinga	**119**	19.47S	42.08W
Carbó	**112**	29.42N	110.58W
Carbondale	**124**	41.34N	75.30W
Carcans, Étang de ⊂	**76**	45.08N	1.08W
Carcassonne	**76**	43.13N	2.21E
Cárdenas	**114**	23.02N	81.12W
Cardiff	**72**	51.29N	3.13W
Cardigan	**72**	52.06N	4.40W
Caribbean Sea ⊤[2]	**114**	15.00N	73.00W
Caripito	**114**	10.08N	63.06W
Carleton Place	**124**	45.08N	76.09W
Carlisle, Eng., U.K.	**72**	54.54N	2.55W
Carlisle, Pa., U.S.	**124**	40.12N	77.11W
Carlsbad	**112**	32.25N	104.13W
Carlsbad Caverns National Park ♦	**112**	32.08N	104.35W
Carmacks	**120**	62.05N	136.18W
Carmarthen	**72**	51.52N	4.19W
Carmona	**78**	37.28N	5.38W
Caroline Islands II	**102**	8.00N	140.00E
Caroní ≃	**114**	8.21N	62.43W
Carpathian Mountains ⋏	**70**	48.00N	24.00E
Carpații Meridionali ⋏	**82**	45.30N	24.15E
Carpentaria, Gulf of ⊂	**106**	14.00S	139.00E
Carrara	**80**	44.05N	10.06E
Carrauntoohill ∧	**72**	52.00N	9.45W
Carrizo Springs	**112**	28.31N	99.51W
Carson City	**126**	39.10N	119.46W
Cartagena, Col.	**116**	10.25N	75.32W
Cartagena, Esp.	**78**	37.36N	0.59W
Cartago	**114**	9.52N	83.55W
Caruaru	**116**	8.17S	35.58W
Carúpano	**114**	10.40N	63.14W
Casablanca (Dar-El-Beida)	**88**	33.39N	7.35W
Casa Grande	**112**	32.52N	111.45W
Casale Monferrato	**80**	45.08N	8.27E
Cascade Point ›	**110**	44.00S	168.22E

Name	Page No.	Lat.	Long.
Cascade Range ⋏	**122**	49.00N	120.00W
Cascais	**78**	38.42N	9.25W
Casper	**122**	42.52N	106.18W
Caspian Sea ⊤[2]	**70**	42.00N	50.30E
Cassai (Kasai) ≃	**90**	3.06S	16.57E
Castelo Branco	**78**	39.49N	7.30W
Castile	**124**	42.37N	78.03W
Castletown	**72**	54.04N	4.40W
Castres	**76**	43.36N	2.15E
Castries	**114**	14.01N	61.00W
Catalão	**119**	18.10S	47.57W
Cataluña □[9]	**78**	42.00N	2.00E
Catamarca	**118**	28.28S	65.47W
Catanduanes Island I	**102**	13.45N	124.15E
Catanduva	**119**	21.08S	48.58W
Catania	**80**	37.30N	15.06E
Catanzaro	**80**	38.54N	16.36E
Cat Island I	**114**	24.27N	75.30W
Catoche, Cabo ›	**112**	21.35N	87.05W
Catskill Mountains ⋏	**124**	42.10N	74.30W
Caucasus → Bol'šoj Kavkaz ⋏	**70**	42.30N	45.00E
Caxambu	**119**	21.59S	44.56W
Caxias do Sul	**118**	29.10S	51.11W
Cayenne	**116**	4.56N	52.20W
Cayman Islands □[2]	**114**	19.30N	80.40W
Cayuga Lake ⊜	**124**	42.45N	76.45W
Cazaux, Étang de ⊂	**76**	44.30N	1.10W
Čeboksary	**70**	56.09N	47.15E
Cebu	**102**	10.18N	123.54E
Čechy □[9]	**74**	49.50N	14.00E
Cedar City	**122**	37.40N	113.03W
Cedar Rapids	**122**	42.00N	91.38W
Cegléd	**74**	47.10N	19.48E
Čel'abinsk	**70**	55.10N	61.24E
Celaya	**112**	20.31N	100.49W
Celebes → Sulawesi I	**102**	2.00S	121.00E
Celebes Sea ⊤[2]	**102**	3.00N	122.00E
Celestún	**112**	20.52N	90.24W
Celinograd	**86**	51.10N	71.30E
Čelkar	**70**	47.50N	59.36E
Celle	**74**	52.37N	10.05E
Čel'uskin, Mys ›	**86**	77.45N	104.20E
Cenderawasih, Teluk ⊂	**102**	2.30S	135.20E
Central, Cordillera ⋏	**116**	8.00S	77.00W
Central, Massif ⋏	**76**	45.00N	3.10E
Central, Planalto ⋏[1]	**116**	18.00S	47.00W
Central, Sistema ⋏	**78**	40.30N	5.00W
Central African Republic □[1]	**88**	7.00N	21.00E
Čeremchovo	**86**	53.09N	103.05E
Čerepovec	**84**	59.08N	37.54E
Cereté	**114**	8.53N	75.48W
Čerkassy	**70**	49.26N	32.04E
Černigov	**70**	51.30N	31.18E
Černogorsk	**86**	53.49N	91.18E
Černovcy	**70**	48.18N	25.56E
Cerritos	**112**	22.26N	100.17W
Cerro de Pasco	**116**	10.41S	76.16W
Čerskogo, Chrebet ⋏	**86**	65.00N	144.00E
Cesena	**80**	44.08N	12.15E
České Budějovice	**74**	48.59N	14.28E
Ceuta	**88**	35.53N	5.19W
Chabarovsk	**86**	48.27N	135.06E
Chad □[1]	**88**	15.00N	19.00E
Chad, Lake (Lac Tchad) ⊜	**88**	13.20N	14.00E
Chadron	**122**	42.49N	103.00W
Chaidamupendi ≚[1]	**98**	37.00N	95.00E
Chalbi Desert ◆[2]	**92**	3.00N	37.20E
Chalmette	**112**	29.56N	89.57W
Châlons-sur-Marne	**76**	48.57N	4.22E
Chalon-sur-Saône	**76**	46.47N	4.51E

Name	Page No.	Lat.	Long.
Ciudad del Carmen	112	18.38N	91.50W
Ciudad de México (Mexico City)	112	19.24N	99.09W
Ciudad de Valles	112	21.59N	99.01W
Ciudad de Villaldama	112	26.30N	100.26W
Ciudad Guayana	116	8.22N	62.40W
Ciudad Guerrero	112	28.33N	107.30W
Ciudad Ixtepec	112	16.34N	95.06W
Ciudad Jiménez	112	27.08N	104.55W
Ciudad Juárez	112	31.44N	106.29W
Ciudad Madero	112	22.16N	97.50W
Ciudad Mante	112	22.44N	98.57W
Ciudad Melchor Múzquiz	112	27.53N	101.31W
Ciudad Obregón	112	27.29N	109.56W
Ciudad Ojeda	114	10.12N	71.19W
Ciudad Real	78	38.59N	3.56W
Ciudad Victoria	112	23.44N	99.08W
Clanwilliam	90	32.11S	18.54E
Claremont	124	43.22N	72.20W
Clarksburg	124	39.16N	80.20W
Clearfield	124	41.01N	78.26W
Clear Lake ⊜ [1]	126	39.02N	122.50W
Clermont-Ferrand	76	45.47N	3.05E
Cleveland, Oh., U.S.	124	41.29N	81.41W
Cleveland, Tx., U.S.	112	30.20N	95.05W
Clifton Forge	124	37.48N	79.49W
Clinton, Mi., U.S.	124	42.04N	83.58W
Clinton, Ok., U.S.	122	35.30N	98.58W
Clio	122	31.42N	85.36W
Cloncurry	106	20.42S	140.30E
Clonmel	72	52.21N	7.42W
Clovis	122	34.24N	103.12W
Cluj-Napoca	82	46.47N	23.36E
Clyde	120	70.25N	68.30W
Clyde, Firth of ⊂ [1]	72	55.42N	5.00W
Coalinga	126	36.08N	120.21W
Coast Mountains ⋀	120	55.00N	129.00W
Coast Ranges ⋀	122	41.00N	123.30W
Coaticook	124	45.08N	71.48W
Coatzacoalcos	112	18.09N	94.25W
Cobija	116	11.02S	68.44W
Cobourg	124	43.58N	78.10W
Coburg	74	50.15N	10.58E
Cochabamba	116	17.24S	66.09W
Cochin	94	9.58N	76.15E
Coco ≃	114	15.00N	83.10W
Coco Channel ꞩ	104	13.45N	93.00E
Cod, Cape ≻	124	41.42N	70.15W
Cognac	76	45.42N	0.20W
Coiba, Isla de I	114	7.27N	81.45W
Coimbatore	95	11.00N	76.58E
Coimbra	78	40.12N	8.25W
Čojbalsan	98	48.34N	114.50E
Colatina	116	19.32S	40.37W
Coldwater	124	40.28N	84.37W
Coleman	124	43.45N	84.35W
Coleraine	72	55.08N	6.40W
Colima	112	19.14N	103.43W
Cologne → Köln	74	50.56N	6.59E
Colombia □ [1]	116	4.00N	72.00W
Colombo	95	6.56N	79.51E
Colón	114	9.22N	79.54W
Colón, Archipiélago de (Galapagos Islands) II	66	0.30S	90.30W
Colonia Dora	118	28.36S	62.57W
Colonia Las Heras	118	46.33S	68.57W
Colorado □ [3]	122	39.30N	105.30W
Colorado ≃, Arg.	118	39.50S	62.08W
Colorado ≃, N.A.	122	31.54N	114.57W
Colorado ≃, Tx., U.S.	112	28.36N	95.58W
Colorado Springs	122	38.50N	104.49W
Columbia, Md., U.S.	124	39.14N	76.50W
Columbia, S.C., U.S.	122	34.00N	81.02W
Columbia ≃	120	46.15N	124.05W
Columbia, Mount ∧	120	52.09N	117.25W
Columbia Plateau ⋀ [1]	126	44.00N	117.30W
Columbus, Ga., U.S.	122	32.29N	84.59W
Columbus, Ne., U.S.	122	41.25N	97.22W
Columbus, Oh., U.S.	124	39.57N	82.59W
Colville ≃	128	70.25N	150.30W
Comitán [de Domínguez]	112	16.15N	92.08W
Communism Peak → Kommunizma, Pik ∧	94	38.57N	72.01E
Como	80	45.47N	9.05E
Como, Lago di ⊜	80	46.00N	9.20E
Comodoro Rivadavia	118	45.52S	67.30W
Comorin, Cape ≻	95	8.04N	77.34E
Comoros □ [1]	90	12.10S	44.10E
Compiègne	76	49.25N	2.50E
Conakry	88	9.31N	13.43W
Concepción, Bol.	116	16.15S	62.04W
Concepción, Chile	118	36.50S	73.03W
Concepción, Para.	118	23.25S	57.17W
Concepción de la Vega	114	19.13N	70.31W
Concepción del Uruguay	118	32.29S	58.14W
Conchos ≃	112	29.35N	104.25W
Concord	124	43.12N	71.32W
Congo □ [1]	90	1.00S	15.00E
Congo (Zaïre) ≃	90	6.04S	12.24E
Connaught □ [9]	72	53.45N	9.00W
Connecticut □ [3]	122	41.45N	72.45W
Connemara ◆ [1]	72	53.25N	9.45W
Connersville	124	39.38N	85.15W
Constanța	82	44.11N	28.39E
Constantine	88	36.22N	6.37E
Contas, Rio de ≃	119	14.17S	39.01W
Conway, N.H., U.S.	124	43.58N	71.07W
Conway, S.C., U.S.	122	33.50N	79.02W
Cook, Mount ∧	110	43.36S	170.10E
Cook Inlet ⊂	128	60.30N	152.00W
Cook Islands □ [2]	66	20.00S	158.00W
Cook Strait ꞩ	110	41.15S	174.30E
Cooktown	106	15.28S	145.15E
Cooperstown	124	42.42N	74.55W
Coos Bay	126	43.22N	124.12W
Copenhagen → København	73	55.40N	12.35E
Copiapó	118	27.22S	70.20W
Copper ≃	128	60.30N	144.50W
Coral Sea ▾ [2]	66	20.00S	158.00E
Córdoba, Arg.	118	31.24S	64.11W
Córdoba, Esp.	78	37.53N	4.46W
Córdoba, Méx.	112	18.53N	96.56W
Cordova	128	60.33N	145.46W
Corfu → Kérkira I	82	39.40N	19.42E
Corinth, Gulf of → Korinthiakós Kólpos ⊂	82	38.19N	22.04E
Cork	72	51.54N	8.28W
Çorlu	82	41.09N	27.48E
Corner Brook	120	48.57N	57.57W
Corning	124	42.08N	77.03W
Cornwall	124	45.02N	74.44W
Coro	116	11.25N	69.41W
Coromandel Coast ⚬ [2]	95	14.00N	80.10E
Coromandel Peninsula ≻ [1]	110	36.50S	175.35E
Coronel Pringles	118	37.58S	61.22W
Corpus Christi	122	27.48N	97.23W
Corrientes	118	27.28S	58.50W
Corrientes, Cabo ≻, Col.	116	5.30N	77.34W
Corrientes, Cabo ≻, Cuba	114	21.45N	84.31W
Corrientes, Cabo ≻, Méx.	112	20.25N	105.42W
Corry	124	41.55N	79.38W
Corse (Corsica) I	80	42.00N	9.00E

Name	Page No.	Lat.	Long.
Dehiwala-Mount Lavinia	95	6.51N	79.52 E
Dehra Dūn	96	30.19N	78.02 E
Dej	82	47.09N	23.52 E
Delano	126	35.46N	119.14W
Delaware □³	122	39.10N	75.30W
Delaware ≃	124	39.20N	75.25W
Delaware Bay c	124	39.05N	75.15W
Delhi	96	28.40N	77.13 E
Delicias	112	28.13N	105.28W
Del Rio	122	29.21N	100.53W
Demirci	82	39.03N	28.40 E
Denain	76	50.20N	3.23 E
Denali National Park ♦	128	63.30N	150.00W
Den Helder	74	52.54N	4.45 E
Denison	122	33.45N	96.32W
Denizli	82	37.46N	29.06 E
Denmark □¹	70	56.00N	10.00 E
Denpasar	102	8.39S	115.13 E
Denton	124	38.53N	75.49W
D'Entrecasteaux Islands ‖	106	9.30S	150.40 E
Denver	122	39.44N	104.59W
Dera Ghāzi Khān	94	30.03N	70.38 E
Dera Ismāīl Khān	96	31.50N	70.54 E
Derby	72	52.55N	1.29W
Derby Line	124	45.00N	72.05W
Dese	92	11.05N	39.41 E
Des Moines	122	41.36N	93.36W
Des Moines ≃	122	40.22N	91.26W
Dessau	74	51.50N	12.14 E
Detmold	74	51.56N	8.52 E
Detroit	124	42.20N	83.03W
Deutsche Bucht c	74	54.30N	7.30 E
Deva	82	45.53N	22.55 E
Deventer	74	52.15N	6.10 E
Devon Island ‖	120	75.00N	87.00W
Devonport	110	36.49S	174.48 E
Dexter	124	45.01N	69.17W
Dezfūl	92	32.23N	48.24 E
Dhaka	96	23.43N	90.25 E
Dhodhekánisos (Dodecanese) ‖	82	36.30N	27.00 E
Dhorāji	96	21.44N	70.27 E
Diable, Île du ‖	116	5.17N	52.35W
Diablo Range ⋆	126	37.00N	121.20W
Diamantina	116	18.15S	43.36W
Diamond Peak ⋀	126	43.33N	122.09W
Dieppe	76	49.56N	1.05 E
Digby	120	44.37N	65.46W
Dijon	76	47.19N	5.01 E
Dili	102	8.33S	125.35 E
Dillingham	128	59.02N	158.29W
Dillon	122	45.12N	112.38W
Dimashq (Damascus)	93	33.30N	36.18 E
Dimitrovgrad	82	42.03N	25.36 E
Dimlang ⋀	88	8.24N	11.47 E
Dinant	74	50.16N	4.55 E
Dinara (Dinaric Alps) ⋆	80	43.50N	16.35 E
Dingle	72	52.08N	10.15W
Dingwall	72	57.35N	4.29W
Dire Dawa	92	9.37N	41.52 E
Diriamba	114	11.51N	86.14W
Disappointment, Cape ‣	122	46.18N	124.03W
Disappointment, Lake ⊜	106	23.30S	122.50 E
Diu	96	20.42N	70.59 E
Diu □³	96	20.42N	70.59 E
Divinópolis	116	20.09S	44.54W
Diyarbakir	70	37.55N	40.14 E
Dja ≃	88	2.02N	15.12 E
Djerba, Île de ‖	88	33.48N	10.54 E
Djibouti	92	11.36N	43.09 E
Djibouti □¹	92	11.30N	43.00 E
Dnepr ≃	70	46.30N	32.18 E
Dnepropetrovsk	70	48.27N	34.59 E
Dnestr ≃	70	46.18N	30.17 E
Doberai, Jazirah ⟩¹	102	1.30S	132.30 E
Dodecanese → Dhodhekánisos ‖	82	36.30N	27.00 E
Dodge City	122	37.45N	100.01W
Dodoma	90	6.11S	35.45 E
Doha → Ad-Dawḥah	92	25.17N	51.32 E
Dolbeau	120	48.53N	72.14W
Dolisie	90	4.12S	12.41 E
Dolomiti ⋆	80	46.25N	11.50 E
Dominica □¹	114	15.30N	61.20W
Dominican Republic □¹	114	19.00N	70.40W
Don ≃	70	47.04N	39.18 E
Donau → Danube ≃	74	45.20N	29.40 E
Don Benito	78	38.57N	5.52W
Dondra Head ⟩	95	5.55N	80.35 E
Doneck	70	48.00N	37.48 E
Donegal	72	54.39N	8.07W
Donga ≃	88	8.19N	9.58 E
Dongara	106	29.15S	114.56 E
Dongtinghu ⊜	98	29.20N	112.54 E
Dordogne ≃	76	45.02N	0.35W
Dordrecht	74	51.49N	4.40 E
Dores do Indaiá	119	19.27S	45.36W
Dortmund	74	51.31N	7.28 E
Dothan	122	31.13N	85.23W
Douala	88	4.03N	9.42 E
Doubtless Bay c	110	34.55S	173.25 E
Douglas	72	54.09N	4.28W
Dourados	119	22.13S	54.48W
Douro (Duero) ≃	78	41.08N	8.40W
Dover, Eng., U.K.	72	51.08N	1.19 E
Dover, De., U.S.	124	39.09N	75.31W
Dover, N.H., U.S.	124	43.11N	70.52W
Dover, Strait of (Pas de Calais) ⊔	76	51.00N	1.30 E
Dra, Hamada du ◄²	88	29.00N	6.45W
Drâa, Oued ∨	88	28.43N	11.09W
Drachten	74	53.06N	6.05 E
Drakensberg ⋆	90	27.00S	30.00 E
Drake Passage ⊔	69	58.00S	70.00W
Dráma	82	41.09N	24.08 E
Drammen	73	59.44N	10.15 E
Dranov, Ostrovul ‖	82	44.52N	29.15 E
Drava (Dráva) (Drau) ≃	74	45.33N	18.55 E
Dresden	74	51.03N	13.44 E
Drina ≃	82	44.53N	19.21 E
Drobeta-Turnu-Severin	82	44.38N	22.39 E
Drogheda	72	53.43N	6.21W
Drummondville	124	45.53N	72.29W
Duarte, Pico ⋀	114	19.02N	70.59W
Dubayy	92	25.18N	55.18 E
Dubbo	106	32.15S	148.36 E
Dublin (Baile Átha Cliath)	72	53.20N	6.15W
Du Bois	124	41.07N	78.45W
Dubrovnik	82	42.38N	18.07 E
Duero (Douro) ≃	78	41.08N	8.40W
Dufourspitze ⋀	76	45.55N	7.52 E
Dugi Otok ‖	80	44.00N	15.04 E
Duisburg	74	51.25N	6.46 E
Duluth	122	46.45N	92.07W
Dumfries	72	55.04N	3.37W
Dumyāṭ	93	31.25N	31.48 E
Duna → Danube ≃	74	45.20N	29.40 E
Dunaj → Danube ≃	74	45.20N	29.40 E
Dunaújváros	74	46.58N	18.57 E
Dundalk	72	54.01N	6.25W
Dundee	72	56.28N	3.00W

Name	Page No.	Lat.	Long.
Dunedin	110	45.52S	170.30 E
Dungarvan	72	52.05N	7.37W
Dunkirk, In., U.S.	124	40.22N	85.12W
Dunkirk, N.Y., U.S.	124	42.28N	79.20W
Dunkirk, Oh., U.S.	124	40.47N	83.38W
Dun Laoghaire	72	53.17N	6.08W
Dunnville	124	42.54N	79.36W
Durance ≃	78	43.55N	4.44 E
Durango	112	24.02N	104.40W
Durban	90	29.55S	30.56 E
Durham	124	44.10N	80.49W
Durmitor ∧	82	43.08N	19.01 E
Durness	72	58.33N	4.45W
Durrësi	82	41.19N	19.26 E
D'Urville Island I	110	40.50S	173.52 E
Dušanbe	94	38.35N	68.48 E
Düsseldorf	74	51.12N	6.47 E
Dzaoudzi	90	12.47S	45.17 E
Dzierżoniów (Reichenbach)	74	50.44N	16.39 E

E

Name	Page No.	Lat.	Long.
Eagle Pass	122	28.42N	100.29W
East Aurora	124	42.46N	78.36W
East Cape ≻	110	37.41S	178.33 E
East China Sea ⊤ 2	98	30.00N	126.00 E
Eastern Ghāts ⋌	95	14.00N	78.50 E
East Falkland I	118	51.55S	59.00W
East Lansing	124	42.44N	84.29W
East Liverpool	124	40.37N	80.34W
East London (Oos-Londen)	90	33.00S	27.55 E
Eastmain	120	52.15N	78.30W
Easton	124	40.41N	75.13W
East Stroudsburg	124	40.59N	75.10W
East Tawas	124	44.16N	83.29W
Eau Claire	122	44.48N	91.29W
Eberswalde	74	52.50N	13.49 E
Ebro ≃	78	40.43N	0.54 E
Ebro, Delta del ≃ 2	78	40.43N	0.54 E
Écija	78	37.32N	5.05W
Ecuador □ 1	116	2.00S	77.30W
Edinburg, Tx., U.S.	112	26.18N	98.09W
Edinburg, Va., U.S.	124	38.49N	78.33W
Edinburgh	72	55.57N	3.13W
Edirne	82	41.40N	26.34 E
Edmonton	120	53.33N	113.28W
Edremit	82	39.35N	27.01 E
Edson	120	53.35N	116.26W
Eel ≃	126	40.40N	124.20W
Efate I	111b	17.40S	168.25 E
Eganville	124	45.32N	77.06W
Eger	74	47.54N	20.23 E
Egypt □ 1	88	27.00N	30.00 E
Eindhoven	74	51.26N	5.28 E
Eisenach	74	50.59N	10.19 E
Eisenhüttenstadt	74	52.10N	14.39 E
Eisenstadt	74	47.51N	16.32 E
Eisleben	74	51.31N	11.32 E
Ekibastuz	86	51.42N	75.22 E
Ekwan ≃	120	53.14N	82.13W
El Aaiún	88	27.09N	13.12W
El Asnam (Orléansville)	78	36.10N	1.20 E
Elat	93	29.33N	34.57 E
Elba, Isola d' I	80	42.46N	10.17 E
El Banco	114	9.00N	73.58W
Elbasani	82	41.06N	20.05 E
Elbe (Labe) ≃	74	53.50N	9.00 E
Elbląg (Elbing)	74	54.10N	19.25 E
El'brus, Gora ∧	70	43.21N	42.26 E
El Cajon	126	32.47N	116.57W
El Campo	112	29.11N	96.16W
El Capitan ∧	122	46.01N	114.23W
Elche	78	38.15N	0.42W

Name	Page No.	Lat.	Long.
Elda	78	38.29N	0.47W
El Djouf ◆ 2	88	20.30N	8.00W
El Dorado	122	33.12N	92.39W
Eldoret	90	0.31N	35.17 E
El Encanto	116	1.37S	73.14W
Elephant Mountain ∧	124	44.46N	70.46W
El Estor	114	15.32N	89.21W
Eleuthera I	114	25.10N	76.14W
Elgin	72	57.39N	3.20W
Elizabeth City	122	36.18N	76.13W
Elk	74	53.50N	22.22 E
El Kairouan	80	35.41N	10.07 E
El Kef	80	36.11N	8.43 E
Elkins	124	38.55N	79.50W
Elko	126	40.49N	115.45W
Elk Rapids	124	44.53N	85.24W
Elkton	124	39.36N·	75.50W
Ellesmere Island I	68	81.00N	80.00W
Ellsworth	124	44.32N	68.25W
Elmer	124	39.35N	75.10W
Elmira	124	42.05N	76.48W
Elmore	108	36.30S	144.37 E
Elmshorn	74	53.45N	9.39 E
El Nevado, Cerro ∧	118	35.35S	68.30W
El Palmar	114	7.58N	61.53W
El Paso	122	31.45N	106.29W
El Progreso	114	15.21N	87.49W
El Salvador □ 1	114	13.50N	88.55W
El Sauce	114	12.53N	86.32W
El Tigre	116	8.55N	64.15W
El Turbio	118	51.41S	72.05W
Elvas	78	38.53N	7.10W
Ely	126	39.14N	114.53W
Embarcación	118	23.13S	64.06W
Emden	74	53.22N	7.12 E
Emerald	106	23.32S	148.10 E
Empoli	80	43.43N	10.57 E
Emporia	122	38.24N	96.10W
Emporium	124	41.30N	78.14W
Encarnación	118	27.20S	55.54W
Encontrados	114	9.03N	72.14W
Enderby Land ◆ 1	69	67.30S	53.00 E
Endicott	124	42.05N	76.02W
Engel's	70	51.30N	46.07 E
England □ 8	72	52.30N	1.30W
English Channel (La Manche) ⋃	76	50.20N	1.00W
Enns ≃	80	48.14N	14.32 E
Enschede	74	52.12N	6.53 E
Ensenada	112	31.52N	116.37W
Entebbe	90	0.04N	32.28 E
Enugu	88	6.27N	7.27 E
Eolie, Isole II	80	38.30N	15.00 E
Épinal	76	48.11N	6.27 E
Equatorial Guinea □ 1	88	2.00N	9.00 E
Erechim	118	27.38S	52.17W
Erfurt	74	50.58N	11.01 E
Erie	124	42.07N	80.05W
Erie, Lake ☺	122	42.15N	81.00W
Eritrea □ 9	92	15.20N	39.00 E
Erlangen	74	49.36N	11.01 E
Eromanga I	111b	18.45S	169.05 E
Erzurum	70	39.55N	41.17 E
Esbjerg	73	55.28N	8.27 E
Esch-sur-Alzette	74	49.30N	5.59 E
Escondido	126	33.07N	117.05W
Escuintla	114	14.18N	90.47W
Eşfahān	92	32.40N	51.38 E
Eskilstuna	73	59.22N	16.30 E
Eskimo Point	120	61.07N	94.03W
Eskişehir	70	39.46N	30.32 E
Esmeraldas	116	0.59N	79.42W
Esperance	106	33.51S	121.53 E

Name	Page No.	Lat.	Long.
Espinhaço, Serra do ⋌	116	17.30 S	43.30 W
Espiritu Santo ▮	111b	15.50 S	166.50 E
Espoo (Esbo)	73	60.13 N	24.40 E
Esquel	118	42.54 S	71.19 W
Essen	74	51.28 N	7.01 E
Estados, Isla de los ▮	118	54.47 S	64.15 W
Estelí	114	13.05 N	86.23 W
Estonskaja Sovetskaja Socialističeskaja Respublika ◻³	70	59.00 N	26.00 E
Estrela ⋏	78	40.19 N	7.37 W
Ethiopia ◻¹	92	9.00 N	39.00 E
Etna, Monte ⋏¹	80	37.46 N	15.00 E
Ettelbruck	74	49.52 N	6.05 E
Eucla	106	31.43 S	128.52 E
Eugene	122	44.03 N	123.05 W
Eugenia, Punta ⵀ	122	27.50 N	115.05 W
Euphrates (Al-Furāt) ≃	92	31.00 N	47.25 E
Eureka, Ca., U.S.	126	40.48 N	124.09 W
Eureka, Nv., U.S.	126	39.30 N	115.57 W
Europa, Île ▮	90	22.20 S	40.22 E
Europe ⋆¹	66	50.00 N	20.00 E
Evansville	122	37.58 N	87.33 W
Everest, Mount ⋏	96	27.59 N	86.56 E
Everglades National Park ✦	114	25.27 N	80.53 W
Évora	78	38.34 N	7.54 W
Évreux	76	49.01 N	1.09 E
Evrótas ≃	82	36.48 N	22.40 E
Évvoia ▮	82	38.34 N	23.50 E
Exeter	72	50.43 N	3.31 W
Exuma Sound ⊔	114	24.15 N	76.00 W
Eyre North, Lake ⌀	108	28.40 S	137.10 E
Eyre Peninsula ⵀ¹	108	34.00 S	135.45 E
Eyre South, Lake ⌀	108	29.30 S	137.20 E

F

Fada	88	17.14 N	21.33 E
Faenza	80	44.17 N	11.53 E
Faeroe Islands ◻²	70	62.00 N	7.00 W
Fairbanks	128	64.51 N	147.43 W
Fairfield, Ca., U.S.	126	38.14 N	122.02 W
Fairfield, Oh., U.S.	124	39.20 N	84.33 W
Fairlie	110	44.06 S	170.50 E
Fairmont	124	39.29 N	80.08 W
Fairview	124	44.43 N	84.03 W
Fairweather, Mount ⋏	120	58.54 N	137.32 W
Fais ▮	102	9.46 N	140.31 E
Faisalabad	94	31.25 N	73.05 E
Falevai	111e	13.55 S	171.59 W
Falfurrias	112	27.13 N	98.08 W
Falkland Islands ◻²	118	51.45 S	59.00 W
Falköping	73	58.10 N	13.31 E
Fallon	126	39.28 N	118.46 W
Fall River	124	41.42 N	71.09 W
Falun	73	60.36 N	15.38 E
Fan-si-pan ⋏	104	22.15 N	103.46 E
Faradofay	90	25.02 S	47.00 E
Farāh	94	32.22 N	62.07 E
Farewell, Cape ⵀ	110	40.30 S	172.41 E
Fargo	122	46.52 N	96.47 W
Farmington	122	36.43 N	108.13 W
Faro	78	37.01 N	7.56 W
Farquhar Group ▮▮	90	10.10 S	51.10 E
Farvel, Kap ⵀ	120	59.45 N	44.00 W
Farwell	124	43.50 N	84.52 W
Fayetteville	122	35.03 N	78.52 W
Fazzān (Fezzan) ➤¹	88	26.00 N	14.00 E
Feira de Santana	116	12.15 S	38.57 W
Fenton	124	42.47 N	83.42 W
Fernando de Noronha, Ilha ▮	116	3.51 S	32.25 W
Fernandópolis	119	20.16 S	50.14 W

Name	Page No.	Lat.	Long.
Fernando Póo → Bioko ▮	88	3.30 N	8.40 E
Ferrara	80	44.50 N	11.35 E
Fès	88	34.05 N	4.57 W
Feuilles, Rivière aux ≃	120	58.47 N	70.04 W
Feyzābād	94	35.01 N	58.46 E
Fianarantsoa	90	21.26 S	47.05 E
Fichtelberg ⋏	74	50.26 N	12.57 E
Figueira da Foz	78	40.09 N	8.52 W
Figueras	78	42.16 N	2.58 E
Fiji ◻¹	66	18.00 S	175.00 W
Filchner Ice Shelf ⌀	69	79.00 S	40.00 W
Findlay	124	41.02 N	83.39 W
Finland ◻¹	70	64.00 N	26.00 E
Finland, Gulf of ⊂	73	60.00 N	27.00 E
Firenze (Florence)	80	43.46 N	11.15 E
Fitchburg	124	42.35 N	71.48 W
Fitzroy, Monte (Cerro Chaltel) ⋏	118	49.17 S	73.05 W
Flagstaff	122	35.11 N	111.39 W
Flemingsburg	124	38.25 N	83.44 W
Flensburg	74	54.47 N	9.26 E
Flinders Island ▮	108	40.00 S	148.00 E
Flinders Range ⋌	106	31.00 S	139.00 E
Flin Flon	120	54.46 N	101.53 W
Flint	124	42.59 N	83.45 W
Florence → Firenze	80	43.46 N	11.15 E
Florencia	116	1.36 N	75.36 W
Flores ▮	102	8.30 S	121.00 E
Flores, Laut (Flores Sea) ⵴²	102	8.00 S	120.00 E
Florianópolis	118	27.35 S	48.34 W
Florida	114	21.32 N	78.14 W
Florida ◻³	122	28.00 N	82.00 W
Florida, Straits of ⊔	114	25.00 N	79.45 W
Florida Keys ▮▮	122	24.45 N	81.00 W
Fly ≃	102	8.30 S	143.41 E
Focşani	82	45.41 N	27.11 E
Foggia	80	41.27 N	15.34 E
Folkestone	72	51.05 N	1.11 E
Fond du Lac	120	59.19 N	107.10 W
Fontainebleau	76	48.24 N	2.42 E
Fontur ⵀ	70	66.23 N	14.30 W
Formiga	119	20.27 S	45.25 W
Formosa	118	26.11 S	58.11 W
Forrest	106	30.51 S	128.06 E
Forst	74	51.44 N	14.39 E
Fortaleza	116	3.43 S	38.30 W
Fort Chipewyan	120	58.42 N	111.08 W
Fort-de-France	114	14.36 N	61.05 W
Fort Fitzgerald	120	59.53 N	111.37 W
Fort Franklin	120	65.11 N	123.46 W
Fort-George	120	53.50 N	79.00 W
Fort Good Hope	120	66.15 N	128.38 W
Forth, Firth of ⊂¹	72	56.05 N	2.55 W
Fort-Lamy → N'Djamena	88	12.07 N	15.03 E
Fort Lauderdale	122	26.07 N	80.08 W
Fort Macleod	120	49.43 N	113.25 W
Fort McMurray	120	56.44 N	111.23 W
Fort Myers	114	26.38 N	81.52 W
Fort Nelson	120	58.49 N	122.39 W
Fort Norman	120	64.54 N	125.34 W
Fort Peck Lake ⌀¹	120	47.45 N	106.50 W
Fort Reliance	120	62.42 N	109.08 W
Fort Resolution	120	61.10 N	113.40 W
Fort Saint John	120	56.15 N	120.51 W
Fort Simpson	120	61.52 N	121.23 W
Fort Smith	122	35.23 N	94.23 W
Fort Stockton	122	30.53 N	102.52 W
Fort Wayne	122	41.07 N	85.07 W
Fort Worth	122	32.43 N	97.19 W

Name	Page No.	Lat.	Long.
Geraldton, On., Can.	120	49.44N	86.57W
Gerlachovský Štít ʌ	74	49.12N	20.08 E
German Democratic Republic (East Germany) □¹	70	52.00N	12.30 E
Germany, Federal Republic of (West Germany) □¹	70	51.00N	9.00 E
Gerona	78	41.59N	2.49 E
Ghana □¹	88	8.00N	2.00 W
Ghanzi	90	21.38S	21.45 E
Gharbīyah, Aṣ-Ṣaḥrā' al- (Western Desert) ➡²	88	27.00N	27.00 E
Ghardaïa	88	32.31N	3.37 E
Ghazāl, Baḥr al- ≃	88	9.31N	30.25 E
Ghaznī	96	33.33N	68.26 E
Ghazzah (Gaza)	93	31.30N	34.28 E
Gia-dinh	104	10.48N	106.42 E
Gibeon	90	25.09S	17.43 E
Gibraltar	78	36.09N	5.21W
Gibraltar □²	70	36.11N	5.22W
Gibraltar, Strait of (Estrecho de Gibraltar) ⊍	78	35.57N	5.36W
Gibson Desert ➡²	106	24.30S	126.00 E
Giessen	74	50.35N	8.40 E
Gifu	100	35.25N	136.45 E
Gijón	78	43.32N	5.40W
Gimli	120	50.38N	96.59W
Gironde c¹	76	45.20N	0.45W
Gisborne	110	38.40S	178.01 E
Gizo	111a	8.06S	156.51 E
Gjirokastra	82	40.05N	20.10 E
Gjoa Haven	120	68.38N	95.57W
Glace Bay	120	46.12N	59.57W
Glacier Bay National Park ♦	128	58.45N	136.30W
Gladwin	124	43.58N	84.29W
Glåma ≃	73	59.12N	10.57 E
Glasgow	72	55.53N	4.15W
Glenns Ferry	126	42.57N	115.18W
Glens Falls	124	43.18N	73.38W
Glittertinden ʌ	73	61.39N	8.33 E
Glorieuses, Îles II	90	11.30S	47.20 E
Gloucester, Eng., U.K.	72	51.53N	2.14W
Gloucester, Ma., U.S.	124	42.36N	70.39W
Gloversville	124	43.03N	74.20W
Gniezno	74	52.31N	17.37 E
Goa □⁸	95	14.20N	74.00 E
Gobi ➡²	98	43.00N	105.00 E
Godāvari ≃	95	17.00N	81.45 E
Godhavn	120	69.15N	53.33W
Godthåb	66	64.11N	51.44W
Godwin Austen → K2 ʌ	96	35.53N	76.30 E
Goiânia	116	16.40S	49.16W
Gökçeada I	82	40.10N	25.50 E
Gómez Palacio	112	25.34N	103.30W
Gonaïves	114	19.27N	72.41W
Gonâve, Golfe de la c	114	19.00N	73.30W
Gonâve, Île de la I	114	18.51N	73.03W
Gonder	92	12.40N	37.30 E
Good Hope, Cape of ⊁	90	34.24S	18.30 E
Good Hope Mountain ʌ	120	51.09N	124.10W
Gooding	126	42.56N	114.42W
Goodland	122	39.21N	101.42W
Goose Bay	120	53.20N	60.25W
Gorakhpur	96	26.45N	83.22 E
Gore, Ityo.	92	8.08N	35.33 E
Gore, N.Z.	110	46.06S	168.58 E
Gorgān	70	36.50N	54.29 E
Gorki → Gor'kij ʌ	84	56.20N	44.00 E
Gor'kij (Gorky)	84	56.20N	44.00 E
Gorontalo	102	0.33N	123.03 E
Göteborg (Gothenburg)	73	57.43N	11.58 E
Gotland I	73	57.30N	18.33 E
Göttingen	74	51.32N	9.55 E
Gottwaldov	74	49.13N	17.41 E
Gouin, Réservoir ◖¹	120	48.38N	74.54W
Governador Valadares	116	18.51S	41.56W
Gowanda	124	42.27N	78.56W
Goya	118	29.08S	59.16W
Graaff-Reinet	90	32.14S	24.32 E
Gracias a Dios, Cabo ⊁	114	15.00N	83.10W
Grafton	106	29.41S	152.56 E
Grampian Mountains ⋌	72	56.45N	4.00W
Granada, Esp.	78	37.13N	3.41W
Granada, Nic.	114	11.56N	85.57W
Granby	124	45.24N	72.44W
Gran Canaria I	88	28.00N	15.36W
Gran Chaco ≃	118	23.00S	60.00W
Grand Bahama I	114	26.38N	78.25W
Grand Bank	120	47.06N	55.46W
Grand Bend	124	43.15N	81.45W
Grande ≃	119	19.52S	50.20W
Grande, Bahía c³	118	50.45S	68.45W
Grande, Ilha I	119	23.09S	44.14W
Grande, Rio (Bravo del Norte) ≃	122	25.55N	97.09W
Grand Erg de Bilma ➡²	88	18.30N	14.00 E
Grand Erg Occidental ➡²	88	30.30N	0.30 E
Grand Erg Oriental ➡²	88	30.30N	7.00 E
Grande-Terre I	114	16.20N	61.25W
Grand Forks, B.C., Can.	120	49.02N	118.27W
Grand Forks, N.D., U.S.	122	47.55N	97.01W
Grand Island	122	40.55N	98.20W
Grand Junction	122	39.03N	108.33W
Grand Rapids, Mb., Can.	120	53.08N	99.20W
Grand Rapids, Mi., U.S.	124	42.58N	85.40W
Grand-Saint-Bernard, Tunnel du ➡⁵	76	45.51N	7.11 E
Grand Teton ʌ	122	43.44N	110.48W
Grand Turk	114	21.28N	71.08W
Granollers	78	41.37N	2.18 E
Grants Pass	126	42.26N	123.19W
Grantsville	124	38.55N	81.05W
Gravenhurst	124	44.55N	79.22W
Grayling	124	44.39N	84.42W
Graz	74	47.05N	15.27 E
Great Abaco I	114	26.28N	77.05W
Great Artesian Basin ≃¹	108	25.00S	143.00 E
Great Astrolabe Reef ⊹²	111c	18.52S	178.31 E
Great Australian Bight c³	106	35.00S	130.00 E
Great Barrier Island I	110	36.10S	175.25 E
Great Barrier Reef ⊹²	106	18.00S	145.50 E
Great Basin ≃¹	122	40.00N	117.00W
Great Bear Lake ◖	120	66.00N	120.00W
Great Channel ⊍	104	6.25N	94.20 E
Great Dividing Range ⋌	106	25.00S	147.00 E
Greater Antilles II	114	20.00N	74.00W
Greater Sunda Islands II	102	2.00S	110.00 E
Great Exuma I	122	23.32N	75.50W
Great Falls	122	47.30N	111.17W
Great Himalaya Range ⋌	96	29.00N	83.00 E
Great Inagua I	114	21.05N	73.18W
Great Indian Desert (Thar Desert) ➡²	96	28.00N	72.00 E
Great Karroo ⋌¹	90	32.25S	22.40 E
Great Salt Lake ◖	122	41.10N	112.30W
Great Salt Lake Desert ➡²	126	40.40N	113.30W
Great Sandy Desert ➡², Austl.	106	21.30S	125.00 E
Great Sandy Desert ➡², Or., U.S.	126	43.35N	120.15W
Great Slave Lake ◖	120	61.30N	114.00W
Great Victoria Desert ➡²	106	28.30S	127.45 E

Name	Page No.	Lat.	Long.
Great Yarmouth	72	52.37N	1.44 E
Gréboun, Mont ʌ	88	20.00N	8.35 E
Greece □¹	70	39.00N	22.00 E
Green Bay	122	44.31N	88.01W
Greenfield	124	42.35N	72.36W
Greenland □²	66	70.00N	40.00W
Greenland Sea ᴛ²	68	77.00N	1.00W
Green Mountains ⩗	124	43.45N	72.45W
Greenock	72	55.57N	4.45W
Greensboro	122	36.04N	79.47W
Greensburg	124	40.18N	79.32W
Greenville, Mi., U.S.	124	43.10N	85.15W
Greenville, S.C., U.S.	122	34.51N	82.23W
Greenville, Tx., U.S.	122	33.08N	96.06W
Greenwood	122	33.30N	90.10W
Greifswald	74	54.05N	13.23 E
Grenada □¹	114	12.07N	61.40W
Grenoble	76	45.10N	5.43 E
Greymouth	110	42.28S	171.12 E
Grey Range ⩗	108	27.00S	143.35 E
Grimsby	72	53.35N	0.05W
Grodno	84	53.41N	23.50 E
Groningen	74	53.13N	6.33 E
Groote Eylandt I	106	14.00S	136.40 E
Grosseto	80	42.46N	11.08 E
Grossglockner ʌ	74	47.04N	12.42 E
Grove City	124	41.09N	80.05W
Groznyj	70	43.20N	45.42 E
Grudziądz	74	53.29N	18.45 E
Gruzinskaja Sovetskaja Socialisticeskaja Respublika □³	70	42.00N	44.00 E
Guadalajara, Esp.	78	40.38N	3.10W
Guadalajara, Méx.	112	20.40N	103.20W
Guadalcanal I	111a	9.32S	160.12 E
Guadalquivir ≃	78	36.47N	6.22W
Guadalupe	112	25.41N	100.15W
Guadalupe Peak ʌ	112	31.50N	104.52W
Guadeloupe □²	114	16.15N	61.35W
Guadiana ≃	78	37.14N	7.22W
Guam □²	102	13.28N	144.47 E
Guanajuato	112	21.01N	101.15W
Guangzhou (Canton)	98	23.06N	113.16 E
Guantánamo	114	20.08N	75.12W
Guaratinguetá	119	22.49S	45.13W
Guardafui, Cape ⊁	92	11.48N	51.22 E
Guatemala	114	14.38N	90.31W
Guatemala □¹	114	15.30N	90.15W
Guayaquil	116	2.10S	79.50W
Guayaquil, Golfo de c	116	3.00S	80.30W
Guaymas	112	27.56N	110.54W
Gubkin	70	51.18N	37.32 E
Guelma	80	36.28N	7.26 E
Guernsey □²	76	49.28N	2.35W
Guildford	72	51.14N	0.35W
Guilin	98	25.11N	110.09 E
Guinea □¹	88	11.00N	10.00W
Guinea, Gulf of c	88	2.00N	2.30 E
Guinea-Bissau □¹	88	12.00N	15.00W
Güines	114	22.50N	82.02W
Güiria	114	10.34N	62.18W
Guiyang	98	26.35N	106.43 E
Gujarat □³	96	22.00N	72.00 E
Gujrānwāla	94	32.26N	74.33 E
Gujrāt	94	32.34N	74.05 E
Gulfport	112	30.22N	89.05W
Guntūr	95	16.18N	80.27 E
Gurjev	70	47.07N	51.56 E
Guyana □¹	116	5.00N	59.00W
Gwalior	96	26.13N	78.10 E
Gwanda	90	20.57S	29.01 E
Gweru	90	19.27S	29.49 E
Gydanskaja Guba c	86	71.20N	76.30 E

Name	Page No.	Lat.	Long.
Gyöngyös	74	47.47N	19.56 E
Györ	74	47.42N	17.38 E

H

Haarlem	74	52.23N	4.38 E
Haast	110	43.53S	169.03 E
Hachinohe	100	40.30N	141.29 E
Hachiōji	100	35.39N	139.20 E
Hadera	93	32.26N	34.55 E
Ha-dong	104	20.58N	105.46 E
Hadūr Shu'ayb ʌ	92	15.18N	43.59 E
Hagerstown	124	39.37N	77.45W
Ha-giang	104	22.50N	104.59 E
Haikou	98	20.06N	110.21 E
Hainan □⁴	98	19.00N	109.30 E
Hainandao I	104	19.00N	109.30 E
Hai-phong	104	20.52N	106.41 E
Haiti □¹	114	19.00N	72.25W
Hakodate	100a	41.45N	140.43 E
Halab (Aleppo)	93	36.12N	37.10 E
Haleakala Crater ≛⁶	127	20.43N	156.13W
Halifax	120	44.39N	63.36W
Halle	74	51.29N	11.58 E
Hallowell	124	44.17N	69.47W
Halls Creek	106	18.16S	127.46 E
Halmahera I	102	1.00N	128.00 E
Halmstad	73	56.39N	12.50 E
Haltiatunturi ʌ	73	69.18N	21.16 E
Hamadān	92	34.48N	48.30 E
Hamāh	93	35.08N	36.45 E
Hamamatsu	100	34.42N	137.44 E
Hamar	73	60.48N	11.06 E
Hamburg	74	53.33N	9.59 E
Hämeenlinna	73	61.00N	24.27 E
Hameln	74	52.06N	9.21 E
Hamhŭng	98	39.54N	127.32 E
Hamilton, Ber.	122	32.17N	64.46W
Hamilton, On., Can.	120	43.15N	79.51W
Hamilton, N.Z.	110	37.45S	175.17 E
Hamilton, Oh., U.S.	124	39.23N	84.33W
Hammamet, Golfe de c	80	36.05N	10.40 E
Hammam Lif	80	36.44N	10.20 E
Hammerfest	73	70.40N	23.42 E
Hammond	112	30.30N	90.27W
Handan	98	36.37N	114.29 E
Hangzhou	98	30.15N	120.10 E
Hannover	74	52.24N	9.44 E
Ha-noi	104	21.02N	105.51 E
Hanover	124	39.48N	76.59W
Hanzhong	98	32.59N	107.11 E
Harare	90	17.50S	31.03 E
Harbin	98	45.45N	126.41 E
Hardangerfjorden c²	73	60.10N	6.00 E
Harer	92	9.18N	42.08 E
Hargeysa	92	9.30N	44.03 E
Harlingen	112	26.11N	97.41W
Harney Basin ≥¹	126	43.15N	120.40W
Härnösand	73	62.38N	17.56 E
Harrisburg	124	40.16N	76.53W
Harrison, Cape ⊁	120	54.55N	57.55W
Harrisonburg	124	38.26N	78.52W
Harrisville, Mi., U.S.	124	44.39N	83.17W
Harrisville, N.Y., U.S.	124	43.35N	75.31W
Harstad	73	68.46N	16.30 E
Hartford	124	41.46N	72.41W
Harts ≃	90	28.24S	24.17 E
Haryana □³	96	29.20N	76.20 E
Haskovo	82	41.56N	25.33 E
Hastings, N.Z.	110	39.38S	176.51 E
Hastings, Eng., U.K.	72	50.51N	0.36 E
Hattiesburg	122	31.19N	89.17W
Hat Yai	104	7.01N	100.28 E

Name	Page No.	Lat.	Long.
Haugesund	73	59.25N	5.18 E
Havana			
→ La Habana	114	23.08N	82.22W
Havelock	124	44.26N	77.53W
Haverhill	124	42.46N	71.04W
Havre-Saint-Pierre	120	50.14N	63.36W
Hawaii □ 3	127	20.00N	157.45W
Hawaii I	127	19.30N	155.30W
Hawaiian Islands II	66	24.00N	167.00W
Hawera	110	39.35S	174.17 E
Hawick	72	55.25N	2.47W
Hawke Bay c	110	39.20S	177.30 E
Hawthorne	126	38.31N	118.37W
Hay	106	34.30S	144.51 E
Hayden Peak ∧	126	42.59N	116.39W
Hayrabolu	82	41.12N	27.06 E
Hay River	120	60.51N	115.40W
Hays	122	38.52N	99.19W
Hazleton	124	40.57N	75.58W
Hearst	120	49.41N	83.40W
Hebrides II	70	57.00N	6.30W
Hebron	120	58.12N	62.38W
Hecate Strait ʯ	120	53.00N	131.00W
Ḥefa (Haifa)	93	32.50N	35.00 E
Hefei	98	31.51N	117.17 E
Hegang	98	47.24N	130.17 E
Heidelberg	74	49.25N	8.43 E
Heidenheim	74	49.01N	10.44 E
Heilbronn	74	49.08N	9.13 E
Heilongjiang (Amur) ≃	86	52.56N	141.10 E
Helena	122	46.35N	112.02W
Helen Island I	102	2.58N	131.49 E
Hellín	78	38.31N	1.41W
Helmand ≃	94	31.12N	61.34 E
Helmsdale	72	58.07N	3.40W
Helsingborg	73	56.03N	12.42 E
Helsinki (Helsingfors)	73	60.10N	24.58 E
Hengyang	98	26.51N	112.30 E
Henzada	104	17.38N	95.28 E
Herät	94	34.20N	62.07 E
Hereford	72	52.04N	2.43W
Herford	74	52.06N	8.40 E
Hermosillo	112	29.04N	110.58W
Herning	73	56.08N	8.59 E
Hibbing	122	47.25N	92.56W
Hidalgo del Parral	112	26.56N	105.40W
Hilo	127	19.43N	155.05W
Himachal Pradesh □ 8	96	32.00N	77.00 E
Himalayas ⋌	96	28.00N	84.00 E
Himeji	100	34.49N	134.42 E
Hims (Homs)	93	34.44N	36.43 E
Hindu Kush ⋌	96	36.00N	71.30 E
Hinganghät	95	20.34N	78.50 E
Hinnøya I	73	68.30N	16.00 E
Hinton	120	53.25N	117.34W
Hirosaki	100	40.35N	140.28 E
Hiroshima	100	34.24N	132.27 E
Hispaniola I	114	19.00N	71.00W
Hitachi	100	36.36N	140.39 E
Hjørring	73	57.28N	9.59 E
Hobart	106	42.53S	147.19 E
Hobbs	112	32.42N	103.08W
Hochalmspitze ∧	74	47.01N	13.19 E
Hochschwab ∧	74	47.37N	15.09 E
Hódmezővásárhely	74	46.25N	20.20 E
Hōfu	100	34.03N	131.34 E
Hohe Tauern ⋌	74	47.10N	12.30 E
Hokitika	110	42.43S	170.58 E
Hokkaidō I	100a	44.00N	143.00 E
Holbrook	122	34.54N	110.09W
Holden	124	37.49N	82.03W
Holguín	114	20.53N	76.15W
Hollister	126	36.51N	121.24W
Holstebro	73	56.21N	8.38 E
Holy Cross	128	62.12N	159.47W
Holyhead	72	53.19N	4.38W
Holyoke	124	42.12N	72.37W
Hombori Tondo ∧	88	15.16N	1.40W
Homer	128	59.39N	151.33W
Honduras □ 1	114	15.00N	86.30W
Honduras, Gulf of c	114	16.10N	87.50W
Hønefoss	73	60.10N	10.18 E
Honesdale	124	41.34N	75.15W
Hon-gay	104	20.57N	107.05 E
Hong Kong □ 2	98	22.15N	114.10 E
Honguedo, Détroit d' ʯ	120	49.15N	64.00W
Honiara	111a	9.26S	159.57 E
Honolulu	127	21.18N	157.51W
Honshū I	100	36.00N	138.00 E
Hood, Mount ∧	122	45.23N	121.41W
Hooghly ≃	96	21.56N	88.04 E
Hoonah	128	58.07N	135.26W
Hooper Bay	128	61.31N	166.06W
Hoover Dam ⇀ 6	126	36.00N	114.27W
Hopedale	120	55.28N	60.13W
Hormuz, Strait of ʯ	92	26.34N	56.15 E
Horn, Cape			
→ Hornos, Cabo de ⋋	118	55.59S	67.16W
Hornell	124	42.19N	77.39W
Hornos, Cabo de (Cape			
Horn) ⋋	118	55.59S	67.16W
Hospitalet	78	41.22N	2.08 E
Hot Springs National Park	122	34.30N	93.04W
Houghton Lake	124	44.18N	84.45W
Houston	122	29.45N	95.21W
Howard City	124	43.23N	85.28W
Howe, Cape ⋋	106	37.31S	149.59 E
Howell	124	42.36N	83.55W
Howland	124	45.14N	68.39W
Howrah	96	22.35N	88.20 E
Hradec Králové	74	50.12N	15.50 E
Hranice	74	49.33N	17.44 E
Hsinchu	98	24.48N	120.58 E
Hsinkao Shan ∧	98	23.28N	120.57 E
Hua Hin	104	12.34N	99.58 E
Huainan	98	32.40N	117.00 E
Huallanca	116	8.49S	77.52W
Huambo	90	12.44S	15.47 E
Huancayo	116	12.04S	75.14W
Huanghe ≃	98	37.32N	118.19 E
Huangshi	98	30.13N	115.05 E
Huánuco	116	9.55S	76.14W
Huaras	116	9.32S	77.32W
Huascarán, Nevado ∧	116	9.07S	77.37W
Huasco	118	28.28S	71.14W
Hudiksvall	73	61.44N	17.07 E
Hudson	124	42.15N	73.47W
Hudson ≃	124	40.42N	74.02W
Hudson Bay	120	52.52N	102.25W
Hudson Bay c	120	60.00N	86.00W
Hudson Strait ʯ	120	62.30N	72.00W
Hue	104	16.28N	107.36 E
Huehuetenango	114	15.20N	91.28W
Huelva	78	37.16N	6.57W
Huesca	78	42.08N	0.25W
Hughenden	106	20.51S	144.12 E
Huhehaote	98	40.51N	111.40 E
Huixtla	112	15.09N	92.28W
Hull	124	45.26N	75.43W
Humboldt ≃	126	40.02N	118.31W
Humboldt, Mont ∧	111b	21.53S	166.25 E
Humphreys Peak ∧	122	35.20N	111.40W
Hunedoara	82	45.45N	22.54 E
Hungary □ 1	70	47.00N	20.00 E
Hunkurāb, Ra's ⋋	93	24.34N	35.10 E
Huntington	124	38.25N	82.26W

Name	Page No.	Lat.	Long.
Kholm	96	36.42N	67.41 E
Khon Kaen	104	16.26N	102.50 E
Khulna	96	22.48N	89.33 E
Khunjerab Pass)(	96	36.52N	75.27 E
Khyber Pass)(	96	34.05N	71.10 E
Kiel	74	54.20N	10.08 E
Kielce	74	50.52N	20.37 E
Kieler Bucht c	74	54.35N	10.35 E
Kiev			
→ Kijev	70	50.26N	30.31 E
Kigali	90	1.57S	30.04 E
Kijev	70	50.26N	30.31 E
Kikinda	82	45.50N	20.28 E
Kikládhes II	82	37.30N	25.00 E
Kikwit	90	5.02S	18.49 E
Kilauea Crater ± [6]	127	19.25N	155.17W
Kilimanjaro ▲	90	3.04S	37.22 E
Kilkenny	72	52.39N	7.15W
Killarney	124	45.58N	81.31W
Killeen	122	31.07N	97.43W
Kilmarnock	72	55.36N	4.30W
Kimberley	90	28.43S	24.46 E
Kimberley Plateau ⋊ [1]	106	17.00S	127.00 E
Kimch'aek	98	40.41N	129.12 E
Kinabalu, Gunong ▲	102	6.05N	116.33 E
Kindersley	120	51.27N	109.10W
Kindu	90	2.57S	25.56 E
King Island I	108	39.50S	144.00 E
Kingman	126	35.11N	114.03W
Kings Canyon National			
Park ♦	126	36.48N	118.30W
King's Lynn	72	52.45N	0.24 E
Kingston, On., Can.	120	44.14N	76.30W
Kingston, Jam.	114	18.00N	76.48W
Kingston, N.Z.	110	45.20S	168.42 E
Kingston, N.Y., U.S.	124	41.55N	73.59W
Kingston upon Hull	72	53.45N	0.20W
Kingstown	114	13.09N	61.14W
Kingsville	112	27.30N	97.51W
Kinshasa (Léopoldville)	90	4.18S	15.18 E
Kinyeti ▲	92	3.57N	32.54 E
Kiparissiakós Kólpos c	82	37.37N	21.24 E
Kira Kira	111a	10.27S	161.55 E
Kirensk	86	57.46N	108.08 E
Kiribati □ [1]	66	4.00S	175.00 E
Kirínia	93	35.20N	33.19 E
Kirinyaga ▲	90	2.43N	36.51 E
Kirkcaldy	72	56.07N	3.10W
Kırklareli	82	41.44N	27.12 E
Kirksville	122	40.11N	92.34W
Kirkük	92	35.28N	44.28 E
Kirkwall	72	58.59N	2.58W
Kirov	84	54.05N	34.20 E
Kirovabad	70	40.40N	46.22 E
Kirovograd	70	48.30N	32.18 E
Kīrthar Range ⋊	96	27.00N	67.10 E
Kiruna	73	67.51N	20.16 E
Kiryū	100	36.24N	139.20 E
Kisangani (Stanleyville)	90	0.30N	25.12 E
Kishiwada	100	34.28N	135.22 E
Kišin'ov	70	47.00N	28.50 E
Kiskörei-víztároló ☷ [1]	74	47.35N	20.40 E
Kiskunfélegyháza	74	46.43N	19.52 E
Kiskunhalas	74	46.26N	19.30 E
Kismaayo	90	0.23S	42.30 E
Kissidougou	88	9.11N	10.06W
Kita	88	13.03N	9.29W
Kitakyūshū	100	33.53N	130.50 E
Kitami	100a	43.48N	143.54 E
Kitchener	120	43.27N	80.29W
Kíthira I	82	36.20N	22.58 E
Kitwe	90	12.49S	28.13 E
Kjustendil	82	42.17N	22.41 E
Kladno	74	50.08N	14.05 E
Klagenfurt	74	46.38N	14.18 E
Klamath ≃	126	41.33N	124.04W
Klamath Falls	122	42.13N	121.46W
Klamath Mountains ⋊	126	41.40N	123.20W
Klarälven ≃	73	59.23N	13.32 E
Klerksdorp	90	26.58S	26.39 E
Klincy	84	52.47N	32.14 E
Kłodzko	74	50.27N	16.39 E
Klondike □ [9]	128	63.30N	139.00W
Kl'učevskaja Sopka,			
Vulkan ▲ [1]	86	56.04N	160.38 E
Kneža	82	43.30N	24.05 E
Knoxville	122	35.57N	83.55W
Kōbe	100	34.41N	135.10 E
København (Copenhagen)	73	55.40N	12.35 E
Koblenz	74	50.21N	7.35 E
Kōchi	100	33.33N	133.33 E
Kodiak	128	57.48N	152.23W
Kodiak Island I	128	57.30N	153.30W
Koes	90	25.59S	19.08 E
Kōfu	100	35.39N	138.35 E
Kokkola (Gamlakarleby)	73	63.50N	23.07 E
Koksoak ≃	120	58.32N	68.10W
Kola Peninsula			
→ Kol'skij Poluostrov ➤ [1]	86	67.30N	37.00 E
Kolhāpur	95	16.42N	74.13 E
Koliganek	128	59.48N	157.25W
Köln (Cologne)	74	50.56N	6.59 E
Kolovrat, Mount ▲	111a	9.10S	161.05 E
Kolpaševo	86	58.20N	82.50 E
Kol'skij Poluostrov (Kola			
Peninsula) ➤ [1]	86	67.30N	37.00 E
Kolwezi	90	10.43S	25.28 E
Kolyma ≃	86	69.30N	161.00 E
Komárno	74	47.45N	18.09 E
Komatsu	100	36.24N	136.27 E
Komló	74	46.12N	18.16 E
Kommunizma, Pik			
(Communism Peak) ▲	94	38.57N	72.01 E
Komotiní	82	41.08N	25.25 E
Komsomolec, Ostrov I	86	80.30N	95.00 E
Komsomol'sk-na-Amure	86	50.35N	137.02 E
Kona Coast ± [2]	127	19.25N	155.55W
Koné	111b	21.04S	164.52 E
Kŏng, Kaôh I	104	11.20N	103.00 E
Königsberg			
→ Kaliningrad	84	54.43N	20.30 E
Konin	74	52.13N	18.16 E
Könkämäälven ≃	73	68.29N	22.17 E
Konstanz	74	47.40N	9.10 E
Kontagora	88	10.24N	5.28 E
Konya	70	37.52N	32.31 E
Kor'akskoje Nagorje ⋊	86	62.30N	172.00 E
Korça	82	40.37N	20.46 E
Korea, North □ [1]	98	40.00N	127.00 E
Korea, South □ [1]	98	36.30N	128.00 E
Korinthiakós Kólpos c	82	38.19N	22.04 E
Kórinthos (Corinth)	82	37.56N	22.56 E
Korolevu	111c	18.13S	177.44 E
Koro Sea ⊤ [2]	111c	18.00S	179.50 E
Korsør	73	55.20N	11.09 E
Kortrijk (Courtrai)	74	50.50N	3.16 E
Kos I	82	36.50N	27.10 E
Kosciusko, Mount ▲	108	36.27S	148.16 E
Košice	74	48.43N	21.15 E
Kosovska Mitrovica	82	42.53N	20.52 E
Kostroma	84	57.46N	40.55 E
Koszalin (Köslin)	74	54.12N	16.09 E
Kota Baharu	104	6.08N	102.15 E
Kota Kinabalu	102	5.59N	116.04 E
Kotel'nyj, Ostrov I	86	75.45N	138.44 E
Kotka	73	60.28N	26.55 E

Name	Page No.	Lat.	Long.
Kotuj ≃	86	71.55N	102.05 E
Kotzebue Sound ⋓	128	66.20N	163.00W
Koussi, Emi ⋀	88	19.50N	18.30 E
Kouvola	73	60.52N	26.42 E
Kowloon (Jiulong)	98	22.18N	114.10 E
Koyukuk ≃	128	64.56N	157.30W
Koza	101b	26.20N	127.50 E
Kra, Isthmus of ⋆ ³	104	10.20N	99.00 E
Krâchéh	104	12.29N	106.01 E
Kragerø	73	58.52N	9.25 E
Kragujevac	82	44.01N	20.55 E
Kraków	74	50.03N	19.58 E
Kraljevo	82	43.43N	20.41 E
Kranj	80	46.15N	14.21 E
Krasnodar	70	45.02N	39.00 E
Krasnojarsk	86	56.01N	92.50 E
Krasnokamsk	70	58.04N	55.48 E
Krasnoural`sk	86	58.21N	60.03 E
Krems an der Donau	74	48.25N	15.36 E
Kričov	84	53.42N	31.43 E
Kristiansand	73	58.10N	8.00 E
Kristianstad	73	56.02N	14.08 E
Kristiansund	73	63.07N	7.45 E
Kríti I	82	35.29N	24.42 E
Kritikón Pélagos ⊤ ²	82	35.46N	23.54 E
Krivoj Rog	70	47.55N	33.21 E
Krnov	74	50.05N	17.41 E
Kroonstad	90	27.46S	27.12 E
Kropotkin	86	58.30N	115.17 E
Krung Thep (Bangkok)	104	13.45N	100.31 E
Kruševac	82	43.35N	21.20 E
Ksar-el-Kebir	78	35.01N	5.54W
Kuala Lumpur	104	3.10N	101.42 E
Kuala Terengganu	104	5.20N	103.08 E
Kuantan	104	3.48N	103.20 E
Kuching	104	1.33N	110.20 E
Kuhmo	73	64.08N	29.31 E
Kujbyšev, S.S.S.R.	70	53.12N	50.09 E
Kujbyšev, S.S.S.R.	86	55.27N	78.19 E
Kula Kangri ⋀	96	28.03N	90.27 E
Kumagaya	100	36.08N	139.23 E
Kumamoto	100	32.48N	130.43 E
Kumanovo	82	42.08N	21.43 E
Kumasi	88	6.41N	1.35W
Kumo	88	10.03N	11.13 E
Kumon Range ⋌	104	26.30N	97.15 E
Kunlunshanmai ⋌	96	36.30N	88.00 E
Kunming	98	25.05N	102.40 E
Kuopio	73	62.54N	27.41 E
Kupang	102	10.10S	123.35 E
Kupino	86	54.22N	77.18 E
Kurashiki	100	34.35N	133.46 E
Kure	100	34.14N	132.34 E
Kurgan	86	55.26N	65.18 E
Kuril`skije Ostrova (Kuril Islands) II	86	46.10N	152.00 E
Kurmuk	88	10.33N	34.17 E
Kursk	70	51.42N	36.12 E
Kuruman	90	27.28S	23.28 E
Kurume	100	33.19N	130.31 E
Kuskokwim ≃	128	60.17N	162.27W
Kustanaj	70	53.10N	63.35 E
Kūstī	88	13.10N	32.40 E
Kutch, Gulf of c	96	22.36N	69.30 E
Kutno	74	52.15N	19.23 E
Kuwait □¹	92	29.30N	47.45 E
Kuybyshev → Kujbyšev	86	55.27N	78.19 E
Kwangju	98	35.09N	126.54 E
Kwekwe	90	18.55S	29.49 E
Kyle of Lochalsh	72	57.17N	5.43W
Kyoga, Lake ⊜	90	1.30N	33.00 E
Kyōto	100	35.00N	135.45 E

Name	Page No.	Lat.	Long.
Kyūshū I	100	33.00N	131.00 E
Kyzyl	86	51.42N	94.27 E

L

Name	Page No.	Lat.	Long.
Labe (Elbe) ≃	74	53.50N	9.00 E
La Blanquilla I	114	11.51N	64.37W
Labrador ◆¹	120	54.00N	62.00W
Labrador City	120	52.57N	66.55W
Labrador Sea ⊤²	120	57.00N	53.00W
Labutta	104	16.09N	94.46 E
Laccadive Islands II	95	10.00N	73.00 E
Laccadive Sea ⊤²	95	8.00N	75.00 E
La Ceiba	114	15.47N	86.50W
Lac-giao	104	12.40N	108.03 E
Lachlan ≃	108	34.21S	143.57 E
La Chorrera	114	8.53N	79.47W
Lac la Biche	120	54.46N	111.58W
Lac-Mégantic	124	45.36N	70.53W
Laconia	124	43.31N	71.28W
La Coruña	78	43.22N	8.23W
La Crosse	122	43.48N	91.14W
Ladožskoje Ozero (Lake Ladoga) ⊜	73	61.00N	31.30 E
Ladysmith	90	28.34S	29.45 E
Lafayette	122	30.13N	92.01W
Laghouat	88	33.50N	2.59 E
Lagos	88	6.27N	3.24 E
Lagrange	124	41.39N	85.25W
La Gran Sabana ≚	116	5.30N	61.30W
La Guajira, Península de ⋋¹	116	12.00N	71.40W
Laguna Beach	126	33.32N	117.46W
Lagunillas	116	19.38S	63.43W
La Habana (Havana)	114	23.08N	82.22W
Lahaina	127	20.52N	156.40W
Lahore	94	31.35N	74.18 E
Lahti	73	60.58N	25.40 E
Laingsburg	90	33.11S	20.51 E
Lake Charles	122	30.13N	93.13W
Lake Harbour	120	62.51N	69.53W
Lake Havasu City	126	34.29N	114.19W
Lake Placid	124	44.16N	73.58W
Lake Pleasant	124	43.28N	74.25W
Lakeview	126	42.11N	120.20W
Lakonikós Kólpos c	82	36.25N	22.37 E
Lakshadweep □³	95	10.00N	73.00 E
La Loche	120	56.29N	109.27W
La Mancha ◆¹	78	39.05N	3.00W
La Manche (English Channel) ⋓	76	50.20N	1.00W
Lamap	111b	16.26S	167.43 E
Lambaréné	88	0.42S	10.13 E
Lambasa	111c	16.26S	179.24 E
Lambert's Bay	90	32.05S	18.17 E
Lamesa	112	32.44N	101.57W
Lamía	82	38.54N	22.26 E
Lamont	126	35.15N	118.54W
Lampang	104	18.18N	99.31 E
Lamphun	104	18.35N	99.01 E
Lamu	90	2.16S	40.54 E
Lanai I	127	20.50N	156.55W
Lanai City	127	20.49N	156.55W
Lancaster, On., Can.	124	45.15N	74.30W
Lancaster, Eng., U.K.	72	54.03N	2.48W
Lancaster, Ca., U.S.	126	34.41N	118.08W
Lancaster, Oh., U.S.	124	39.43N	82.36W
Lancaster, Pa., U.S.	124	40.02N	76.18W
Lancaster Sound ⋓	120	74.13N	84.00W
Lanchow → Lanzhou	98	36.03N	103.41 E
Land's End ⋋	72	50.03N	5.44W
Landshut	74	48.33N	12.09 E

Name	Page No.	Lat.	Long.
Langenhagen	74	52.27N	9.44 E
Langsa	104	4.28N	97.58 E
L'Annonciation	124	46.25N	74.52W
Lansing	124	42.43N	84.33W
Lanzhou	98	36.03N	103.41 E
Laos □ [1]	102	18.00N	105.00 E
La Palma	114	8.25N	78.09W
La Paragua	116	6.50N	63.20W
La Paz, Bol.	116	16.30S	68.09W
La Paz, Méx.	112	24.10N	110.18W
La Perouse Strait (Sōya-kaikyō) ṳ	100a	45.45N	142.00 E
La Piedad [Cavadas]	112	20.21N	102.00W
Lapland ◆ [1]	73	68.00N	25.00 E
La Plata, Arg.	118	34.55S	57.57W
La Plata, Md., U.S.	124	38.31N	76.58W
Lappeenranta	73	61.04N	28.11 E
Laptevych, More (Laptev Sea) ᵜ [2]	86	76.00N	126.00 E
La Quiaca	118	22.06S	65.37W
L'Aquila	80	42.22N	13.22 E
Larache	78	35.12N	6.10W
Laramie	122	41.18N	105.35W
Laredo	122	27.30N	99.30W
La Rioja	118	29.26S	66.51W
Lárisa	82	39.38N	22.25 E
Lārkāna	96	27.33N	68.13 E
La Rochelle	76	46.10N	1.10W
La Roche-sur-Yon	76	46.40N	1.26W
La Ronge	120	55.06N	105.17W
La Sarre	120	48.48N	79.12W
Las Cruces	112	32.18N	106.46W
La Serena	118	29.54S	71.16W
Las Flores	118	36.03S	59.07W
Las Lomitas	118	24.42S	60.36W
Las Minas, Cerro ▲	114	14.33N	88.39W
Las Palmas de Gran Canaria	88	28.06N	15.24W
La Spezia	80	44.07N	9.50 E
Lassen Peak ▲ [1]	126	40.29N	121.31W
Las Vegas	126	36.10N	115.08W
La Tortuga, Isla I	114	10.56N	65.20W
La Tuque	120	47.26N	72.47W
Lātūr	95	18.24N	76.35 E
Latvijskaja Sovetskaja Socialističeskaja Respublika □ [3]	70	57.00N	25.00 E
Lauchhammer	74	51.30N	13.47 E
Lau Group II	111c	18.20S	178.30W
Launceston	106	41.26S	147.08 E
La Union	114	13.20N	87.57W
Laurel	112	31.41N	89.07W
Lausanne	76	46.31N	6.38 E
Lautoka	111c	17.37S	177.27 E
Laval, P.Q., Can.	124	45.33N	73.44W
Laval, Fr.	76	48.04N	0.46W
Lavapié, Punta ➤	118	37.09S	73.35W
La Vela, Cabo de ➤	114	12.13N	72.11W
Lavras	119	21.14S	45.00W
Lawrenceburg	124	39.05N	84.51W
Lawton	122	34.36N	98.23W
Lead	122	44.21N	103.45W
Leamington	124	42.03N	82.36W
Lebanon, N.H., U.S.	124	43.38N	72.15W
Lebanon, Pa., U.S.	124	40.20N	76.24W
Lebanon □ [1]	93	33.50N	35.50 E
Lecce	80	40.23N	18.11 E
Lecco	80	45.51N	9.23 E
Leeds	72	53.50N	1.35W
Leeuwarden	74	53.12N	5.46 E
Leeward Islands II	114	17.00N	63.00W
Legnica (Liegnitz)	74	51.13N	16.09 E
Le Havre	76	49.30N	0.08 E
Lehighton	124	40.50N	75.42W
Leicester	72	52.38N	1.05W
Leinster □ [9]	72	53.05N	7.00W
Leipzig	74	51.19N	12.20 E
Leland	124	45.01N	85.45W
Lemanmanu Mission	111a	5.02S	154.35 E
Le Mans	76	48.00N	0.12 E
Leme	119	22.12S	47.24W
Lemesós (Limassol)	93	34.40N	33.02 E
Lemmon	122	45.56N	102.09W
Lena ≈	86	72.25N	126.40 E
Lenakel	111b	19.32S	169.16 E
Leninakan	70	40.48N	43.50 E
Leningrad	84	59.55N	30.15 E
Leninsk-Kuzneckij	86	54.38N	86.10 E
Lens	76	50.26N	2.50 E
Leoben	74	47.23N	15.06 E
León, Esp.	78	42.36N	5.34W
León, Nic.	114	12.26N	86.53W
León [de los Aldamas]	112	21.07N	101.40W
Leonora	106	28.53S	121.20 E
Leopoldina	119	21.32S	42.38W
Lérida	78	41.37N	0.37 F
Lerwick	72	60.09N	1.09W
Lesbos → Lésvos I	82	39.10N	26.20 E
Les Cayes	114	18.12N	73.45W
Leskovac	82	42.59N	21.57 E
Lesotho □ [1]	90	29.30S	28.30 E
Lesozavodsk	86	45.28N	133.27 E
Lesser Antilles II	114	15.00N	61.00W
Lesser Sunda Islands II	102	9.00S	120.00 E
Lésvos I	82	39.10N	26.20 E
Leszno	74	51.51N	16.35 E
Letea, Ostrovul I	82	45.20N	29.20 E
Lethbridge	120	49.42N	112.50W
Lethem	116	3.23N	59.48W
Leticia	116	4.09S	69.57W
Levanger	73	63.45N	11.18 E
Leverkusen	74	51.03N	6.59 E
Levin	110	40.37S	175.17 E
Levkás I	82	38.39N	20.27 E
Lewis, Isle of I	72	58.10N	6.40W
Lewiston, Id., U.S.	122	46.25N	117.01W
Lewiston, Me., U.S.	124	44.06N	70.12W
Lewistown	124	40.35N	77.34W
Lexington, Ky., U.S.	124	38.02N	84.30W
Lexington, Ma., U.S.	124	42.26N	71.13W
Lexington Park	124	38.16N	76.27W
Leyte I	102	10.50N	124.50 E
Leyte Gulf c	102	10.50N	125.25 E
Lhasa	98	29.40N	91.09 E
Liaoyuan	98	42.54N	125.07 E
Liberal	122	37.02N	100.55W
Liberec	74	50.46N	15.03 E
Liberia	114	10.38N	85.27W
Liberia □ [1]	88	6.00N	10.00W
Libertad	114	8.20N	69.37W
Lībīyah, Aş-Şaḥrā' al- (Libyan Desert) ◆ [2]	88	24.00N	25.00 E
Libreville	90	0.23N	9.27 E
Libya □ [1]	88	27.00N	17.00 E
Licata	80	37.05N	13.56 E
Lichinga	90	13.18S	35.14 E
Liechtenstein □ [1]	70	47.09N	9.35 E
Liège	74	50.38N	5.34 E
Lier	74	51.08N	4.34 E
Liezen	74	47.35N	14.15 E
Lifou, Île I	111b	20.53S	167.13 E
Ligurian Sea ᵜ [2]	76	43.00N	8.00 E
Lihue	127	21.58N	159.22W
Likasi (Jadotville)	90	10.59S	26.44 E
Lille	76	50.38N	3.04 E

Name	Page No.	Lat.	Long.
Luzon I	102	16.00N	121.00 E
Luzon Strait ⩗	102	20.30N	121.00 E
L'vov	70	49.50N	24.00 E
Lynch, Lac ⊜	124	46.25N	77.05W
Lynn	124	42.28N	70.57W
Lynn Lake	120	56.51N	101.03W
Lyon	76	45.45N	4.51 E

M

Name	Page No.	Lat.	Long.
Ma'ān	93	30.12N	35.44 E
Maastricht	74	50.52N	5.43 E
McAdam	124	45.36N	67.20W
Macaé	119	22.23S	41.47W
McAlester	122	34.56N	95.46W
McAllen	112	26.12N	98.13W
Macapá	116	0.02N	51.03W
Macau (Aomen)	98	22.14N	113.35 E
Macau □²	98	22.10N	113.33 E
McComb	112	31.14N	90.27W
McConnellsburg	124	39.55N	77.59W
McCook	122	40.12N	100.37W
Macdonnell Ranges ⋌	106	23.45S	133.20 E
Macedonia □⁹	82	41.00N	23.00 E
Maceió	116	9.40S	35.43W
Macerata	80	43.18N	13.27 E
McGill	126	39.24N	114.46W
Mcgrath	128	62.58N	155.38W
Machačkala	70	42.58N	47.30 E
Machias	124	44.42N	67.27W
Machupicchu	116	13.07S	72.34W
Macina ➝¹	88	14.30N	5.00W
Mackay	106	21.09S	149.11 E
Mackay, Lake ⊜	106	22.30S	129.00 E
Mackenzie ⥲	120	69.15N	134.08W
Mackenzie Bay c	120	69.00N	136.30W
Mackenzie Mountains ⋌	120	64.00N	130.00W
Mackinac, Straits of ⩗	122	45.49N	84.42W
Mackinaw City	124	45.47N	84.43W
McKinley, Mount ⋀	128	63.30N	151.00W
McLoughlin, Mount ⋀	126	42.27N	122.19W
Mâcon, Fr.	76	46.18N	4.50 E
Macon, Ga., U.S.	122	32.50N	83.37W
Madagascar □¹	90	19.00S	46.00 E
Madeira ⥲	116	3.22S	58.45W
Madeira, Arquipélago da (Madeira Islands) II	88	32.40N	16.45W
Mädelegabel ⋀	80	47.18N	10.18 E
Madera	126	36.57N	120.03W
Madhya Pradesh □³	96	23.00N	79.00 E
Madison, W.V., U.S.	124	38.04N	81.49W
Madison, Wi., U.S.	122	43.04N	89.24W
Madiun	102	7.37S	111.31 E
Madras	95	13.05N	80.17 E
Madre, Laguna c, Méx.	112	25.00N	97.40W
Madre, Laguna c, Tx., U.S.	112	27.00N	97.35W
Madre, Sierra ⋌	112	15.30N	92.35W
Madre del Sur, Sierra ⋌	112	17.00N	100.00W
Madre Occidental, Sierra ⋌	112	25.00N	105.00W
Madre Oriental, Sierra ⋌	112	22.00N	99.30W
Madrid	78	40.24N	3.41W
Madura I	102	7.00S	113.20 E
Madurai	95	9.56N	78.07 E
Madyan ➝¹	93	27.40N	35.35 E
Maebashi	100	36.23N	139.04 E
Maewo I	111b	15.10S	168.10 E
Magadan	86	59.34N	150.48 E
Magallanes, Estrecho de (Strait of Magellan) ⩗	118	54.00S	71.00W
Magangué	116	9.14N	74.45W
Magdalena	116	13.20S	64.08W
Magdalena ⥲	116	11.06N	74.51W

Name	Page No.	Lat.	Long.
Magdeburg	74	52.07N	11.38 E
Maghāghah	93	28.39N	30.50 E
Magnitogorsk	70	53.27N	59.04 E
Magog	124	45.16N	72.09W
Magwe	104	20.09N	94.55 E
Mahābhārat Range ⋌	96	27.40N	84.30 E
Mahajanga	90	15.43S	46.19 E
Mahārāshtra □³	95	19.00N	76.00 E
Mahia Peninsula ⋋¹	110	39.10S	177.53 E
Mahón	78	39.53N	4.15 E
Maiduguri	88	11.51N	13.10 E
Mai-Ndombe, Lac ⊜	90	2.00S	18.20 E
Maine □³	122	45.15N	69.15W
Mainland I	72	59.00N	3.10W
Mainz	74	50.01N	8.16 F
Maipo, Volcán ⋀¹	118	34.10S	69.50W
Maipú	118	36.52S	57.52W
Maiquetía	114	10.36N	66.57W
Majorca → Mallorca I	78	39.30N	3.00 E
Makasar, Selat (Makassar Strait) ⩗	102	2.00S	117.30 E
Makat	70	47.39N	53.19 E
Makgadikgadi Pans ⋈	90	20.45S	25.30 E
Makinsk	86	52.37N	70.26 E
Makkah (Mecca)	92	21.27N	39.49 E
Makó	74	46.13N	20.29 E
Makunudu Atoll I¹	95	6.20N	72.36 E
Makurdi	88	7.45N	8.32 E
Malabar Coast ⋅²	95	10.00N	76.15 E
Malabo	88	3.45N	8.47 E
Malacca, Strait of ⩗	104	2.30N	101.20 E
Málaga	78	36.43N	4.25W
Malaita I	111a	9.00S	161.00 E
Malakāl	88	9.31N	31.39 E
Malang	102	7.59S	112.37 E
Malange	90	9.32S	16.20 E
Malatya	70	38.21N	38.19 E
Malawi □¹	90	13.30S	34.00 E
Malaya □⁹	104	4.00N	102.00 E
Malay Peninsula ⋋¹	104	6.00N	101.00 E
Malaysia □¹	102	2.30N	112.30 E
Malbork	74	54.02N	19.01 E
Maldive Islands II	95	5.00N	73.00 E
Maldives □¹	95	3.15N	73.00 E
Malekula I	111b	16.15S	167.30 E
Malheur, South Fork ⥲	126	43.33N	118.10W
Mali □¹	88	17.00N	4.00W
Malik, Wādī al- V	88	18.02N	30.58 E
Malino, Bukit ⋀	102	0.45N	120.47 E
Malkara ⟋	82	40.53N	26.54 E
Mallaig	72	57.00N	5.50W
Mallawī	88	27.44N	30.50 E
Mallorca I	78	39.30N	3.00 E
Malmö	73	55.36N	13.00 E
Małopolska ➝¹	74	50.10N	21.30 E
Malpelo, Isla de I	116	3.59N	81.35W
Malta □¹	70	35.50N	14.35 E
Malta I	80	35.53N	14.27 E
Maluku (Moluccas) II	102	2.00S	128.00 E
Maluku, Laut (Molucca Sea) ⊤²	102	0.00	125.00 E
Mamagota	111a	6.46S	155.24 E
Manado	102	1.29N	124.51 E
Managua	114	12.09N	86.17W
Manakara	90	22.08S	48.01 E
Manaus	116	3.08S	60.01W
Manawai	111a	9.05S	161.11 E
Manchester, Eng., U.K.	72	53.30N	2.15W
Manchester, N.H., U.S.	124	42.59N	71.27W
Manchester, Vt., U.S.	124	43.09N	73.04W
Manchuria □⁹	98	47.00N	125.00 E
Mandal	73	58.02N	7.27 E

Name	Page No.	Lat.	Long.
Mandalay	104	22.00N	96.05 E
Mandeb, Bāb el- ꭡ	92	12.40N	43.20 E
Manfredonia	80	41.38N	15.55 E
Manfredonia, Golfo di c	80	41.35N	16.05 E
Mangalore	95	12.52N	74.53 E
Manhattan	122	39.11N	96.34W
Manhuaçu	119	20.15S	42.02W
Manila	102	14.35N	121.00 E
Manipur □ 8	96	25.00N	94.00 E
Manitoba □ 4	120	54.00N	97.00W
Manitoba, Lake ⊜	120	51.00N	98.45W
Manitoulin Island I	124	45.45N	82.30W
Manizales	116	5.05N	75.32W
Mankato	122	44.09N	93.59W
Mannar, Gulf of c	95	8.30N	79.00 E
Mannheim	74	49.29N	8.29 E
Mannington	124	39.31N	80.20W
Manono	90	7.18S	27.25 E
Manresa	78	41.44N	1.50 E
Mansfield	124	40.45N	82.30W
Mansfield, Mount ʌ	124	44.33N	72.49W
Manta	116	0.57S	80.44W
Mantes-la-Jolie	76	48.59N	1.43 E
Manton	124	44.24N	85.23W
Mantova	80	45.09N	10.48 E
Manzanares	78	39.00N	3.22W
Manzanillo, Cuba	114	20.21N	77.07W
Manzanillo, Méx.	112	19.03N	104.20W
Maoke, Pegunungan ʌ	102	4.00S	138.00 E
Mapire	114	7.45N	64.42W
Maputo (Lourenço Marques)	90	25.58S	32.35 E
Maracaibo	116	10.40N	71.37W
Maracaibo, Lago de ⊜	114	9.50N	71.30W
Maracay	116	10.15N	67.36W
Maragogipe	119	12.46S	38.55W
Maramureşului, Munţii ʌ	82	47.50N	24.45 E
Marañón ≃	116	4.30S	73.27W
Marathon	120	48.40N	86.25W
Maravovo	111a	9.17S	159.38 E
Marcy, Mount ʌ	124	44.07N	73.56W
Mardān	96	34.12N	72.02 E
Mar del Plata	118	38.00S	57.33W
Maré, Île I	111b	21.30S	168.00 E
Margarita, Isla de I	114	11.00N	64.00W
Margherita Peak ʌ	90	0.22N	29.51 E
Mariana Islands II	102	16.00N	145.30 E
Marianao	114	23.05N	82.26W
Marías, Islas II	112	21.25N	106.28W
Maribor	80	46.33N	15.39 E
Maricourt (Wakeham Bay)	120	61.36N	71.58W
Mariental	90	24.36S	17.59 E
Marietta	124	39.24N	81.27W
Marília	119	22.13S	49.56W
Marinette	122	45.06N	87.37W
Maringá	118	23.25S	51.55W
Marion, Mi., U.S.	124	44.06N	85.08W
Marion, Oh., U.S.	124	40.35N	83.07W
Maripa	114	7.26N	65.09W
Mariscal Estigarribia	118	22.02S	60.38W
Maritime Alps ʌ	76	44.15N	7.10 E
Markham, Mount ʌ	69	82.51S	161.21 E
Marlborough	124	42.20N	71.33W
Marmara Denizi (Sea of Marmara) ⲧ 2	82	40.40N	28.15 E
Marmara Gölü ⊜	82	38.37N	28.02 E
Marmet	124	38.14N	81.34W
Marne ≃	76	48.49N	2.24 E
Maroa	116	2.43N	67.33W
Maromokotro ʌ	90	14.01S	48.59 E
Maroua	88	10.36N	14.20 E
Marovoay	90	16.06S	46.39 E
Marquette	122	46.32N	87.23W
Marrah, Jabal ʌ	88	14.04N	24.21 E
Marrakech	88	31.38N	8.00W
Marsabit	92	2.20N	37.59 E
Marsala	80	37.48N	12.26 E
Marseille	76	43.18N	5.24 E
Marshall	122	32.32N	94.22W
Marsh Island I	112	29.35N	91.53W
Marsing	126	43.32N	116.48W
Martaban, Gulf of c	104	16.30N	97.00 E
Martha's Vineyard I	124	41.25N	70.40W
Martigny	76	46.06N	7.04 E
Martigues	76	43.24N	5.03 E
Martin	74	49.05N	18.55 E
Martinique □ 2	114	14.40N	61.00W
Martinsburg	124	39.27N	77.57W
Maryborough	106	25.32S	152.42 E
Maryland □ 3	122	39.00N	76.45W
Marysville	126	39.08N	121.35W
Masai Steppe ʌ 1	90	4.45S	37.00 E
Mascarene Islands II	90	21.00S	57.00 E
Masherbrum ʌ	96	35.38N	76.18 E
Mason City	122	43.09N	93.12W
Masqat (Muscat)	92	23.37N	58.35 E
Massa	80	44.01N	10.09 E
Massachusetts □ 3	122	42.15N	71.50W
Massachusetts Bay c	124	42.20N	70.50W
Massena	124	44.55N	74.53W
Massillon	124	40.48N	81.32W
Masterton	110	40.57S	175.40 E
Matadi	90	5.49S	13.27 E
Matagalpa	114	12.55N	85.55W
Matagorda Island I	112	28.15N	96.30W
Matamoros	112	25.53N	97.30W
Matanzas	114	23.03N	81.35W
Matías Romero	112	16.53N	95.02W
Mato Grosso, Planalto do ʌ 1	116	15.30S	56.00W
Matsue	100	35.28N	133.04 E
Matsumoto	100	36.14N	137.58 E
Matsuyama	100	33.50N	132.45 E
Mattagami ≃	120	50.43N	81.29W
Mattawamkeag	124	45.30N	68.21W
Matterhorn ʌ	76	45.59N	7.43 E
Matthew Town	114	20.57N	73.40W
Maturín	116	9.45N	63.11W
Maubeuge	76	50.17N	3.58 E
Maug Islands II	102	20.01N	145.13 E
Maui I	127	20.45N	156.15W
Maumee	124	41.33N	83.39W
Mauna Loa ʌ 1	127	19.29N	155.36W
Maunath Bhanjan	96	25.57N	83.33 E
Mauritania ≃	88	20.00N	12.00W
Mauritius □ 1	90	20.17S	57.33 E
Mayaguana I	114	22.23N	72.57W
Mayagüez	114	18.12N	67.09W
Maymyo	104	22.02N	96.28 E
Mayotte □ 2	90	12.50S	45.10 E
Mayotte I	90	12.50S	45.10 E
Maysville	124	38.38N	83.44W
Mazara del Vallo	80	37.39N	12.36 E
Mazār-e-Sharīf	96	36.42N	67.06 E
Mazatlán	112	23.13N	106.25W
Mazury ⬅	74	53.45N	21.00 E
Mbabane	90	26.18S	31.06 E
Mbala	90	8.50S	31.22 E
Mbale	90	1.05N	34.10 E
Mbandaka (Coquilhatville)	90	0.04N	18.16 E
Mbomou (Bomu) ≃	88	4.08N	22.26 E
Mbuji-Mayi (Bakwanga)	90	6.09S	23.38 E
M'Clintock Channel ꭡ	120	71.00N	101.00W
Mead, Lake ⊜ 1	126	36.05N	114.25W
Meadville	124	41.38N	80.09W
Meander River	120	59.02N	117.42W

Name	Page No.	Lat.	Long.
Meath □ 9	72	53.36N	6.54W
Mecca			
→ Makkah	92	21.27N	39.49 E
Mechelen	74	51.02N	4.28 E
Mecklenburg □ 9	74	53.30N	13.00 E
Medan	102	3.35N	98.40 E
Médéa	78	36.12N	2.50 E
Medellín	116	6.15N	75.35W
Médenine	88	32.21N	10.30 E
Medford	126	42.19N	122.52W
Medgidia	82	44.15N	28.16 E
Medicine Hat	120	50.03N	110.40W
Mediterranean Sea ⊤ 2	66	35.00N	20.00 E
Medjerda, Monts de la ⋏	80	36.35N	8.15 E
Meekatharra	106	26.36S	118.29 E
Meerut	96	28.59N	77.42 E
Meiktila	104	20.52N	95.52 E
Meiningen	74	50.34N	10.25 E
Meissen	74	51.10N	13.28 E
Mekambo	90	1.01N	13.56 E
Mekong ≃	104	10.33N	105.24 E
Melaka	104	2.12N	102.15 E
Melanesia II	66	13.00S	164.00 E
Melbourne, Austl.	106	37.49S	144.58 E
Melbourne, Fl., U.S.	122	28.04N	80.36W
Melby House	72	60.18N	1.39W
Melilla	88	35.19N	2.58W
Melita	120	49.16N	101.00W
Melitopol'	70	46.50N	35.22 E
Melville Island I, Austl.	106	11.40S	131.00 E
Melville Island I, N.T., Can.	120	75.15N	110.00W
Melville Peninsula ⋎ 1	120	68.00N	84.00W
Memmingen	74	47.59N	10.11 E
Memphis	122	35.08N	90.02W
Mendocino, Cape ⋎	126	40.25N	124.25W
Mendoza	118	32.53S	68.49W
Menorca I	78	40.00N	4.00 E
Mentawai, Kepulauan II	102	2.00S	99.30 E
Menzel Bourguiba	80	37.10N	9.48 E
Merano (Meran)	80	46.40N	11.09 E
Merced	126	37.18N	120.28W
Mercedes	118	33.40S	65.28W
Mergui (Myeik)	104	12.26N	98.36 E
Mergui Archipelago II	104	12.00N	98.00 E
Mérida, Esp.	78	38.55N	6.20W
Mérida, Méx.	112	20.58N	89.37W
Mérida, Ven.	114	8.30N	71.10W
Mérida, Cordillera de ⋏	116	8.40N	71.00W
Meriden	124	41.32N	72.48W
Meridian	122	32.21N	88.42W
Merseburg	74	51.21N	11.59 E
Mersin	93	36.48N	34.38 E
Merthyr Tydfil	72	51.46N	3.23W
Mesa	122	33.25N	111.49W
Mesewa (Massaua)	92	15.38N	39.28 E
Mesopotamia ⬥ 1	92	34.00N	44.00 E
Mesquite	126	36.48N	114.03W
Messina, It.	80	38.11N	15.33 E
Messina, S. Afr.	90	22.23S	30.00 E
Metán	118	25.29S	64.57W
Metz	76	49.08N	6.10 E
Meuse (Maas) ≃	74	51.49N	5.01 E
Mexicali	112	32.40N	115.29W
Mexico	122	39.10N	91.52W
Mexico □ 1	112	23.00N	102.00W
Mexico, Gulf of c	112	24.00N	93.00W
Mexico City			
→ Ciudad de México	112	19.24N	99.09W
Meymaneh	96	35.55N	64.47 E
Miami	122	25.46N	80.11W
Miānwāli	96	32.35N	71.33 E
Miass	70	54.59N	60.06 E
Michigan □ 3	122	44.00N	85.00W
Michigan, Lake ⊜	122	44.00N	87.00W
Micronesia II	66	11.00N	159.00 E
Mičurinsk	84	52.54N	40.30 E
Middelburg	90	31.30S	25.00 E
Middlebury	124	44.00N	73.10W
Middlesbrough	72	54.35N	1.14W
Middletown, N.Y., U.S.	124	41.26N	74.25W
Middletown, Oh., U.S.	124	39.30N	84.23W
Midland, On., Can.	124	44.45N	79.53W
Midland, Mi., U.S.	124	43.36N	84.14W
Midland, Tx., U.S.	122	31.59N	102.04W
Mielec	74	50.18N	21.25 E
Miguel Alemán, Presa ⊜ 1	112	18.13N	96.32W
Mihajlovgrad	82	43.25N	23.13 E
Mikkeli	73	61.41N	27.15 E
Milan			
→ Milano, It.	80	45.28N	9.12 E
Milan, Mi., U.S.	124	42.05N	83.40W
Milano (Milan)	80	45.28N	9.12 E
Mildura	106	34.12S	142.09 E
Miles City	122	46.24N	105.50W
Milford	124	38.54N	75.25W
Milford Haven	72	51.40N	5.02W
Millau	76	44.06N	3.05 E
Millinocket	124	45.39N	68.42W
Milltown Malbay	72	52.52N	9.23W
Mílos I	82	36.41N	24.15 E
Milparinka	106	29.44S	141.53 E
Milwaukee	122	43.02N	87.54W
Minas	118	34.23S	55.14W
Minas, Sierra de las ⋏	114	15.10N	89.40W
Minatitlán	112	17.59N	94.31W
Mindanao I	102	8.00N	125.00 E
Minden	112	32.36N	93.17W
Mindoro I	102	12.50N	121.05 E
Mineral Wells	122	32.48N	98.06W
Minho (Miño) ≃	78	41.52N	8.51W
Minneapolis	122	44.58N	93.15W
Minnesota □ 3	122	46.00N	94.15W
Miño (Minho) ≃	78	41.52N	8.51W
Minorca			
→ Menorca I	78	40.00N	4.00 E
Minot	122	48.13N	101.17W
Minsk	84	53.54N	27.34 E
Minto, Lac ⊜	120	51.00N	73.37W
Minūf	93	30.28N	30.56 E
Mirtóön Pélagos ⊤ 2	82	36.51N	23.18 E
Miskolc	74	48.06N	20.47 E
Mississippi □ 3	122	32.50N	89.30W
Mississippi ≃	122	29.00N	89.15W
Mississippi Delta ≃ 2	122	29.10N	89.15W
Missoula	122	46.52N	113.59W
Missouri □ 3	122	38.30N	93.30W
Missouri ≃	122	38.50N	90.08W
Mistassini, Lac ⊜	120	51.00N	73.37W
Mitilíni	82	39.06N	26.32 E
Mito	100	36.22N	140.28 E
Mitú	116	1.08N	70.03W
Mitumba, Monts ⋏	90	6.00S	29.00 E
Miyakonojō	100	31.44N	131.04 E
Miyazaki	100	31.54N	131.26 E
Mizoram □ 8	96	23.30N	93.00 E
Mladá Boleslav	74	50.23N	14.59 E
Mobile	122	30.41N	88.02W
Moçambique	90	15.03S	40.42 E
Mochudi	90	24.28S	26.05 E
Mococa	119	21.28S	47.01W
Modena	80	44.40N	10.55 E
Modesto	126	37.38N	120.59W
Moffat	72	55.20N	3.27W
Moga	96	30.48N	75.10 E
Mogaung	104	25.18N	96.56 E
Mogil'ov	84	53.54N	30.21 E

Name	Page No.	Lat.	Long.
Murfreesboro	122	35.50N	86.23W
Murmansk	70	68.58N	33.05 E
Murom	84	55.34N	42.02 E
Muroran	100a	42.18N	140.59 E
Murray ≃	108	35.22S	139.22 E
Murraysburg	90	31.58S	23.47 E
Murrumbidgee ≃	108	34.43S	143.12 E
Murupara	110	38.28S	176.42 E
Mürzzuschlag	74	47.36N	15.41 E
Mūsā, Jabal (Mount Sinai)			
∧	93	28.32N	33.59 E
Musala ∧	82	42.11N	23.34 E
Muscat			
→ Masqat	92	23.37N	58.35 E
Mustafakemalpaşa	82	40.02N	28.24 E
Mutá, Ponta do ⋗	119	13.52S	38.56W
Mutare	90	18.58S	32.40 E
Mwanza	90	2.31S	32.54 E
Myanaung	104	18.17N	95.19 E
Myingyan	104	21.28N	95.23 E
Myitkyinā	104	25.23N	97.24 E
Mymensingh	96	24.45N	90.24 E
Myrtle Point	126	43.03N	124.08W
Mysore	95	12.18N	76.39 E

N

Name	Page No.	Lat.	Long.
Naalehu	127	19.03N	155.35W
Naas	72	53.13N	6.39W
Nabeul	80	36.27N	10.44 E
Nābulus	93	32.13N	35.16 E
Nacogdoches	122	31.36N	94.39W
Næstved	73	55.14N	11.46 E
Naga	102	13.37N	123.11 E
Nāgāland □ 3	96	26.00N	95.00 E
Nagano	100	36.39N	138.11 E
Nagaoka	100	37.27N	138.51 E
Nagasaki	100	32.48N	129.55 E
Nagoya	100	35.10N	136.55 E
Nāgpur	96	21.09N	79.06 E
Nagykanizsa	74	46.27N	17.00 E
Naha	101b	26.13N	127.40 E
Nain	120	56.32N	61.41W
Nairobi	90	1.17S	36.49 E
Najin	98	42.15N	130.18 E
Nakhon Pathom	104	13.49N	100.03 E
Nakhon Ratchasima	104	14.58N	102.07 E
Nakhon Sawan	104	15.41N	100.07 E
Nakhon Si Thammarat	104	8.26N	99.58 E
Nakuru	90	0.17S	36.04 E
Nal'čik	70	43.29N	43.37 E
Namangan	94	41.00N	71.40 E
Nam-dinh	104	20.25N	106.10 E
Namib Desert ◄ 2	90	23.00S	15.00 E
Namibe	90	15.10S	12.09 E
Namibia □ 2	90	22.00S	17.00 E
Nampa	122	43.32N	116.33W
Namp'o	98	38.45N	125.23 E
Nampula	90	15.07S	39.15 E
Namsos	73	64.29N	11.30 E
Nanchang	98	28.41N	115.53 E
Nanchong	98	30.48N	106.04 E
Nancy	76	48.41N	6.12 E
Nanda Devi ∧	96	30.23N	79.59 E
Nānga Parbat ∧	96	35.15N	74.36 E
Nanjing (Nanking)	98	32.03N	118.47 E
Nanling ⋏	98	25.00N	112.00 E
Nanning	98	22.48N	108.20 E
Nansei-shotō (Ryukyu Islands) II	98	26.30N	128.00 E
Nantes	76	47.13N	1.33W
Nantong	98	32.02N	120.53 E
Nantucket Island I	124	41.16N	70.03W

Name	Page No.	Lat.	Long.
Nanuque	116	17.50S	40.21W
Napanee	124	44.15N	76.57W
Napier	110	39.29S	176.55 E
Naples			
→ Napoli	80	40.51N	14.17 E
Napo ≃	116	3.20S	72.40W
Napoleon	124	41.23N	84.07W
Napoli (Naples)	80	40.51N	14.17 E
Nara	100	34.41N	135.50 E
Narathiwat	104	6.26N	101.50 E
Nārāyanganj	96	23.37N	90.30 E
Narbonne	76	43.11N	3.00 E
Narew ≃	74	52.26N	20.42 E
Narmada ≃	96	21.38N	72.36 E
Narodnaja, Gora ∧	86	65.04N	60.09 E
Narva	84	59.23N	28.12 E
Narvik	73	68.26N	17.25 E
Nashua	124	42.45N	71.28W
Nashville	122	36.09N	86.47W
Nāsik	95	19.59N	73.48 E
Nassau	114	25.05N	77.21W
Nasser, Lake ◙ 1	92	22.40N	32.00 E
Natal	116	5.47S	35.13W
Natchez	122	31.33N	91.24W
Natchitoches	112	31.45N	93.05W
Natuna Besar I	104	4.00N	108.15 E
Naumburg	74	51.09N	11.48 E
Nausori	111c	18.02S	175.32 E
Navojoa	112	27.06N	109.26W
Nawābganj	96	24.36N	88.17 E
Nawābshāh	96	26.15N	68.25 E
Náxos I	82	37.02N	25.35 E
Nazaré	119	13.02S	39.00W
Nazca	116	14.50S	74.57W
Naze	101b	28.23N	129.30 E
Nazilli	82	37.55N	28.21 E
N'Djamena (Fort-Lamy)	88	12.07N	15.03 E
Ndola	90	12.58S	28.38 E
Néa Páfos (Paphos)	93	34.45N	32.25 E
Near Islands II	128	52.40N	173.30 E
Nebraska □ 3	122	41.30N	100.00W
Nechí	114	8.07N	74.46W
Neepawa	120	50.13N	99.29W
Negele	92	5.20N	39.36 E
Negombo	95	7.13N	79.50 E
Negra, Punta ⋗	116	6.06S	81.09W
Negro ≃, Arg.	118	41.02S	62.47W
Negro ≃, S.A.	116	3.08S	59.55W
Negros I	102	10.00N	123.00 E
Neimenggu Zizhiqu (Inner Mongolia) □ 4	98	43.00N	115.00 E
Neisse ≃	74	52.04N	14.46 E
Neiva	116	2.56N	75.18W
Nelson, B.C., Can.	120	49.29N	117.17W
Nelson, N.Z.	110	41.17S	173.17 E
Neman (Nemunas) ≃	84	55.18N	21.23 E
Nemunas (Neman) ≃	84	55.18N	21.23 E
Nemuro	100a	43.20N	145.35 E
Nemuro Strait ⋃	100a	44.00N	145.20 E
Nenana	128	64.34N	149.07W
Nepal □ 1	94	28.00N	84.00 E
Nerastro, Sarīr ◄ 2	88	24.20N	20.37 E
Ness, Loch ◙	72	57.15N	4.30W
Netherlands □ 1	70	52.15N	5.30 E
Netherlands Antilles □ 2	114	12.15N	69.00W
Neubrandenburg	74	53.33N	13.15 E
Neuchâtel, Lac de ◙	76	46.52N	6.50 E
Neumünster	74	54.04N	9.59 E
Neunkirchen	74	49.20N	7.10 E
Neusiedler See ◙	80	47.50N	16.46 E
Neustrelitz	74	53.21N	13.04 E
Neutral Zone □ 2	92	29.10N	45.30 E
Nevada □ 3	122	39.00N	117.00W

Name	Page No.	Lat.	Long.
Novaja Sibir', Ostrov **I**	86	75.00N	149.00 E
Novaja Zeml'a **II**	86	74.00N	57.00 E
Nova Lima	119	19.59S	43.51W
Nova Lisboa			
→ Huambo	90	12.44S	15.47 E
Novara	76	45.28N	8.38 E
Nova Scotia □ **4**	120	45.00N	63.00W
Nové Zámky	74	47.59N	18.11 E
Novgorod	84	58.31N	31.17 E
Novi Pazar, Blg.	82	43.21N	27.12 E
Novi Pazar, Jugo.	82	43.08N	20.31 E
Novi Sad	82	45.15N	19.50 E
Novokuzneck	86	53.45N	87.06 E
Novomoskovsk	84	54.05N	38.13 E
Novorossijsk	70	44.45N	37.45 E
Novosibirsk	86	55.02N	82.55 E
Novosibirskije Ostrova **II**	86	75.00N	142.00 E
Novyj Port	86	67.40N	72.52 E
Nowa Sól (Neusalz)	74	51.48N	15.44 E
Nowy Sącz	74	49.38N	20.42 E
Nubian Desert ◆ ²	92	20.30N	33.00 E
Nueces ≃	112	27.50N	97.30W
Nueva Rosita	112	27.57N	101.13W
Nueva San Salvador	114	13.41N	89.17W
Nueve de Julio	118	35.27S	60.52W
Nuevitas	114	21.33N	77.16W
Nuevo Laredo	112	27.30N	99.31W
Numazu	100	35.06N	138.52 E
Nunivak Island **I**	128	60.00N	166.30W
Nürnberg	74	49.27N	11.04 E
Nyala	88	12.03N	24.53 E
Nyanda	90	20.05S	30.50 E
Nyasa, Lake ⊜	90	12.00S	34.30 E
Nyaunglebin	104	17.57N	96.44 E
Nyíregyháza	74	47.59N	21.43 E
Nykøbing	73	55.55N	11.41 E
Nyköping	73	58.45N	17.00 E
Nyngan	108	31.34S	147.11 E
Nysa	74	50.29N	17.20 E
Nzérékoré	88	7.45N	8.49W

O

Name	Page No.	Lat.	Long.
Oahu **I**	127	21.30N	158.00W
Oak Hill	124	37.58N	81.08W
Oakland, Ca., U.S.	126	37.48N	122.16W
Oakland, Or., U.S.	126	43.25N	123.17W
Oakville	124	43.27N	79.41W
Oamaru	110	45.06S	170.58 E
Oaxaca [de Juárez]	112	17.03N	96.43W
Ob' ≃	86	66.45N	69.30 E
Oberwart	74	47.17N	16.13 E
Obihiro	100a	42.55N	143.12 E
Obskaja Guba **c**	86	69.00N	73.00 E
Ocaña	114	8.15N	73.20W
Occidental, Cordillera ⋏	116	10.00S	77.00W
Ocean City, Md., U.S.	124	38.20N	75.05W
Ocean City, N.J., U.S.	124	39.16N	74.34W
Oceanside	126	33.11N	117.22W
Ochotsk	86	59.23N	143.18 E
Ocotlán	112	20.21N	102.46W
Ōdate	100	40.16N	140.34 E
Odawara	100	35.15N	139.10 E
Ödemiş	82	38.13N	27.59 E
Odense	73	55.24N	10.23 E
Oder (Odra) ≃	74	53.32N	14.38 E
Odessa, S.S.S.R.	70	46.28N	30.44 E
Odessa, Tx., U.S.	122	31.50N	102.22W
Odra (Oder) ≃	74	53.32N	14.38 E
Offenbach	74	50.08N	8.47 E
Ōgaki	100	35.21N	136.37 E
Ogallala	122	41.07N	101.43W
Ogbomosho	88	8.08N	4.15 E

Name	Page No.	Lat.	Long.
Ogden	122	41.13N	111.58W
Ogdensburg	124	44.41N	75.29W
Ohio □ ³	122	40.15N	82.45W
Ohio ≃	122	36.59N	89.08W
Ohrid, Lake ⊜	82	41.02N	20.43 E
Oil City	124	41.26N	79.42W
Oildale	126	35.25N	119.01W
Ōita	100	33.14N	131.36 E
Ojos del Salado, Nevado ⋏	118	27.06S	68.32W
Oka ≃	84	56.20N	43.59 E
Okahandja	90	21.59S	16.58 E
Okaihau	110	35.19S	173.47 E
Okavango (Cubango) ≃	90	18.50S	22.25 E
Okavango Swamp ⩳	90	18.45S	22.45 E
Okayama	100	34.39N	133.55 E
Okazaki	100	34.57N	137.10 E
Okeechobee, Lake ⊜	122	26.55N	80.45W
Okhotsk, Sea of (Ochotskoje More) ₸ ²	86	53.00N	150.00 E
Oki-guntō **II**	100	36.15N	133.15 E
Okinawa-jima **I**	101b	26.30N	128.00 E
Oklahoma □ ³	122	35.30N	98.00W
Oklahoma City	122	35.28N	97.30W
Oksskolten ⋏	73	65.59N	14.15 E
Okt'abr'skoj Revol'ucii, Ostrov **I**	86	79.30N	97.00 E
Öland **I**	73	56.45N	16.38 E
Olcott	124	43.20N	78.42W
Old Bahama Channel ⋃	114	22.30N	78.50W
Old Crow	120	67.35N	139.50W
Oldenburg	74	53.08N	8.13 E
Old Forge	124	43.42N	74.58W
Old Town	124	44.56N	68.38W
Olean	124	42.04N	78.25W
Oléron, Île d' **I**	76	45.56N	1.15W
Olimarao **I** ¹	102	7.41N	145.52 E
Ólimbos ⋏, Ellás	82	40.05N	22.21 E
Ólimbos ⋏, Kípros	93	34.56N	32.52 E
Olímpia	119	20.44S	48.54W
Olinda	116	8.01S	34.51W
Oliveira	119	20.41S	44.49W
Ollagüe	118	21.14S	68.16W
Olmos	116	5.59S	79.46W
Olomouc	74	49.36N	17.16 E
Olsztyn (Allenstein)	74	53.48N	20.29 E
Olt ≃	82	43.43N	24.51 E
Olympia	122	47.02N	122.53W
Olympus, Mount → Ólimbos ⋏	82	40.05N	22.21 E
Olympus, Mount ⋏	122	47.48N	123.43W
Omagh	72	54.36N	7.18W
Omaha	122	41.15N	95.56W
Oman □ ¹	92	22.00N	58.00 E
Oman, Gulf of **c**	92	24.30N	58.30 E
Omarama	110	44.29S	169.58 E
Ometepe, Isla de **I**	114	11.30N	85.35W
Ōmiya	100	35.54N	139.38 E
Omsk	86	55.00N	73.24 E
Ōmuta	100	33.02N	130.27 E
Ondangua	90	17.55S	16.00 E
Oneida	124	43.05N	75.39W
Oneida Lake ⊜	124	43.13N	76.00W
Oneonta	124	42.27N	75.03W
Onslow	106	21.39S	115.06 E
Ontario	122	44.01N	116.57W
Ontario □ ⁴	120	51.00N	85.00W
Ontario, Lake ⊜	122	43.45N	78.00W
Ooldea	106	30.27S	131.50 E
Oostende (Ostende)	74	51.13N	2.55 E
Opava	74	49.56N	17.54 E
Opelousas	112	30.32N	92.04W
Opole (Oppeln)	74	50.41N	17.55 E
Opotiki	110	38.00S	177.17 E

Name	Page No.	Lat.	Long.
Paraguaná, Península de ▸[1]	114	11.55N	70.00W
Paraguarí	118	25.38S	57.09W
Paraguay □[1]	118	23.00S	58.00W
Paraíba do Sul ≃	119	21.37S	41.03W
Paramaribo	116	5.50N	55.10W
Paraná	118	31.44S	60.32W
Paraná ≃, Bra.	119	12.30S	48.14W
Paraná ≃, S.A.	118	33.43S	59.15W
Paranaguá	118	25.31S	48.30W
Paranavaí	119	23.04S	52.28W
Pardubice	74	50.02N	15.47 E
Parecis, Chapada dos ⋌	116	13.00S	60.00W
Parent	120	47.55N	74.37W
Parepare	102	4.01S	119.38 E
Paris, Fr.	76	48.52N	2.20 E
Paris, Ky., U.S.	124	38.12N	84.15W
Parker	126	34.09N	114.17W
Parkersburg	124	39.16N	81.33W
Parma, It.	80	44.48N	10.20 E
Parma, Oh., U.S.	124	41.24N	81.43W
Parnaíba	116	2.54S	41.47W
Pärnu	84	58.24N	24.32 E
Paro	94	27.26N	89.25 E
Páros I	82	37.08N	25.12 E
Parry Sound	120	45.21N	80.02W
Parsons	122	37.20N	95.15W
Pasadena	126	34.08N	118.08W
Paso de Indios	118	43.52S	69.06W
Passau	74	48.35N	13.28 E
Passo Fundo	118	28.15S	52.24W
Passos	119	20.43S	46.37W
Pasto	116	1.13N	77.17W
Patagonia ◂[1]	118	44.00S	68.00W
Paternò	80	37.34N	14.54 E
Paterson	124	40.55N	74.10W
Pátmos I	82	37.20N	26.33 E
Patna	96	25.36N	85.07 E
Patos de Minas	119	18.35S	46.32W
Patquía	118	30.03S	66.53W
Pátrai	82	38.15N	21.44 E
Patrocínio	119	18.57S	46.59W
Patuca ≃	114	15.50N	84.17W
Pau	76	43.18N	0.22W
Paulo Afonso	116	9.21S	38.14W
Paungde	104	18.29N	95.30 E
Pavlodar	86	52.18N	76.57 E
Paysandú	118	32.19S	58.05W
Pazardžik	82	42.12N	24.20 E
Peace River	120	56.14N	117.17W
Pearl ≃	112	30.11N	89.32W
Pearl Harbor c	127	21.22N	157.58W
Peć	82	42.40N	20.19 E
Pečora	86	65.10N	57.11 E
Pečora ≃	86	68.13N	54.15 E
Pecos	112	31.25N	103.29W
Pecos ≃	112	29.42N	101.22W
Pécs	74	46.05N	18.13 E
Pedregal	114	11.01N	70.08W
Pedro Juan Caballero	119	22.34S	55.37W
Peekskill	124	41.17N	73.55W
Pegasus Bay c	110	43.20S	173.00 E
Pegu	104	17.20N	96.29 E
Peking → Beijing	98	39.55N	116.25 E
Pelagie, Isole II	80	35.40N	12.40 E
Pelée, Montagne ⋀	114	14.48N	61.10W
Pelly Mountains ⋌	120	62.00N	133.00W
Pelopónnisos (Peloponnesus) ◂[1]	82	37.30N	22.00 E
Pelotas	118	31.46S	52.20W
Pematangsiantar	102	2.57N	99.03 E
Pemba	90	12.58S	40.30 E
Pemba Island I	90	7.31S	39.25 E
Pembroke	120	45.49N	77.07W
Penápolis	119	21.24S	50.04W
Pennines ⋌	72	54.10N	2.05W
Pennsylvania □[3]	122	40.45N	77.30W
Penobscot ≃	124	44.30N	68.50W
Pensacola	122	30.25N	87.13W
Pentecost Island I	111b	15.42S	168.10 E
Penza	70	53.13N	45.00 E
Peoria	122	40.41N	89.35W
Pereira	116	4.49N	75.43W
Périgueux	76	45.11N	0.43 E
Perijá, Sierra de ⋌	114	10.00N	73.00W
Perm'	70	58.00N	56.15 E
Pernik	82	42.36N	23.02 E
Perpignan	76	42.41N	2.53 E
Perryville	128	55.54N	159.10W
Persian Gulf c	92	27.00N	51.00 E
Perth, Austl.	106	31.56S	115.50 E
Perth, Scot., U.K.	72	56.24N	3.28W
Perth Amboy	124	40.30N	74.15W
Peru □[1]	116	10.00S	76.00W
Perugia	80	43.08N	12.22 E
Pesaro	80	43.54N	12.55 E
Pescara	80	42.28N	14.13 E
Peshāwar	96	34.01N	71.33 E
Petaluma	126	38.13N	122.38W
Peterborough, Austl.	106	32.58S	138.50 E
Peterborough, On., Can.	120	44.18N	78.19W
Peterborough, Eng., U.K.	72	52.35N	0.15W
Petersburg	128	56.49N	132.57W
Petoskey	124	45.22N	84.57W
Petrič	82	41.24N	23.13 E
Petrolina	116	9.24S	40.30W
Petropavlovsk	86	54.54N	69.06 E
Petropavlovsk-Kamčatskij	86	53.01N	158.39 E
Petrópolis	116	22.31S	43.10W
Petroșani	82	45.25N	23.22 E
Petrozavodsk	70	61.47N	34.20 E
Pforzheim	74	48.54N	8.42 E
Phan-rang	104	11.34N	108.59 E
Phan-thiet	104	10.56N	108.06 E
Phet Buri	104	13.06N	99.57 E
Philadelphia	124	39.57N	75.09W
Philippi	124	39.09N	80.02W
Philippines □[1]	102	13.00N	122.00 E
Philippine Sea ⟂[2]	66	20.00N	135.00 E
Philipsburg	124	40.53N	78.13W
Phitsanulok	104	16.50N	100.15 E
Phnum Pénh	104	11.33N	104.55 E
Phoenix	122	33.26N	112.04W
Phôngsali	104	21.41N	102.06 E
Phra Nakhon Si Ayutthaya	104	14.21N	100.33 E
Phuket	104	7.53N	98.24 E
Phu-vinh	104	9.56N	106.20 E
Piacenza	80	45.01N	9.40 E
Piatra-Neamț	82	46.56N	26.22 E
Picardie □[9]	76	50.00N	3.30 E
Pickford	124	46.09N	84.21W
Pidurutalagala ⋀	95	7.00N	80.46 E
Piedras Negras, Guat.	114	17.11N	91.15W
Piedras Negras, Méx.	112	28.42N	100.31W
Pieksämäki	73	62.18N	27.08 E
Pielinen ⊜	73	63.15N	29.40 E
Pierre	122	44.22N	100.21W
Pietermaritzburg	90	29.37S	30.16 E
Pietersburg	90	23.54S	29.25 E
Pietrosu, Vîrful ⋀, Rom.	82	47.36N	24.38 E
Pietrosu, Vîrful ⋀, Rom.	82	47.08N	25.11 E
Pikes Peak ⋀	122	38.51N	105.03W
Piła (Schneidemühl)	74	53.10N	16.44 E
Pilica ≃	74	51.52N	21.17 E

Name	Page No.	Lat.	Long.
Pinang			
→ George Town	104	5.25N	100.20 E
Pinar del Río	114	22.25N	83.42 W
Píndhos óros ⋌	82	39.49N	21.14 E
Pine Bluff	122	34.13N	92.00 W
Pins, Île des I	111b	22.37S	167.30 E
Pinsk	84	52.07N	26.04 E
Piombino	80	42.55N	10.32 E
Piotrków Trybunalski	74	51.25N	19.42 E
Pipmouacane, Réservoir			
🝙¹	120	49.35N	70.30 W
Piqua	124	40.08N	84.14 W
Piracicaba	119	22.43S	47.38 W
Piraiévs (Piraeus)	82	37.57N	23.38 E
Piraju	119	23.12S	49.23 W
Pirapora	119	17.21S	44.56 W
Pirmasens	74	49.12N	7.36 E
Pisa	80	43.43N	10.23 E
Pisco	116	13.42S	76.13 W
Pisticci	80	40.23N	16.34 E
Piteå	73	65.20N	21.30 E
Pitești	82	44.52N	24.52 E
Pittsburgh	124	40.26N	79.59 W
Pittsfield	124	42.27N	73.14 W
Piura	116	5.12S	80.38 W
Placetas	114	22.19N	79.40 W
Planeta Rica	114	8.25N	75.36 W
Plata, Río de la ⊂¹	118	35.00S	57.00 W
Platte ≌	122	39.16N	94.50 W
Plattsburgh	124	44.41N	73.27 W
Plauen	74	50.30N	12.08 E
Plenty, Bay of ⊂	110	37.40S	177.00 E
Plétipi, Lac 🝙	120	51.44N	70.06 W
Pleven	82	43.25N	24.37 E
Płock	74	52.33N	19.43 E
Ploiești	82	44.56N	26.02 E
Plovdiv	82	42.09N	24.45 E
Plymouth, Eng., U.K.	72	50.23N	4.10 W
Plymouth, Ma., U.S.	124	41.57N	70.40 W
Plzeň	74	49.45N	13.23 E
Po ≌	80	44.57N	12.04 E
Pobeda, Gora ⋀	86	65.12N	146.12 E
Pocatello	122	42.52N	112.26 W
Poços de Caldas	119	21.48S	46.34 W
Podlasie ➡¹	74	52.30N	23.00 E
Podol'sk	84	55.26N	37.33 E
Podor	88	16.40N	14.57 W
Pofadder	90	29.10S	19.22 E
Poiana Ruscăi, Munții ⋌	82	45.41N	22.30 E
Pointe-à-Pitre	114	16.14N	61.32 W
Pointe-Noire	90	4.48S	11.51 E
Point Pleasant	124	40.04N	74.04 W
Point Reyes National			
Seashore ✦	126	38.00N	122.58 W
Poitiers	76	46.35N	0.20 E
Poland □¹	70	52.00N	19.00 E
Polevskoj	70	56.26N	60.11 E
Poltava	70	49.35N	34.34 E
Poltimore	124	45.47N	75.43 W
Polynesia II	66	4.00S	156.00 W
Pomerania □⁹	74	54.00N	16.00 E
Pomeranian Bay ⊂	74	54.00N	14.15 E
Ponca City	122	36.42N	97.05 W
Ponce	114	18.01N	66.37 W
Pondicherry □⁸	95	11.56N	79.50 E
Ponta Grossa	118	25.05S	50.09 W
Ponte Nova	119	20.24S	42.54 W
Pontevedra	78	42.26N	8.38 W
Pontiac	124	42.38N	83.17 W
Pontianak	102	0.02S	109.20 E
Poopó, Lago 🝙	116	18.45S	67.07 W
Popayán	116	2.27N	76.36 W
Poplar Bluff	122	36.45N	90.23 W
Popocatépetl, Volcán ⋀¹	112	19.02N	98.38 W
Popomanaseu, Mount ⋀	106	9.42S	160.04 E
Poprad	74	49.03N	20.18 E
Pordenone	80	45.57N	12.39 E
Pori	73	61.29N	21.47 E
Porlamar	114	10.57N	63.51 W
Poronajsk	86	49.14N	143.04 E
Portadown	72	54.26N	6.27 W
Portage	124	42.12N	85.34 W
Port Allegany	124	41.48N	78.16 W
Port Arthur	122	29.53N	93.55 W
Port Augusta	106	32.30S	137.46 E
Port-au-Prince	114	18.32N	72.20 W
Port Austin	124	44.02N	82.59 W
Port Blair	104	11.40N	92.45 E
Port Clyde	124	43.55N	69.15 W
Port Elgin	124	44.26N	81.24 W
Port Elizabeth	90	33.58S	25.40 E
Port Ellen	72	55.39N	6.12 W
Porterville	126	36.03N	119.00 W
Port-Gentil	90	0.43S	8.47 E
Port Harcourt	88	4.43N	7.05 E
Port Hedland	106	20.19S	118.34 E
Port Henry	124	44.02N	73.27 W
Port Huron	124	42.58N	82.25 W
Portland, Austl.	106	38.21S	141.36 E
Portland, Me., U.S.	124	43.39N	70.15 W
Portland, Or., U.S.	122	45.31N	122.40 W
Port Lavaca	112	28.36N	96.37 W
Port Lincoln	106	34.44S	135.52 E
Port Louis	90	20.10S	57.30 E
Port Macquarie	106	31.26S	152.55 E
Port Moresby	106	9.30S	147.10 E
Port Nolloth	90	29.17S	16.51 E
Port-Nouveau-Québec	120	58.32N	65.54 W
Porto	78	41.11N	8.36 W
Pôrto Alegre	118	30.04S	51.11 W
Porto Amboim	90	10.44S	13.44 E
Portobelo	114	9.33N	79.39 W
Port of Spain	114	10.39N	61.31 W
Porto-Novo	88	6.29N	2.37 E
Port Orford	126	42.44N	124.29 W
Porto-Vecchio	80	41.35N	9.16 E
Pôrto Velho	116	8.46S	63.54 W
Port Pirie	106	33.11S	138.01 E
Port Said			
→ Būr Saʿīd	88	31.16N	32.18 E
Port Shepstone	90	30.46S	30.22 E
Portsmouth, Eng., U.K.	72	50.48N	1.05 W
Portsmouth, N.H., U.S.	124	43.04N	70.45 W
Portsmouth, Oh., U.S.	124	38.43N	82.59 W
Porttipahdan tekojärvi 🝙¹	73	68.08N	26.40 E
Portugal □¹	70	39.30N	8.00 W
Portugalete	78	43.19N	3.01 W
Posadas	118	27.23S	55.53 W
Potenza	80	40.38N	15.49 E
Potgietersrus	90	24.15S	28.55 E
Potomac ≌	124	38.00N	76.18 W
Potosí	116	19.35S	65.45 W
Potsdam	74	52.24N	13.04 E
Poughkeepsie	124	41.42N	73.55 W
Poume	111b	20.14S	164.02 E
Pouso Alegre	119	22.13S	45.56 W
Poüthisăt	104	12.32N	103.55 E
Povungnituk	120	60.02N	77.10 W
Powassan	124	46.05N	79.22 W
Powell, Lake 🝙¹	122	37.25N	110.45 W
Poza Rica de Hidalgo	112	20.33N	97.27 W
Poznań	74	52.25N	16.55 E
Prague			
→ Praha	74	50.05N	14.26 E
Praha (Prague)	74	50.05N	14.26 E

Name	Page No.	Lat.	Long.
Preparis North Channel ʯ	104	15.27N	94.05 E
Preparis South Channel ʯ	104	14.40N	94.00 E
Presidente Epitácio	119	21.46S	52.06W
Presidente Prudente	116	22.07S	51.22W
Presidio	112	29.33N	104.22W
Prešov	74	49.00N	21.15 E
Prespa, Lake ⊜	82	40.55N	21.00 E
Presque Isle	122	46.40N	68.00W
Preston, Eng., U.K.	72	53.46N	2.42W
Preston, Id., U.S.	122	42.05N	111.52W
Pretoria	90	25.45S	28.10 E
Prey Vêng	104	11.29N	105.19 E
Příbram	74	49.42N	14.01 E
Prievidza	74	48.47N	18.37 E
Prilep	82	41.20N	21.33 E
Prince Albert	120	53.12N	105.46W
Prince Edward Island □⁴	120	46.20N	63.20W
Prince George	120	53.55N	122.45W
Prince of Wales Island I, N.T., Can.	120	72.40N	99.00W
Prince of Wales Island I, Ak., U.S.	128	55.47N	132.50W
Prince Rupert	120	54.19N	130.19W
Princeton	124	40.20N	74.39W
Prinzapolca	114	13.24N	83.34W
Priština	82	42.39N	21.10 E
Prizren	82	42.12N	20.44 E
Proctor	124	43.39N	73.02W
Prokopjevsk	86	53.53N	86.45 E
Prome (Pyè)	104	18.49N	95.13 E
Prostějov	74	49.29N	17.07 E
Provence □⁹	76	44.00N	6.00 E
Providence	124	41.49N	71.24W
Providence, Cape ⋗	110	46.01S	166.28 E
Provincetown	124	42.03N	70.10W
Provo	122	40.14N	111.39W
Prudhoe Bay c	128	70.20N	148.20W
Pruszków	74	52.11N	20.48 E
Prut ≃	82	45.30N	28.12 E
Przemyśl	74	49.47N	22.47 E
Pskov	84	57.50N	28.20 E
Puapua	111e	13.34S	172.09W
Pucallpa	116	8.23S	74.32W
Pudukkottai	95	10.23N	78.49 E
Puebla [de Zaragoza]	112	19.03N	98.12W
Pueblo	122	38.15N	104.36W
Puerto Aisén	118	45.24S	72.42W
Puerto Armuelles	114	8.17N	82.52W
Puerto Asís	116	0.30N	76.31W
Puerto Barrios	114	15.43N	88.36W
Puerto Berrío	116	6.29N	74.24W
Puerto Cabello	114	10.28N	68.01W
Puerto Cabezas	114	14.02N	83.23W
Puerto Carreño	116	6.12N	67.22W
Puerto Casado	118	22.20S	57.55W
Puerto Cortés, C.R.	114	8.58N	83.32W
Puerto Cortés, Hond.	114	15.48N	87.56W
Puerto Cumarebo	114	11.29N	69.21W
Puerto de Nutrias	116	8.05N	69.18W
Puerto Deseado	118	47.45S	65.54W
Puerto la Cruz	116	10.13N	64.38W
Puerto Leguízamo	116	0.12S	74.46W
Puertollano	78	38.41N	4.07W
Puerto Lobos	118	42.00S	65.06W
Puerto Madryn	118	42.46S	65.03W
Puerto Maldonado	116	12.36S	69.11W
Puerto Montt	118	41.28S	72.57W
Puerto Natales	118	51.44S	72.31W
Puerto Rico □²	114	18.15N	66.30W
Puerto Vallarta	112	20.37N	105.15W
Pula	80	44.52N	13.50 E
Pulaski	124	43.34N	76.07W
Puławy	74	51.25N	21.57 E
Pune (Poona)	95	18.32N	73.52 E
Punjab □³	96	31.00N	75.30 E
Puno	116	15.50S	70.02W
Punta Arenas	118	53.09S	70.55W
Puntarenas	114	9.58N	84.50W
Punto Fijo	116	11.42N	70.13W
Puri	96	19.48N	85.51 E
Purnea	96	25.47N	87.31 E
Purus (Purús) ≃	116	3.42S	61.28W
Pusan	98	35.06N	129.03 E
Puto	111a	5.41S	154.43 E
Putumayo (Içá) ≃	116	3.07S	67.58W
Puy de Sancy ʌ	76	45.32N	2.49 E
Pyinmana	104	19.44N	96.13 E
P'yŏngyang	98	39.01N	125.45 E
Pyramid Lake ⊜	126	40.00N	119.35W
Pyrenees ⋋	78	42.40N	1.00 E
Pyu	104	18.29N	96.26 E

Q

Name	Page No.	Lat.	Long.
Qalāt	96	32.07N	66.54 E
Qamar, Ghubbat al- c	92	16.00N	52.30 E
Qandahār	96	31.32N	65.30 E
Qatar □¹	92	25.00N	51.10 E
Qinā	93	26.10N	32.43 E
Qingdao (Tsingtao)	98	36.06N	120.19 E
Qinhuangdao	98	39.56N	119.36 E
Qiqihaer (Tsitsihar)	98	47.19N	123.55 E
Qom	92	34.39N	50.54 E
Quanzhou	98	24.54N	118.35 E
Quartzsite	126	33.39N	114.13W
Québec	120	46.49N	71.14W
Quebec (Québec) □⁴	120	52.00N	72.00W
Quedlinburg	74	51.48N	11.09 E
Queen Charlotte Islands II	120	53.00N	132.00W
Queen Charlotte Sound ʯ	120	51.30N	129.30W
Queen Maud Land ➡¹	69	72.30S	12.00 E
Queen Maud Mountains ⋋	69	86.00S	160.00W
Queensland □³	106	22.00S	145.00 E
Queenstown, N.Z.	110	45.02S	168.40 E
Queenstown, S. Afr.	90	31.52S	26.52 E
Quelimane	90	17.53S	36.51 E
Querétaro	112	20.36N	100.23W
Quetta	96	30.12N	67.00 E
Quezon City	102	14.38N	121.00 E
Quibdó	116	5.42N	76.40W
Quilpie	106	26.37S	144.15 E
Quimper	76	48.00N	4.06W
Quincemil	116	13.16S	70.38W
Qui-nhon	104	13.46N	109.14 E
Quiros, Cape ⋗	111b	14.55S	167.01 E
Quito	116	0.13S	78.30W
Qūs	93	25.55N	32.45 E

R

Name	Page No.	Lat.	Long.
Rabat, Magreb	88	34.02N	6.51W
Rabat (Victoria), Malta	80	36.02N	14.14 E
Rach-gia	104	10.01N	105.05 E
Racibórz (Ratibor)	74	50.06N	18.13 E
Radom	74	51.25N	21.10 E
Radomsko	74	51.05N	19.25 E
Raetihi	110	39.26S	175.17 E
Rafaela	118	31.16S	61.29W
Rafah	93	31.18N	34.15 E
Ragusa	80	36.55N	14.44 E
Raḥīmyār Khān	96	28.25N	70.18 E
Raiatea ⊜	111d	16.50S	151.25W
Rāichūr	95	16.12N	77.22 E
Raipur	96	21.14N	81.38 E
Rājahmundry	95	16.59N	81.47 E
Rajang ≃	102	2.04N	111.12 E

Name	Page No.	Lat.	Long.
Rājapālaiyam	95	9.27N	77.34 E
Rājasthān □⁴	96	27.00N	74.00 E
Rajčichinsk	86	49.46N	129.25 E
Rājkot	96	22.18N	70.47 E
Raleigh	122	35.46N	78.38W
Rama	114	12.09N	84.15W
Ramm, Jabal ⋀	93	29.35N	35.24 E
Rāmpur	96	28.49N	79.02 E
Ramree Island I	104	19.06N	93.48 E
Ramu ≃	102	5.00S	144.40 E
Rancagua	118	34.10S	70.45W
Rānchī	96	23.21N	85.20 E
Randers	73	56.28N	10.03 E
Randolph	124	43.55N	72.39W
Rangeley	124	44.57N	70.38W
Rangitikei ≃	110	40.18S	175.14 E
Rangoon	104	16.47N	96.10 E
Rangpur	96	25.45N	89.15 E
Rankin Inlet	120	62.45N	92.10W
Rann of Kutch ≃	96	24.00N	70.00 E
Rantauprapat	104	2.06N	99.50 E
Rapid City	122	44.04N	103.13W
Ras Dashen ⋀	92	13.10N	38.26 E
Rasht	70	37.16N	49.36 E
Rat Islands II	128	52.00N	178.00 E
Ratlām	96	23.19N	75.04 E
Rauma	73	61.08N	21.30 E
Ravena	124	42.28N	73.49W
Ravenna	80	44.25N	12.12 E
Ravensburg	74	47.47N	9.37 E
Ravenshoe	106	17.37S	145.29 E
Ravensthorpe	106	33.35S	120.02 E
Rāwalpindi	96	33.36N	73.04 E
Rawson	118	43.18S	65.06W
Raz, Pointe du ⋗	76	48.02N	4.44W
R'azan'	84	54.38N	39.44 E
Razgrad	82	43.32N	26.31 E
Ré, Île de I	76	46.12N	1.25W
Reading, Eng., U.K.	72	51.28N	0.59W
Reading, Pa., U.S.	124	40.20N	75.55W
Real, Cordillera ⋌	116	19.00S	66.30W
Realicó	118	35.02S	64.15W
Recherche, Cape ⋗	111a	10.11S	161.19 E
Recife	116	8.03S	34.54W
Recklinghausen	74	51.36N	7.13 E
Red (Hong-ha) (Yuanjiang)			
≃, Asia	104	20.17N	106.34 E
Red ≃, U.S.	122	31.00N	91.40W
Red Deer	120	52.16N	113.48W
Redding	126	40.35N	122.23W
Red Lake	120	51.03N	93.49W
Red Sea ᵥ²	92	20.00N	38.00 E
Reed City	124	43.52N	85.30W
Reefton	110	42.07S	171.52 E
Regensburg	74	49.01N	12.06 E
Reggio di Calabria	80	38.07N	15.39 E
Reggio nell'Emilia	80	44.43N	10.36 E
Regina	120	50.25N	104.39W
Rehoboth Beach	124	38.43N	75.04W
Rehovot	93	31.54N	34.49 E
Reims	76	49.15N	4.02 E
Remada	88	32.19N	10.24 E
Rendsburg	74	54.18N	9.40 E
Renfrew	124	45.28N	76.41W
Rennes	76	48.05N	1.41W
Reno	126	39.31N	119.48W
Reschenpass)(	76	46.50N	10.30 E
Resistencia	118	27.27S	58.59W
Reșița	82	45.17N	21.53 E
Réthimnon	82	35.22N	24.29 E
Reunion □²	90	21.06S	55.36 E
Reus	78	41.09N	1.07 E
Reutlingen	74	48.29N	9.11 E

Name	Page No.	Lat.	Long.
Revelstoke	120	50.59N	118.12W
Revillagigedo, Islas II	112	19.00N	111.30W
Rewa	96	24.32N	81.18 E
Rewāri	96	28.11N	76.37 E
Rey, Isla del I	114	8.22N	78.55W
Reyes	116	14.19S	67.23W
Reykjavík	70	64.09N	21.51W
Reynosa	112	26.07N	98.18W
Rhaetian Alps ⋌	76	46.30N	10.00 E
Rhein			
→ Rhine ≃	74	51.52N	6.02 E
Rheine	74	52.17N	7.26 E
Rhine (Rhein) (Rhin) ≃	74	51.52N	6.02 E
Rhinelander	122	45.38N	89.24W
Rhode Island □³	122	41.40N	71.30W
Rhodes			
→ Ródhos I	82	36.10N	28.00 E
Rhodope Mountains ⋌	82	41.30N	24.30 E
Rhône ≃	76	43.20N	4.50 E
Riau, Kepulauan II	104	1.00N	104.30 E
Ribeirão Prêto	116	21.10S	47.48W
Riberalta	116	10.59S	66.06W
Richfield, Id., U.S.	126	43.02N	114.09W
Richfield, Ut., U.S.	122	38.46N	112.05W
Richmond, In., U.S.	124	39.49N	84.53W
Richmond, Ky., U.S.	124	37.44N	84.17W
Richmond, Va., U.S.	122	37.33N	77.27W
Richwood	124	38.13N	80.32W
Riesa	74	51.18N	13.17 E
Rieti	80	42.24N	12.51 E
Rif ⋌	78	35.00N	4.00W
Rift Valley V	90	3.00S	29.00 E
Rīga	84	56.57N	24.06 E
Riga, Gulf of			
→ Rižskij Zaliv c	84	57.30N	23.35 E
Rigestān ⬥¹	94	31.00N	65.00 E
Rijeka	80	45.20N	14.27 E
Rimini	80	44.04N	12.34 E
Ringgold Isles II	111c	16.15S	179.25W
Ringvassøya I	73	69.55N	19.15 E
Riobamba	116	1.40S	78.38W
Rio Branco	116	9.58S	67.48W
Rio Cuarto	118	33.08S	64.21W
Rio de Janeiro	116	22.54S	43.14W
Río Gallegos	118	51.38S	69.13W
Río Grande, Arg.	118	53.47S	67.42W
Rio Grande, Bra.	118	32.02S	52.05W
Ríohacha	116	11.33N	72.55W
Río Hato	114	8.23N	80.10W
Río Mayo	118	45.41S	70.16W
Rio Verde	119	17.43S	50.56W
Ripley	124	38.49N	81.42W
Ritter, Mount ⋀	126	37.42N	119.12W
Rivas	114	11.26N	85.50W
Rivera	118	30.54S	55.31W
Riverhead	124	40.55N	72.39W
Riverina ⬥¹	108	35.30S	145.30 E
Riverside	126	33.57N	117.23W
Riyadh			
→ Ar-Riyāḍ	92	24.38N	46.43 E
Rižskij Zaliv (Rīgas Jūras			
Līcis) (Gulf of Riga) c	84	57.30N	23.35 E
Rizzuto, Capo ⋗	80	38.54N	17.06 E
Roanne	76	46.02N	4.04 E
Roanoke	122	37.16N	79.56W
Roberts Peak ⋀	120	52.57N	120.32W
Roberval	120	48.31N	72.13W
Roboré	116	18.20S	59.45W
Rocha	118	34.29S	54.20W
Rochefort	76	45.57N	0.58W
Rochester, Mn., U.S.	122	44.01N	92.28W
Rochester, N.H., U.S.	124	43.18N	70.58W
Rochester, N.Y., U.S.	124	43.09N	77.36W

Name	Page No.	Lat.	Long.
Rockefeller Plateau ⚲ [1]	69	80.00S	135.00W
Rockford, Il., U.S.	122	42.16N	89.05W
Rockford, Mi., U.S.	124	43.07N	85.33W
Rockhampton	106	23.23S	150.31 E
Rock Island	122	41.30N	90.34W
Rockland	124	44.06N	69.06W
Rock Springs	122	41.35N	109.12W
Rockville	124	39.05N	77.09W
Rocky Mountains ⚲	66	48.00N	116.00W
Rodez	76	44.21N	2.35 E
Ródhos (Rhodes)	82	36.26N	28.13 E
Ródhos I	82	36.10N	28.00 E
Roebourne	106	20.47S	117.09 E
Roeselare	74	50.57N	3.08 E
Rogue ≃	126	42.26N	124.25W
Rohtak	96	28.54N	76.34 E
Roma (Rome)	80	41.54N	12.29 E
Roman	82	46.55N	26.56 E
Romania ◻ [1]	70	46.00N	25.30 E
Romans [-sur-Isère]	76	45.03N	5.03 E
Rome			
→ Roma, It.	80	41.54N	12.29 E
Rome, Ga., U.S.	122	34.15N	85.09W
Rome, N.Y., U.S.	124	43.12N	75.27W
Romeo	124	42.48N	83.00W
Roncador, Serra do ⚲ [1]	116	12.00S	52.00W
Ron-ma, Mui ➤	104	18.07N	106.22 E
Ronne Ice Shelf ⋈	69	78.30S	61.00W
Roosevelt Island I	69	79.30S	162.00W
Roraima, Mount ᴧ	116	5.12N	60.44W
Rosario	118	32.57S	60.40W
Roscommon	72	53.38N	8.11W
Roseau	114	15.18N	61.24W
Roseburg	126	43.13N	123.20W
Rosenheim	74	47.51N	12.07 E
Ross Ice Shelf ⋈	69	81.30S	175.00W
Rossijskaja Sovetskaja			
Federativnaja			
Socialističeskaja			
Respublika ◻ [3]	70	60.00N	45.00 E
Rosslare	72	52.17N	6.23W
Ross Sea ▼ [2]	69	76.00S	175.00W
Rostock	74	54.05N	12.07 E
Rostov-na-Donu	70	47.14N	39.42 E
Roswell	122	33.23N	104.31W
Rotorua	110	38.09S	176.15 E
Rotterdam	74	51.55N	4.28 E
Roubaix	76	50.42N	3.10 E
Rouen	76	49.26N	1.05 E
Rouyn	120	48.15N	79.01W
Rovaniemi	73	66.34N	25.48 E
Rovno	70	50.37N	26.15 E
Royan	76	45.37N	1.01W
Ruapehu ᴧ	110	39.17S	175.34 E
Rubcovsk	86	51.33N	81.10 E
Ruby	128	64.44N	155.30W
Ruby Lake ≡	126	40.10N	115.30W
Rudolf, Lake ⊜	92	3.30N	36.00 E
Rügen I	74	54.25N	13.24 E
Rukwa, Lake ⊜	90	8.00S	32.25 E
Rump Mountain ᴧ	124	45.12N	71.04W
Rupert	126	42.37N	113.40W
Ruse	82	43.50N	25.57 E
Rüsselsheim	74	50.00N	8.25 E
Rutland	124	43.36N	72.58W
Ruvuma (Rovuma) ≃	90	10.29S	40.28 E
Rwanda ◻ [1]	90	2.30S	30.00 E
Rybinsk	84	58.03N	38.52 E
Rybinskoje Vodochranilišče			
⊜ [1]	84	58.30N	38.25 E
Rysy ᴧ	74	49.12N	20.04 E
Ryukyu Islands			
→ Nansei-shotō II	98	26.30N	128.00 E

Name	Page No.	Lat.	Long.
Rzeszów	74	50.03N	22.00 E
S			
Saarbrücken	74	49.14N	6.59 E
Saaremaa I	84	58.25N	22.30 E
Sab, Tônlé ⊜	104	13.00N	104.00 E
Sabinas Hidalgo	112	26.30N	100.10W
Sabine ≃	112	30.00N	93.45W
Sable, Île de I	106	19.15S	159.56 E
Sachalin, Ostrov (Sakhalin)			
I	86	51.00N	143.00 E
Šachty	70	47.42N	40.13 E
Sacramento	126	38.34N	121.29W
Sacramento ≃	126	38.03N	121.56W
Sacramento Valley ∨	126	39.15N	122.00W
Sado I	100	38.00N	138.25 E
Saga	100	33.15N	130.18 E
Sagami-nada c	100	35.00N	139.30 E
Sägar	96	23.50N	78.45 E
Saginaw	124	43.25N	83.56W
Saginaw Bay c	124	43.50N	83.40W
Sagua de Tánamo	114	20.35N	75.14W
Sagua la Grande	114	22.49N	80.05W
Saguaro National			
Monument ◆	112	32.12N	110.38W
Sagunto	78	39.41N	0.16W
Sahara ↦ [2]	88	26.00N	13.00 E
Sahāranpur	96	29.58N	77.33 E
Saidpur	96	25.47N	88.54 E
Sai-gon			
→ Thanh-pho Ho Chi			
Minh	104	10.45N	106.40 E
Saint Anthony	120	51.22N	55.35W
Saint Augustine	122	29.53N	81.18W
Saint-Augustin-Saguenay	120	51.14N	58.39W
Saint-Brieuc	76	48.31N	2.47W
Saint Catharines	124	43.10N	79.15W
Saint-Chamond	76	45.28N	4.30 E
Saint Christopher			
(Saint Kitts) I	114	17.20N	62.45W
Saint-Christopher-Nevis ◻ [1]	114	17.20N	62.45W
Saint Clair	124	42.48N	82.29W
Saint Croix I	114	17.45N	64.45W
Saint-Denis, Fr.	76	48.56N	2.22 E
Saint-Denis, Réu.	90	20.52S	55.28 E
Saint-Dizier	76	48.38N	4.57 E
Saint Elias, Mount ᴧ	128	60.18N	140.55W
Saint-Étienne	76	45.26N	4.24 E
Saint George	106	28.02S	148.35 E
Saint George's	114	12.03N	61.45W
Saint George's Bay c	120	48.20N	59.00W
Saint George's Channel ⋃	72	52.00N	6.00W
Saint Helier	76	49.12N	2.37W
Saint-Hyacinthe	124	45.38N	72.57W
Saint James	124	45.45N	85.30W
Saint James, Cape ➤	120	51.56N	131.01W
Saint-Jean	124	45.19N	73.16W
Saint-Jérôme	124	45.46N	74.00W
Saint John	120	45.16N	66.03W
Saint John, Cape ➤	120	50.00N	55.32W
Saint John's	120	47.34N	52.43W
Saint Johnsbury	124	44.25N	72.00W
Saint Joseph	122	39.46N	94.50W
Saint Joseph, Lake ⊜	120	51.05N	90.35W
Saint-Jovite	124	46.07N	74.36W
Saint Kilda I	72	57.49N	8.36W
Saint Kitts			
→ Saint Christopher I	114	17.20N	62.45W
Saint Lawrence ≃	120	49.30N	67.00W
Saint Lawrence, Gulf of c	120	48.00N	62.00W
Saint Lawrence Island I	128	63.30N	170.30W
Saint-Lô	76	49.07N	1.05W

Name	Page No.	Lat.	Long.
Saint-Louis, Sén.	88	16.02N	16.30W
Saint Louis, Mo., U.S.	122	38.37N	90.11W
Saint Lucia □¹	114	13.53N	60.58W
Saint-Malo	76	48.39N	2.01W
Saint-Malo, Golfe de ⊂	76	48.45N	2.00W
Sainte-Marie, Cap ⊁	90	25.36S	45.08 E
Saint Marys	124	41.25N	78.33W
Saint-Nazaire	76	47.17N	2.12W
Saint Paul	122	44.57N	93.05W
Saint Peter Port	76	49.27N	2.32W
Saint Petersburg	122	27.46N	82.40W
Saint Pierre and Miquelon □²	120	46.55N	56.10W
Saint-Quentin	76	49.51N	3.17 E
Saintes	76	45.45N	0.52W
Saint Thomas	124	42.47N	81.12W
Saint Vincent, Gulf ⊂	108	35.00S	138.05 E
Saint Vincent and the Grenadines □¹	114	13.15N	61.12W
Saipan I	102	15.12N	145.45 E
Sairecábur, Cerro ∧	116	22.43S	67.54W
Saito	100	32.06N	131.24 E
Sajama, Nevado ∧	116	18.06S	68.54W
Sakai	100	34.35N	135.28 E
Sakata	100	38.55N	139.50 E
Sakau	111b	16.49S	168.24 E
Sakhalin → Sachalin, Ostrov I	86	51.00N	143.00 E
Saku	100	36.09N	138.26 E
Sakurai	100	34.30N	135.51 E
Salamanca	78	40.58N	5.39W
Saldanha	90	33.00S	17.56 E
Salem, Ma., U.S.	124	42.31N	70.53W
Salem, Oh., U.S.	124	40.54N	80.51W
Salem, Or., U.S.	122	44.56N	123.02W
Salerno	80	40.41N	14.47 E
Salgótarján	74	48.07N	19.48 E
Salihli	82	38.29N	28.09 E
Salinas	126	36.40N	121.39W
Salinas ≃	126	36.45N	121.48W
Salisbury, Eng., U.K.	72	51.05N	1.48W
Salisbury, Md., U.S.	124	38.21N	75.35W
Salmon River Mountains ⋌	122	44.45N	115.00W
Salonika → Thessaloníki	82	40.38N	22.56 E
Sal'sk	70	46.28N	41.33 E
Salta	118	24.47S	65.25W
Saltillo	112	25.25N	101.00W
Salt Lake City	122	40.45N	111.53W
Salto	118	31.23S	57.58W
Salton Sea ⊜	126	33.19N	115.50W
Salvador	116	12.59S	38.31W
Salween (Nujiang) ≃	104	16.31N	97.37 E
Salyersville	124	37.45N	83.04W
Salzburg	74	47.48N	13.02 E
Salzgitter	74	52.10N	10.25 E
Samar I	102	12.00N	125.00 E
Samarinda	102	0.30S	117.09 E
Samarkand	94	39.40N	66.48 E
Sambalpur	96	21.27N	83.58 E
Samoa Islands II	111e	14.00S	171.00W
Sámos I	82	37.48N	26.44 E
Samothráki (Samothrace) I	82	40.30N	25.32 E
Sam Rayburn Reservoir ⊜¹	122	31.27N	94.37W
Samsun	70	41.17N	36.20 E
Samui, Ko I	104	9.30N	100.00 E
Samut Prakan	104	13.36N	100.36 E
San ≃	74	50.45N	21.51 E
San'ä'	92	15.23N	44.12 E
San Agustin, Cape ⊁	102	6.16N	126.11 E
San Andrés	114	12.35N	81.42W
San Andrés, Isla de I	114	12.32N	81.42W
San Angelo	122	31.27N	100.26W
San Antonio	122	29.25N	98.29W
San Antonio, Cabo ⊁	114	21.52N	84.57W
San Antonio Oeste	118	40.44S	64.56W
San Benedetto del Tronto	80	42.57N	13.53 E
San Benito	114	16.55N	89.54W
San Bernardino	126	34.07N	117.18W
San Bernardino Mountains ⋌	126	34.10N	117.00W
San Blas, Cape ⊁	122	29.40N	85.22W
San Carlos	114	11.07N	84.47W
San Carlos de Bariloche	118	41.09S	71.18W
San Carlos del Zulia	114	9.01N	71.55W
San Carlos de Río Negro	116	1.55N	67.04W
San Clemente	126	33.25N	117.36W
San Clemente Island I	126	32.54N	118.29W
San Cristóbal	116	7.46N	72.14W
San Cristóbal I	111a	10.36S	161.45 E
Sancti-Spíritus	114	21.56N	79.27W
Sandakan	102	5.50N	118.07 E
Sandia	116	14.17S	69.26W
San Diego	126	32.42N	117.09W
Sandnes	73	58.51N	5.44 E
Sandusky, Mi., U.S.	124	43.25N	82.49W
Sandusky, Oh., U.S.	124	41.26N	82.42W
Sandviken	73	60.37N	16.46 E
Sandy Hook	124	38.05N	83.07W
Sandy Lake ⊜	120	53.00N	93.07W
San Felipe	114	10.20N	68.44W
San Fernando, Esp.	78	36.28N	6.12W
San Fernando, Trin.	114	10.17N	61.28W
San Fernando de Apure	116	7.54N	67.28W
San Fernando de Atabapo	116	4.03N	67.42W
Sanford	124	43.26N	70.46W
San Francisco	126	37.46N	122.25W
San Francisco de Macorís	114	19.18N	70.15W
San Gabriel Mountains ⋌	126	34.20N	118.00W
Sāngli	95	16.52N	74.34 E
San Gottardo, Passo del)(	76	46.33N	8.34 E
San Jacinto	114	9.50N	75.08W
San Joaquin ≃	126	38.03N	121.50W
San Joaquin Valley ∨	126	37.00N	120.10W
San Jorge, Golfo ⊂	118	46.00S	67.00W
San José, C.R.	114	9.56N	84.05W
San Jose, Ca., U.S.	126	37.20N	121.53W
San José de Chiquitos	116	17.51S	60.47W
San José de Guanipa	114	8.54N	64.09W
San José del Guaviare	116	2.35N	72.38W
San Juan, Arg.	118	31.32S	68.31W
San Juan, P.R.	114	18.28N	66.07W
San Juan ≃	114	10.56N	83.42W
San Juan del Norte	114	10.55N	83.42W
San Juan de los Cayos	114	11.10N	68.25W
San Juan de los Morros	114	9.55N	67.21W
San Julián	118	49.18S	67.43W
San Justo	118	30.47S	60.35W
Sankt Gallen	76	47.25N	9.23 E
Sankt Moritz	76	46.30N	9.50 E
Sankt Pölten	74	48.12N	15.37 E
San Lucas, Cabo ⊁	112	22.52N	109.53W
San Luis, Guat.	114	16.14N	89.27W
San Luis, Ven.	114	11.07N	69.42W
San Luis Obispo	126	35.16N	120.39W
San Luis Potosí	112	22.09N	100.59W
San Luis Río Colorado	112	32.29N	114.48W
San Marcos	122	29.52N	97.56W
San Marino	80	43.55N	12.28 E
San Marino □¹	70	43.56N	12.25 E
San Mateo, Ca., U.S.	126	37.33N	122.19W
San Mateo, Ven.	114	9.45N	64.33W
San Miguel	114	13.29N	88.11W
San Miguel de Tucumán	118	26.49S	65.13W
San Nicolas Island I	126	33.15N	119.31W

Name	Page No.	Lat.	Long.	Name	Page No.	Lat.	Long.
San Onofre	114	9.44N	75.32W	Sarajevo	82	43.52N	18.25 E
San Pedro, Punta ➤	118	25.30S	70.38W	Saransk	70	54.11N	45.11 E
San Pedro de las Colonias	112	25.45N	102.59W	Sarapul	70	56.28N	53.48 E
San Pedro de Macorís	114	18.27N	69.18W	Sarasota	122	27.20N	82.31W
San Pedro Sula	114	15.27N	88.02W	Saratoga Springs	124	43.04N	73.47W
San Rafael, Arg.	118	34.36S	68.20W	Saratov	70	51.34N	46.02 E
San Rafael, Méx.	112	25.01N	100.33W	Sardegna (Sardinia) I	80	40.00N	9.00 E
San Remo	80	43.49N	7.46 E	Sargodha	96	32.05N	72.40 E
San Salvador	114	13.41N	89.17W	Sarh	88	9.09N	18.23 E
San Salvador de Jujuy	118	24.11S	65.18W	Sarmiento	118	45.36S	69.05W
San Sebastián	78	43.19N	1.59W	Sarnia	120	42.58N	82.23W
San Severo	80	41.41N	15.23 E	Saronikós Kólpos c	82	37.54N	23.12 E
Santa Ana, Bol.	116	15.31S	67.30W	Sarthe ≃	76	47.30N	0.32W
Santa Ana, Hond.	114	13.59N	89.34W	Sasamungga	111a	7.02S	156.47 E
Santa Ana, Ca., U.S.	126	33.44N	117.52W	Sasebo	100	33.10N	129.43 E
Santa Barbara	126	34.25N	119.42W	Saskatchewan □4	120	54.00N	105.00W
Santa Barbara Channel ⋃	126	34.15N	119.55W	Saskatoon	120	52.07N	106.38W
Santa Catalina, Gulf of c	126	33.20N	117.45W	Sassandra ≃	88	4.58N	6.05W
Santa Clara, Cuba	114	22.24N	79.58W	Sassari	80	40.44N	8.33 E
Santa Clara, Ca., U.S.	126	37.20N	121.56W	Sātāra	95	17.41N	73.59 E
Santa Cruz, Bol.	116	17.48S	63.10W	Sataua	111e	13.28S	172.40W
Santa Cruz, Ca., U.S.	126	36.58N	122.01W	Satna	96	24.35N	80.50 E
Santa Cruz de Tenerife	88	28.27N	16.14W	Satsunan-shotō II	101b	29.00N	130.00 E
Santa Cruz Island I	126	34.01N	119.45W	Satu Mare	82	47.48N	22.53 E
Santa Fe, Arg.	118	31.38S	60.42W	Saudi Arabia □1	92	25.00N	45.00 E
Santa Fe, N.M., U.S.	122	35.41N	105.56W	Sauerland ➤1	74	51.10N	8.00 E
Santa Isabel I	111a	8.00S	159.00 E	Saugerties	124	42.04N	73.57W
Santa Lucia Range ⋌	126	36.00N	121.20W	Sault Sainte Marie, On.,			
Santa Maria, Bra.	118	29.41S	53.48W	Can.	120	46.31N	84.20W
Santa Maria, Ca., U.S.	126	34.57N	120.26W	Sault Sainte Marie, Mi.,			
Santa Maria, Cabo de ➤	90	13.25S	12.32 E	U.S.	122	46.30N	84.21W
Santa María Island I	111b	14.15S	167.30 E	Saumur	76	47.16N	0.05W
Santa Marta	116	11.15N	74.13W	Saurimo	90	9.39S	20.24 E
Santana do Livramento	118	30.53S	55.31W	Sava ≃	82	44.50N	20.26 E
Santander	78	43.28N	3.48W	Savai'i I	111e	13.35S	172.25W
Santarém	116	2.26S	54.42W	Savannah	122	32.05N	81.06W
Santa Rosa, Arg.	118	36.37S	64.17W	Savannakhét	104	16.33N	104.45 E
Santa Rosa, Arg.	118	32.20S	65.12W	Savona	80	44.17N	8.30 E
Santa Rosa, Ca., U.S.	126	38.26N	122.42W	Savusavu	111c	16.15S	179.21 E
Santa Rosa Island I	126	33.58N	120.06W	Sawdā', Qurnat as- ⋌	93	34.18N	36.07 E
Santiago	118	33.27S	70.40W	Sawhāj	88	26.33N	31.42 E
Santiago de Compostela	78	42.53N	8.33W	Sawu, Laut (Savu Sea) ⊤2	106	9.40S	122.00 E
Santiago de Cuba	114	20.01N	75.49W	Sayan Mountains (Sajany)			
Santiago del Estero	118	27.47S	64.16W	⋌	86	52.45N	96.00 E
Santiago [de los				Sayaxché	114	16.31N	90.10W
Caballeros]	114	19.27N	70.42W	Schaffhausen	76	47.42N	8.38 E
Santo André	119	23.40S	46.31W	Schefferville	120	54.48N	66.50W
Santo Ângelo	118	28.18S	54.16W	Schenectady	124	42.48N	73.56W
Santo Antônio de Jesus	119	12.58S	39.16W	Schleswig	74	54.31N	9.33 E
Santo Domingo	114	18.28N	69.54W	Schwaben □9	74	48.20N	10.30 E
Santos	116	23.57S	46.20W	Schwäbisch Gmünd	74	48.48N	9.47 E
San Valentín, Cerro ⋌	118	46.36S	73.20W	Schwarzwald ⋌	74	48.00N	8.15 E
San Vicente	114	13.38N	88.48W	Schwedt	74	53.03N	14.17 E
San Vicente de Baracaldo	78	43.18N	2.59W	Schweinfurt	74	50.03N	10.14 E
San Vito, Capo ➤	80	38.11N	12.43 E	Schwerin	74	53.38N	11.25 E
São Carlos	119	22.01S	47.54W	Sciacca	80	37.30N	13.06 E
São Francisco ≃	116	10.30S	36.24W	Scotland □8	72	57.00N	4.00W
São José do Rio Prêto	116	20.48S	49.23W	Scott Islands II	120	50.48N	128.40W
São José dos Campos	119	23.11S	45.53W	Scottsbluff	122	41.52N	103.40W
São Leopoldo	118	29.46S	51.09W	Scranton	124	41.24N	75.39W
São Luís	116	2.31S	44.16W	Scutari, Lake ⊜	82	42.12N	19.18 E
São Mateus	116	18.44S	39.51W	Searsport	124	44.27N	68.55W
Saône ≃	74	46.05N	4.45 E	Seattle	122	47.36N	122.19W
São Paulo	116	23.32S	46.37W	Sebastian, Cape ➤	126	42.19N	124.26W
São Roque, Cabo de ➤	116	5.29S	35.16W	Sebastián Vizcaíno, Bahía			
São Sebastião, Ilha de I	119	23.50S	45.18W	c	112	28.00N	114.30W
São Sebastião, Ponta ➤	90	22.07S	35.30 E	Ségou	88	13.27N	6.16W
São Tomé	90	0.20N	6.44 E	Segovia	78	40.57N	4.07W
São Tomé, Cabo de ➤	119	21.59S	40.59W	Seguin	112	29.34N	97.57W
Sao Tome and Principe □1	90	1.00N	7.00 E	Seine, Baie de la ≃	76	49.30N	0.30W
São Vicente, Cabo de ➤	78	37.01N	9.00W	Sekondi-Takoradi	88	4.59N	1.43W
Sapitwa ⋌	90	15.57S	35.36 E	Selawik	128	66.37N	160.03W
Sapporo	100a	43.03N	141.21 E	Seldovia	128	59.27N	151.43W

Name	Page No.	Lat.	Long.
Sioux City	122	42.30N	96.24W
Sioux Falls	122	43.33N	96.42W
Sioux Lookout	120	50.06N	91.55W
Siple, Mount ∧	69	73.15S	126.06W
Siracusa	80	37.04N	15.17 E
Sirājganj	96	24.27N	89.43 E
Siret ≏	82	45.24N	28.01 E
Sirhān, Wādī as- ∨	93	30.30N	38.00 E
Sisak	80	45.29N	16.23 E
Siskiyou Pass)(	126	42.03N	122.36W
Sitka	128	57.03N	135.02W
Sittwe (Akyab)	104	20.09N	92.54 E
Sivas	70	39.45N	37.02 E
Skagerrak ɰ	73	57.45N	9.00 E
Skagway	128	59.28N	135.19W
Skarzysko-Kamienna	74	51.08N	20.53 E
Skeldon	116	5.53N	57.08W
Skelleftea	73	64.46N	20.57 E
Skellefteälven ≏	73	64.42N	21.06 E
Skien	73	59.12N	9.36 E
Skíros	82	38.53N	24.33 E
Skíros I	82	38.53N	24.32 E
Skopje	82	41.59N	21.26 E
Skye, Island of I	72	57.15N	6.10W
Slanské Vrchy ⋌	74	48.50N	21.30 E
Slavgorod	86	53.00N	78.40 E
Slavonija ◆[1]	80	45.00N	18.00 E
Slavonski Brod	82	45.10N	18.01 E
Sligo	72	54.17N	8.28W
Sliven	82	42.40N	26.19 E
Słupsk (Stolp)	74	54.28N	17.01 E
Smederevo	82	44.40N	20.56 E
Smiths Falls	124	44.54N	76.01W
Smithton	106	40.51S	145.07 E
Smokey Dome ∧	126	43.29N	114.56W
Smolensk	84	54.47N	32.03 E
Smoljan	82	41.35N	24.41 E
Smythe, Mount ∧	120	57.54N	124.53W
Snake ≏	122	46.12N	119.02W
Snake River Plain ≅	126	43.00N	113.00W
Snina	74	48.59N	22.07 E
Snøtinden ∧	73	66.38N	14.00 E
Snow Hill	124	38.10N	75.23W
Snyder	112	32.43N	100.55W
Sobat ≏	92	9.22N	31.33 E
Sobral	116	3.42S	40.21W
Soči	70	43.35N	39.45 E
Société, Îles de la (Society Islands) II	111d	17.00S	150.00W
Söderhamn	73	61.18N	17.03 E
Sofija (Sofia)	82	42.41N	23.19 E
Sognafjorden c[2]	73	61.06N	5.10 E
Soissons	76	49.22N	3.20 E
Söke	82	37.45N	27.24 E
Sokoto	88	13.04N	5.16 E
Solbad Hall in Tirol	74	47.17N	11.31 E
Soligorsk	84	52.48N	27.32 E
Solikamsk	70	59.39N	56.47 E
Solimões → Amazon ≏	116	0.05S	50.00W
Solomon Islands □[1]	66	8.00S	159.00 E
Solomon Sea ∓[2]	106	8.00S	155.00 E
Solothurn	76	47.13N	7.32 E
Somalia □[1]	92	10.00N	49.00 E
Sombor	82	45.46N	19.07 E
Somerset	122	37.05N	84.36W
Somerset Island I	120	73.15N	93.30W
Someşu Mic ≏	82	47.09N	23.55 E
Somosomo	111c	16.46S	179.58W
Songkhla	104	7.12N	100.36 E
Sonneberg	74	50.22N	11.10 E
Sopron	74	47.41N	16.36 E
Sorel	124	46.02N	73.07W
Sorocaba	119	23.29S	47.27W
Sorol I[1]	102	8.08N	140.23 E
Sørøya I	73	70.36N	22.46 E
Sorsatunturi ∧	73	67.24N	29.38 E
Souk Ahras	80	36.23N	8.00 E
Sŏul (Seoul)	98	37.33N	126.58 E
Sousse	80	35.49N	10.38 E
South Africa □[1]	90	30.00S	26.00 E
South America ±[1]	66	15.00S	60.00W
Southampton	72	50.55N	1.25W
Southampton Island I	120	64.20N	84.40W
South Australia □[3]	106	30.00S	135.00 E
Southbridge	110	43.49S	172.15 E
South Cape ⊁	111c	17.01S	179.55 E
South Carolina □[3]	122	34.00N	81.00W
South China Sea ∓[2]	98	19.00N	115.00 E
South Dakota □[3]	122	44.15N	100.00W
Southend-on-Sea	72	51.33N	0.43 E
Southern Alps ⋌	110	43.30S	170.30 E
Southern Cross	106	31.13S	119.19 E
South Georgia I	118	54.15S	36.45W
South Indian Lake	120	56.46N	98.57W
South Island I	110	43.00S	171.00 E
South Orkney Islands II	69	60.35S	45.30W
South Platte ≏	122	41.07N	100.42W
South Point ⊁	108	39.00S	146.20 E
South Pole ◆	69	90.00S	0.00
Southport, Austl.	108	27.58S	153.25 E
Southport, Eng., U.K.	72	53.39N	3.01W
South Sandwich Islands II	69	57.45S	26.30W
South Shetland Islands II	69	62.00S	58.00W
South West Cape ⊁	108	43.34S	146.02 E
Sovetskaja Gavan'	86	48.58N	140.18 E
Soviet Union → Union of Soviet Socialist Republics □[1]	66	60.00N	80.00 E
Spain □[1]	70	40.00N	4.00W
Spanish North Africa □[2]	78	35.53N	5.19W
Spanish Town	114	17.59N	76.57W
Sparks	126	39.32N	119.45W
Spárti (Sparta)	82	37.05N	22.27 E
Spassk-Dal'nij	86	44.37N	132.48 E
Spencer Gulf c	108	34.00S	137.00 E
Speyer	74	49.19N	8.26 E
Split	80	43.31N	16.27 E
Spokane	122	47.39N	117.25W
Spoleto	80	42.44N	12.44 E
Springbok	90	29.43S	17.55 E
Springdale	120	49.30N	56.04W
Springfield, Il., U.S.	122	39.48N	89.38W
Springfield, Ma., U.S.	124	42.06N	72.35W
Springfield, Mo., U.S.	122	37.12N	93.17W
Springfield, Oh., U.S.	124	39.55N	83.48W
Springfontein	90	30.19S	25.36 E
Springhill	120	45.39N	64.03W
Springs	90	26.13S	28.25 E
Spruce Knob ∧	124	38.42N	79.32W
Squillace, Golfo di c	80	38.50N	16.50 E
Srednesibirskoje Ploskogorje ⋌[1]	86	65.00N	105.00 E
Sri Lanka □[1]	94	7.00N	81.00 E
Sri Lanka I	95	7.00N	81.00 E
Srīnagar	96	34.05N	74.49 E
Stade	74	53.36N	9.28 E
Stafford	72	52.48N	2.07W
Stalingrad → Volgograd	70	48.44N	44.25 E
Stamford	124	41.03N	73.32W
Standish	124	43.58N	83.57W
Stanke Dimitrov	82	42.16N	23.07 E
Stanley Falls → Boyoma Falls ∟	90	0.15N	25.30 E

Name	Page No.	Lat.	Long.
Takada	100	37.06N	138.15 E
Takaka	110	40.51S	172.48 E
Takamatsu	100	34.20N	134.03 E
Takaoka	100	36.45N	137.01 E
Takapuna	110	36.47S	174.47 E
Takasaki	100	36.20N	139.01 E
Takatsuki	100	34.51N	135.37 E
Takefu	100	35.54N	136.10 E
Takêv	104	10.59N	104.47 E
Takla Makan			
→ Talimupendi ◆ ²	98	39.00N	83.00 E
Takuam, Mount ∧	111a	6.27S	155.36 E
Talara	116	4.34S	81.17W
Talaud, Kepulauan II	102	4.20N	126.50 E
Talavera de la Reina	78	39.57N	4.50W
Talca	118	35.26S	71.40W
Talcahuano	118	36.43S	73.07W
Talimupendi (Takla Makan)			
◆ ²	98	39.00N	83.00 E
Tallahassee	122	30.26N	84.16W
Tallinn	84	59.25N	24.45 E
Tamale	88	9.25N	0.50W
Tamanrasset	88	22.56N	5.30 E
Tambov	84	52.43N	41.25 E
Tamel Aike	118	48.19S	70.58W
Tamil Nadu □ ³	95	11.00N	78.15 E
Tampa	122	27.56N	82.27W
Tampere	73	61.30N	23.45 E
Tampico	112	22.13N	97.51W
Tamworth	106	31.05S	150.55 E
Tana, Lake ❸	92	12.00N	37.20 E
Tananarive			
→ Antananarivo	90	18.55S	47.31 E
Tandil	118	37.19S	59.09W
Tando Ādam	96	25.46N	68.40 E
Tanega-shima I	101b	30.40N	131.00 E
Tanga	90	5.04S	39.06 E
Tanganyika, Lake ❸	90	6.00S	29.30 E
Tanger (Tangier)	88	35.48N	5.45W
Tangshan	98	39.38N	118.11 E
Tanimbar, Kepulauan II	102	7.30S	131.30 E
Tanjungbalai	104	2.58N	99.48 E
Tanjungpinang	104	0.55N	104.27 E
Tanoriki	111b	14.59S	168.09 E
Tanțā	88	30.47N	31.00 E
Tanzania □ ¹	90	6.00S	35.00 E
Tapachula	112	14.54N	92.17W
Tapajós ≃	116	2.24S	54.41W
Tāpi ≃	95	21.06N	72.41 E
Tapuaenuku ∧	110	42.00S	173.40 E
Tara	86	56.54N	74.22 E
Tarābulus (Tripoli), Lībiyā	88	32.54N	13.11 E
Tarābulus (Tripoli), Lubnān	93	34.26N	35.51 E
Tarābulus (Tripolitania) ◆¹	88	31.00N	15.00 E
Taranto	80	40.28N	17.15 E
Taranto, Golfo di c	80	40.10N	17.20 E
Târgoviște	82	43.15N	26.34 E
Tarija	116	21.31S	64.45W
Tarnów	74	50.01N	21.00 E
Tarragona	78	41.07N	1.15 E
Tarrasa	78	41.34N	2.01 E
Tartu	84	58.23N	26.43 E
Tarutung	104	2.01N	98.58 E
Tashi Gang Dzong	96	27.19N	91.34 E
Tasikmalaya	102	7.20S	108.12 E
Taškent	94	41.20N	69.18 E
Tasman Bay c	110	41.00S	173.20 E
Tasmania □ ³	106	43.00S	147.00 E
Tasman Sea ▼ ²	106	30.00S	157.00 E
Taštagol	86	52.47N	87.53 E
Tatabánya	74	47.34N	18.26 E
Tatarsk	86	55.13N	75.58 E
Taumarunui	110	38.52S	175.17 E

Name	Page No.	Lat.	Long.
Taunggyi	104	20.47N	97.02 E
Taupo	110	38.41S	176.05 E
Taupo, Lake ❸	110	38.49S	175.55 E
Tauranga	110	37.42S	176.10 E
Tauroa Point ⟩	110	35.10S	173.04 E
Tautira	111d	17.44S	149.09W
Tavda	86	58.03N	65.15 E
Tavoy	104	14.05N	98.12 E
Tawkar	88	18.26N	37.44 E
Tbilisi	70	41.43N	44.49 E
Tchibanga	90	2.51S	11.02 E
Te Anau	110	45.25S	167.43 E
Te Anau, Lake ❸	110	45.12S	167.48 E
Tébessa	80	35.28N	8.09 E
Tecuci	82	45.50N	27.26 E
Tegucigalpa	114	14.06N	87.13W
Tehrān	70	35.40N	51.26 E
Tehuacán	112	18.27N	97.23W
Tehuantepec	112	16.20N	95.14W
Tehuantepec, Golfo de c	112	16.00N	94.50W
Tehuantepec, Istmo de ▲ ³	112	17.00N	95.00W
Tejo			
→ Tagus ≃	78	38.40N	9.24W
Tekirdağ	82	40.59N	27.31 E
Te Kuiti	110	38.20S	175.10 E
Tel Aviv-Yafo	93	32.04N	34.46 E
Telén	118	36.16S	65.30W
Teleño ∧	78	42.21N	6.23W
Telescope Peak ∧	126	36.10N	117.05W
Telok Anson	104	4.02N	101.01 E
Tembeling ≃	104	4.04N	102.20 E
Temirtau	86	50.05N	72.56 E
Temple	112	31.05N	97.20W
Temuco	118	38.44S	72.36W
Tenāli	95	16.15N	80.35 E
Tende, Col de)(	76	44.09N	7.34 E
Ténéré ◆ ²	88	19.00N	10.30 E
Tenerife I	88	28.19N	16.34W
Tennant Creek	106	19.40S	134.10 E
Tennessee □ ³	122	35.50N	85.30W
Tenterfield	106	29.03S	152.01 E
Teófilo Otoni	119	17.51S	41.30W
Tepelena	82	40.18N	20.01 E
Tepic	112	21.30N	104.54W
Teramo	80	42.39N	13.42 E
Teresina	116	5.05S	42.49W
Terre Haute	122	39.28N	87.24W
Tete	90	16.13S	33.35 E
Tetiaroa I ¹	111d	17.05S	149.32W
Tétouan	78	35.34N	5.23W
Tetovo	82	42.01N	20.58 E
Tevere (Tiber) ≃	76	41.44N	12.14 E
Texarkana	122	33.25N	94.02W
Texas □ ³	122	31.30N	99.00W
Texas City	112	29.23N	94.54W
Thabazimbi	90	24.41S	27.21 E
Thailand □ ¹	102	15.00N	100.00 E
Thailand, Gulf of c	104	10.00N	101.00 E
Thai-nguyen	104	21.36N	105.50 E
Thames	110	37.08S	175.33 E
Thames ≃	72	51.28N	0.43 E
Thamesville	124	42.33N	81.59W
Thāmir, Jabal ∧	92	13.53N	45.30 E
Thāna	95	19.12N	72.58 E
Thanh-hoa	104	19.48N	105.46 E
Thanh-pho Ho Chi Minh			
(Sai-gon)	104	10.45N	106.40 E
Thar Desert (Great Indian			
Desert) ◆ ²	94	27.00N	71.00 E
Thásos I	82	40.41N	24.47 E
Thaton	104	16.55N	97.22 E
Thayetmyo	104	19.19N	95.11 E
The Everglades ≈	114	26.00N	81.00W

Name	Page No.	Lat.	Long.
The Hague			
→ 's-Gravenhage	74	52.06N	4.18 E
Theodore	106	24.57S	150.05 E
Thermaïkós Kólpos c	82	40.23N	22.47 E
The Slot ↯	111a	8.00S	158.10 E
Thessalía ◆ ¹	82	39.30N	22.00 E
Thessalon	124	46.15N	83.34W
Thessaloníki (Salonika)	82	40.38N	22.56 E
Thetford Mines	124	46.05N	71.18W
Thiel Mountains ⊀	69	85.15S	91.00W
Thielsen, Mount ⋀	126	43.09N	122.04W
Thimbu	98	27.28N	89.39 E
Thionville	76	49.22N	6.10 E
Thíra I	82	36.24N	25.29 E
Thisted	73	56.57N	8.42 E
Thívai (Thebes)	82	38.21N	23.19 E
Thongwa	104	16.46N	96.32 E
Thonze	104	17.38N	95.47 E
Thrakikón Pélagos ᵥ²	82	40.15N	24.28 E
Thunder Bay	120	48.23N	89.15W
Thüringer Wald ⊀	76	50.30N	10.30 E
Tianjin (Tientsin)	98	39.08N	117.12 E
Tibasti, Sarīr ◆²	88	24.15N	17.15 E
Tiber			
→ Tevere ⇌	76	41.44N	12 14 E
Tibesti ⊀	88	21.30N	17.30 E
Tibet			
→ Xizang Zizhiqu □⁹	98	31.00N	88.00 E
Tiburón, Isla I	112	29.00N	112.23W
Tichoreck	70	45.51N	40.09 E
Ticonderoga	124	43.50N	73.25W
Tien Shan ⊀	98	42.00N	80.00 E
Tientsin			
→ Tianjin	98	39.08N	117.12 E
Tierra de Campos ◆¹	78	42.10N	4.50W
Tierra del Fuego, Isla			
Grande de I	118	54.00S	69.00W
Tietê ⇌	119	20.40S	51.35W
Tifton	122	31.27N	83.30W
Tigre ⇌	116	4.26S	74.05W
Tigris (Dijlah) ⇌	92	31.00N	47.25 E
Tīh, Jabal at- ⊀¹	93	29.30N	34.00 E
Tijuana	112	32.32N	117.01W
Tilburg	74	51.34N	5.05 E
Tillabéry	88	14.13N	1.27 E
Timaru	110	44.24S	171.15 E
Timbuktu			
→ Tombouctou	88	16.46N	3.01W
Timişoara	82	45.45N	21.13 E
Timmins	120	48.28N	81.20W
Timor I	102	9.00S	125.00 E
Timor Sea ᵥ²	106	11.00S	128.00 E
Tinaco	114	9.42N	68.26W
Tinian I	102	15.00N	145.38 E
Tínos I	82	37.38N	25.10 E
Tinsukia	96	27.30N	95.22 E
Tipperary	72	52.29N	8.10W
Tiquisate	114	14.17N	91.22W
Tirana	82	41.20N	19.50 E
Tire	82	38.04N	27.45 E
Tîrgovişte	82	44.56N	25.27 E
Tîrgu-Jiu	82	45.02N	23.17 E
Tîrgu Mureş	82	46.33N	24.33 E
Tîrgu-Ocna	82	46.15N	26.37 E
Tiruchchirāppalli	95	10.49N	78.41 E
Tirunelveli	95	8.44N	77.42 E
Tiruppur	95	11.06N	77.21 E
Tiruvannāmalai	95	12.13N	79.04 E
Tisza (Tisa) ⇌	82	45.15N	20.17 E
Titicaca, Lago ⊜	116	15.50S	69.20W
Titograd	82	42.26N	19.14 E
Titovo Užice	82	43.51N	19.51 E
Tivoli	80	41.58N	12.48 E
Tlemcen	88	34.52N	1.15W
Tlētē Ouāte Gharbī, Jabal			
⋀	93	35.20N	39.13 E
Toamasina	90	18.10S	49.23 E
Toba, Danau ⊜	104	2.35N	98.50 E
Tobago I	114	11.15N	60.40W
Tocantins ⇌	116	1.45S	49.10W
Togo □¹	88	8.00N	1.10 E
Toiyabe Range ⊀	126	39.10N	117.10W
Tōkamachi	100	37.08N	138.46 E
Toki	100	35.21N	137.11 E
Tokushima	100	34.04N	134.34 E
Tokuyama	100	34.03N	131.49 E
Tōkyō	100	35.42N	139.46 E
Tolbuhin	82	43.34N	27.50 E
Toledo, Esp.	78	39.52N	4.01W
Toledo, Oh., U.S.	124	41.39N	83.33W
Toliara	90	23.21S	43.40 E
Toljatti	70	53.31N	49.26 E
Tomakomai	100a	42.38N	141.36 E
Tomaniivi, Mount ⋀	111c	17.37S	178.01 E
Tomaszów Mazowiecki	74	51.32N	20.01 E
Tombigbee ⇌	122	31.04N	87.58W
Tombouctou (Timbuktu)	88	16.46N	3.01W
Tomini, Teluk c	102	0.20S	121.00 E
Tomsk	86	56.30N	84.58 E
Tone ⇌	100	35.44N	140.51 E
Tonga □¹	66	20.00S	175.00W
Tonkin, Gulf of c	104	20.00N	108.00 E
Tonopah	126	38.04N	117.13W
Tønsberg	73	59.17N	10.25 E
Toowoomba	106	27.33S	151.57 E
Topeka	122	39.02N	95.40W
Torino (Turin)	80	45.03N	7.40 E
Torneträsk ⊜	73	68.20N	19.10 E
Torokina	111a	6.14S	155.03 E
Toronto	120	43.39N	79.23W
Toros Dağları ⊀	93	37.00N	33.00 E
Torquay (Torbay)	72	50.28N	3.30W
Torrens, Lake ⊜	106	31.00S	137.50 E
Torreón	112	25.33N	103.26W
Torres Islands II	111b	13.15S	166.37 E
Torres Strait ↯	106	10.25S	142.10 E
Torrington	124	41.48N	73.07W
Tortona	80	44.54N	8.52 E
Toruń	74	53.02N	18.35 E
Tostado	118	29.14S	61.46W
Tottori	100	35.30N	134.14 E
Toubkal, Jbel ⋀	88	31.05N	7.55W
Touggourt	88	33.10N	6.00 E
Toulon	76	43.07N	5.56 E
Toulouse	76	43.36N	1.26 E
Toungoo	104	18.56N	96.26 E
Tours	76	47.23N	0.41 E
Townsville	106	19.16S	146.48 E
Toyama	100	36.41N	137.13 E
Toyohashi	100	34.46N	137.23 E
Toyota	100	35.05N	137.09 E
Tracy	126	37.44N	121.25W
Tralee	72	52.16N	9.42W
Trancas	118	26.13S	65.17W
Transkei □⁹	90	31.20S	29.00 E
Transylvania □⁹	82	46.30N	24.00 E
Transylvanian Alps			
→ Carpaţii Meridionali ⊀	82	45.30N	24.15 E
Trapani	80	38.01N	12.31 E
Traverse City	124	44.45N	85.37W
Treinta y Tres	118	33.14S	54.23W
Trelew	118	43.15S	65.18W
Tremblant, Mont ⋀	124	46.16N	74.35W
Trenčín	74	48.54N	18.04 E
Trento	80	46.04N	11.08 E
Trenton, On., Can.	124	44.06N	77.35W

Name	Page No.	Lat.	Long.
Uncompahgre Peak ʌ	122	38.04N	107.28W
Undu Cape ⟩	111c	16.08S	179.57W
Ungava, Péninsule d' ⟩[1]	120	60.00N	74.00W
Ungava Bay c	120	59.30N	67.30W
Unimak Island I	128	54.50N	164.00W
Union of Soviet Socialist Republics □[1]	66	60.00N	80.00 E
Uniontown	124	39.54N	79.44W
United Arab Emirates □[1]	92	24.00N	54.00 E
United Kingdom □[1]	70	54.00N	2.00W
United States □[1]	122	38.00N	97.00W
Uozu	100	36.48N	137.24 E
Upata	114	8.01N	62.24W
Upington	90	28.25S	21.15 E
Upolu I	111e	13.55S	171.45W
Upper Arlington	124	40.00N	83.03W
Upper Klamath Lake ⊜	126	42.23N	122.55W
Upper Volta → Burkina Faso □[1]	88	13.00N	2.00W
Uppsala	73	59.52N	17.38 E
Ural ≃	70	47.00N	51.48 E
Ural'skije Gory ⋌	86	66.00N	63.00 E
Urbana	124	40.06N	83.45W
Urfa	93	37.08N	38.46 E
Uruapan [del Progreso]	112	19.25N	102.04W
Uruguaiana	118	29.45S	57.05W
Uruguay □[1]	118	33.00S	56.00W
Uruguay (Uruguai) ≃	118	34.12S	58.18W
Usa	100	33.31N	131.22 E
Uşak	82	38.41N	29.25 E
Ushibuka	100	32.11N	130.01 E
Ushuaia	118	54.48S	68.18W
Ussuri (Wusulijiang) ≃	86	48.27N	135.04 E
Ussurijsk	86	43.48N	131.59 E
Ust'-Čaun	86	68.47N	170.30 E
Ústí nad Labem	74	50.40N	14.02 E
Ust'-Kamenogorsk	86	49.58N	82.38 E
Ust'-Kut	86	56.46N	105.40 E
Usuki	100	33.08N	131.49 E
Usumacinta ≃	112	18.24N	92.38W
Utah □[3]	122	39.30N	111.30W
Utica	124	43.06N	75.13W
Utrecht	74	52.05N	5.08 E
Utsunomiya	100	36.33N	139.52 E
Uttar Pradesh □[3]	96	27.00N	80.00 E
Uvalde	112	29.12N	99.47W
Uvéa, Île I	111b	20.30S	166.35 E
Uwajima	100	33.13N	132.34 E
'Uwaynāt, Jabal al- ʌ	88	21.54N	24.58 E
Uyuni	116	20.28S	66.50W
Uzunköprü	82	41.16N	26.41 E

V

Vaasa (Vasa)	73	63.06N	21.36 E
Vác	74	47.47N	19.08 E
Vadsø	73	70.05N	29.46 E
Vaduz	76	47.09N	9.31 E
Vaganski Vrh ʌ	80	44.22N	15.31 E
Vaileka	111c	17.23S	178.09 E
Vākhān ≃	96	37.00N	72.40 E
Valdez	128	61.07N	146.16W
Valdivia	118	39.48S	73.14W
Valdosta	122	30.49N	83.16W
Valença	119	13.22S	39.05W
Valence	76	44.56N	4.54 E
Valencia, Esp.	78	39.28N	0.22W
Valencia, Ven.	116	10.11N	68.00W
Valencia □[9]	78	39.30N	0.40W
Valencia, Golfo de c	78	39.50N	0.30 E
Valenciennes	76	50.21N	3.32 E
Valentine	122	42.52N	100.33W
Valera	116	9.19N	70.37W

Name	Page No.	Lat.	Long.
Valkeakoski	73	61.16N	24.02 E
Valladolid	78	41.39N	4.43W
Valle de la Pascua	114	9.13N	66.00W
Valledupar	114	10.29N	73.15W
Vallejo	126	38.06N	122.15W
Vallenar	118	28.35S	70.46W
Valletta	80	35.54N	14.31 E
Valleyfield	124	45.15N	74.08W
Valparaíso	118	33.02S	71.38W
Vancouver	120	49.16N	123.07W
Vancouver Island I	120	49.45N	126.00W
Vanderbilt	124	45.08N	84.39W
Vandergrift	124	40.36N	79.33W
Vänern ⊜	73	58.55N	13.30 E
Vangunu, Mount ʌ	111a	8.42S	158.00 E
Vannes	76	47.39N	2.46W
Vanrhynsdorp	90	31.36S	18.44 E
Vanua Levu I	111c	16.33S	179.15 E
Vanuatu □[1]	111b	16.00S	167.00 E
Vārānasi (Benares)	96	25.20N	83.00 E
Varangerfjorden c[2]	73	70.00N	30.00 E
Varangerhalvøya ⟩[1]	73	70.25N	29.30 E
Varaždin	80	46.19N	16.20 E
Vardar (Axiós) ≃	82	40.31N	22.43 E
Vardø	73	70.21N	31.02 E
Varese	80	45.48N	8.48 E
Varkaus	73	62.19N	27.55 E
Varna	82	43.13N	27.55 E
Varunga Point ⟩	111a	7.11S	157.17 E
Vassar	124	43.22N	83.35W
Västerås	73	59.37N	16.33 E
Vatican City (Città del Vaticano) □[1]	80	41.54N	12.27 E
Vatnajökull ⊠	70	64.25N	16.50W
Vättern ⊜	73	58.24N	14.36 E
Vatu-i-Ra Channel ⥥	111c	17.17S	178.31 E
Växjö	73	56.52N	14.49 E
Velika Morava ≃	82	44.43N	21.03 E
Velikije Luki	84	56.20N	30.32 E
Veliki Vitorog ʌ	80	44.07N	17.03 E
Veliko Târnovo	82	43.04N	25.39 E
Vellore	95	12.56N	79.08 E
Venado Tuerto	118	33.45S	61.58W
Venezia (Venice)	80	45.27N	12.21 E
Venezuela □[1]	116	8.00N	66.00W
Venezuela, Golfo de c	116	11.30N	71.00W
Venice → Venezia	80	45.27N	12.21 E
Venice, Gulf of c	80	45.15N	13.00 E
Ventura	126	34.16N	119.17W
Veracruz [Llave]	112	19.12N	96.08W
Verāval	96	20.54N	70.22 E
Vercelli	80	45.19N	8.25 E
Verchojanskij Chrebet ⋌	86	67.00N	129.00 E
Verdun, P.Q., Can.	124	45.27N	73.34W
Verdun, Fr.	76	49.10N	5.23 E
Vereeniging	90	26.38S	27.57 E
Vermont □[3]	122	43.50N	72.45W
Vernon	124	41.49N	72.28W
Véroia	82	40.31N	22.12 E
Verona	80	45.27N	11.00 E
Versailles, Fr.	76	48.48N	2.08 E
Versailles, Ky., U.S.	124	38.03N	84.43W
Verviers	74	50.35N	5.52 E
Vesterålen II	73	68.45N	15.00 E
Vestfjorden c[2]	73	68.08N	15.00 E
Vesuvio ʌ[1]	80	40.49N	14.26 E
Veszprém	74	47.06N	17.55 E
Viangchan (Vientiane)	104	17.58N	102.36 E
Viareggio	80	43.52N	10.14 E
Viborg	73	56.26N	9.24 E
Vicenza	80	45.33N	11.33 E
Vichy	76	46.08N	3.26 E

Name	Page No.	Lat.	Long.
Warsaw			
→ Warszawa, Pol.	**74**	52.15N	21.00 E
Warsaw, Ky., U.S.	**124**	38.47N	84.54W
Warsaw, Va., U.S.	**124**	37.57N	76.45W
Warszawa (Warsaw)	**74**	52.15N	21.00 E
Washington, D.C., U.S.	**124**	38.53N	77.02W
Washington, Pa., U.S.	**124**	40.10N	80.14W
Washington □³	**122**	47.30N	120.30W
Washington, Mount ʌ	**124**	44.15N	71.15W
Washington Court House	**124**	39.32N	83.26W
Waspán	**114**	14.44N	83.58W
Waterbury	**124**	41.33N	73.02W
Waterford	**72**	52.15N	7.06W
Waterloo, On., Can.	**124**	43.28N	80.31W
Waterloo, Ia., U.S.	**122**	42.29N	92.20W
Watertown, N.Y., U.S.	**124**	43.58N	75.54W
Watertown, S.D., U.S.	**120**	44.53N	97.06W
Waterville	**124**	44.33N	69.37W
Watrous	**120**	51.40N	105.28W
Watson Lake	**120**	60.07N	128.48W
Wāw	**88**	7.42N	28.00 E
Wawa	**120**	47.59N	84.47W
Waycross	**122**	31.12N	82.21W
Waynesboro, Pa., U.S.	**124**	39.45N	77.34W
Waynesboro, Va., U.S.	**124**	38.04N	78.53W
Weatherford	**112**	32.45N	97.47W
Webster Springs	**124**	38.28N	80.24W
Weddell Sea ᴠ²	**69**	72.00S	45.00W
Weiden in der Oberpfalz	**74**	49.41N	12.10 E
Weifang	**98**	36.42N	19.04 E
Weirton	**124**	40.25N	80.35W
Welkom	**90**	27.59S	26.45 E
Wellington	**110**	41.18S	174.47 E
Wellington, Isla ı	**118**	49.20S	74.40W
Wells	**126**	41.06N	114.57W
Wellsford	**110**	36.17S	174.31 E
Wellston	**124**	39.07N	82.31W
Wels	**74**	48.10N	14.02 E
Wendover	**126**	40.44N	114.02W
Wenzhou	**98**	28.01N	120.39 E
West Bengal □³	**96**	24.00N	88.00 E
Westerly	**124**	41.22N	71.49W
Western Australia □³	**106**	25.00S	122.00 E
Western Ghāts ⋌	**95**	14.00N	75.00 E
Western Sahara □²	**88**	24.30N	13.00 E
Western Samoa □¹	**111e**	13.55S	172.00W
Westerville	**124**	40.07N	82.55W
West Falkland ı	**118**	51.50S	60.00W
Westfield	**124**	42.19N	79.34W
West Indies ıı	**114**	19.00N	70.00W
West Liberty	**124**	37.55N	83.15W
Westminster	**124**	39.34N	76.59W
West Palm Beach	**122**	26.42N	80.03W
Westport	**110**	41.45S	171.36 E
West Virginia □³	**122**	38.45N	80.30W
Wetaskiwin	**120**	52.58N	113.22W
Wexford	**72**	52.20N	6.27W
Weymouth	**72**	50.36N	2.28W
Whangarei	**110**	35.43S	174.19 E
Whataroa	**110**	43.17S	170.25 E
Wheeler Peak ʌ, Nv., U.S.	**126**	38.59N	114.19W
Wheeler Peak ʌ, N.M., U.S.	**122**	36.34N	105.25W
Wheeling	**124**	40.03N	80.43W
Whitehaven	**72**	54.33N	3.35W
Whitehorse	**120**	60.43N	135.03W
White Mountains ⋌	**124**	44.10N	71.35W
White Nile (Al-Bahr al-Abyaḍ) ≏	**92**	15.38N	32.31 E
White Plains	**124**	41.02N	73.45W
White Sands National Monument ✦	**112**	32.48N	106.20W
White Volta (Volta Blanche) ≏	**88**	9.10N	1.15W
Whitney, Mount ʌ	**126**	36.35N	118.18W
Whyalla	**108**	33.02S	137.35 E
Wichita	**122**	37.41N	97.20W
Wichita Falls	**122**	33.54N	98.29W
Wielkopolska ◂¹	**74**	51.50N	17.20 E
Wien (Vienna)	**74**	48.13N	16.20 E
Wiener Neustadt	**74**	47.49N	16.15 E
Wieprz ≏	**74**	51.34N	21.49 E
Wieprz-Krzna, Kanał ᴤ	**74**	51.56N	22.56 E
Wiesbaden	**74**	50.05N	8.14 E
Wilhelm, Mount ʌ	**102**	5.45S	145.05 E
Wilhelmshaven	**74**	53.31N	8.08 E
Wilkes-Barre	**124**	41.14N	75.52W
Wilkes Land ◂¹	**69**	69.00S	120.00 E
Willard	**124**	41.03N	82.44W
Willemstad	**114**	12.06N	68.56W
Williams Lake	**120**	52.08N	122.09W
Williamsport	**124**	41.14N	76.59W
Williston	**122**	48.08N	103.38W
Wilmington, De., U.S.	**124**	39.44N	75.32W
Wilmington, N.C., U.S.	**122**	34.13N	77.56W
Wiluna	**106**	26.36S	120.13 E
Winchester, In., U.S.	**124**	40.10N	84.58W
Winchester, Va., U.S.	**124**	39.11N	78.10W
Windhoek	**90**	22.34S	17.06 E
Windsor, N.S., Can.	**120**	44.59N	64.08W
Windsor, On., Can.	**120**	42.18N	83.01W
Windsor, P.Q., Can.	**124**	45.34N	72.00W
Windsor, Eng., U.K.	**72**	51.29N	0.38W
Windward Islands ıı	**114**	13.00N	61.00W
Windward Passage ⥮	**122**	20.00N	73.50W
Winisk	**120**	55.15N	85.12W
Winisk Lake ⊜	**120**	52.55N	87.22W
Winnemucca	**126**	40.58N	117.44W
Winnfield	**112**	31.55N	92.38W
Winnipeg	**120**	49.53N	97.09W
Winnipeg, Lake ⊜	**120**	52.00N	97.00W
Winnipesaukee, Lake ⊜	**124**	43.35N	71.20W
Winslow	**124**	44.32N	69.37W
Winston-Salem	**122**	36.05N	80.14W
Winterport	**124**	44.38N	68.51W
Winton, Austl.	**106**	22.23S	143.02 E
Winton, N.Z.	**110**	46.09S	168.20 E
Wisconsin □³	**122**	44.45N	89.30W
Wisła ≏	**74**	5.42N	18.55 E
Wismar, D.D.R.	**74**	53.53N	11.28 E
Wismar, Guy.	**116**	6.00N	58.18W
Wittenberg	**74**	51.52N	12.39 E
Wittenberge	**74**	53.00N	11.44 E
Woleai ı¹	**102**	7.21N	143.52 E
Wolfsberg	**74**	46.51N	14.51 E
Wolfsburg	**74**	52.25N	10.47 E
Wollongong	**108**	34.25S	150.54 E
Wŏnsan	**98**	39.09N	127.25 E
Woodbridge	**124**	38.39N	77.15W
Woodland	**126**	38.40N	121.46W
Woodlark Island ı	**106**	9.05S	152.50 E
Woods, Lake of the ⊜	**122**	49.15N	94.45W
Woodstock	**124**	43.08N	80.45W
Woodsville	**124**	44.09N	72.02W
Woodville	**110**	40.20S	175.52 E
Woomera	**106**	31.31S	137.10 E
Woonsocket	**124**	42.00N	71.30W
Worcester, Eng., U.K.	**72**	52.11N	2.13W
Worcester, Ma., U.S.	**124**	42.15N	71.48W
Wrangell	**128**	56.28N	132.23W
Wrangell Mountains ⋌	**128**	62.00N	143.00W
Wrexham	**72**	53.03N	3.00W
Wrocław (Breslau)	**74**	51.06N	17.00 E
Wuhan	**98**	30.36N	114.17 E
Wuhu	**98**	31.21N	118.22 E

ne	Page No.	Lat.	Long.	Name	Page No.	Lat.	Long.
⌐⌐ ńska Wola	74	51.36N	18.57 E	Žlobin	84	52.54N	30.03 E
Zeerust	90	25.33S	26.06 E	Znojmo	74	48.52N	16.02 E
Zeja	86	53.45N	127.15 E	Zomba	90	15.23S	35.18 E
Zelee, Cape ⟩	111a	9.45S	161.34 E	Zudañez	116	19.06S	64.44W
Zgierz	74	51.52N	19.25 E	Zugspitze ⋏	74	47.25N	10.59 E
Zhangjiakou (Kalgan)	98	40.50N	114.53 E	Zuiderzee			
Zhangzhou	98	24.33N	117.39 E	→ IJsselmeer ⊤ [2]	74	52.45N	5.25 E
Zhanjiang	98	21.16N	110.28 E	Zululand □ [9]	90	28.10S	32.00 E
Zhengzhou	98	34.48N	113.39 E	Zunyi	98	27.39N	106.57 E
Zhuzhou	98	27.50N	113.09 E	Zürich	76	47.23N	8.32 E
Zigong	98	29.24N	104.47 E	Zvolen	74	48.35N	19.08 E
Ziguinchor	88	12.35N	16.16W	Zwettl	74	48.37N	15.10 E
Žilina	74	49.14N	18.46 E	Zwickau	74	50.44N	12.29 E
Zimbabwe □ [1]	90	20.00S	30.00 E	Zwolle	74	52.30N	6.05 E
Žitomir	70	50.16N	28.40 E				